Red Silk

Harvard East Asian Monographs 431

Red Silk

Class, Gender, and Revolution in China's Yangzi Delta Silk Industry

Robert Cliver

Published by the Harvard University Asia Center
Distributed by Harvard University Press
Cambridge (Massachusetts) and London 2020

Printed in the United States of America

The Harvard University Asia Center publishes a monograph series and, in coordination with the Fairbank Center for Chinese Studies, the Korea Institute, the Reischauer Institute of Japanese Studies, and other faculties and institutes, administers research projects designed to further scholarly understanding of China, Japan, Vietnam, Korea, and other Asian countries. The Center also sponsors projects addressing multidisciplinary and regional issues in Asia.

Library of Congress Cataloging-in-Publication Data
Names: Cliver, Robert, author.
Title: Red silk : class, gender, and revolution in China's Yangzi delta silk industry / Robert Cliver.
Description: First Edition. | Cambridge : Harvard University Asia Center, 2020. | Includes bibliographical references and index. |
Identifiers: LCCN 2019044017 | ISBN 9780674244467 (hardcover)
Subjects: LCSH: Silk industry—China—Yangtze River—History—20th century. | Women silk industry workers—China—Yangtze River. | Women—Employment—China—Yangtze River. | Women and socialism—China—Yangtze River. | Work environment—China—Yangtze River.
Classification: LCC HD9926.C63 C55 2020 | DDC 331.4/87739124209512—dc23
LC record available at https://lccn.loc.gov/2019044017

Index by Jac Nelson
Printed on acid-free paper
Last figure below indicates year of this printing

26 25 24 23 22 21 20

For my family

Contents

Illustrations and Tables

Illustrations

Tables

Acknowledgments

Writing this book has been a protracted process, one that would not have been possible without the support of a great many people and institutions. I am first of all grateful to my Harvard classmates for their friendship and collegiality and for many hours of reading, discussing, and criticizing my graduate work leading up to my Ph.D. in History in 2007. The focus on gender in *Red Silk* emerged from discussions with my graduate classmates, who recognized before I did its centrality in my study of Chinese workers. I am equally grateful to my professors, who guided me through my first forays into Chinese archives and the process of researching and writing the dissertation upon which this book is based. I am especially indebted to the members of my dissertation committee—Elizabeth Perry, Andrew Gordon, and William Kirby—who read drafts and met with me many times despite their busy schedules. I would also like to thank other faculty at Harvard and elsewhere who encouraged and influenced my work, especially Sven Beckert, Terry Martin, John Womack, Michael McCormick, Peter Bol, Henrietta Harrison, Michael Puett, Rana Mitter, and Toby Lincoln. These scholars continue to inspire and encourage me.

In the lengthy process of revising the dissertation to produce the current manuscript I have been extremely fortunate to have had the tireless support and excellent suggestions of some of the leading scholars in the field of modern Chinese labor history. S. A. Smith read my first revision of the dissertation and offered insightful suggestions and unflinching support. I am deeply appreciative of the work of the two external reviewers for Harvard University Asia Center—Jacob Eyferth and Joshua Howard. Both of them devoted an impressive amount of time and effort to reading two revisions of the manuscript and provided invaluable suggestions and criticisms; they also asked questions that forced me to address inconsistencies, conceptual ambiguities, and points of confusion. I am likewise indebted to Kristen Wanner for her excellent editing skills and unrelenting efforts to help me produce a readable manuscript that accomplishes what I set out to do. These individuals have helped me to make this book the best it could be. Any remaining flaws and errors are entirely my own responsibility.

Research for this project began with a trip to the Yangzi Delta in 2002, and since that time, grants and funding from several institutions have made continued research possible. I am very grateful for the support and guidance I received from the Harvard University Graduate School of Arts and Sciences Office of Financial Aid. The staff there greatly assisted my efforts to obtain funding through a Sheldon Traveling Fellowship in 2002, and History Department Research and Travel Grants in 2001, 2004, and 2005. I am also grateful to the U.S. Department of State for the award of an IIE Cultural Exchange Fulbright Fellowship for 2002–2004, which supported a two-year stay in China to conduct archival research. I would also like to express my appreciation to the American Historical Association, which awarded me a Schmitt Grant for research travel in 2005, and the California State University's Wang Family Stipend, which supported summer research travel to China in 2008.

My current employer, Humboldt State University in California, has provided unwavering support for my scholarly work even through difficult financial times. HSU's support has included a Research, Scholarship, and Creative Activities Grant in 2011 and Emeritus and Retired Faculty Association (ERFA) Grant Awards in 2010 and 2012, for which I am very grateful. I would also like to express my appreciation to the Association for Asian Studies for awarding me a China and Inner-Asia Council Small Grant in 2014. Finally, I am most appreciative of a generous grant from the Chiang Ching-kuo Foundation in 2014, which allowed me to travel to Taiwan, the PRC, and Japan in 2015 to present my work at conferences, conduct additional research in Chinese archives, and complete the second round of revisions on this manuscript. It would not have been possible for me to access the sources I have used or refine this manuscript without the support of these institutions. I am forever grateful.

My ability to conduct the research for this manuscript has depended on the support and cooperation of several institutions in the People's Republic of China. The History Department at Beijing University and the Center for Contemporary Chinese History Studies at East China Normal University both hosted me for research trips and workshops, which greatly facilitated my engagement with Chinese archives and scholarship. Professor Yang Kuisong and Professor Feng Xiaocai at ECNU have been especially helpful and supportive of my work. Other organizations and institutions to which I would like to express my gratitude include the Shanghai Academy of Social Sciences, Shanghai Library, Shanghai Municipal Archives, Zhejiang Provincial Archives, Beijing Municipal Archives, Xi'an Municipal Archives, and Wuxi Municipal Archives. The staff and administrators at these institutions have been generous and helpful to me in my efforts to obtain historical materials for this book, which would be a much poorer work if not for their support.

Finally, I thank my friends, family, students, and colleagues, who have encouraged and supported me over the years. I am especially grateful to my colleagues at Humboldt State University for granting me the sabbatical time to work on this and other projects, and for the many opportunities to present and discuss my work in a critical but supportive environment. My research assistant Meghan Ueland was also very helpful in completing the final revisions. I could not have produced such fine work without their support. Any remaining shortcomings are solely my own responsibility.

—Robert Cliver, Arcata, CA

Abbreviations Used in the Text and Footnotes

ACFTU	All-China Federation of Trade Unions
CCP	Chinese Communist Party
CCSC	Central China Sericulture Company (Huazhong cansi gongsi, est. 1938)
CLA	Chinese Labor Association
CPPCC	Chinese People's Political Consultative Congress
CSC	China Sericulture Company (Zhongguo cansi gongsi), est. 1946 and renamed China Silk Company (Zhongguo sichou gongsi) in 1953
GLU	General Labor Union
GMD	Guomindang (Nationalist Party)
GVIO	Gross Value of Industrial Output
LCCC	Labor-Capital Consultative Conference
MCC	Military Control Commission
NCDN	*North China Daily News*
NCNA	New China News Agency (Xinhua)
NRC	National Resources Commission
PMC	Production Management Committee
PRC	People's Republic of China
RMB	Renminbi
SAB	Social Affairs Bureau
SCMP	Survey of China Mainland Press

SMA	Shanghai Municipal Archives
USD	United States dollars
USSR	Union of Soviet Socialist Republics
WMA	Wuxi Municipal Archives
ZPA	Zhejiang Provincial Archives

Conventions

The Hanyu Pinyin romanization system is used throughout the text to transcribe Chinese names and terms. The exception to this rule is Chiang Kai-shek, whose name is not transliterated into *pinyin*. See the glossary for Chinese character equivalents of major terms and names used in the text.

Chinese units of measurement are used in most cases, in particular the *dan* (a unit of weight equivalent to about 110 lbs. or 50 kg) and *jin* (1.1 lbs. or 500 g), as well as the *mu* (a measure of land area for farming, equivalent to about 0.1647 acre). Where the original statistics are given in other units, such as tons, the original units are used. Several currencies were in use in China in the mid-twentieth century, including the Nationalist government's *fabi* yuan, the Gold Yuan note issued in October 1948, and both the old and the new Renminbi (RMB) yuan of the People's Republic of China. (The Old RMB were converted to New RMB in 1955 at the rate of 10,000 to 1.) World market prices reported in newspapers are given in US dollars, and some Chinese export statistics are measured in US dollars or Russian rubles.

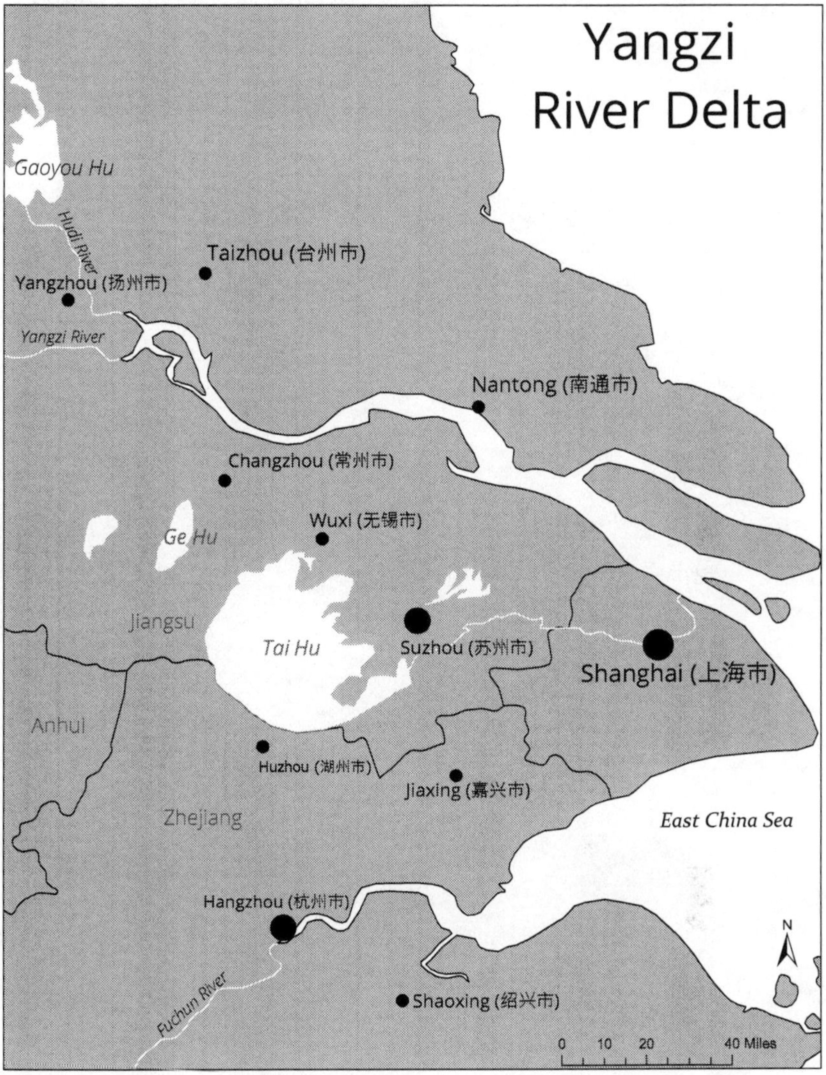

Map of the Yangzi River Delta. Map created with Natural Earth by Ryan Aufdermarsh.

INTRODUCTION

Class and Gender in the Chinese Revolution

In the spring of 1949, as the People's Liberation Army moved south to take the cities of the Yangzi River Delta, a Communist silk weaver named Zhang Qi and his fellow workers in Shanghai welcomed the approach of the Red forces. Having suffered under occupation, economic crisis, and political repression for many years, these men and women now participated enthusiastically in the Communist seizure of power. Committed to the party's goals and capable of taking the initiative to improve working conditions and labor relations in the city's silk industry, Communist silk weavers like Zhang won great improvements for their fellow workers and took up positions of responsibility and leadership in the new order. Zhang became a vice chairman of the Shanghai Federation of Trade Unions after 1949, and in 1991 he wrote and published a book on the Shanghai labor movement.[1]

In contrast, Shen Gendi, a young woman working in a silk thread mill in the city of Wuxi, saw few changes in her situation following the Communist seizure of power. Although the economy stabilized and new institutions such as trade unions and women's federations appeared, Shen and silk workers like her experienced Liberation (*jiefang* in Chinese—a term to describe the Communist revolution) primarily as a new political discourse, one that their antagonists in the mills manipulated against them. In the silk filatures of the Yangzi River

1. Zhang Qi, *Shanghai gongyun jishi.*

Delta in the early 1950s, male supervisors continued to use brutal methods, including physical beatings and other forms of abuse and exploitation, to manage young female workers. It was not until Shen Gendi was beaten to death by her supervisor in August 1951 that the Communist Party authorities took steps to reform the abusive management system prevalent in most Yangzi Delta filatures, including those administered by the new party-state.

Unlike Zhang Qi, her male weaver counterpart in Shanghai, who is still famous among Chinese labor leaders, Shen Gendi's name is entirely unknown to later generations of Chinese workers. One possible reason is that she was an ordinary young woman and not a male Communist leader. Or perhaps it was because she lived upriver in Wuxi, not in the metropolis of Shanghai. Even so, her story would seem to make her a good revolutionary martyr, perfect for propaganda purposes. Perhaps it is because her brutal death at the hands of her male supervisor occurred in a state-run factory only recently appropriated from agencies of the Nationalist government. Regardless of why Zhang Qi and Shen Gendi experienced such different revolutions, the fact of their divergent experiences despite otherwise similar circumstances creates an opportunity for a comparative history of the Chinese revolution.

If a history of revolution can liberate itself from the search for first causes, it can become a study of change and continuity. Which goals of the revolution were realized, and which were not? What factors conditioned the actions of revolutionaries, counter-revolutionaries, and ordinary men and women as they pursued their interests in a rapidly changing context? *Red Silk* is a social history of the silk reeling and weaving industry in China's Yangzi River Delta during the tumultuous years of war and revolution in the mid-twentieth century. Specifically, it is a case study of revolutionary transformation in an important export industry under Chinese Communist Party (CCP) leadership.

I take a historical and comparative approach in examining changes in labor organizing, factory management, business practices, and state-society relations in silk reeling and weaving factories to determine what factors most strongly affected the outcomes of state policies. I also examine the ways in which the actions of silk workers and their employers influenced the early construction of socialism in China. *Red*

Silk presents a multifaceted narrative of how the Yangzi Delta silk industry came to be "red" in the first decade of Communist rule. It was not a linear process, and the Communists' efforts to transform the industry in the protean context of revolution, combined with the legacies of the labor movement and business practices developed in times of war and economic crisis, produced diverse and sometimes contradictory outcomes in different localities and different branches of the silk industry.

The geographical setting for this study is the Lower Yangzi region, or Jiangnan, which includes the southern parts of Jiangsu Province and the northern parts of Zhejiang, downriver from Anhui Province. In the mid-twentieth century, the Yangzi Delta produced by far the greatest proportion of Chinese silk, and the industry provided livelihoods for hundreds of thousands of men and women in cities and in the countryside. Most cities in the region possessed both silk thread mills and weaving factories. This study focuses on two cities, Shanghai and Wuxi. Shanghai was a major center for silk weaving throughout the twentieth century, and Wuxi was the largest center for thread production in the region. There were sizable silk industries in other cities, such as Hangzhou, Nanjing, Huzhou, and Suzhou, but none reached the scale and importance of these two.[2]

The topics covered in this book—work, business, and politics in the Yangzi Delta silk industry during the middle decades of the twentieth century—present an excellent opportunity to examine and better understand the complexities and diverse outcomes of the Chinese revolution. In the mid-twentieth century the two branches of the silk industry, thread and cloth production, faced broadly similar market and policy conditions but differed greatly in other ways, such as in their gendered division of labor and their relationships with state agencies.

2. My research focuses on silk workers employed in urban, mechanized factories and does not examine the tens of thousands of handicraft silk weavers who worked at home throughout the Yangzi Delta region. Rural handicraft weavers were subject to a different set of policies, and studying that group of workers would require different sources and methods than the comparison of urban, industrial silk reeling and weaving undertaken here. For an illuminating example of rural deindustrialization in the 1950s and 1960s, see Eyferth, *Eating Rice from Bamboo Roots*.

Because of this diversity within commonality, the silk industry allows us to examine the processes that led to divergent outcomes as different branches of the industry attempted to implement similar state-policy directives. Based on this example, we can determine what factors influenced the course of revolutionary change in other contexts. This comparative approach can help to explain the diverse results of a wide array of policies, including union organizing, labor-capital cooperation, state-contracted production, welfare provision, political mobilization, and the integration of private firms into the socialist economy. Furthermore, this approach can clarify the nature of the revolutionary state and the effects it had on society in the first years of the People's Republic of China (PRC).

Early studies of the PRC written during the Cold War focused on the ideology and organization of the Communist Party and the visions and decisions of the party's top leaders. The works of political scientists and sociologists in the West generally treated Chinese society as the object of action by the party. I owe a great debt to those pioneering works, which provide valuable analyses of party documents, published materials, and the official structure of power in the PRC.[3] However, because of the limitations of the sources, these early studies could not examine the complex processes and unintended consequences of revolutionary initiatives in different localities and among various groups of people.[4]

Scholars of the Chinese revolution have also shown great interest in the historical and social origins of the Chinese Communist Party

3. Two examples of early scholarship on PRC politics and society that have been very influential for this project are MacFarquhar, *Origins of the Cultural Revolution*, and Schurmann, *Ideology and Organization*.

4. In her 1985 dissertation, Kathrin Sears expresses this problem well, stating, "Studies of the post-1949 period in China tend to emphasize the role of government and party leaders and reflect their desire to appear in control of the policy process as a whole. Analysis of nationalization in the Shanghai cotton textile industry provides a new perspective on the ways in which existing factors and implementing processes may limit central leaders' policy choices and ability to control the pace of change." Sears, "Shanghai's Textile Capitalists," 2–3.

itself. Given the party's longtime rural base and the importance of "the peasant problem," studies of state-society relations in China have focused more on rural society than on urban residents and industrial workers.[5] The body of literature on Chinese urban society in the 1950s has expanded rapidly in recent years, including some valuable studies of the labor movement and the transformation of private businesses.[6] Nevertheless, much of this scholarship continues to focus on the policies of the party-state more than on the results of implementation or popular responses to state initiatives.[7]

Early emphasis in both Western and Chinese scholarship on the party and its policies was also a result of restrictions on historical scholarship in China. For decades, the necessity of relying on published and official sources limited scholars' avenues of inquiry and restricted the kinds of questions they could address.[8] The limited information about events at the level of the city and the factory, combined with Cold War political cleavages within academia, inclined many Western scholars to accept the claims in official party documents without questioning the extent to which the policies were reactive, contingent, or simply unsuccessful.[9]

Scholars based in China have enjoyed better access to historical materials, but restrictions imposed by the Communist party-state have

5. On the rural revolution, see Chan, Madsen, and Unger, *Chen Village under Mao and Deng*; Friedman et al., *Chinese Village, Socialist State*; Hinton, *Fanshen*; Johnson, *Women, the Family, and Peasant Revolution*; Selden, *The Yenan Way*; Shue, *Peasant China in Transition*; and Stacey, *Patriarchy and Socialist Revolution*.

6. For example: Frazier, *Chinese Industrial Workplace*; Vogel, *Canton under Communism*; James Gao, *Communist Takeover of Hangzhou*; Tao, Zheng, and Mow, *Holding Up Half the Sky*; Brown and Pickowicz, *Dilemmas of Victory*.

7. For example, Kaple, *Dream of a Red Factory*.

8. Some early scholars of the Chinese revolution, such as Kenneth Lieberthal, A. Doak Barnett, Ezra Vogel, and Stephen Uhalley, also made use of interviews with émigrés from the PRC to Hong Kong. This method carried its own attendant problems, however, and often resulted in a mirror image of the party's claims, transforming unalloyed successes into unmitigated disasters.

9. For a typical example of anti-Communist Cold War scholarship, see Shih, *Life of Workers under Chinese Communist Persecution*. For examples of a more pro-Maoist bias, see Myrdal, *Report from a Chinese Village*; Breth, *Mao's China*; and some of the chapters in Schram and Bastid, *Authority, Participation and Cultural Change*.

limited the range of historical interpretation.[10] Histories of the revolution in China have thus more often looked to the ideology and stated goals of party leaders, imagining in them a coherent plan, and neglected the possibility that policy implementation was substantially conditioned and transformed (even opposed) through interaction with diverse social groups.[11] Despite recent criticisms of non-party historians engaging in "historical nihilism," a code for histories that contradict the CCP's own narrative, the possibilities open to scholars of the early People's Republic have expanded dramatically in the twenty-first century.[12] The conditions for historical research in China are now more open and relaxed than they were for most of the twentieth century, as demonstrated by the frequently critical scholarship on the Chinese revolution published in China in recent years.[13] Chinese archives are more accessible to both foreign and Chinese scholars now than they were thirty years ago (although that window may be closing as the current leadership tightens restrictions on scholarship again). Generally speaking, however, it has become possible in the past twenty or thirty years to write a deeper and more complex social history of the

10. For an example of Chinese history as hagiography, see Chen Boda, *Mao Tse-tung on the Chinese Revolution*. Much of historical writing published during the Mao years was similarly politicized and forced into a mold of class struggle and Stalinist stages of history.

11. As Christopher Howe writes, "In attempting to reconstruct Chinese economic policy in the 1950s, one has constantly to avoid the temptation of linking together policy statements and administrative measures to give them an appearance of design and coherence that exaggerates the degree to which, in reality, they comprised an articulate and fully comprehended plan." Howe, *Employment and Economic Growth*, 122.

12. For example, see Xinhua, "Party History Researcher Warns against 'Historical Nihilism.'"

13. Scholars at the East China Normal University (ECNU) Center for Contemporary Chinese History, such as Han Gang, Yang Kuisong, Feng Xiaocai, and Zhang Jishun, and their students, are doing some excellent research on the history of the Maoist period. From symposia such as the Academic Symposium on China's Social Culture in the 1950s to such publications as the journal *Zhongguo dangdai shi yanjiu* (Research in contemporary Chinese history), ECNU is making great strides in Chinese-language scholarship and international cooperation in this field.

early PRC, and thereby to reassess the roles and significance of government agencies and diverse social groups in the Chinese revolution.[14]

Of course, any attempt to write a social history of the Chinese revolution must include some understanding of the CCP's leaders, ideology, and policies.[15] It is nonetheless increasingly possible to investigate the changes and continuities in Chinese society in the 1950s without assuming that the visions and preferences of party leaders were the most significant factors. In other words, it is possible to "bring society back in"—to study how ordinary people resisted, embraced, and adapted to changing political and economic conditions to protect and advance their interests.[16] In this view, Chinese socialism was not simply a product of the party leaders' ideology or policies. Many factors shaped the project of "socialist construction" and revolutionary transformation, including the recent legacies of political disintegration, war, and economic collapse, and the diverse perceptions, interests, and ambitions of groups and individuals.[17]

Methods and Approaches

As a study of revolutionary transformation in the Yangzi Delta silk industry, *Red Silk* examines the interaction between the goals and policies of the party-state and the diverse responses of the men and women

14. Some important recent works based on archival research include Diamant, *Revolutionizing the Family*; Perry, *Patrolling the Revolution*; and Hershatter, *Gender of Memory*. This body of archive- and interview-based history continues to grow rapidly as scholars take advantage of the accessibility of archives from the 1950s.

15. As evidence of how important Mao and his ideas remain in our understanding of the People's Republic, two popular textbooks on China are Meisner, *Mao's China and After*, and Walder, *China under Mao*.

16. Apologies to Theda Skocpol for paraphrasing her now famous statement about "bringing the state back in," in *States and Social Revolutions*.

17. On the topic of leaders' frustration with the ineffectiveness of even their own party organization in policy implementation, Andrew Walder writes, "Orders from the top reverberated through a large national bureaucracy and a new social structure, and in the process their intended impacts were diverted, distorted, or magnified in unanticipated ways." Walder, *China under Mao*, xii. Walder does not, however, look to popular opposition or cooptation of regime initiatives as an explanation for divergent outcomes.

engaged in silk production. The story of how Chinese silk became "red" describes not only the process of political revolution but also how silk workers were reeducated in Communist Party politics and how silk factories were integrated into the emerging socialist economy, not always with the results that party leaders had expected. The socialist silk industry developed out of the complex interaction between the processes of state formation and revolutionary transformation, on the one hand, and the efforts of workers and capitalists to adapt to changing conditions, on the other. In protecting and pursuing their interests, the actors involved—agents of the state, union organizers, factory owners, and workers—were simultaneously constrained and enabled by the legacies of the recent past and the changes that followed in the wake of China's Communist revolution.

Contrary to Chairman Mao's claim in 1958 that China was a "blank sheet of paper," China's cultural traditions have proved extremely resilient, even under the pressures of radical revolution.[18] In the context of the 1950s silk industry, the newer "traditions" that had developed in business practices, labor relations, and political struggle since the 1920s strongly influenced the ways in which silk weavers, filature workers, and their employers responded to the challenges and opportunities of revolution. Many tricks of the trade and strategies for collective action from the decades before 1949 persisted into the PRC period, while others were suppressed, abandoned, or adapted to fit changing conditions.

To implement its policies, the revolutionary party also had to adapt to the complex social and economic realities of the Yangzi Delta silk industry. Revolutionary leaders had to accommodate, to some extent, the aspirations and expectations of China's industrial workers and "national capitalists" (*minzu zibenjia*). In dialectical fashion, workers' and employers' adaptations and responses forced leaders to modify

18. For "blank sheet of paper," see Mao Zedong, *Selected Readings*, 499–500. Mao was speaking on the topic of agricultural cooperatives. For a comparative study of revolutionary regimes' ability to overcome the historical conditions constraining revolutionary transformation, see Kirchheimer, "Confining Conditions and Revolutionary Breakthroughs."

existing policies or initiate new ones, which in turn elicited unpredictable responses from different social groups, leading to further modifications of policy. As Mark Frazier points out in his study of labor management practices in Shanghai and Guangzhou factories in the 1950s: "Imposed from above, state solutions to the problems of workforce organization and mobilization did not always take shape in their intended form and function. The preferences of workers and managers substantially altered such institutional designs of the state."[19] Similarly, in her study of the nationalization of Shanghai's cotton textiles industry, Kathrin Sears writes, "Nationalization involved a dynamic interaction between central leaders' policy goals and priorities, the capabilities and preferences of local actors, and factors arising during the implementation process."[20]

Class: Workers and Capitalists

In this book, I emphasize the agency of local actors and highlight continuities in China's socialist work-unit system that derived from the economic, political, and military crises preceding the Communist takeover.[21] But unlike the shipyards and cotton mills Frazier and Sears studied, silk factories were overwhelmingly privately owned in 1949; they were also smaller in scale. Silk reeling filatures were generally medium-size enterprises with hundreds of employees, and they were more closely integrated with state agencies even before the Communist takeover. Silk weaving factories were usually little more than workshops with a dozen looms, and they had much more limited connections to state agencies before the 1950s. The labor-capital relationship was far more important in this context than in state-run shipyards and massive textile combines, which were, to some extent, already integrated into the state-run economy under Nationalist Party rule. For this reason, socioeconomic

19. Frazier, *Chinese Industrial Workplace*, 13–14.

20. Sears, "Shanghai's Textile Capitalists," 2.

21. Howard, *Workers at War*, exemplifies the new Chinese labor history, which recognizes continuities across the 1949 divide.

classes and class relations are prominent categories in *Red Silk*, both as frameworks for analysis and as fields of contestation among capitalists, workers, and Communists (categories that sometimes came together in a single person). Workers, employers, and party cadres struggled to define what it meant to be "bourgeois" or "proletarian" and to place their interests within these rhetorical categories.

In his 2003 article "Beyond Chesneaux," the historian and China scholar Arif Dirlik makes a convincing argument for the continued importance of class in contemporary and historical analyses of China's society and political economy.[22] Of course, other forces besides class conflict, including colonialism, imperialism, and war, shaped China's modern history. Nevertheless, Marxist class analysis was vitally important for the CCP and its ideology, and these ideas had tremendous importance for Chinese people's lives in the twentieth century. Dirlik points out that the Chinese Communists used class not only as an analytical category but also as an operational category that determined individuals' status in the new socialist society. At the same time, workers and employers struggled over the meaning and applicability of class terminology as the Chinese economy underwent wholesale restructuring during the 1950s.[23] Class identities in China were fluid and historical before the regime began to use Marxist categories to assign political status. When used operationally, according to Richard Kraus, class categories became frozen "fossils" of historical classes, especially after the "socialist transformation" in 1956.[24] By the end of the decade, political labels were more important than individuals' roles in

22. Dirlik, "Beyond Chesneaux," 79–99. Recognizing the complexities introduced to the concept of class in China in labor histories written in the decades since the 1968 publication of Jean Chesneaux's *The Chinese Labor Movement*, Dirlik expresses the hope that scholars can illuminate the diversity, agency, and historical origins of China's working class. He calls for a more sophisticated understanding of how class intersected with other bases of identity and action among Chinese workers—native place, gender, nationalism, localism, craft, and industry—sometimes supplanting and sometimes supplementing class-based identities. He further suggests that class remains a category of central importance for understanding China's modern history and its contemporary role in the global capitalist economy.

23. Dirlik, "Beyond Chesneaux," 93–94.

24. Richard Kraus, *Class Conflict in Chinese Socialism*, 29–30, 58–61.

production for defining one's status in the new society. Nonetheless, class remained an important concept for social and political analysis.

For decades, scholars in China and the West have studied China's industrial working class from a variety of disciplinary approaches. Common themes in this body of scholarship include working-class formation and fragmentation, and the basis for collective action among Chinese workers. Marxist historians have searched for a consistently broad-based and class-conscious labor movement in China, but they have rarely found one, either before or after the 1949 revolution. Major crises that affected the whole of Chinese society—conflicts with European imperialists, the Great Depression, the Japanese occupation from 1937 to 1945, and the postwar inflation—elicited united action across broad segments of the working class. However, the rhetoric of those movements rarely expressed an obviously Marxist class consciousness.[25]

In their groundbreaking studies, Charles Hoffmann and Andrew Walder describe the "creation" (or re-creation) of China's working class under Communist-led industrialization.[26] More recent research reveals that, far from being "essentially passive participants" in the transformations of the 1950s, as Walder claims, Chinese workers continued to assert their interests and to attempt to use historically viable forms of organization and action, even as those methods were discredited and prohibited during the 1950s.[27] Neither Chinese workers' traditions of organizing nor factory management practices were a "blank sheet of paper"; rather, they were palimpsests over which the Communists wrote new scripts.

25. S. A. Smith expresses the "class-inflected anti-imperialist nationalism" of some Shanghai workers by quoting a statement from August 1925 in which members of the Cotton Workers Federation said they sought to "concentrate our forces, resist imperialist oppression, struggle for the sovereignty of the nation (*minzu*), and seek the emancipation of the working class." S. A. Smith, *Like Cattle and Horses*, 190.

26. Hoffmann, *Chinese Worker*, 180; Walder, *Communist Neo-Traditionalism*, 85.

27. Walder, "Remaking the Chinese Working Class," 11. When Walder claims in his article that "the new Chinese regime literally created, almost from scratch, a new tradition of labor relations" that resulted in a docile, passive proletariat, he overstates the case. Sheehan, *Chinese Workers*, 19; F. Chen, "Labor Protests."

Unlike the Soviet Union in the 1920s, the CCP regime in China does not seem to have resorted to widespread repression or coercion to "discipline" the industrial working class in the 1950s.[28] Walder contends that, in relation to the working class, the party-state used positive incentives and political controls rather than repression and coercion. His claim that the "meshing of economic and political power on the structured incentives offered by the party" kept at least the most privileged groups of workers loyal to the CCP is undoubtedly accurate.[29] However, his focus on the most privileged workers employed in state-owned enterprises neglects the vast majority of working-class people and overlooks evidence of ongoing conflict between the CCP and its proletarian constituents. Other scholars, such as Jackie Sheehan and Elizabeth Perry, are more inclined to highlight instances of conflict between workers and the party-state, thus revealing a much more fraught relationship and less passivity among Chinese workers.[30]

All these scholars recognize that China's working class was historically fragmented, both before and after 1949.[31] They differ, however, in their conclusions about workers' collective action. Walder focuses on workers (such as steelworkers and silk weavers) who benefited most from the Communist seizure of power, while recognizing that CCP policy created new divisions within the working class. In his 1984 article, he identifies multiple divisions among Chinese workers and details stratification among state-socialist employees, workers in the collective sector, and contract and temporary laborers, especially rural peasant workers.[32] By the 1970s these divisions had developed into "a pattern of sectoral inequality—especially within the industrial labor

28. Walder, *China under Mao*, 70, mentions the CCP "curbing" organized labor but provides no examples or evidence of the suppression of workers' actions during the Mao period. In a 2014 article, F. Chen details numerous worker protests against CCP policies but makes no mention of suppression, stating that "the government was largely conciliatory toward the protestors" ("Labor Protests," 507).

29. Walder, *Communist Neo-Traditionalism*, 6.

30. See especially Sheehan, *Chinese Workers*, 9–11.

31. For an informed discussion of how the previously divergent working conditions and protest actions of state- and privately employed workers may be converging in contemporary China, see Hurst, "Chinese Labor," 127–36.

32. Walder, "Remaking the Chinese Working Class," 40.

force—whose rigidity has never been equaled in the USSR." In Walder's view, the lack of working-class unity further supports the idea that Chinese workers under CCP rule were largely passive, accepting, and disciplined: "The revolution has ushered in the *unmaking* of the Chinese working class."[33]

Such divisions, however, were not the product of the 1950s revolution. Many labor historians have observed that the Chinese working class has been frustratingly lacking in solidarity and class consciousness since its inception. The question then arises as to whether the obvious fragmentation of the Chinese working class by industrial sector, skill, native place, language, and gender inhibited workers' collective action or, alternatively, served as the basis for political action. Similarly, historians have asked whether and how class struggle developed between Chinese proletarians and the Chinese or imperialist bourgeoisie, or even between the working class and the "new class" of the Communist party-state bureaucracy.

In contrast with scholars who have sought a classically class-conscious proletariat in modern China, Elizabeth Perry has eschewed Marxist class analysis in favor of more specific and historical categories, such as the "politics of place" and the "politics of production." In *Shanghai on Strike*, published in 1993, she shows that the enduring divisions within Shanghai's working class formed the "basis for politically influential working-class action."[34] Perry offers a historical ethnography of workers' actions in pre-1949 Shanghai that describes "traditions of protest" specific to different groups of workers. In her view, "fragmentation" and "divergent norms" do not imply passivity or a lack of awareness of one's collective interests, even if they are distinct from those of other workers.[35] Perry concludes that Chinese workers' diverse traditions of collective action survived the crises of the mid-twentieth century, and workers continued to draw on those traditions into the Maoist era and beyond.

33. Walder, "Remaking the Chinese Working Class," 41–42. Italics in the original.
34. Perry, *Shanghai on Strike*, 1.
35. Perry, *Shanghai on Strike*, 5–6.

Shanghai on Strike compares different groups of Chinese workers in the twentieth century and even focuses on some of the same workers—silk weavers and filature workers in Shanghai—studied in this book. Our conclusions are understandably similar. When common crises brought their circumstances into closer convergence, different groups of workers, whether privileged male weavers or exploited female mill hands, could make common cause and join forces against employers and the state. Divisions within the Chinese working class did not prevent coordinated action, despite the fact that historians do not generally identify the emergence of a united and class-conscious proletariat in twentieth-century China.[36] Focusing on workers' collective action in the 1920s and 1930s, Perry demonstrates that, despite fragmentation, diverse groups of workers could engage in struggle, even politically powerful struggle, despite, or even on the basis of, divisions and inequalities.

Jackie Sheehan's work reveals that this pattern persisted into the 1950s, 1960s, and 1970s, as workers responded to inequalities and conflicts with party-state administrators with a form of "class struggle."[37] Sheehan theorizes that the CCP's rhetoric of class unity and the benefits of socialism, directed at industrial workers after 1949, contrasted starkly with the inequalities and injustices built into the PRC's employment system. Working-class fragmentation fostered a type of class consciousness in which people were painfully aware of the gap between CCP rhetoric and the working conditions they experienced. This was especially apparent when workers compared claims concerning working-class unity and worker control with the obvious stratification of China's socialist working class and the clear lack of worker control in

36. In *"Cent Fleurs" à l'usine*, 2, Francois Gipouloux comments that the labor movement was mostly suppressed in pre-1949 China, "except perhaps during the second half of the 1940s when the movement in opposition to the civil war gained in strength." Contra Walder, Gipouloux furthermore states that, as a result of Communist-led industrialization, "the proletariat, the favored child of the new regime, would again emerge as a social force in the milieu of the 1950s." I am grateful to my student Ryan Thomas for translating the introduction to this book from the French original.

37. Sheehan, *Chinese Workers*.

most Chinese factories.[38] She argues that the inequalities of the socialist system and conflicts between industrial workers and bureaucratic administrators created the basis for collective action and even class struggle between workers and the "new class" of the party apparatus resulting in frequent conflict between industrial workers and the party-state throughout the latter half of the twentieth century.[39]

The CCP's distinction between "class conscious" political action and workers' "economistic" demands is hugely important for understanding the CCP's effort to transform Chinese workers into "socialist men and women."[40] In his 1974 study of Chinese workers, Charles Hoffmann describes the CCP's conception of workers' "class struggle" after 1949 as an effort to transform earlier economistic class consciousness into the collectivist, nationalist, self-sacrificing ethos of the party activist. However, the party's efforts at "human socialization" of workers through "class struggle," particularly struggle against the "stubborn persistence of narrow individualism," often conflicted with the goals of industrialization and improving productivity through "scientific management."[41] In this view, in the absence of a unified, class-conscious proletariat, class struggle after 1949 was whatever the party said it was; it served the industrializing goals of the regime, leaving little room for workers to define their interests in class terms.

According to both Perry and Sheehan, however, seemingly economic demands over wages, benefits, and working conditions could become the basis for effective and influential political action, as among "labor aristocrats" in the 1930s and among temporary and contract workers during the Cultural Revolution of the 1960s.[42] Because of the

38. Sheehan, *Chinese Workers*, 229–31. Whereas Walder claims that working-class divisions, combined with the provision of socialist welfare benefits for the most privileged workers, created a passive and compliant working class, Sheehan highlights many instances of conflict between Chinese workers and the party-state, often based on the same divisions. F. Chen, "Labor Protests," 490, similarly states that "the discrepancy between the state's socialist promises and . . . the practices of its agencies often disappointed and disillusioned workers and became a major source of workers' grievances."

39. Sheehan, *Chinese Workers*, 9.

40. Hoffmann, *Chinese Worker*, 9–11.

41. Hoffmann, *Chinese Worker*, 24. See also F. Chen, "Labor Protests," 507–9.

42. See, for example, Perry and Li, *Proletarian Power*.

managerial role of party administrators in industry, Sheehan argues, all *economic* issues (working conditions, wages, inequalities) became *political* issues. Conflict between the rhetoric and the realities of Chinese socialism, as in the claim that workers are "masters of the factory" (*gongchang de zhurenweng*) through institutions for "democratic management" (*minzhu guanli*) could create a basis for collective political action, at least among segments of the Chinese working class.[43] That there were differences in the ways groups of Chinese workers mobilized around such issues after 1949 indicates that the CCP had not succeeded in replacing their earlier traditions of organizing, which persisted for many decades.

Contrary to official CCP history, conflict between proletarians and China's vanguard party continued despite, and even because of, divisions among workers. Sheehan claims that workers' awareness of inequality and the gap between socialist rhetoric and reality was often expressed as antagonism toward CCP administrators rather than toward more-privileged workers. This implies that the CCP's policies created not only new divisions within the working class, as Walder notes, but also a class-conscious awareness of conflict between proletarians and the new class of administrators. Sheehan puts it this way: "Workers in every decade from the 1950s returned to this basic dichotomy between those with power and those without, tracing to this their other myriad grievances about status, conditions, pay, representation, and participation, and thus turning virtually every major dispute with the authorities into a political confrontation."[44]

Fragmented workers in the Shanghai silk industry were motivated to action because of these obvious disparities and injustices. If the silk weavers after 1949 more closely resemble Walder's co-opted, privileged, and passive workers under state socialism, the filature workers are more like the disenfranchised but outspoken workers that Sheehan identifies. As we will see in chapters 6 and 7, the young women employed in

43. Sheehan, *Chinese Workers*, 9–11.

44. Sheehan, *Chinese Workers*, 231. Burawoy and Lukács, *Radiant Past*, makes the point that exploitation, and thus the target of labor action, is much more obvious in a socialist system in which the state is management and the expropriator of surplus value, rather than capital and the market.

Jiangnan filatures continued to engage in direct actions, such as strikes and walkouts, even after the party-state had condemned and disallowed those earlier forms of struggle. Their actions, including spontaneous strikes as late as 1957, derived from obvious inequalities and injustices in their circumstances, but unlike in the late 1940s, they received little support or solidarity from other groups of workers.

There are also important differences in the circumstances of Shanghai silk weavers in the 1950s as compared with the weavers of the 1930s whom Perry studied. After 1949, the alliance of Shanghai silk weavers and the Communist Party strengthened the weavers' position vis-à-vis silk factory owners. As discussed in chapter 4, Shanghai silk weavers benefited greatly from the Communist seizure of power, but they were not directly managed by agents of the state. Instead, from 1949 to 1957, they continued to engage with private factory owners while enjoying considerable political, economic, and rhetorical support from the party-state. Of course, this changed after 1956 and the "socialist transformation of industry and commerce" described in chapter 7.

The Gender Divide

Gender differences, particularly divisions between male and female workers, is one axis of working-class fragmentation that has received little attention in the literature to date. Walder, Sheehan, Hoffmann, and Chesneaux make almost no mention of gender, even though entire industries, including silk production, were subject to a gendered division of labor. Perry's *Shanghai on Strike* discusses women workers and the role of gender in setting wages and identifying certain professions as skilled or unskilled.[45] Although there are some excellent books on Chinese women workers before 1949, there is still remarkably little historical literature on the intersection of class and gender in modern China, especially after 1949.[46]

In contrast, gender features prominently in *Red Silk*, both as a framework of analysis and as an important locus of revolutionary

45. Perry, *Shanghai on Strike*, 48–60.

46. Honig, *Sisters and Strangers*, and Hershatter, *Workers of Tianjin*, both discuss women workers in depth.

struggle. The prominence of women's liberation in CCP ideology and policy provided opportunities for women workers to advance their interests, but it also contributed to raised expectations and disappointed hopes. Like the contested redefinition of class, the construction of the socialist man and woman involved negotiation, struggle, co-optation, and coercion, and produced diverse outcomes among different social groups. In her 2017 study of "state feminists" in the PRC, Wang Zheng reveals how activist leaders of the Women's Federation adopted the tactics of "hidden scripts" and the "politics of concealment" to advance a feminist agenda and avoid being criticized as "rightists."[47] She calls for a completely new paradigm in how we view PRC history:

> The conceptual chasm and methodological difference in dealing with "state feminism" are symptomatic of a lingering Cold War paradigm of a "totalitarian Communist party-state" in the field of Chinese studies. By ignoring fissures, contradictions, gaps, and conflicts inherently embedded in the formation of the socialist state, and by assuming the impossibility of expressions of feminist agency in the male-dominated power structure, a masculinist fixation on power struggles among top male leaders in high politics has effectively worked to erase feminist contentions in the socialist state.[48]

Similarly, in her 1998 book, *Gender and the South China Miracle*, Ching Kwan Lee critiques Michael Burawoy's concept of the "factory regime" and calls for a "theory of gendered labor control."[49] The term "factory regime" comes from *The Politics of Production*, in which Burawoy describes "despotic" and "hegemonic" regimes of factory management.[50] Building on Burawoy's model, Lee introduces elements of gender and locality to her study of factory regimes in two very

47. Wang Zheng, *Finding Women*, 17.

48. Wang Zheng, *Finding Women*, 7.

49. Ching Kwan Lee, *Gender and the South China Miracle*, 20.

50. Burawoy's conceptualization of the politics of production and the economic roles of the state is also applicable to the historical Chinese case. For Burawoy's sociological-historical analysis of factory regimes in Western industry (both capitalist and socialist), see Burawoy, *Politics of Production*, especially chapter 3.

similar electronics factories in Hong Kong and Shenzhen in the 1990s. Although the regulatory context, division of labor, product mix, and production technologies were entirely similar in both factories, management employed two very different regimes of control, which Lee describes as "localistic despotism" (Shenzhen) and "familial hegemony" (Hong Kong). She attributes these differences to diverging labor market structures, but also views them as "inextricably connected to gender."[51] Lee best expresses the importance of gender for understanding labor processes when she writes, "Cultural constructions of women's gender are the recurrent references by which labor-management relations are conceived, legitimated, and criticized." These constructions are, moreover, "not purely ideational, as they have material roots in shop-floor organization and are shaped by a set of social institutions outside the shop floors in the labor market, the family, kin networks, and even the state."[52] This point is especially important for understanding the gendered differences in silk-factory regimes in the early PRC.

In *Red Silk* I apply Burawoy's term "factory regime" to describe management and labor relations in the Yangzi Delta silk industry. Because of its gendered division of labor, the Yangzi Delta silk industry presents an excellent case study of the intersection of class and gender in the Chinese revolution. Silk weavers were mostly adult men who shared with their employers the hegemonic (to use Burawoy's term) masculine culture of Jiangnan silk weaving. In contrast, silk filatures employed young women, who worked under the supervision of older male managers in a despotic, patriarchal factory regime that had persisted since the 1920s. Because of gendered differences in workforces and managerial regimes, when the party attempted to implement the same policies in different types of factories the results could vary dramatically.[53] Viewing the Chinese revolution through the combined lenses of class and gender provides unique insights into the complex

51. Ching Kwan Lee, *Gender and the South China Miracle*, 159–63.

52. Ching Kwan Lee, *Gender and the South China Miracle*, 28.

53. For evidence that male workers were better able than their female counterparts to participate in institutions for "democratic management" in Chinese factories in the 1950s, see Cliver, "*Minzhu guanli.*"

processes and divergent outcomes of policy initiatives, including policy failure, that would otherwise be invisible or incomprehensible.

Because of their importance to the revolutionary regime as a focus of organizing efforts and propaganda, women workers should be an important subject of analysis for historians of the Chinese revolution. However, Western scholarship on Chinese women has devoted relatively little attention to female proletarians.[54] This is unfortunate, because the experiences of women workers provide important insights into the nature of "liberation," the limits of revolutionary social transformation in modern China, and the relationship between the CCP and China's complex and diverse working class.

One point that Delia Davin's 1976 book, *Woman Work*, makes very well is that although the unions established under Communist leadership after 1949 focused considerable attention on women workers, they were also generally ineffective in addressing their needs and interests. CCP policy and ideology emphasized women's liberation, particularly the need to protect and advance the interests of women workers. But these efforts encountered persistent resistance from employers, male workers, and party and union cadres. Women in the Wuxi filatures were disadvantaged, even compared with workers in Shanghai filatures, because unlike the Shanghai Silk Workers Union, filature unions in Wuxi were controlled by managerial personnel who were extremely hostile to women's liberation. Furthermore, compared with Shanghai, the city of Wuxi was much more limited in the

54. Some excellent histories of women workers before 1949 are cited later in this book and in the bibliography. There has been surprisingly little research, however, on working-class women in the early PRC. A happy exception is Delia Davin's *Woman Work*, which recognizes that "though numerically a small group, [women workers] were given a disproportionate amount of attention by the Party, the Women's Federation and the trade unions at the time of liberation." Davin goes so far as to state, "More importance was attached to the mobilization of women factory workers than of any other group, in part because they were members of what the Party taught was now to be the leading class in China, and also because they had an immediate role to play in the restoration of the economy" (174). This does not mean, however, that the CCP effectively addressed many issues that women workers confronted. A more recent (2014) article on working-class women in Beijing by Zhao Ma echoes this appraisal, stating, "Female workers, though few in number, were given a conspicuous and powerful place in the nascent Communist political order." Zhao, "Female Workers," 580.

material and political resources that could be enlisted to advance the welfare of women workers.[55]

Locality is thus another important axis of analysis in this history of silk workers. Most Yangzi Delta cities, including Shanghai and Wuxi, possessed both thread mills and weaving factories. Although Shanghai dominated silk weaving and Wuxi was the largest producer of silk thread in China, there were also filatures in Shanghai and silk weaving factories in Wuxi. These exceptions are very useful for distinguishing the effects of gender, industry, and locality. For example, the thread mills of Shanghai were managed differently from their counterparts in Wuxi: shop-floor supervisors in Shanghai were usually older women, whereas in Wuxi they were men. In addition, women working in the thread mills of Shanghai belonged to the same citywide industrial union as the privileged and powerful Shanghai silk weavers, and Shanghai filature workers benefited from their association with that group. They also benefited from living in the metropolis of Shanghai, which enjoyed more financial and physical resources (such as clinics and childcare facilities) and political resources, in the form of responsible and capable leadership, than other Yangzi Delta cities. The more numerous filature workers of Wuxi faced a much more despotic factory regime, were forced into unions dominated by male supervisors and factory owners, and did not have access to the same resources as their counterparts in Shanghai. This multilayered comparison highlights the differences created by gender, factory regime, and locality in specific instances, and helps to identify the most salient conditions influencing workers' experiences and actions.

The Dynamic Context of Revolution

The changes brought about by the Communist seizure of power provided opportunities for some workers, such as Shanghai's silk weavers, to define and pursue their interests better than ever before. At the same

55. This is also apparent in comparison with female workers in Beijing, to whom the party devoted impressive organizational and personnel resources, despite their relatively small numbers. Zhao, "Female Workers," 559–66.

time, those changes disadvantaged other groups, including filature workers and factory owners, by making previously successful strategies like spontaneous strikes and tax evasion less viable. Individuals and groups preserved, adapted, or replaced earlier strategies in response to the actions of the party-state. In turn, their responses affected state policies and the developmental path of the revolution, as Chinese people chose which politics and policies to pursue most energetically, which to conform to as a formality, and which to ignore entirely.

The early 1950s, the focus of the book's core chapters, present a dynamic context that changed quickly in response to developments both domestic and international. The Communist Party's policies concerning inflation, land reform, and the treatment of "counter-revolutionaries" produced results and responses that required more policies to deal with new problems and unintended outcomes. Events outside the party leadership's control, such as the February Sixth Bombing of Shanghai's main power plant in 1950, conditioned the possibilities open to both the revolutionary state and the Chinese populace. In the same way, the party's implementation of political campaigns, the First Five-Year Plan, and the "General Line for the Transition to Socialism" elicited, restricted, or redirected popular responses. The revolutionary process in China often produced conflict and competition among social groups and shifted suddenly in response to events outside the leadership's control, including unintended results of the party's own policies.

By the end of the decade, the potential for action was more restricted and the range of opportunities had narrowed. As the socialist system developed, the decisions and compromises made in the 1950s were "locked in," limiting the possibilities for advancing collective interests and exercising autonomy and influence.[56] Those who criticized the regime after 1957 risked being labeled as "rightists" and punished with exile, imprisonment, or even death. Ironically, by the end of the 1950s, with the establishment of the socialist system of state-administered work units known as *danwei*, the remaining means of advancing one's interests were highly individualistic—political activism, party membership, status as a labor model, and attaching oneself

56. On the phenomenon of lock-in and increasing returns in an economic context, see Brian Arthur's 1989 article, "Competing Technologies, Increasing Returns."

to networks of patronage in return for the benefits of socialism.[57] After the expropriation of capitalists' factories in 1956, the concept of class lost any meaning outside of revolutionary discourse and, as defined and legitimized by the party-state, rarely supported the autonomous pursuit of collective interests. By 1959, many of the collective identities based on native place, religion, and kinship had been suppressed, discredited, or co-opted, leaving workers with little basis for defining and pursuing their interests outside of the political, social, and economic system dominated by the party-state.[58] These end-of-the-decade outcomes were shaped by the vagaries of the mass campaigns of the previous ten years, even if the results of those campaigns were often not what any of the actors involved, including party leaders, had desired or expected.

The impact of social forces on the processes of revolution and state formation in the 1950s, the sites of contestation, and the unintended outcomes of such processes are nearly invisible if we adopt a top-down approach centered on China's revolutionary leaders. By examining many individual histories in detail, in a comparative framework, *Red Silk* highlights the resources and limitations that different social groups brought to their participation in the revolutionary project. Comparing the experiences of Wuxi filature workers and Shanghai silk weavers in the early years of Communist Party rule reveals the variable influences of gender, locality, factory regime, and recent history on the reception and manipulation of revolutionary politics. Comparative analysis of archival sources also reveals the broad diversity in people's relationships to political power and their ability to define and pursue individual and collective interests. These relationships highlight the extent and limits of social transformation in China's Communist revolution.

57. On the work units, see Lü and Perry, *Danwei*. See also Walder, *Communist Neo-Traditionalism*, and Bian, *Making of the State Enterprise System*.

58. Although often subsumed in the official discourse of class and nation, alternative identities, especially those based on native place and region, did not disappear entirely. Rather, they continued to form the basis for collective action when opportunities presented themselves, as during the Cultural Revolution. See, for example, Perry and Li, *Proletarian Power*.

Sources

Research into the Chinese revolution of the past thirty years has had the advantage of including previously inaccessible archival sources as well as oral interviews. Of course, like other sources, these have their own perspectives and biases, but newly available archival materials reveal many issues and events that had never previously appeared in public documents. Thus, they bring us one step closer to understanding how workers conceived of themselves and their relationships to other groups in Chinese society in the 1950s.

The sources for this study come mainly from municipal archives in the cities of the Yangzi Delta, especially Shanghai and Wuxi. Other source materials include contemporary newspaper articles, professional journals, and published reports, as well as interviews with former workers and managers in the Yangzi Delta silk industry. I conducted interviews with several men and women who lived in Shanghai and worked in the silk industry in the 1950s; the interviews gave me superb insights into the mentalities and experiences of silk industry workers and managers. Their recollections of how work was organized, how political campaigns developed, and how policies were implemented provided a more human and personal perspective than the official reports and published accounts. I am very grateful to the individuals who agreed to be interviewed, and I enjoyed immensely hearing their stories and gaining their insights into historical questions.[59]

The most revealing sources were archival documents produced by the unions (workers' organizations) and industry associations (employers' organizations) of Shanghai and Wuxi. These archival collections include internal reports on a wide range of subjects; individuals' letters, petitions, and confessions; and detailed records of meetings and discussions among workers, employers, and state officials. Meeting minutes, an extraordinarily rich source, often remarkably frank, pro-

59. In interviewing workers and managers retired from Shanghai silk factories, I encountered an interesting mix of nostalgia and vindication, identification with the regime and resistance to it, similar to findings in other research that has drawn on memories of the Maoist era, such as Unger and Chan, "Memories and the Moral Economy," and Ching Kwan Lee, "What Was Socialism." See also Hershatter, *Gender of Memory*, which makes extensive use of oral interviews.

vide novel insights into the complexities of labor relations and state-private relations. They also reveal specific details of the processes of revolutionary transformation rarely presented in such published sources as state directives and newspaper accounts. Documents from the unions and the employers' associations of the Yangzi Delta silk industry make up a rich base from which to examine the complex and varied experiences and perspectives of workers and employers in the first decade of the PRC.[60]

In comparing the lives of male silk weavers and female filature workers, I have attempted to construct a multilayered narrative and analysis that captures the diversity, complexity, and contingency of human experiences in the Chinese revolution. This approach reveals the many ways in which individuals and groups accepted, rejected, or manipulated the party's initiatives, and makes the point that life in revolutionary China did not begin and end in the headquarters of the Communist Party. This historical and humanistic approach also shows how people's perceptions and interests changed over time; for many people, earlier options became unviable or irrelevant and new opportunities appeared. To trace the many stories in this book, I do not follow a strictly linear narrative; instead, I often return to the same events of the 1950s in order to view them through different lenses and thereby present multiple perspectives.

Summary of Chapters

The first two chapters of *Red Silk* provide the historical background for developments following the Communist seizure of power in 1949. Chapter 1 presents the early history of China's modern silk industry

60. Working with these sources brought to mind a similar realization by Gail Hershatter in her research on workers in Tianjin: "The Tianjin working class was deeply fragmented, with significant numbers of handicraft workers, freight haulers, and casual laborers in addition to the millhands I had hoped to study. The material commanded an attentiveness to fragmentation, divisiveness, a changing sexual division of labor, and growth that proceeded in a distressingly nonlinear fashion." Hershatter, *Workers of Tianjin*, 7. I believe that this kind of nonlinearity and diversity helps us gain a better understanding of how political processes in the early PRC produced divergent outcomes in different contexts.

and the social structures, business practices, and government institutions that evolved from the industry's beginnings through the Japanese occupation and the postwar crisis. During the 1940s, the role of the state in administering the silk industry expanded dramatically while economic chaos and rampant inflation undermined the livelihoods of workers and employers alike. Chapter 2 examines the labor movements among Yangzi Delta silk workers during the same period; it also traces the organizations and tactics that workers developed to protect their interests during the difficult years of economic depression, war, and revolution. Although filature workers and silk weavers participated in these movements in different ways, on the eve of the Communist takeover the circumstances of exploited female mill workers and privileged male weavers had converged, owing to economic collapse and hyperinflation.

Chapter 3 presents a multilayered treatment of the transition to Communist rule in the early 1950s. It first chronicles the party's initial attempts to influence urban society and labor relations in private industry, as well as the Communists' efforts to restore production and employment in the Yangzi Delta silk industry. Next, it describes popular responses to the party's policies of Liberation (*Jiefang*) and New Democracy (*Xin minzhuzhuyi*) and details the CCP's efforts to organize unions and industry associations under Communist leadership. Chapter 4, focusing on workers in Shanghai's silk weaving industry, examines the ways in which silk weavers and their employers adapted to the crises precipitated by the Communist takeover and the outbreak of war in Korea. Well positioned to take advantage of the opportunities presented by the revolution and the restoration of silk weaving through state-contracted production for export to the Soviet Union, Shanghai silk weavers achieved many of the cherished goals of the labor movement, including job security, a living wage, medical benefits, and influence over managerial decisions and working conditions. The operations of the Shanghai Silk Weaving Industry Labor-Capital Consultative Conference, one of the most successful examples of "democratic management" in the early PRC, reveals the extent to which silk weavers benefited from the Communist seizure of power as one of the most privileged groups of workers in the Chinese revolution.

Chapter 5 describes the transition from "New Democracy" to a "Campaign Society" during the Korean War, from 1950 to 1953. Through political mobilization and production campaigns, the party-state attempted to redirect worker politics and transform labor relations, but workers and employers often took these campaigns in unanticipated directions. Even mobilization efforts to educate or suppress certain segments of the population, such as the campaign to implement the Marriage Law of 1950 or the Campaign to Suppress Counter-revolutionaries, produced unanticipated outcomes as men and women, workers and capitalists seized the opportunity to express, define, and pursue their own interests by manipulating the goals and methods of the campaigns. Popular attempts to manipulate political campaigns, although sometimes unsuccessful, influenced their outcomes and necessitated subsequent campaigns to deal with the new problems created.

Unlike the Shanghai silk weavers, the filature workers described in chapter 6 found their earlier tactics of spontaneous strikes and walkouts, which had often been very powerful, suppressed in the new political context. New Democracy emphasized restoring production and economic health through labor-capital cooperation rather than through radical efforts at liberation and social transformation. Taking advantage of this, filature management quickly dominated the unions established under Communist Party leadership, and little changed in the difficult (even hostile) working conditions of the thread mills. Indeed, before 1952 almost nothing changed for these workers except the intensification of filature work under the patriotic production competitions of the Korean War. After 1949 these women continued to work under a harsh and brutal factory regime in which male supervisors physically and verbally abused them. This gendered factory regime, based on patriarchal violence, persisted even in filatures administered by the revolutionary party-state. When change finally did come to the thread mills in the autumn of 1951, it came in the form of a party-led campaign for "Democratic Reform" of the unions that sought more to suppress the party's political enemies than to empower filature workers to pursue their own interests as workers and women.

Chapter 7 details the process of establishing state administration and control of silk production and redefining labor relations and state-society relations in line with the model of a planned socialist economy. More broadly, it examines the shift away from a mixed economy during the First Five-Year Plan through the socialist transformation of 1955–56. The continued focus on working conditions, labor relations, and state-society relations at the factory level helps to clarify the unintended (and often disappointing) results that socialization brought for silk workers, their former employers, and agents of the state. Although the institutional context changed dramatically after 1956, with agents of the state playing a much more prominent role in formerly private factories, the words and actions of silk workers and former capitalists continued to affect the outcomes of policy implementation and political campaigns.

With their voices increasingly suppressed in the years following the socialist transformation of 1956, former capitalists, male silk weavers, and female filature workers nonetheless continued to make their needs known and pursue their interests, sometimes going against the party regime. The fact that people continued to voice criticisms (sometimes just sarcastic comments) after the suppression of "rightists" in 1957 reveals the continuing conflict between labor and management, even under an economy and factory regime that was theoretically socialist. Chapter 7 also briefly summarizes the fate of the silk industry and its workers from the disasters of the Great Leap Forward of 1958–61 through the industry's rise to global dominance in the 1980s.

The topics explored in this book are of interest not only to historians of the Chinese revolution but also to scholars whose work focuses on labor and gender issues in contemporary China. Readers of sociological and political studies of Chinese workers in the past twenty years, such as Ching Kwan Lee's *Gender and the South China Miracle* and Lee's 2007 book, *Against the Law: Labor Protests in China's Rustbelt and Sunbelt*, will find useful connections and insights here, because contemporary social divisions have grown out of those of the Maoist period.[61]

61. Ching Kwan Lee, *Against the Law*. For just a few more examples of this literature, see Chan, *China's Workers under Assault*; Leslie Chang, *Factory Girls*; Hurst, *Chinese Workers after Socialism*; Philion, *Workers' Democracy*; and Pun, *Made in China*.

There are also many parallels between the Chinese revolution of 1949 and the Russian revolution of 1917. Despite the very different origins of the two Communist parties, the results of the two revolutions for Russian and Chinese workers and farmers were distressingly similar. The Chinese Communists modeled a great many of their institutions and policies on the Soviet example, contributing to what some scholars have described as the "Stalinization" of China under Mao—although even the Soviet Union was never as Stalinized as it appeared to outside observers, and the totalitarian project was even less complete in China.[62] However, there were also a great many unintended consequences common to both revolutions that cannot be explained solely by conscious imitation. The experiences of Chinese workers in the 1950s provide an intriguing comparison with those of Soviet workers in earlier decades.[63]

We are very fortunate now, in the early twenty-first century, to have gained access to a wealth of new sources while many of those who participated in these events are still alive and willing to speak to researchers. As a result, it has become possible to write a social history of the Chinese revolution from the ground up. *Red Silk* presents a history of the Chinese revolution that is more inclusive and complex than the versions related in either the official Chinese Communist historiography or the Cold War and postsocialist histories of the PRC published in the West. I hope that it will inspire more historians to go down to the factories to learn from the workers and enhance our understanding of the Chinese revolution.

62. For examples of the literature on Stalinization, see Hua-yu Li, *Economic Stalinization of China*; Meliksetov and Pantsov, "Stalinization of the People's Republic," 198–233; Walder, *China under Mao*; and Kaple, *Dream of a Red Factory*.

63. In contast with Chinese workers, the scholarship on workers in the Russian revolution and Stalin era is massive. Two works that are especially useful in this comparative context are Pirani, *Revolution in Retreat*, and S. A. Smith, *Revolution and the People*.

CHAPTER ONE

The Development of China's Modern Silk Industry

From the days of the Silk Road to the present age of global markets, few products have been as important as silk for China's domestic economy and foreign trade. Synonymous with China since ancient times,[1] silk was an important source of revenue for imperial governments from the Qin (221–206 BCE) to the Qing (1644–1911 CE). In the nineteenth and twentieth centuries, silk played a central role in China's industrialization, serving as a locus of mechanization, capital accumulation, and class formation. The history of China's modern silk industry exhibits change, diversity, and creativity in response to political turmoil, foreign occupation, and economic crisis. The practices that evolved in China's modern silk industry, born out of firms' difficult relationships with successive political regimes and developments in labor relations, persisted into the 1950s and beyond.

The Japanese occupation of China from 1937 to 1945, and the inflation and economic instability of the postwar period, are particularly important for our understanding of the silk industry policies of the early PRC. Not only did the Communists preserve the administrative organs established in the 1940s to govern the silk industry, but many of the Communists' early policies—such as state-contracted production in private factories, government-sponsored labor unions,

1. The English word "silk" is derived from the Greek *serikos*. The Greeks used the related term *Seres* to refer to China.

enterprise-based welfare provision, and the policy of labor-capital cooperation—have their origins in the years before 1949. Business practices and labor conflicts in the early PRC also exhibited continuities with the wartime and postwar periods. Incentives for firms to hold on to precious supplies and inventories intensified, and a highly politicized and class-conscious labor movement expanded during the Chinese Civil War and the inflationary crisis of the late 1940s. This chapter examines the emergence and development of China's modern silk reeling and weaving industries from the late nineteenth century through the crises of the 1930s and 1940s. The next chapter describes working conditions and the labor movement during the same period.

Chinese Silk from Ancient Times

According to legend, the Empress Leizu, wife of the Yellow Emperor, discovered sericulture (silk farming) almost five thousand years ago when a silkworm cocoon dropped into her bath, unraveling its lustrous fibers. Mulberry silkworms (*Bombyx mori*) were domesticated in China by 3000 BCE, and archaeologists have discovered images of silkworms and remains of cocoons, thread, and silk cloth at Neolithic sites dating from seven to ten thousand years ago.[2] Aside from boiling the cocoons to remove the sericin shell and release the fibers, the key innovation in sericulture was baking the chrysalides before they could hatch and eat their way out of the cocoon. Baked cocoons produced long, continuous fibers that could be reeled into thread by a simple mechanical process and then woven into cloth.

People around the world have prized silk for its qualities. Silk takes dyes well, and the rich depth of color combines beautifully with its lustrous sheen. It naturally breathes and absorbs moisture and is 20 percent warmer than goose down. Silk is also one of the strongest natural fibers on Earth, stronger than a steel filament of the same diameter. It is no surprise that silk quickly became a prized luxury good, lending its name to the trade routes that united Eurasia from ancient

2. Joan Lewis, "Chinese Empress Discovers Silk"; Zhu Xinyu, *Zhejiang sichou shi*, 1–3.

times. Not only was silk an important export for Chinese dynasties, the imperial state also collected silk as tax and used it as currency.

For centuries, women weavers in northwest China produced most of the world's silk cloth. But with the southern shift in population and production during the Song dynasty (960–1279), Jiangnan (the Lower Yangzi River region) became China's main source of silk. The rise of Jiangnan as a silk center from around 1000 CE accompanied a gradual commercialization of silk production. By the eighteenth century, male-dominated guilds had formed, resulting in a partial "masculinization" of commercial silk weaving that persisted into the twentieth century, with men and women weaving at home, and male workers employed in urban weaving workshops.[3]

Machinery for textiles production developed rapidly in imperial China under the stimulus of trade and government support. By the early fourteenth century, silk producers were using water-powered machinery to manufacture silk thread and complex pattern-making looms to weave many varieties of silk cloth. The Mongol Yuan dynasty (1271–1368) imposed a system of government-managed production and procurement for major commodities. At the height of the Mongol occupation, the government collected over 500 tons of raw silk (thread) annually. The Yuan furthermore established an imperial textiles system employing hereditary bonded weavers. Some of these state enterprises were very large in scale and employed hundreds of workers. For example, the Dongxi Silk Department in Jinling (present-day Nanjing) had 3,000 workers, 145 looms, and an annual production of 4,527 bolts requiring almost six tons of raw silk.[4]

The government of the Ming dynasty (1368–1644) preserved the Yuan policies with some important modifications. Hereditary weavers were allowed to work commercially but were still obliged to provide service to the state on a rotating basis. This continued until the system began to break down under abuses in the early sixteenth century, when artisans were permitted to commute their labor service to cash payment. Other Ming policies, especially the "Single Whip" tax reforms

3. On Chinese textiles between 1000 and 1800, see Bray, *Technology and Gender*, 175–272.

4. Zhu Xinyu, *Zhongguo sichou shi*, 263–68.

of 1581, encouraged the further expansion of silk production by private households. In some cases, large landowners expropriated the labor of their female bondservants to produce silk for the state and the market, and in the late Ming the imperial production system increasingly utilized independent contractors. It is estimated that the dynasty's annual demand for silk exceeded 280,000 bolts, which the Ming used as payment to military and government officials. Ming China also exchanged cloth for Tibetan and Mongolian horses and exported large amounts of silk to Southeast Asia and Spanish Manila.[5]

Under the Manchu rulers of the Qing dynasty (1644–1911), the trend toward commercial silk production accelerated. In an edict of 1645, the Shunzhi Emperor released all remaining hereditary artisans from bondage, making them ordinary subjects with no special obligation to the state. The imperial silk factories continued to hire weavers on a wage basis. Although by the end of the seventeenth century the annual output of government textiles factories exceeded that of the Ming, imperial production declined as a proportion of total textiles production.[6] Commercial silk production in the Yangzi Delta flourished under the Qing reforms. Silk weaving was managed by accounting houses (*zhangfang*) that did not operate factories, but acted as middlemen, guaranteeing the work and purchasing the product of dispersed household weavers on behalf of silk brokers who supplied thread. There were also urban silk factories in Qing China. In Jiangnan cities like Suzhou, male silk weavers gathered each morning under guild auspices to await work in the shops of the master weavers or the imperial factories. Hiring practices were conditioned by the needs of the imperial workshops and guild traditions, but these weavers' lives were as insecure as those of modern migrant workers. A late seventeenth-century source describes their existence this way: "Like vagrants, they gather together, and after having rice gruel, they scatter and return [whence they came]. If the master weavers should reduce their output, this group will have no

5. Zhu Xinyu, *Zhongguo sichou shi*, 302–6.

6. Zhang Yan, *Qingdai jingji jianshi*, 419–66, 609–15. For an overview of Chinese cotton and silk production from the seventeenth century to the present, see Cliver, "China," 103–39.

sources of food and clothing."[7] Much like modern proletarians, the weavers employed in commercial silk workshops of the eighteenth and nineteenth centuries proved sufficiently conscious and well-organized to engage in strikes for higher wages and job security.[8]

The military conflicts and violent uprisings of the nineteenth century dramatically curtailed these trends by disrupting trade and sericulture. The Taiping Rebellion (1851–64) left millions dead and destroyed urban silk weaving centers of the Yangzi Delta such as Nanjing. Toward the end of the rebellion, the Taiping leaders ordered acres of mulberry trees cut down, a catastrophe that contributed to the subsequent expansion of silk production in South China.[9] Jiangnan sericulture, silk reeling, and weaving only began to recover in the last decade of the nineteenth century.

The Development of China's Modern Silk Industry

In China, steam power developed earlier in the silk industry than in cotton textiles because of the two fabrics' different relationships with the world economy. Fueled by demand from European silk weavers, Chinese exports of hand-reeled silk increased rapidly from the 1830s. When French and Italian sericulture collapsed due to an epidemic of pébrine silkworm disease in the 1860s, demand for Chinese silk expanded. Beginning in the late nineteenth century, raw silk comprised one-quarter of the gross value of exports from Qing China, consistently occupying first or second place among exported commodities. Even as late as 1930, raw silk comprised nearly 15 percent of China's exports.[10] International trade in silk had several important effects on Chinese silk production in the nineteenth century; among these were the expansion of sericulture to the southern province of Guangdong, and the introduction of steam-powered reeling.

7. Quoted in Lillian Li, *China's Silk Trade*, 49. See also Eng, *Economic Imperialism in China*, 149–50.

8. Zhang Yan, *Qingdai jingji jianshi*, 455–64.

9. Koo, *Tariff and the Cotton Industry*, 74–79.

10. Xu Xinwu, *Zhongguo jindai saosi gongye*, 575; Yan Zhongping, *Zhongguo jindai jingji*, 74–76.

Partly due to the influence of international markets, sericulture and the silk industries followed different paths in Guangdong and Jiangnan. For example, whereas sericulturalists in Jiangnan tended to dedicate at least half of their land to rice, farmers in the new sericulture regions in the south grew dependent on silk alone, leaving them vulnerable to fluctuations in world markets and exchange rates. Steam-powered silk reeling appeared later in Jiangnan than in Guangdong and was more strongly influenced by the needs of the local silk weaving industry. The relationship between sericulturalists and silk filatures (the English term for silk thread mills) was also different in the two regions.

In the early nineteenth century, much of the raw silk exported from China was hand-reeled in sericulturalists' homes; the thread they produced was often of uneven thickness and was discolored by smoke from charcoal fires used for boiling cocoons. In both Shanghai and Guangzhou, European and American merchants dominated the silk export trade. Chinese merchants, though essential to the marketing process, were unwilling and unable to engage in the export trade directly. This created a separation between production and sales that inhibited foreign merchants' efforts to improve quality.[11] To encourage the production of high-quality raw silk of even width and color, foreign exporters attempted to set up steam filatures in Shanghai in the 1860s, but lacking a sufficient supply of cocoons, these filatures failed.[12] As US demand increased with the development of the silk and ribbon industries in places like Paterson, New Jersey, exporters sought to improve supplies through partnerships with silk producers in South China. This led to the introduction of French and Italian silk reeling technology and the establishment of steam-powered filatures, first in Guangdong and later in the Yangzi Delta.

The first successful steam filature in South China was established in 1874 by Chen Jiyuan, who had studied French silk reeling technology in Vietnam. Although opposition from household silk reelers stymied his first effort, once the local gentry in his native Nanhai realized that machine-reeled silk brought prices 30–60 percent higher

11. Hu Minjian, "Waishang yanghang," 45–62.
12. Bergère, *Shanghai*, 59–60, 69.

than hand-reeled silk, they invited him to set up another filature. Southern silk production developed rapidly under the leadership of local gentry, who used their status as landowners to encourage tenant farmers to engage in sericulture and utilized lineage organizations to legitimize the employment of young women in steam-powered filatures. By offering high prices for cocoons to ensure a stable supply and recruiting women workers from within lineage networks, Chen's rural factory quickly expanded to employ some three hundred workers. Within ten years there were ten such filatures in Guangdong Province, with a total of 2,400 basins for boiling cocoons. By century's end, virtually all the province's silk exports came from steam filatures, which numbered eighty-six, utilizing 34,600 basins.[13]

Steam filatures also flourished in the Yangzi Delta in the last decades of the nineteenth century. Chinese entrepreneurs successfully established filatures in Shanghai beginning in the 1880s, and by 1901 there were more than 20 filatures operating 7,800 basins.[14] Three years later, local elites in the Jiangnan town of Wuxi, many of whom already operated filatures in Shanghai, constructed filatures locally. Enjoying cheaper labor and better access to cocoons, filatures proliferated in smaller Yangzi Delta cities in the early twentieth century.[15] By 1928, there were 162 filatures in the Jiangnan region, of which 95 were in Shanghai. Supported by foreign capital and better connected to export markets, Shanghai's silk reeling industry expanded dramatically in the 1920s, and at its peak in 1930 there were more than 100 filatures there, operating more than 25,000 basins.[16] At its zenith in 1926, the southern silk reeling industry in the Canton Delta counted 202 filatures, but this industry declined steadily from 1929 to 1935 as international silk markets collapsed.[17]

13. Xu Xinwu, *Zhongguo jindai saosi gongye*, 627; Alvin So, *South China Silk District*, 112–18.

14. Xu Xinwu, *Zhongguo jindai saosi gongye*, 615.

15. Bell, *One Industry, Two Chinas*, 89–108. See also Gao and Yan, *Jindai Wuxi cansiye*, 54–188.

16. Xu Xinwu, *Zhongguo jindai saosi gongye*, 617; Lillian Li, *China's Silk Trade*, 163–73.

17. Eng, *Economic Imperialism in China*, 49–50.

China's silk weaving industry did not receive the same stimulus from world demand as the filature industry. On the contrary, as Robert Eng argues, export demand for raw silk had a deleterious effect on handicraft silk weaving. The weaving industry was also structured very differently. The mid-Qing commercial revolution of the eighteenth century led to a flourishing of household and workshop silk weaving. Predominantly male weavers served as the dispersed producers in a complex commercial network, or as wage laborers in manufactories that varied in scale and form of ownership. As silk exports increased and steam filatures developed in the late nineteenth century, it became increasingly difficult for weavers to obtain raw materials. This was due both to increased demand for Chinese silk overseas and to the fact that hand-reeled silk was softer and easier to weave using traditional wooden looms. In general, filature silk was exported, while the diminishing supplies of hand-reeled thread went to Chinese weavers. As steam filatures' demand for cocoons drove prices higher, sericulturalists increasingly focused on cocoon production and only returned to hand reeling when cocoon prices fell. These changes in Chinese silk production elicited violent protests and machine-wrecking among some communities of weavers in the 1870s and 1880s.[18]

Although the development of steam reeling for export adversely affected household weaving in South China, silk weaving remained relatively stable in other parts of China, and overall production of silk cloth increased in the early twentieth century.[19] The technology and structure of the silk weaving industry changed markedly, however. From the end of the nineteenth century rural handicraft weaving faced competition from factories employing iron looms equipped with Jacquard devices for setting complex designs.[20] Initially imported from Japan, these looms doubled productivity and were better suited to using the more brittle steam-filature thread.

18. Bell, *One Industry, Two Chinas*, 79; Eng, *Economic Imperialism in China*, 152–53. On the 1881 uprising of Nanhai silk weavers, see Eng, 1–3.

19. Lillian Li, *China's Silk Trade*, 120.

20. A French innovation of the late eighteenth century, Jacquard looms are fitted with an apparatus that has perforated cards to facilitate the weaving of figured and brocaded fabrics containing elaborate patterns.

As earnings from household handicrafts continued to decline, more and more Jiangnan weavers flocked to cities seeking work in mechanized silk factories. During the first two decades of the twentieth century, silk production spread from the old imperial silk center of Nanjing to smaller Jiangnan cities like Hangzhou, Suzhou, and Huzhou. In the 1910s and 1920s, Hangzhou witnessed the rapid electrification of silk weaving through the purchase of inexpensive Japanese power looms, affordable even to small workshops. The scale of production was generally very small, with most factories employing only ten or twenty weavers. But factories with over two hundred looms also appeared, demonstrating that silk weaving could attract substantial capital investment.

Hangzhou's Zhenxin Silk Factory introduced the first electric-powered looms in 1915, and within a few years there were more than eight hundred such looms in Hangzhou. The larger factories also adopted electric-powered equipment for processes such as twisting, spooling, and warp preparation. However, even small workshops could adopt electric-powered looms for weaving, as the technology was inexpensive and similar to hand-powered Jacquard looms. The weaving boom in Hangzhou stimulated the establishment of steam filatures there, and before the 1920s Hangzhou's silk weaving industry consumed more than 80 percent of the cocoons raised and reeled locally.[21]

In the 1920s, large weaving companies such as Meiya (the largest silk weaving company in China—sometimes called Mayar in English) and Meiwen in Shanghai, Lihua and Dachang in Huzhou, and Zhenya and Tiansun in Suzhou also adopted electric-powered looms. As the provincial silk factories went into decline after 1927 due to shrinking demand, power-loom silk weaving became concentrated in Shanghai. The treaty-port metropolis emerged as the major center for silk weaving in the Yangzi Delta due to its many advantages, including lower taxes and interest rates, as well as access to electric power, imported synthetic fibers, and export markets.

21. Zhu Xinyu, *Zhejiang sichou shi*, 184; D. K. Lieu, *Silk Industry of China*, 162. On the question of whether demand for raw silk from weavers held back development of steam filatures in Jiangnan, contrast Lillian Li, *China's Silk Trade*, 118–29, and Alvin So, *South China Silk District*, 111.

By 1931, Shanghai's silk weaving industry counted five hundred workshops (as opposed to just fifty-one in 1928) with some six thousand power looms. That year, the Meiya Company, which operated several silk factories in the Jiangnan region, employed a total of 2,368 personnel utilizing 927 looms, and produced 192,794 bolts of silk cloth. The scale of Jiangnan silk factories varied widely, however, and large firms like Meiya coexisted with hundreds of small workshops employing fewer than thirty workers. Whereas Meiya was organized as a limited liability company, most silk weaving factories were family-owned or simple partnerships with minimal capital, often established by veteran weavers.[22]

Shanghai's silk weaving industry went into steep decline in the 1930s. These were hard times for China's silk weavers, who exported 60 percent of their product annually and found it increasingly difficult to compete with Japanese products as international markets evaporated.[23] Competition between China and Japan in world silk markets reflected broader trends in the early decades of the twentieth century. From 1909, Japan surpassed China as the world's leading exporter of silk, and by the 1920s, Japan provided almost 80 percent of silk imports to the United States, the world's largest market for silk at that time. Responding to US demand, the quality and cost of Japanese silk improved from the late nineteenth century. Shipping costs to the United States from China were 20–30 percent higher than costs from Japan, and Japanese producers enjoyed the additional advantages of lower production costs and higher labor productivity.

One of Japan's greatest advantages was the high quality and low cost of Japanese cocoons. By 1930, Japanese cocoons cost 30 percent less than Chinese cocoons. When combined with higher productivity, this translated into prices for Japanese silk that were less than half of Chinese prices. Japanese filatures' direct connections and financial arrangements with sericulturalists furthermore enabled them to promote improved techniques and hybrid strains. Both the silk capitalists and the Japanese government were far more effective than their Chinese

22. Xu Xinwu, *Jindai Jiangnan sizhi gongye*, 310; D. K. Lieu, *Silk Industry of China*, 173–84.

23. D. K. Lieu, *Silk Industry of China*, 163–72; *Shanghai sichou zhi*, 172.

counterparts at improving sericulture and silk production. Between 1897 and 1920, the Japanese government passed several laws to regulate and improve cocoon quality. Government funding of sericulture schools, egg research and production stations, and silk inspection stations at trading ports facilitated scientific improvements in Japanese silk production and established mechanisms for the enforcement of quality standards.[24]

In contrast, in the early twentieth century, China lacked a strong central government that could implement similar policies effectively or even prevent the export of thousands of tons of cocoons to Japan in the 1920s.[25] Export taxes on raw silk disadvantaged Chinese silk in competition with Japanese products and synthetic fibers. At the same time, China's Customs Administration taxed imports of rayon, which was increasingly favored by Chinese weavers, despite the fact that China did not produce its own synthetics.[26] The conflict of interests between Chinese producers and foreign exporters, combined with the lack of effective government leadership, prevented the institution of a recognized silk inspection agency until the establishment of the Silk Department of the Shanghai Bureau of Inspection and Testing of Commercial Commodities in 1929.[27] By that time Chinese producers of silk cloth had all but lost their markets in the United States and Europe and were mainly exporting to Southeast Asia and India. High demand within China, however, continued to support production of silk cloth.

Chinese production of filature silk peaked at more than 16 million tons in 1930, by which time China was exporting more than 10 million tons annually and Japan was exporting more than 30 million tons

24. Eng, *Economic Imperialism in China*, 163–74.

25. Gu and Wang, *Riben qinhua shiqi*, 64–68.

26. In the 1920s, Chinese weavers began using rayon weft, imported from the United States, Italy, and Japan. Synthetics were easy to work with and almost as strong as silk, although they did not take dyes with the same depth and brilliance. When weavers learned the process of starching rayon warp in 1926, the Chinese market for rayon expanded rapidly. With the introduction of soft and fine rayon at low prices in 1929, imports boomed, reaching 29 million yuan in 1931. Rayon contributed to Shanghai's weaving boom, and by the 1930s most Chinese silk products included synthetic fibers. Zhu Xinyu, *Zhejiang sichou shi*, 185–96; D. K. Lieu, *Silk Industry of China*, 166–67.

27. Eng, *Economic Imperialism in China*, 181–87.

annually. Although both countries' silk industries suffered during the Great Depression, between 1930 and 1935, China's silk exports dropped by 50 percent while Japan's only fell by 15 percent. China's share of the lucrative US market fell from 14 percent in 1930 to just 2 percent in 1934, while Japan's share increased to 97 percent. By 1934, the price of Chinese silk in New York was less than one-third the 1930 price.[28] Responding to petitions from silk producers, China's Nationalist government removed the export tax on silk thread in 1933. The National Economic Commission also announced a 30 million yuan bond issue to support sericulture improvement and state purchases of accumulated inventories.[29] But in the context of global economic depression there was little the government could do to halt falling prices and profits.

The decline of China's silk industry in contrast with Japan's success derived in large part from the lack of effective government leadership. Nationalist government programs to develop silk production during the Nanjing Decade (1927–37) failed due to capitalist corruption and peasant mistrust, and the lost export potential of the silk industry, in turn, hindered China's economic development and industrialization. As Robert Eng puts it, "In Japan there was a transition from silk to steel that failed to take place in China."[30] For one thing, the Nationalist government's extortionate policies toward Yangzi Delta businesses exacerbated uncertainties and imposed additional costs. During the "revenue drive" of May 1927, Nationalist Party supporters forced the Shanghai Silk Dealers Union to contribute 100,000 yuan to Chiang Kai-shek's government. The Nationalists' policies toward industry were not entirely exploitative, however. Parks Coble explains that "the Nanking Government did make modest efforts to aid industry and commerce," and in August 1931 the National Industrial and Commercial Conference voted to issue 6 million yuan in bonds to assist the Yangzi Delta silk industry.[31]

28. Ding Kangshi, "Woguo cansi chanxiao gaikuang"; Eng, *Economic Imperialism in China*, 179–80; Liu Dajun, *Zhongguo gongye diaocha baogao*, 2:639. On the decline of Chinese filatures in the 1930s, see Gao and Yan, *Jindai Wuxi cansiye*, 221–47.

29. Eng, *Economic Imperialism in China*, 160. See also Gao and Yan, *Jindai Wuxi cansiye*, 247–380.

30. Eng, *Economic Imperialism in China*, 195.

31. Coble, *Shanghai Capitalists*, 34, 84.

In 1932, China's largest silk manufacturers established the Silk Reform Association (Cansi gailiang hui), which studied advanced Japanese methods and promoted research, training, and dissemination of improved techniques. The Association also established quality standards and an inspection system that offered bonuses for high-quality silk, but its reach was limited.[32] Of greatest potential benefit was the Nationalist government's program to reform sericulture in the villages of the Yangzi Delta. Modeled on Japanese programs, this was an attempt to eliminate pébrine silkworm disease, improve sericultural methods, and provide high-quality, disease-free eggs to silk farmers. The program established egg stations and scientific research institutes, introduced a quality control regime, facilitated access to capital and markets, and assisted sericulturalists in organizing cooperative cocoon ovens to decrease their dependence on the cocoon *hang* brokerage firms.[33] These efforts met with only limited success, however, and the program sometimes created more problems than solutions.

Nowhere were the program's difficulties more evident than in efforts to eliminate pébrine silkworm disease. In the 1920s, 75 to 95 percent of all silkworm eggs were infected, and only about 30 percent of Chinese silkworms survived to produce cocoons.[34] But the 1930s silk reform encountered such mistrust on the part of sericulturalists that disinfecting measures were usually blocked unless the government experts could gain the active support of trusted village elites.[35] Particularly damaging to the program's credibility were repeated failures to supply sufficient numbers of improved egg cards while at the same time forbidding the use of "native" (*tu*) eggs, which yielded about one-third less silk than improved varieties. The practice of selling high-priced, poor-quality egg cards masquerading as improved varieties was widespread, and even sericulture improvement leaders engaged in deception

32. Weidner, "Local Political Work," 70. See also Gao and Yan, *Jindai Wuxi cansiye*, 247–322.

33. Cocoon *hang* were purchasing brokers who acted as middlemen between the cocoon farmers and the filatures. Bell, *One Industry, Two Chinas*, 139–53.

34. Lillian Li, *China's Silk Trade*, 23.

35. Weidner, "Local Political Work," 71–72; Gao and Yan, *Jindai Wuxi cansiye*, 254–58.

and profiteering to the detriment of reform efforts.[36] By 1933, these kinds of abuses incited Jiangnan silk farmers to riot, and they burned egg stations and sericulture centers in districts throughout Zhejiang Province. The Nationalist government's silk reform program ended in violence.[37]

Winning the active support of village leaders was essential for the success of sericulture reform. The domination of the Silk Reform Association and its provincial committees by the owners of large filatures, however, contributed to the effort's failure. Silk industry elites, such as Xue Shouxuan, owner of Wuxi's massive Yongtai Filature, exploited reform efforts to depress cocoon prices and increase profits. Xue established a network of egg breederies that sold improved eggs to sericulturalists, who were contracted to sell their cocoons to Xue's filatures at pre-arranged prices, often below prevailing market rates. Although world prices for raw silk recovered steadily from 1935 to 1937, the prices Xue's filatures offered for cocoons remained artificially low at fifteen to thirty yuan per *dan*. With production costs estimated at about twenty yuan per *dan* of cocoons, sericulturalists were left with painfully slim margins.[38]

Jiangnan filatures claimed that suppressing cocoon prices was necessary to maintain meager profits, but the Nationalist Party organization of Zhejiang Province "disputed the owners' claims of poverty,"[39] and investigators estimated filature profits at 25–35 percent or even higher. For his part, Xue Shouxuan made huge profits from low cocoon prices in the mid-thirties. Taking advantage of the silk reform program and purchasing failing filatures during the depression, the Xue family group by 1934 had expanded to control a combined 2,400

36. Bell, *One Industry, Two Chinas*, 145–52.

37. Weidner, "Local Political Work," 73–74.

38. D. K. Lieu, *Silk Industry of China*, appendix; Weidner, "Local Political Work," 76; Bell, *One Industry, Two Chinas*, 168–70, 174–75. For a moving fictional account of sericulturalists' difficulties, see the 1932 short story by Mao Dun, "Spring Silkworms."

39. Weidner, "Local Political Work," 77.

reeling machines, 20 percent of Wuxi's total silk reeling capacity.[40] The Xue family also modified its corporate structure and strategies, establishing marketing offices in the United States, Britain, Australia, and other countries beginning in 1932. In 1934, Xue Shouxuan sent his brother, Xue Zukang, to set up a branch of the Yongtai Company in New York, which helped to increase exports and profits.[41] The suppression of cocoon prices through domination of the silk reform program was indispensable to the expansion of Xue family assets. By 1937 Xue Shouxuan's company had gained control of two-thirds of Wuxi's cocoon brokers and filatures, and the months before the Japanese invasion of China in July of that year were very profitable.[42]

For most producers of cocoons, thread, and cloth, however, the global depression reversed years of growth in production, profits, and employment.[43] China's silver-based currency had initially protected Chinese exporters from the effects of the global depression following the October 1929 collapse of the New York Stock Exchange. And in many industries, falling prices for Chinese goods compensated for reduced demand in international markets. Silk exports, however, already suffering from Japanese competition, plummeted with collapsing demand. Exports of raw silk, China's largest foreign exchange earner, dropped by one-third in 1929–30 and fell by a further 50 percent in 1931–32, catastrophically reducing revenues in the filature industry.[44]

The silk industry's difficulties worsened with the flooding of the Yangzi River in the summer of 1931, described as "the most disastrous in sixty years."[45] The crisis was further exacerbated by the Japanese seizure of Manchuria in September 1931, followed by fighting in Shanghai's Zhabei District in January 1932. Military conflict between Japanese

40. Bell, *One Industry, Two Chinas*, 170–72; Wang He, "Wei fazhan Zhongguo siye," 184–87.

41. Qian, *Wuxishi sichou gongye*, 21; Coble, *Japan's New Order*, 162.

42. Weidner, "Local Political Work," 78; Bell, *One Industry, Two Chinas*, 172–73.

43. For an analysis of the effects of plummeting world prices on silk farmers in Wujin, Jiangsu, between 1931 and 1934, see the 1937 article by Raeburn and Ko, "Prices in Wuchin, Kiangsu," 251–61.

44. Rawski, *Economic Growth*, 171. As Tim Wright puts it, "Among the consumer goods industries . . . the worst hit was silk." Wright, "World Depression," 651–52.

45. Rawski, *Economic Growth*, 171–72.

and Chinese troops, including aerial bombardment and shelling of this industrial and residential district, wrought destruction on the city's silk industry, with losses estimated at nearly 1.5 million yuan.[46]

In late 1932, international silver prices began to rise, which increased the cost of Chinese exports. US government purchases of silver at high prices in 1934–35 drove up Chinese prices and created a currency crisis as large amounts of silver were smuggled out of China. Although, as Thomas Rawski notes, Chinese price deflation "began later, was less severe, and ended more rapidly" than in the United States, the effects were disastrous for China's silk producers and sericulturalists. By 1936, despite the industry's nascent recovery, Chinese silk production was no greater than it had been in 1912, and exports had declined by about 60 percent when compared with 1926.[47]

The impact of this manufacturing collapse on the finances of silk enterprises and the livelihoods of their workers was catastrophic. A 1933 industrial survey estimated the total number of workers employed in China's silk industries at 194,900 (107,500 in silk reeling and 87,400 in production of silk cloth), a marked decline from 1929. In 1933 an estimated 31,510 silk workers were employed in Shanghai, but more than twice that number may have been unemployed. The number of silk filatures in Shanghai fell from 107 in 1930 to a low of 10 in 1932, recovering to 33 filatures by 1935.[48]

The wave of factory closures Shanghai experienced was replicated in other silk-producing regions, with one-half to two-thirds of filatures throughout China closing their doors between 1929 and 1934. By 1933 only one filature survived in Guangzhou, and more than 10,000 filature workers in Zhejiang Province had lost their jobs.[49] A 1933 survey of industry in seventeen Chinese provinces recorded only 137 filatures employing a total of 86,032 workers, and 204 silk weaving factories

46. On the 1932 conflict in Shanghai, see Henriot, "Neighborhood under Storm," 291–319.

47. Rawski, *Economic Growth*, 173–78, 357–58.

48. Liu Dajun, *Zhongguo gongye diaocha baogao*, 2: 271–72; Liu and Yeh, *Economy of the Chinese Mainland*, 427–32. Yan Zhongping, *Zhongguo jindai jingji*, 162–63, gives somewhat different figures, but the trend is the same.

49. Weidner, "Local Political Work," 68; Lillian Li, *China's Silk Trade*, 123; Eng, *Economic Imperialism in China*, 158.

employing just 19,490 people.[50] Jobless silk workers responded with protests, while silk producers still at work, facing wage reductions and fearful of layoffs, engaged in slowdowns and strikes to protect their livelihoods. The Great Depression thus produced one of the most intense periods of labor unrest in the Yangzi Delta silk industry, to be discussed in more detail in the next chapter.

The Yangzi Delta Silk Industry under Japanese Occupation

The failure of the Nationalist government to improve sericulture and increase China's competitiveness in world silk markets was partly due to an environment of corruption and mistrust. But the unfavorable economic environment during the Great Depression and competition from Japanese producers were additional objective factors that undermined the Nationalists' efforts. In a more favorable environment, with prices and exports beginning to recover in the mid-1930s, Nationalist policies might have succeeded. By 1936, when there was a bumper cocoon harvest, more than 7,000 power looms were weaving silk cloth in Shanghai, and more than 10,000 were operating in other Jiangnan cities. Chinese silk exports had begun to revive. But any positive trends in the Chinese economy were cut short or diverted after 1937.

The Japanese invasion of the Jiangnan region in late 1937 brought significant changes to China's silk industry. The initial devastation of war, followed by years of Japanese occupation, destroyed much of the productive capacity of Jiangnan sericulture and restricted the industry's expansion. Most significantly, the occupation authorities attempted to impose a monopoly on the trade in cocoons and on the production and marketing of silk thread. Although the occupation's monopoly was never complete, and much of Jiangnan silk production remained beyond its control, wartime measures nonetheless restricted Chinese silk production. Occupation policies also reduced the assets

50. Qin Xiaoyi, *Minguo jingji fazhan*, 544. The original 1933 survey data give slightly different numbers for silk weaving—a total of 197 factories employing 18,501 workers and staff. Liu Dajun, *Zhongguo gongye diaocha baogao*, 2: 271–73.

and independence of silk factory owners and laid the foundation for expanded state intervention in the silk industry in the years following the Japanese surrender.

In the late nineteenth century, Japan adopted an aggressive and extortionate policy toward China that by 1932 had resulted in the colonization of Korea, Taiwan, and Manchuria, along with Japan's extraction of heavy reparations and colonial concessions from China. In 1937, Japanese aggression culminated in an invasion of North China following the Marco Polo Bridge Incident of July 7. By August 13, the war had reached Shanghai, where hundreds of thousands of soldiers and civilians perished by the time the Japanese occupied the city in October. Unable to stop the Japanese advance, Chinese forces retreated west. By November, Wuxi and Hangzhou had fallen, and in December Nanjing, the Nationalist capital, fell with numerous atrocities and horrific loss of life.[51]

Japan's invasion of the Yangzi Delta was disastrous for the Jiangnan silk industry. In Shanghai, bombings and fires destroyed over 90 percent of productive capacity in the silk reeling industry, concentrated in the hard-hit Zhabei and Hongkou Districts. According to one account, facing the burning silk factories was like being "in the mouth of a volcano."[52] Of Shanghai's forty-four silk filatures, only the ten located in the relative safety of the Foreign Concessions were spared destruction. A July 1939 report by the Shanghai branch of the Silk Reeling Industry Association stated that only 986 of the city's 10,790 reeling machines survived. The rest were destroyed, with an estimated loss of at least ten million yuan, not including stores of cocoons and reeled silk.[53] As the war progressed up the Yangzi River, the devastation spread to other silk centers. Wuxi lost nearly one-third of its filatures and about one-quarter of its 16,724 reeling machines, and the Japanese

51. Wen-hsin Yeh, *Wartime Shanghai*, 1–2.

52. *Shanghai sichou zhi*, 76–77.

53. SMA S37-1-361. *Shanghai sichou zhi*, 192 gives different figures—7,524 reeling machines either totally or partially destroyed, with only 2,562 surviving, but the total value of losses (10 million) is the same. For more on the initial destruction and rapid recovery of industry in wartime Shanghai, see Henriot, "Shanghai Industries under Japanese Occupation," 17–45.

assault on the city also destroyed eight out of thirteen cocoon warehouses and their contents.[54]

On the eve of the invasion, Shanghai's silk weaving industry counted 480 factories with a total of 7,200 looms producing over two million bolts of silk and satin annually. Most were devastated by aerial bombing, and machinery that was not destroyed outright was confiscated during the occupation. Losses in Shanghai's silk weaving industry were estimated at more than five million yuan. The Meiya Company's Number Ten Factory, one of the newest and most advanced silk weaving factories in China, was laid waste, along with its Number Two Factory and many others on August 13, 1937, the first day of the Japanese assault on Shanghai.[55]

One of the immediate consequences of the invasion was a sharp decline in Chinese silk production just when world demand was recovering. Some Chinese factory owners relocated to Shanghai's Foreign Concessions. Others sought to continue production by obtaining licenses and establishing "joint operations" with the Japanese authorities. Still others attempted to eke out a living on the (loose and wide) margins of the occupation silk monopoly, often moving operations to rural villages to avoid the Japanese authorities.[56] In those parts of Zhejiang, Jiangsu, and Anhui Provinces that the Japanese military held by mid-1938, they went to great lengths to control the production and exchange of major commodities. Unlike many other industries, however, Chinese silk production competed directly with Japan in export markets. Japanese efforts to control Jiangnan silk production therefore exhibited contradictory impulses. On the one hand, the occupation authorities and Japanese capitalists sought to develop and exploit Chinese silk as part of a policy of "using the war to support the war." When this project conflicted with the interests of Japan's silk industry, however, the occupation authorities sought to curtail Chinese silk production and exports.[57]

54. Chen Ciyu, *Zhongguo de jixie saosi*, 115–16; Lincoln, *Urbanizing China*, 130–31.

55. *Shanghai sichou zhi*, 77, 193; *Jiangsusheng cansang sichou zhi*, 250–55.

56. Lincoln, *Urbanizing China*, 132–38.

57. Coble, *Japan's New Order*, 37; Zhu Xinyu, *Zhejiang sichou shi*, 207–8.

The main institution for establishing control over Jiangnan silk production was the Central China Sericulture Company (CCSC) (Huazhong cansi gongsi).[58] The Japanese occupation authorities established the company under the Central China Development Corporation in Shanghai in August 1938 with the following mission: "In controlling sericulture and silk production in this region, the scheme is to coordinate production and exports in Japan and China, to promote the sound development of the two countries' silk industries, so as to make a contribution to the world's silk industry."[59] The CCSC was the product of uneasy cooperation between Japanese industrialists and the military because, unlike industries such as coal and steel, the military leadership found it more practical to invite Japanese capital to invest in the rehabilitation of silk production in occupied Jiangnan.[60] Although the majority of the company's ten million yen investment was nominally from private Japanese firms, most of this was, in fact, loans from the Japanese government. Participation by Japanese capitalists in the CCSC included a total of 218 companies engaged in all aspects of sericulture, silk production, and marketing, especially filatures and exporters. Thirty percent of the CCSC's ten million yen investment came from Chinese sources, mainly in the form of physical plant and fixed assets expropriated from their Chinese owners, who then became junior partners in their own firms.[61]

By the end of 1938, the CCSC was operating 44 offices in 30 Jiangnan counties and cities and directly managing 22 filatures with a total of 6,974 reeling machines.[62] A series of decrees between 1938 and 1940 granted the CCSC monopoly control over all aspects of the production and marketing of silkworm eggs, cocoons, and filature silk in the Jiangnan region.[63] In June 1939, the occupation regime ordered that silk

58. On CCSC policies, see Gao and Yan, *Jindai Wuxi cansiye*, 385–428.

59. Quoted in Chen Ciyu, *Zhongguo de jixie saosi*, 131.

60. Coble, *Japan's New Order*, 42.

61. Chen Ciyu, *Zhongguo de jixie saosi*, 116–18; *Shanghai sichou zhi*, 203–5; Henriot, "Shanghai Industries under Japanese Occupation," 26–35.

62. *Jiangsusheng cansang sichou zhi*, 204; Gu and Wang, *Riben qinhua shiqi*, 102–7.

63. These decrees are reproduced in Gu and Wang, *Riben qinhua shiqi*, 143–47; Shanghai Municipal Archives, *Riben zai Huazhong*, 337–40.

production in the three provinces of Zhejiang, Jiangsu, and Anhui should also come under the control of the CCSC, placing the fate of more than half of Chinese silk production in the hands of China's aggressive rival. Through the CCSC, the occupation authorities established a degree of control over Jiangnan egg breederies, cocoon *hang*, and filatures. For example, the company issued licenses to more than 300 cocoon *hang*, which purchased cocoons on its behalf, sometimes accompanied by military police.[64]

The CCSC's control over silk production nonetheless remained incomplete for several reasons. In 1938 and 1939, the company offered prices for cocoons that amounted to just one-fifth of 1936 prices, and it only paid sericulturalists after the cocoons had been reeled and sold as thread. According to CCSC statistics, Zhejiang cocoon production fell by more than 50 percent from 1936 to 1940. This may reflect the authorities' inability to collect cocoons or information more than it does a real decline in production.[65] Although the CCSC reversed its policies and increased purchasing prices for cocoons in 1940, the outbreak of the Pacific War a year later necessitated reducing Chinese silk output to prevent competition with Japanese producers.[66]

Of the more than one million *dan* of dried cocoons the CCSC purchased between 1938 and 1943, most were reeled in Jiangnan filatures. The CCSC guaranteed cocoon-purchasing loans for filatures, taking equipment and inventories as collateral. This established a pattern of indebtedness among Jiangnan filatures that continued into the postwar years. To further strengthen the occupation's silk monopoly, the Filature Silk Inspection Department, which approved silk thread for export, only accepted silk produced by CCSC-licensed filatures.[67]

Regulations enforcing occupation policies were backed by military force, but in practice the system fell short of a complete monopoly. For one thing, the CCSC's funds were insufficient to dominate cocoon

64. Zhou Dehua, "Lunxian shiqi de Wujiang sichouye," 45–46.

65. Lincoln, *Urbanizing China*, 132–34, argues convincingly that the rapid restoration of sericulture and market networks under autonomous (if cooperative) Chinese leadership hindered later Japanese attempts to impose price controls and licenses.

66. Zhu Xinyu, *Zhejiang sichou shi*, 208–9; Coble, *Japan's New Order*, 37, 59.

67. Chen Ciyu, *Zhongguo de jixie saosi*, 119–20; *Shanghai sichou zhi*, 204.

markets. Given the high prices that filatures in Wuxi's hinterland and Shanghai's Foreign Concessions were willing to pay for dried cocoons, the potential profits to unlicensed cocoon merchants and shipping agents were well worth the risk. The "scramble for cocoons was particularly fierce" in 1941.[68] Resistance fighters were able to disrupt transportation and prevent sales to CCSC-licensed cocoon *hang*. As a result, the occupation monopoly was never able to purchase more than 44 percent of the Jiangnan cocoon harvest, and between 1939 and 1943 the average proportion was only 35 percent.[69] Most Jiangnan cocoons were traded by Chinese brokers and reeled by independent filatures, including a small number of state-run "guerrilla" filatures in the mountains of eastern Zhejiang that remained under Nationalist control.[70] A great deal of silk production during the war thus took place in filatures relocated to rural areas outside Japanese control and operated by workers fleeing the war and the occupied cities.

Because of these factors, the CCSC was only able to control and operate a limited number of silk filatures. In the cities of occupied Zhejiang, only the twenty-one largest filatures continued operations, and their former owners were permitted just a 30 percent stake in the new "joint-venture" companies. The CCSC controlled these firms' supplies of raw materials, credit, and products, and it also attempted to plan production to support Japan's interests, especially controlling as much of the export trade as possible. Another fifty filatures or more operated under CCSC licenses throughout the Yangzi Delta with similar controls in place. Despite the occupation authorities' plans to restore Jiangnan silk production to aid the Japanese war effort, however, by 1940 little more than one-fifth of Wuxi's surviving reeling machines were engaged in production for the CCSC; these employed between ten thousand and twenty thousand workers, compared with more than thirty thousand working in Wuxi's filatures in 1934.[71]

68. Lincoln, *Urbanizing China*, 140–41.

69. *Shanghai sichou zhi*, 86; Gu and Wang, *Riben qinhua shiqi*, 115.

70. Zhu Xinyu, *Zhejiang sichou shi*, 211–14.

71. Lincoln, *Urbanizing China*, 138–39, gives a peak wartime figure of twenty thousand workers employed in Wuxi's filatures in 1939. Chen Ciyu, *Zhongguo de jixie saosi*, 118, 124–25; Zhu Xinyu, *Zhejiang sichou shi*, 209–10.

It is difficult to characterize Chinese capitalists under the Japanese occupation as either collaborators or resisters in any consistent way. As Christian Henriot points out, although Chinese industrialists' refusal to cooperate with the Japanese was "tantamount to having their installations confiscated," factory owners frequently avoided collaboration.[72] Generally speaking, the occupation authorities had little to offer Chinese businesses but unequal partnerships, exploitation, and humiliation.[73] This was especially true for Jiangnan silk industrialists and merchants, who were reluctant to submit to the control of their greatest international rival. Few collaborated actively because cooperation with the occupation authorities provided few benefits. Some simply shut down and retired. Others struggled to restore their factories in areas beyond CCSC control.[74]

An immediate response of many Jiangnan silk capitalists to the Japanese invasion and rising silk prices on world markets was the removal of production facilities to Shanghai's Foreign Concessions, which remained free of Japanese occupation until the end of 1941. By October 1938, fourteen filature owners from Zhejiang and Jiangsu Provinces had reestablished their factories in the "lonely island" (*gudao*) of unoccupied Shanghai. Whereas in 1937 there were only two filatures in the Foreign Concessions, in 1938 there were as many as forty-six.[75] Colonial status provided a degree of protection not only from the devastation of war, but also from the occupation monopoly.

72. Henriot, "Shanghai Industries under Japanese Occupation," 31–33. On collaboration in the context of occupied China, see Brook, *Collaboration*. For a detailed local study of the silk center of Shaoxing, in Zhejiang Province, see Schoppa, "Elite Collaboration in Occupied Shaoxing," 156–79. Schoppa reminds us that "we must go beyond a simple moral interpretation of resistance and collaboration" to achieve a deeper understanding of individuals' allegiances, interests, and motivations.

73. Coble, *Japan's New Order*, 1–3. On the specifics of "joint ownership" under the Japanese occupation, see Barnett, *Economic Shanghai*, 89–96.

74. On the restoration of the silk industry in wartime Wuxi and the role of Chinese leaders willing to work with Japanese occupation forces, see Lincoln, *Urbanizing China*, 132–41.

75. Hinder, *Life and Labour*, 35; Coble, *Japan's New Order*, 23–24; Henriot, "Shanghai Industries under Japanese Occupation," 32–35; Barnett, *Economic Shanghai*, 96.

In a short-lived wartime boom that was due to the migration of factories and workers from other parts of the Yangzi Delta, by 1939 silk production in Shanghai had increased 17 percent as compared with 1936. Exports of raw silk reached a record 4,358 *dan* in November 1938, and international prices continued to increase. From 1939 to 1941, filature silk was Shanghai's most lucrative export.[76]

The CCSC sought to restrict supplies of dried cocoons to filatures in the Foreign Concessions, but Shanghai filatures could obtain cocoons by paying high prices and relying on well-established commercial networks that were antipathetic to the Japanese. Smugglers could earn profits of 30–40 percent delivering cocoons and thread to Shanghai factories.[77] After the occupation regime officially banned the sale of cocoons to filatures in the Foreign Concessions in June 1939, however, it became increasingly difficult to obtain supplies. From late 1939, Shanghai filatures began to close due to lack of raw materials, and by the end of 1940 only four remained, including the Dali Filature.[78]

Shanghai's silk weaving industry similarly enjoyed a brief period of growth in the Foreign Concessions before the outbreak of the Pacific War. For example, the Meiya Company's Number Four and Number Nine Factories, fortuitously located in the Foreign Concessions, restored production in October 1937. Under the leadership of its general manager, Cai Shengbai, Meiya moved equipment from its Shanghai factories to new sites in Hankou, Chongqing, Guangzhou, and Hong Kong.[79] Other silk companies used family members to carry out a similar strategy of dispersing production to avoid losses during the war. Although most silk weaving factories were too small to adopt Meiya's

76. Coble, *Japan's New Order*, 24, 219; *Shanghai sichou zhi*, 77; Barnett, *Economic Shanghai*, 97–99.

77. Chen Ciyu, *Zhongguo de jixie saosi*, 119–20; Lincoln, *Urbanizing China*, 133–34, 141; Zhou Dehua, "Lunxian shiqi de Wujiang sichouye," 46.

78. *Shanghai sichou zhi*, 194–95, 200–201; Tang Kentang, "Dali sichang jianshi," 233–36.

79. This strategy did not save all of Meiya's factories. Its Hankou factory was destroyed in 1941, along with the company's entire archives and accounts from before 1937. Japanese forces seized its Guangzhou factory and confiscated its equipment. When the Japanese attacked Hong Kong in December 1941, Meiya's stores of synthetic fibers were destroyed, causing losses of over HK$200,000. *Shanghai sichou zhi*, 201–3; Feng, *Cai Shengbai*, 70–79.

methods, many found the means to survive, and by the end of 1938, 106 silk weaving factories with an estimated 1,500 looms had restored operations in Shanghai's Foreign Concessions.[80]

Owners of Jiangnan silk factories that were unable to relocate outside occupied territory faced the unappetizing choice of accepting Japanese domination, going out of business, or moving operations to the rural hinterland. Qian Fenggao, a junior partner in the Zhou family's Dingchang Filature, led Wuxi's Sericulture Direction Office from June 1938 and worked with the CCSC. His business operations benefited from the relationship, and at its peak Dingchang operated 512 reeling machines. After the war, however, Qian Fenggao was tried as a traitor.[81]

Under military occupation, urban filature production could not continue at the same scale as before the war. Still, the limitations of the CCSC monopoly provided opportunities for continued commercial silk reeling in the Jiangnan countryside. Licensed thread production lagged far behind market demand, and a new form of production emerged to take advantage of high prices. Beginning in the summer of 1938, "small household filatures" (*jiating xiao sichang*) constituted a "brand new industry."[82] Under occupation law, filatures with twenty reeling machines or fewer were considered "handicraft" workshops and did not come under CCSC control.[83] Many Wuxi filatures broke up their plants and distributed machines in village workshops managed by supervisors from the large Wuxi filatures. These small-scale operations easily attracted investment capital in a wartime economy otherwise barren of business opportunities.[84] As rural factories, they could take advantage of surplus cocoons (in some cases even receiving licensed cocoons from the CCSC) as well as local workers, many of whom had been employed in Wuxi filatures in recent years but had

80. *Shanghai sichou zhi*, 196–97.

81. Lincoln, *Urbanizing China*, 132, 150; Coble, *Japan's New Order*, 161–63.

82. Lincoln, *Urbanizing China*, 136. For materials on micro-filatures in the Wuxi countryside, see Gao and Yan, *Jindai Wuxi cansiye*, 429–43.

83. Gu and Wang, *Riben qinhua shiqi*, 146.

84. As evidence of the popularity of rural micro-filatures, Lincoln, *Urbanizing China*, 136, states that the price of silk reeling machines in Wuxi increased from twenty-five yuan to forty yuan in just one month.

returned to the countryside during the invasion. The result was an interesting case of rural reindustrialization and reintroduction of silk reeling skills to the Wuxi hinterland.[85]

The outdated equipment, bad lighting, and lack of amenities made these "household filatures" unattractive places to work, however, and they were forced to offer high wages to attract skilled workers capable of operating the machines under such poor conditions. Because of quality problems with both raw materials and finished products, skilled cocoon sorters and thread processing workers were in great demand and could command wages 10 to 20 percent higher, and in some cases even 50 percent higher, than those offered in the large, urban, CCSC-licensed filatures. Otherwise, the workers in these "household filatures" were much the same as in the large filatures. Most lived at home rather than in factory dormitories, although those from north of the Yangzi might live on board the boats that had brought them there.[86]

Despite the challenges involved, it was possible to obtain substantial profits in the silk trade, at least before 1941, due to high prices on world markets. The occupation silk company earned net profits amounting to more than 16 million Japanese yen between August 1938 and September 1942 and contributed almost 18 million yen in profits and materials, such as silk floss to line winter coats, for Japan's war effort.[87] Exports of Chinese silk earned more than USD $17 million between 1939 and 1941. In theory, the fourteen Japanese agents that handled the export trade for the CCSC held monopoly rights, but in fact they handled less than half of silk exports from Shanghai in 1939. As world prices for silk increased as much as five times in Chinese yuan terms between 1938 and 1940, foreign silk merchants in Shanghai were willing to pay high prices for smuggled silk despite its generally poor quality. Micro-filatures in Jiangsu Province marketed an estimated 98.2 percent of their product to Shanghai's foreign exporters.[88] Even licensed Japanese exporters purchased about 15 percent of their silk

85. Lincoln, *Urbanizing China*, 143, puts it well, stating that the rise of rural filatures "radically altered the look and feel of towns and villages."

86. Chen Ciyu, *Zhongguo de jixie saosi*, 131–44.

87. Gu and Wang, *Riben qinhua shiqi*, 118–20.

88. *Shanghai sichou zhi*, 79–85.

from filatures operating outside the monopoly system. One of the results of the CCSC's attempt to control exports was that the proportion of Jiangnan silk exports handled by European and American merchants greatly diminished. By 1940, Japanese brokers had come to dominate Chinese silk exports, a fundamental change in the organization of the trade. Unfortunately, only a small proportion of this filature silk was sold domestically for use by Yangzi Delta silk weavers, who found it nearly impossible to obtain alternatives like rayon.[89]

Although capable of doing great damage to China's silk industry, the occupation silk monopoly was never entirely successful in achieving its goals. In 1939, the CCSC operated only 5,972 reeling machines throughout the Jiangnan region, as compared with an estimated 9,700 in rural micro-filatures. In 1940 the CCSC increased purchasing prices for cocoons, which proved more effective than monopolistic edicts. Both the small rural factories and those located in Shanghai's Foreign Concessions began to close for lack of supplies, and in 1941 the Jiangnan silk industry descended into severe depression.[90] The United States, which purchased 96.2 percent of CCSC exports from occupied China, continued to import Japanese silk until the end of 1940. In January 1941, however, the US government prohibited imports of Japanese silk.[91] In July, the Americans imposed an oil embargo and froze all Japanese assets in the United States. In response, Japan's exports shifted to China and Southeast Asia. To avoid competition in shrinking markets, Japanese silk magnates lobbied to restrict Chinese output. In 1941, CCSC-licensed filatures halved the number of machines operating, and again reduced operations by one-third the following year, reducing the total to just over two thousand. By 1942 the CCSC operated only six filatures employing a total of 4,574 workers, down from 16,391 in 1940. As export markets became inaccessible, independent micro-filatures in the Wuxi countryside disappeared almost entirely.[92]

89. Chen Ciyu, *Zhongguo de jixie saosi*, 146–52; *Shanghai sichou zhi*, 82. On May 15, 1941, Dupont began to market its new synthetic, nylon. By the end of June, Dupont had sold 586,000 pairs of nylon stockings.

90. Coble, *Japan's New Order*, 60; Chen Ciyu, *Zhongguo de jixie saosi*, 154, table 3–13.

91. *Shanghai sichou zhi*, 79.

92. Chen Ciyu, *Zhongguo de jixie saosi*, 153–55.

The situation in Shanghai was almost as dire. On December 8, 1941, the Japanese military occupied the Foreign Concessions, bringing an end to "island" Shanghai's brief wartime boom.[93] The disruption of shipping and maritime trade severely curtailed business and manufacturing. Occupation controls on the circulation of currency and basic commodities created desperate circumstances, especially for the urban poor. By 1942, prices for most essential goods including gasoline, lumber, medicine, and metals were centrally regulated, and legal trade in such goods was restricted to licensed merchants. Despite these measures, however, prices continued to rise for the duration of the war.

Contrary to the trend in price controls, the Central China Sericulture Company abandoned its efforts to monopolize the Jiangnan silk trade, and on November 5, 1943, announced its dissolution. Wang Jingwei's government then organized the Chinese Sericulture Company (Zhonghua cansi gongsi), which exercised only limited authority as China's economy sank deeper into crisis.[94] Wang's regime liberalized the production and sale of cocoons and silk thread and allowed Chinese businesses to trade freely. But this change came too late to save the Jiangnan silk industry. By 1943 mulberry acreage and sericulture declined to their lowest levels since the nineteenth century. Occupation policies and the loss of foreign markets had already driven the micro-filatures in the Wuxi area out of business. Shanghai silk reeling collapsed, leaving only a few filatures, none of which could maintain production consistently. As price controls proved ineffective and inflation accelerated, the Yangzi Delta economy failed to provide basic goods or employment.[95] Inflation, warfare, and shortages led to economic stagnation. Sericulturalists, factory owners, and silk workers could only wait in hope that the war's end would bring better times.

93. On occupation policies following the seizure of Shanghai's Foreign Concessions, see Wen-hsin Yeh, *Wartime Shanghai*, 10–12.

94. *Jiangsusheng cansang sichou zhi*, 205. For the company's founding constitution, dated June 21, 1940, and related documents see Gao and Yan, *Jindai Wuxi cansiye*, 430–32.

95. Wen-hsin Yeh, *Wartime Shanghai*, 12–13; Zhu Xinyu, *Zhejiang sichou shi*, 214.

The collapse of the Jiangnan silk industry is typical of the effects of the Sino-Japanese War on China's economy.[96] The initial damage to the silk reeling and weaving industries, especially in Shanghai, was disastrous enough. But more damaging to the industry's long-term recovery were the effects of the war on Jiangnan sericulture. The Japanese military cut down mulberry trees along the Shanghai-Hangzhou Railroad to deny cover to guerrilla fighters and eliminated similar potential cover along other major roads and railways. Because food and fuel were so expensive, mulberry farmers began to plant food crops and sell their mulberry trees as fuel.[97] Mulberry acreage throughout China declined by more than 43 percent, and cocoon supplies declined by 73 percent, between 1936 and 1946.[98] In their forays into Jiangnan villages, Japanese soldiers destroyed equipment used in sericulture, including everything from cocoon ovens to the wicker baskets used for collecting mulberry leaves. Along strategic railways, such as the Shanghai-Nanjing line, the devastation was almost total. Many egg breederies, education and research facilities, warehouses, and filatures were looted and robbed of valuable equipment, much of which was permanently lost.[99]

The war and the decline of sericulture naturally had a devastating effect on the filature industry, despite the intriguing but short-lived phenomenon of rural micro-filatures. By 1946, the majority (62 percent) of Chinese silk thread was reeled by hand rather than in steam filatures, and total production had declined by more than 70 percent. In 1947, the output of raw silk from China's filatures was just 21 percent of 1936 production levels.[100] By the end of the war, only about two-thirds of the silk reeling machines in Zhejiang Province continued production.[101] Whereas Zhejiang produced an estimated three million bolts

96. Kirby, "Chinese War Economy," 185–87. According to estimates by the Nationalist government, total wartime losses to Chinese industry amounted to more than USD $1.19 billion. Gu and Wang, *Riben qinhua shiqi*, 181.

97. Zhou Dehua, "Lunxian shiqi de Wujiang sichouye," 45.

98. Xu and Wu, *Zhongguo zibenzhuyi*, 673; Xu Xinwu, *Zhongguo jindai saosi gongye*, 422, 661.

99. Ma Junya, "Kangzhan shiqi Jiangnan," 44–85; Zhu Xinyu, *Zhejiang sichou shi*, 207, 214.

100. Xu Xinwu, *Zhongguo jindai saosi gongye*, 422, 661.

101. Xu and Wu, *Zhongguo zibenzhuyi*, 673.

of silk cloth in 1936, in 1946 the province only produced about 500,000 bolts, a decrease of more than 80 percent.[102]

The occupation silk monopoly suffered both from divisions among the occupation authorities and from the practical difficulties of controlling Jiangnan silk production and trade at the point of a gun. The occupation initially provided an opportunity for Japanese silk magnates and the military to exploit Chinese labor to compensate for the decline in Japanese production caused by the war. But the CCSC never achieved the level of control that its founders envisioned. If Japanese interests could not exploit the Jiangnan silk industry effectively, however, the occupation authorities could damage it as much as possible, preventing competition in restricted wartime markets and causing devastation from which it took the industry many years to recover. The occupation left other deleterious legacies as well, such as price inflation, diminished purchasing power, transportation problems (96 percent of China's railroads were damaged during the war), indebtedness, and the adaptive preference in business for commodity speculation over productive enterprise.

Another important consequence of the occupation was the greatly increased role of the state in the Chinese economy. Japan's efforts to expropriate, control, and then curtail Jiangnan silk production left a legacy of state predation in an industry previously controlled by private capital. During the war, the Nationalist government in Chongqing established state monopolies for tobacco, matches, sugar, and salt. The Ministry of Economic Affairs, with the National Resources Commission as its core, received an unprecedented mandate to "develop, operate, and control" the state industrial sector, and by 1943 state industry accounted for 35 percent of the total value of industrial production in Nationalist China.[103] The encroachment of the state upon private enterprise was therefore not limited to the occupied territories, but was

102. Zhu Xinyu, *Zhejiang sichou shi*, 214–15.

103. On the Nationalist government's efforts to expand its management of the economy of "Free China" during the war, see the 1940 report to the Institute of Pacific Relations by Ch'ao-ting Chi, *Wartime Economic Development of China*, especially chapter 3, and the discussion of government monopolies in Chongqing newspapers in November 1942 translated in Yung Ying Hsu, *Chinese Views of Wartime Economic Difficulties*, 16–17.

a feature of wartime governance throughout China and much of the rest of the world. Japanese expropriation of light industrial enterprises, such as silk factories, established a foundation for expanded postwar Nationalist economic administration, which had previously been limited mainly to heavy industry, transportation, and military production.[104] When the Nationalist Party reestablished governance in 1946, the state directly controlled nearly 70 percent of China's industrial assets.[105] Unfortunately, state management in the postwar era was no more effective than under Japanese occupation.

The Nationalist "Reconversion" of Occupied Jiangnan and the Silk Industry's Postwar Crisis

The inadequacies of state institutions in Republican China, combined with the impact of the war and the ensuing social and economic crises, were significant challenges that contributed to the downfall of the Nationalist regime in the postwar period. After 1949, these challenges continued to shape the economic institutions developed under Communist rule.[106] Chiang Kai-shek and the Nationalists attempted to restore their prewar prestige following the Japanese surrender in August 1945, but their government soon fell victim to its own corruption, shortsightedness, and mismanagement, providing its Communist opponents a chance to seize power less than four years later. In the years following the liberation of East China from Japanese occupation, the Nationalists ran the economy into the ground with an irresponsible monetary policy that exacerbated expanding budget deficits, while attempting to control and exploit private economic activity to support an unpopular and unsuccessful civil war.

By 1948 Chiang Kai-shek's government had lost the support of most urbanites due to hyperinflation and rampant corruption. The extractive

104. Esherick, "War and Revolution," 10. On wartime changes in state industry, see Bian, "The Sino-Japanese War," 80–123.

105. Kirby, "Chinese War Economy," 185–207.

106. Several historians have noted these factors; see, for example, Eastman, *Seeds of Destruction*; Strauss, *Strong Institutions in Weak Polities*; Fei-ling Wang, *Institutional Change in China*.

policies of state agencies toward private industry undermined support for Chiang's government among both the working class and the bourgeoisie. Nonetheless, many goals the Nationalists pursued after the war—including an expanded economic role for the government, state companies contracting with private producers to stimulate employment, a corporatist vision of labor-capital cooperation through government leadership of unions, and enterprise-based welfare and direct provision of goods to factory workers—were realized only after 1949. Indeed, many of the Nationalist Party's policies came to be identified very strongly with Chinese socialism and the *danwei* work unit system that developed under Communist rule.[107] Similarly, business practices such as tax evasion, hoarding and speculation, and cheating on government contracts, which had developed in response to wartime scarcities, state controls, and inflation, also persisted for years following the Communist seizure of power in 1949. It is therefore worth examining the relationship between the postwar Nationalist government and the Yangzi Delta silk industry in some detail.

The restoration of Nationalist rule in East China after the war certainly represented "liberation" from foreign occupation. But the term *jiefang* does not appear prominently in public pronouncements and accounts of the period. Rather, the terms *shengli* ("victory") and *jieshou* ("to accept or take over," or as it is often translated in this context, "reconvert") were most common. The Nationalist military units and officials that arrived in Chinese cities following the victory over Japan came first and foremost to "reconvert" administrative structures and the assets of the Japanese or their collaborators. The postwar Nationalist government preserved and expanded many of the administrative organs the Japanese military had established to control and exploit sericulture and the Yangzi Delta silk industry. Although the Nationalist government's postwar policies were intended to foster the silk industry's recovery, they were even more exploitative and counter-productive than those of the 1930s. Postwar inflation, which robbed both workers and factory owners of their livelihoods, magnified the deleterious

107. On the continuities between wartime, postwar, and Communist practices, see Lü and Perry, *Danwei*; Bian, *Making of the State Enterprise System*; and Frazier, *Chinese Industrial Workplace*.

effects of the state silk administration's extractive policies and prevented the industry's postwar recovery.

The confusion, corruption, and economic mismanagement that accompanied the Nationalists' return to East China quickly revealed how Chiang Kai-shek's government had degenerated during the war.[108] Surprised by victory, the Nationalist government had not established offices responsible for the restoration of control in East China and the takeover (*jieguan*) of Japanese and collaborationist property. The government initially ordered that all Japanese-owned factories should be closed, warehouses sealed, and occupants of residences evicted.[109] In practice, whichever officials happened to arrive on the scene first occupied factories, warehouses, offices, and residences, and seized vehicles, equipment, and stores of commodities.[110] As Albert Feuerwerker puts it, "The recovered factories were treated like war booty as each civilian and military faction struggled to acquire a share of the loot."[111]

Chiang's government attempted to gain control of the situation and to ensure that reconverted assets were administered properly. In October 1945, the Executive Yuan established a National Reconversion Commission (Guojia jieshou weiyuanhui) with local "disposition bureaus" (*chuliju*) and "deliberation committees" (*shenyi weiyuanhui*) at all levels. But this bureaucratization of the takeover simply increased the number of officials authorized to seize "enemy assets." In Shanghai, no less than sixty government organs, including military departments, were engaged in "reconversion" work. Waves of officials came through Jiangnan cities like locusts, carrying off anything they could find, often to hoard or sell for personal gain.[112]

Chiang Kai-shek recognized the danger and was outraged at the wanton corruption. A telegram dated October 26, 1945, to Shanghai Mayor Qian Dajun expressed Chiang's disgust at reports of corruption,

108. Pepper, *Civil War in China*, 9–16; Melby, *Mandate of Heaven*, 69–70.

109. Ba Tu, *Guomindang jieshou Riwei caichan*, 114; Pepper, *Civil War in China*, 16, 34.

110. China Number Two, "Kangzhan shengli hou," 40.

111. Feuerwerker, *Economic Trends*, 24.

112. China Number Two, "Kangzhan shengli hou," 37; Pepper, *Civil War in China*, 17–19.

theft, bribery, blackmail, prostitution, and gambling on the part of government officials and gave strict orders to curb such behavior:

> To be corrupted to this extent without any self-respect in the recovered areas is a disgrace to the local people, and a sin committed against our heroic martyrs who have been sacrificed in the war. I have been greatly distressed, and have also felt ashamed, on hearing reports of such conditions . . . Upon receipt of this telegram you may give orders to the various departments to strictly forbid prostitution and gambling, and to close all those offices that have opened under the assumed names of various organizations. Any case of blackmailing or illegal occupation of the people's houses must be severely dealt with by the municipal authorities on the one hand, and reported to me on the other. No culprit is to be harbored by personal favors.[113]

The generalissimo's outrage produced few results, however. Although the National Reconversion Commission in Shanghai investigated more than five hundred cases in the two months following its establishment, corruption and misuse of resources continued unabated. Government and military officials competed to occupy textiles factories, flour mills, and office buildings, while the original owners found no recourse. Stores of goods simply disappeared, sold by corrupt military, police, and government officials. In January 1946, Shanghai government officials were charged with illegally selling over four billion *fabi* yuan worth of seized goods. Corruption reached shocking proportions, and the Nationalists soon lost the prestige they enjoyed four months earlier.[114]

Chaos and rampant corruption seriously undermined the government's efforts to restore and administer the economy. According to the regulations, all factories and mines, including all equipment, raw materials, and finished products possessed by the occupation authorities, should be managed by the Ministry of Economic Affairs "so as to

113. Quoted in Pepper, *Civil War in China*, 20.

114. China Number Two, "Kangzhan shengli hou," 38–40; Pepper, *Civil War in China*, 20–28.

increase production."[115] In practice, state economic organs carved out spheres of influence within the economy. The National Resources Commission (NRC), under the leadership of Song Ziwen, took control of most mines and heavy industrial plants, controlling the "commanding heights" of the economy. The "reconversion" of enemy and collaborationist property, however, brought more consumer goods industries under NRC control, including sixty-nine textile factories. These were turned over to the China Textile Company, a joint-stock company under the Ministry of Economic Affairs that enjoyed access to government capital and subsidized US cotton. In the postwar years, the Ministry of Economic Affairs also operated factories producing chemicals, paper, foodstuffs, wool, and silk. As a result, the role of state agencies in China's economy increased dramatically and extended into new sectors. They were, however, primarily concerned with expanding revenue, and as inflation worsened, both state and private enterprises chose to hoard goods rather than accept the government's inflationary currency.[116]

The hyperinflation China experienced in the late 1940s is one of the worst cases in modern history.[117] Between December 1937 and April 1949, prices in China increased roughly one trillion times. Inflationary pressures abated briefly with the end of the war and then accelerated again from November 1945. Scarcity of goods was a contributing factor, especially in the cities. But China's gross output recovered from a 1945 low of 624 million yuan (in 1933 terms) to nearly 1.16 billion yuan by 1947, almost reaching the prewar peak of 1936.[118] The main cause of China's postwar inflation was monetary expansion impelled by the government's large fiscal deficit. The budget deficit grew from

115. China Number Two, "Kangzhan shengli hou," 40.

116. Feuerwerker, *Economic Trends*, 24–25; Westad, *Decisive Encounters*, 87.

117. If one looks only at prices during the period of hyperinflation, beginning from the first month in which prices increased by 50 percent or more, then the situation in China between January 1948 and April 1949, when prices increased about ten million times, was not as severe as Germany in 1922–23, Greece in 1943–44, or Hungary in 1945–46. However, if one examines the real value of money balances, which declined by 99 percent between June 1948 and April 1949, then the Chinese situation is comparable to the Greek and Hungarian cases. Simkin, "Hyperinflation and Nationalist China," 113.

118. John K. Chang, *Industrial Development in Pre-Communist China*, 60–61; Chang Kia-Ngau, *Inflationary Spiral*, 99.

25 percent of government expenditures in 1937 to 60 percent by June 1946.[119] With the outbreak of the Chinese Civil War, the budget deficit again expanded. From June 1946 to the end of 1947, the deficit accounted for more than 80 percent of new note issues, increasing the money supply by more than four times, and prices increased more than ten times. In the first six months of 1948 both the deficit and government expenses increased thirty times.[120]

As the value of the Nationalist government's *fabi* currency plummeted, commodities became a more secure means of storing wealth than bank deposits, leading to frenzied efforts to exchange cash for goods. The first panic came in February 1947, when the monthly rate of price increases jumped from 6 percent to 46 percent. By June 15, 1948, the price of rice in Shanghai was roughly ten thousand times the 1945 price, and the purchasing power of money balances (savings) had declined to just 6 percent of 1937 levels.[121] The government's October 1948 revaluation, the Gold Yuan currency issue, failed to curb inflation, which continued its meteoric rise.[122] Although government leaders blamed capitalists' "hoarding and speculation," these were responses to inflation rather than causes. It was mainly the government's continued note issues (despite promises to the contrary) that undermined the new currency. By January 1949 new currency issues reached nearly fifteen times the promised limit for the Gold Yuan.[123] On February 20,

119. Feuerwerker, *Economic Trends*, 81, 89; Chang Kia-Ngau, *Inflationary Spiral*, 4–8; Teh-wei Hu, "Hyperinflation in China," 186.

120. Simkin, "Hyperinflation and Nationalist China," 116; Chang Kia-Ngau, *Inflationary Spiral*, 101. In contrast with the Communists after 1949, the Nationalist government's sale of bonds (a non-inflationary source of revenue) covered only five percent of expenses during the war and even less in the postwar years. Feuerwerker, *Economic Trends*, 91–92.

121. Teh-wei Hu, "Hyperinflation in China," 188–89, 194–95; Simkin, "Hyperinflation and Nationalist China," 122–23, 128. In his memoir, W. J. Moore recalled that "Nobody kept any cash in hand if it could be helped. The only thing to do was to buy something tangible at once—food, rice, bars of soap, anything." Moore, *Shanghai Century*, 93.

122. Simkin, "Hyperinflation and Nationalist China," 128. On the Gold Yuan currency reform, see Eastman, *Seeds of Destruction*, 185–99; Rowan, *Chasing the Dragon*, 164–65; and US Department of State, *China White Paper*, 278, 401.

123. Simkin, "Hyperinflation and Nationalist China," 128.

1949, the Central Bank of China transferred its gold reserves, fourteen tons worth USD $300–335 million, to Taiwan. This pulled the last support out from under the Gold Yuan. Prices rose 872 percent in February, 510 percent in March, and in April, as the Communist forces crossed the Yangzi River, they rose a dizzying 8,100 percent.[124]

The results for industry and commerce were disastrous. By the end of November 1948, industrial production in Shanghai had fallen by half, even when compared to the miserable state of affairs at the end of 1947. Cigarette and paper factories had mostly discontinued production, and the effects of inflation for the silk industry were especially serious. In addition to inflated production costs, short supplies, and shrinking markets, factory owners found Nationalist administration of the silk industry burdensome and exploitative, and the government's efforts to deal with worker unrest ineffective.

Yangzi Delta silk producers initially greeted the Nationalist liberation of East China with hope and optimism. An alliance of silk merchants, filatures, weaving factories, and household producers in Wujiang, Jiangsu, stated in a missive to the Nationalist government:

> During eight years of occupation [the silk industry] suffered deeply from enemy devastation, which worsened day by day. Because of this, the countryside is impoverished, and the cities languish. In this period of revival, [if we] desire to make the region flourish again, then it is first of all necessary to vigorously develop the silk weaving industry.[125]

Hope quickly turned to despair, however, as war loomed once again, government monetary policies exacerbated inflation, and Nationalist administration proved detrimental to sericulture, filature production, and silk weaving. The economic difficulties caused by the Nationalist government's policies were especially troublesome for industries like silk textiles, rubber, cement, and tobacco, which were affected most severely by the economic downturn from late 1947.[126] The silk industry,

124. Hooton, *The Greatest Tumult*, 152; Melby, *Mandate of Heaven*, 341; Feuerwerker, *Economic Trends*, 92; US Department of State, *China White Paper*, 129, 220–29.

125. *Jiangsusheng cansang sichou zhi*, 301.

126. Chang Kia-Ngau, *Inflationary Spiral*, 353.

a consumer goods industry fraught with risk and tied to volatile export markets, with a politically active workforce and a diversity of firm sizes and structures, illustrates many of the problems businesses faced in China's postwar economic crisis.

Silk was an important source of revenue and foreign exchange, and the postwar government quickly extended its control over this resource by reconverting and expanding the monopolistic agencies of the Japanese occupation.[127] The Nationalists reestablished the China Sericulture Company (CSC) (Zhongguo cansi gongsi) in January 1946, with its head offices in Shanghai. On December 11, 1945, the Legislative Yuan passed legislation detailing the state company's structure, sources of capital, business scope, and purposes. The "Regulations of the China Sericulture Company" stated that, in addition to the assets confiscated from Wang Jingwei's "puppet" regime, the company was invested with 500 million yuan from the Ministry of Economic Affairs and the Ministry of Agriculture and Forestry. The company was granted powers to administer all aspects of silk production, including sericulture; the trade in cocoons; silk reeling; the processing, shipment, and sale of natural silk textiles; academic and scientific research; and the leadership and reward of private silk businesses.[128]

Compared with the cotton textiles industry, there were relatively few Japanese or "collaborator" silk factories. The CSC nonetheless found itself in possession of several "experimental factories" (*shiyanchang*) in the Jiangnan region, including a filature, three silk weaving factories, and three silk spinning factories (*juanfangchang*), as well as several egg breederies, mulberry fields, and research facilities.[129] The company's early activities focused mainly on regulating the production and marketing of cocoons and silk products. Its ostensible purpose was to lead the private sector in restoring and developing production and exports. In practice, however, the CSC faced stronger incentives to contribute revenue to the financial organs that funded

127. For documents relating to the Nationalist "reconversion" of occupation institutions governing the silk industry see Gao and Yan, *Jindai Wuxi cansiye*, 444–48.

128. Zhu Xinyu, *Zhejiang sichou shi*, 216–18.

129. *Shanghai sichou zhi*, 205; Zhu Xinyu, *Zhejiang sichou shi*, 217; James Gao, *Communist Takeover of Hangzhou*, 89.

and controlled it, especially the Central Trust of China (Zhongguo zhongyang xintuoju).[130]

The China Sericulture Company's extractive policies aggravated the problems of short supplies, inflated costs, and unstable markets that silk factories faced. In the inflationary economy, factory managers dedicated much of their time to obtaining raw materials, fuel, and credit, and reacting to price increases and wage demands. Agriculture was less strongly affected, but the amount of produce delivered to urban markets fell as farmers reverted to barter to avoid accepting inflationary currency.[131] Farmers who produced raw materials for industry, such as sericulturalists, faced severe losses. To promote the recovery of mulberry fields, the CSC imported seedlings and extended loans to Jiangnan farmers. Low state purchasing prices for cocoons, however, inhibited the revival of Jiangnan sericulture. The CSC also attempted to restore and control egg production, first by extending loans and providing subsidies and then by importing high-quality egg cards from Japan, Korea, and Taiwan. But loans and subsidies did not even compensate for the increased rate of taxation, let alone rapidly rising production costs, and cocoon production declined precipitously.[132] Some of the decline may reflect sericulturalists' adaptive strategies. As during the occupation, when silk farmers could not receive sufficient compensation for their cocoons, they reeled the thread themselves. Production of home-reeled silk expanded from an estimated 19,195 *dan* in 1946 to 31,824 *dan* in 1947, and contracted only slightly to 30,465 *dan* in 1948. Estimated output of handicraft thread was only 20,920 *dan* in 1949, but this was still more than China's industrial filatures produced that year.[133]

130. During the war, the Central Trust managed trade in railroad and military supplies and gradually took over some functions of the Foreign Trade Commission, handling agricultural export products such as pig bristles, tea, tung oil, and silk. By 1947, the Central Trust had become an independent agency funded directly by the National Treasury and operating under the supervision of the Ministry of Finance. Young, *China's Wartime Finance*, 99, 108, 293.

131. Simkin, "Hyperinflation and Nationalist China," 117; Chang Kia-Ngau, *Inflationary Spiral*, 102, 232, 349.

132. ZPA D1212–104–3–33; *Zhongyang*, 28 Feb. 1946; *Dazhong*, 9 Apr. 1946; *Wenhuibao*, 31 Jan. 1947; Zhu Xinyu, *Zhejiang sichou shi*, 220–22.

133. Xu Xinwu, *Zhongguo jindai saosi gongye*, 422, 661; *Jinrong*, 20 Feb. 1948; *Shangbao*, 31 Dec. 1948.

To promote sericulture and state cocoon purchases, the CSC, in cooperation with the state banks and those filatures that still possessed capital resources, established the Three Province Cocoon-Purchasing Loans Unified Management Office (Sansheng shoujian daikuan lianhe guanli chu), which extended low-interest loans to cover filatures' cocoon purchases. By 1947, state loans provided 90 percent of the capital for cocoon purchases. Filatures sold silk reeled from these cocoons to the state at predetermined prices, selling any surplus on the market.[134] The CSC did not effectively control cocoon prices, however, and as competition drove prices well above the rates at which loans were calculated, filatures were forced to pay exorbitant prices to private cocoon *hang* and take out short-term high-interest loans to pay for cocoons, fuel, and wages, a situation the policy was intended to prevent. By 1947, interest payments amounted to about 30 percent of filatures' costs as compared with only 3 percent before the war.[135]

In addition to loaning money to filatures, the state silk administration also directly supplied private filatures with cocoons to produce silk thread under the policy of "exchanging stores of cocoons for silk reeled on contract, and leading private filatures to restore production" (*cunjian yisi daisao ji fudao minying sichang fuye*). At its peak, the Nationalist government's silk administration supplied almost 40 percent of the total Jiangnan cocoon crop to filatures under this state contracting system.[136] The CSC and government banks controlled cocoon supplies, which were doled out to filatures monthly. Filatures sometimes had to wait days or weeks for new cocoons. When the Lianjia Filature in Shanghai ran out of supplies in August 1947, the owner had to request that the newly established Silk Production and Marketing Assistance and Leadership Commission (Cansi chanxiao xiedao weiyuanhui) release cocoons that Lianjia's own agents had purchased with a government loan. By October, the Silk Commission still had not delivered these cocoons, and Lianjia's owner warned that the filature's workers,

134. ZPA D1212-104-3-29; Zhu Xinyu, *Zhejiang sichou shi*, 217, 225–26.

135. SMA S37-1-168. For documents relating to the Nationalists' governance of the postwar silk industry, see Gao and Yan, *Jindai Wuxi cansiye*, 449–90.

136. *Jiangsusheng cansang sichou zhi*, 252.

who had been left idle and unpaid for months, were on the brink of an uprising.[137]

Despite their intentions, government agencies' handling of contracted thread also created problems for silk filatures. State banks received most filature silk as payment or collateral, and little remained for the filatures to sell independently. Because production costs increased rapidly, the filatures repeatedly petitioned the government to increase the purchasing price for contracted silk. Inflation quickly devoured the Central Trust's reluctant and belated price increases, however, and the filatures' postwar recovery stagnated. Problems appeared as early as 1946. As production costs rose to 4.3 million yuan per *dan* of filature silk, export prices declined, falling to just 2.1 or 2.2 million yuan per *dan*.[138] In October 1947 at an emergency meeting, twenty-three Zhejiang filature owners resolved that the government should purchase silk either at current market prices (when prices were high) or according to actual production costs (when prices were low) rather than at the state-contracted price.[139] The Silk Commission refused to make these changes, however, or to allow filatures to market their silk independently and repay government loans in increasingly worthless cash. With mountains of debt, rapidly rising expenses, an angry workforce, and no certain prospects for the future, by 1948 most filatures could only discontinue operations and close their doors.

The experience of Shanghai's Chang'an Filature is typical. Due to a poor spring cocoon harvest, Chang'an was only able to procure half the supply of cocoons needed in June 1948 and by mid-July petitioned the Silk Commission for more. The filature appealed to the commission's sense of social responsibility, stating that without cocoons, Chang'an would have to lay off its workforce, stripping them of their livelihoods. The filature would be forced to sell raw silk intended for loan repayment to provide workers with severance pay. After more than a month, the Silk Commission had done nothing to relieve the filature's plight, and Chang'an telegrammed the Silk Reeling Industry Association to announce that it had ceased operations. This led to demands for

137. SMA S37–1–165, S37–2–21.

138. SMA S37–1–168, S37–2–20.

139. SMA S37–1–168. Wuxi filature owners held a similar meeting later that month.

reinstatement or severance pay from the mill's employees. In early August, these protests turned violent as more than 520 workers destroyed the filature's doors and windows and precious stores of silk thread. Chang'an's management estimated total losses at more than 4.3 billion yuan and begged for loans from the Agricultural Bank to purchase cocoons or provide severance pay to avoid further violence and losses. In a letter dated September 23, 1948, more than two months after the factory's original appeal for cocoons, the Silk Commission simply stated that it "refused to make a decision in this matter."[140]

One problem Chang'an encountered in its dealings with state companies, commissions, and banks was that these institutions treated cocoons and silk thread as a source of revenue and a speculative commodity, to the detriment of both the filatures and the silk weaving industry. As Chang Kia-Ngau, appointed governor of the Central Bank of China in March 1947, put it in his memoir, "commodity hoarding and speculation became part of the regular business of even the leading financial institutions," and silk was one of the favorite commodities for speculation in the postwar economy.[141] The banks and the Central Trust frequently claimed that filatures had not delivered sufficient amounts of contracted silk, or had delivered inferior quality thread. The Zhenfeng Filature in Hangzhou complained that the CSC demanded additional silk as loan repayment, which the filature claimed already to have delivered to the Agricultural Bank. Shanghai's Qiye Filature faced similar competing claims and resisted for almost a year before finally delivering an additional *dan* of raw silk to the Agricultural Bank. It appears that the efforts of government agencies and banks to squeeze the silk industry denied filatures the capacity to maintain production and sales.[142] It is also possible that extractive policies forced some silk production underground, just as happened during the Japanese occupation. This may account for some of the decline in recorded silk production, which may have shifted toward the black market. In any case, the Nationalist government's exploitative

140. SMA S37-1-244, S37-2-20.

141. Chang Kia-Ngau, *Inflationary Spiral*, 57.

142. *Shanghai sichou zhi*, 87; SMA S37-2-20, S37-1-168; *Wenhuibao*, 11 Oct. 1946; *North China Daily News* (*NCDN*), 15 Dec. 1946.

policies, combined with the inflationary economy, clearly hindered more than helped the silk industry's recovery.

Even though the state silk agencies, the banks, and the Central Trust refused to cede control over supplies of silk thread, much of what they collected simply sat in storage despite silk weavers' desperate need for materials. Filature owners expressed their willingness to provide thread to weavers at official prices, but also complained that they could not obtain sufficient amounts of cocoons and the government could not control prices effectively. Silk farmers refused to sell their cocoons at official prices, holding out for 50 to 100 percent more. Even the state silk agencies were often unwilling to sell cocoons to filatures at official prices, preferring to delay sales in anticipation of increased profits.[143] Market prices for filature silk pursued rising cocoon prices, reaching 240,000 yuan per *dan* by October 1948. Filatures engaged in a frenzy of production using whatever cocoons they could obtain and selling the product to private brokers. In November, when the government abandoned price controls for filature silk, brokers suddenly released stores onto the market. Prices collapsed and filatures suffered heavy losses. By the end of the year, the brief speculative flourishing had ended, and most Jiangnan filatures closed their doors.[144]

The silk weaving industry faced many of the same difficulties as the filature industry, and full recovery proved elusive. Thread prices that rose faster than cloth prices, constricted export markets, and intense conflicts with workers over wages and layoffs quickly dimmed the optimism of 1945. By the end of 1946, Jiangnan production of silk cloth reached only one-third of prewar levels, and production declined thereafter. The larger, well-capitalized Shanghai silk companies such as Meiya and Dacheng initially expanded following Japan's surrender. By 1947, Dacheng operated more than two hundred looms in four factories with over four hundred employees, and marketed its products (mainly checkered emerald crepe and quilt covers) throughout China and abroad. But sales soon stagnated, and the company's liquid assets shrank from 6.9 million yuan in 1947 to just 1.9 million yuan by the end of 1949. The Yunlin Company, owned and operated by the Lou

143. SMA S37-1-351.

144. *Jiangsusheng cansang sichou zhi*, 252–53.

family, also expanded in 1945. But due to rampant inflation, short supplies, and market collapse, only one-quarter of the company's looms were engaged in production by 1949.[145]

Silk weaving factories did not receive the same attention and assistance from the government as the filatures and had great difficulty obtaining supplies of thread. Because of their weaker relationship with state agencies, however, weaving workshops were also less subject to interference and exploitation. Weaving factories' primary inputs were filature silk and synthetic fibers, both of which were expensive and difficult to obtain. Prices for filature silk increased dramatically at the end of 1946. But the Central Trust, anticipating even higher prices, proved reluctant to release supplies of thread, and many weavers could only obtain supplies by purchasing hand-reeled silk directly from sericulturalists.[146]

This is another indication that postwar Nationalist policies may have driven some silk production underground and beyond the reach of official statistics. It is likely, however, that rising costs and shrinking markets simply made silk weaving unviable as an economic activity. Many weaving factories closed due to lack of raw materials or turned to trade instead of production. Although the city of Huzhou counted five hundred power looms and about fifteen hundred old-style pattern-making looms, only one-fifth of these were engaged in production. By early 1947 most weaving factories were only operating about one-third of their looms, and mass layoffs, strikes, and protests had become regular features of the Jiangnan silk industry.[147]

The pattern throughout the postwar period was that thread prices rose faster than cloth prices in Shanghai, which rose faster than cloth prices in the interior, making it extremely difficult for Shanghai weaving factories to survive. In the fall of 1947, the CSC responded by inaugurating a three-month experiment with contracted supply and production of thirteen types of silk cloth. State-contracted supplies met

145. Xu Xinwu, *Jindai Jiangnan sizhi gongye*, 407–8; *Shanghai sichou zhi*, 209–10.

146. *Zhengyan*, 16 Dec. 1946; *Xinwenbao*, 20 Dec. 1946; *Dagongbao*, 5 Feb. 1947; Zhu Xinyu, *Zhejiang sichou shi*, 230–31.

147. Zhu Xinyu, *Zhejiang sichou shi*, 232; *Jiangsusheng cansang sichou zhi*, 302.

less than one-quarter of demand, however, and most factories continued to purchase expensive thread from unlicensed merchants.[148] The experiment in state-contracted silk weaving was halted in November 1947, causing the financial collapse of those Jiangnan silk weaving factories that had altered their equipment and hired new workers in anticipation of expanded state contracts.[149]

In January 1948, Shanghai's Dali Filature and twenty-two other Jiangnan silk mills complained to the Agricultural Bank that the policy of taking 20 percent of the value of cocoon-purchasing loans in product as collateral prevented silk thread from reaching desperate weavers. The filatures requested that they be allowed to repay their loans in cash in the amount of 80 percent of the market value of their product, which would enable them to market silk thread directly to weaving factories.[150] Revenue needs, however, inclined the banks to resist this solution. In May 1948, the Central Bank supplied a handful of Shanghai weaving factories with two hundred *dan* of filature silk at US market prices, which were substantially lower than Chinese domestic prices. But even this price was beyond the means of most cash-strapped weaving factories, and the total amount of filature silk distributed for contract weaving in 1948 was only four hundred *dan*.[151] In China's crisis-ridden postwar economy, control of thread supplies by revenue-hungry banks inhibited the circulation of goods and capital between filatures and weaving factories, causing disaster for the Yangzi Delta silk industry.

In a letter to the Silk Reeling Industry Association dated September 10, 1948, the Silk Weaving Industry Associations of Shanghai, Zhejiang, Jiangsu, and Nanjing requested the filatures' assistance in restoring thread supplies. The letter stated that since the government had begun to implement contract reeling, the weaving factories' main source of thread was the Central Trust. But supplies always fell short of demand,

148. *Shenbao*, 23 Oct. 1946; *Dazhong*, 20 Nov. 1946; *Shishi*, 22 Nov. 1946; Xu Xinwu, *Jindai Jiangnan sizhi gongye*, 408; *Jiangsusheng cansang sichou zhi*, 302.

149. *Shangbao*, 9 Feb. 1948.

150. SMA S37–1–168. Newspaper editorials suggested that the government supply filature silk on contract to produce cloth for export markets. *Shangbao*, 29 Nov. 1947, 9 Feb. 1948.

151. *Shenbao*, 19 May 1948; *Shangbao*, 27 Mar. 1949.

and weaving factories had to seek additional materials at great expense. Under recent rounds of currency reform, supplies had dried up entirely, causing "widespread panic." The weaving factories thus appealed to the filatures to restore supplies of silk "in the spirit of pulling together in times of trouble." The Silk Reeling Industry Association agreed to this proposal in principle, but their response stated that this would require a change in government policy.[152]

The Zhejiang branch of the Silk Weaving Industry Association requested that the provincial government, banks, and state companies assess inventories of filature silk and market those stores at reasonable prices. The Zhejiang Provincial Government agreed to these proposals, emphasizing in a letter to the Central Bank that tens of thousands of Zhejiang residents depended on weaving for their livelihoods. The provincial government also recognized, however, that silk produced from cocoons purchased with government loans was the property of the banks, the Central Trust, and the state silk company, and the filatures had no right to market this thread independently. Pleading with the filatures, the Silk Weaving Industry Association asked them, "Why haven't you distributed the silk as you said you would? Most of us have stopped production due to lack of raw materials. Our stores of cloth have long since run out and there is nothing left to market."[153] As a result, by the end of 1948 the Yangzi Delta silk weaving industry was nearly extinct.[154]

Silk industrialists' last hope was that the government could help silk producers to recover their old export markets or open new ones. In 1946, silk exports amounted to USD $30 million out of USD $39 million total textiles exports, making silk China's third largest export commodity. But over the next three years supply exceeded demand.[155] Chinese filature silk cost two to five times as much to produce as the US market price, which fell from USD $8 per pound in 1946 to just USD $3.5 per pound in 1948. By March 1949, the price of raw silk in New

152. SMA S37-1-317.

153. SMA S37-1-317.

154. *Shanghai sichou zhi*, 210; *Jiangsusheng cansang sichou zhi*, 301.

155. D. K. Lieu, *China's Economic Reconstruction*, 117–20; *Dagongbao*, 20 Sep. 1946; *Wenhuibao*, 7 Nov. 1946; Xu and Wu, *Zhongguo zibenzhuyi*, 672.

York was only USD $2.6 per pound, just one-fifth of Chinese production costs, and Japanese silk enjoyed a virtual monopoly in US markets.[156] Industry advocates in China repeatedly complained that the government was not doing enough to promote exports through diplomatic means, but there was little the Nationalists could do under the circumstances. Total exports of silk cloth in 1948 earned a meager USD $7,106.[157]

By the end of 1948, Wuxi's 104 filatures, employing more than 10,000 workers, had all discontinued operations.[158] Even as late as April 1949, with Nanjing already fallen to the Communists, the Qingji Textile Company in Shanghai pleaded with the Central Bank to purchase its silk so the company could pay its employees.[159] There was no reply. The Nationalist government was struggling for its existence and could spare nothing to save China's silk industry. By May 1949, as Communist forces surrounded Shanghai, only three silk filatures remained in operation, and these had to shut down amid the chaos that accompanied the city's second liberation in four years.[160]

The situation in the silk weaving industry was similarly grim. Despite limited attempts to provide silk thread to weavers through state-contracted production in 1947, hyperinflation drove up production costs and inhibited the flow of goods and capital. The banks, the Central Trust, and state companies all preferred to use stores of filature silk for speculative purposes rather than to supply thread to weavers at affordable prices. As a result, by the end of 1948, fewer than half of the

156. *Shangbao*, 7 Sep. 1947; *Dalu*, 24 & 25 Mar. 1949; SMA S37-1-317; *Shangbao*, 6 Jul. 1949. *NCDN*, 15 Oct. 1946, claimed that the United States Government planned to sell 5,600 bales of Japanese silk by tender on October 16, while silk exported to New York from China, a US ally, remained unsold due to inflated prices. Documents collected in Gao and Yan, *Jindai Wuxi cansiye*, 481–82, make similar claims, in one case referring to US officials' explanations that the United States desired to support the Japanese economy to reduce expenses for the occupation forces there.

157. *Xinwenbao*, 29 Apr. 1947; *Dalu*, 4 Jun. 1946, 21 Oct. 1947; *Dagongbao*, 1 Feb. 1948; *Tianjin minguo*, 13 Oct. 1948; *Heping*, 9 Oct. & 10 Dec. 1948. On the ill-fated efforts of the Unified Silk Production and Export Company from 1947 to 1949, see SMA S39-1-52 and *Jinrong*, 14 Jan. 1948.

158. Qian, *Wuxishi sichou gongye*, 22, 88.

159. SMA S37-2-20.

160. SMA S37-1-351.

silk looms in Jiangsu Province could continue production. By July 1949, only about 3,100 of Shanghai's 6,418 silk looms were engaged in production.[161] Thousands of silk weavers were left idle, either let go temporarily or simply left to swell the ranks of the unemployed in China's increasingly volatile cities.

As damaging as it was for China's silk industry, the postwar crisis did not prevent banks and state companies from earning considerable revenue from their administration of the silk industry. In 1946, the China Sericulture Company made a profit of 1.38 billion yuan. In 1947, the company earned USD $2.86 million and 700 billion yuan (recognizing that Chinese yuan had become almost worthless) from exports of raw silk.[162] But government policy failed to foster the sustained growth of production and employment. Whether driven underground or into bankruptcy, silk production declined precipitously under soaring costs, shrinking markets, and government agencies' extractive practices. Despite the shortcomings in postwar policies, many in the press nonetheless clamored for direct state management of the silk industry, as well as cooperation between silk capitalists and workers for mutual survival.[163] Such arrangements would have to wait, however, for a government more capable of and committed to fostering economic recovery and ensuring the welfare of China's industrial workers.

Conclusion

The development of China's modern silk reeling and weaving industries is broadly representative of the modern transformation of China's economy and society. Local entrepreneurs responding to foreign demand established new industries oriented toward export markets. Novel imports like rayon thread and electric-powered looms impelled the expansion of industrial silk weaving. Given the uncertain political, military, and economic situation in China and worldwide in the first decades of the twentieth century, factory owners tried to displace risk onto sericulturalists and workers by suppressing cocoon prices and

161. *Jiangsusheng cansang sichou zhi*, 302; *Shangbao*, 29 Jul. 1949.
162. Zhu Xinyu, *Zhejiang sichou shi*, 238.
163. *Shenbao*, 12 May 1946; *Wenhuibao*, 12 Sep. 1946.

wages, and laying off workers whenever demand fell. With stronger government leadership and more effective policies, such as were implemented in Japan, Chinese sericulture and silk production might have flourished in the 1930s. But China lacked a unified and capable central government capable of implementing the needed reforms, and lost ground to Japanese producers in world markets, especially the United States, even before the war.

The eight-year Sino-Japanese War and occupation by Japan's military devastated sericulture and the silk industry, but it also established a new relationship between silk producers and the state that carried over into the postwar years. The postwar Nationalist government attempted to foster the industry's growth by expanding the administrative structures established during the occupation. However, civil war, deficit spending, and reckless monetary policies threw manufacturing and commerce into chaos. As a means of restoring production and employment in the Yangzi Delta silk industry, the Nationalist government provided loans and production contracts to silk filatures. But these proved ineffective and created headaches for factory owners, and the exploitative practices of the state banks and the Central Trust further undermined the effectiveness of state production contracts.

Factory owners found the Nationalists' attempts to organize and manipulate the labor movement equally frustrating, as evidenced by repeated complaints that the government was "soft" on labor and encouraged worker militancy. Wars and economic crises not only devastated the silk industry, but also affected labor relations and the labor movement in unanticipated ways that undermined the Nationalists' position and aided their Communist opponents. The next chapter outlines the history of the labor movement among Chinese silk workers.

CHAPTER TWO

Yangzi Delta Silk Workers in War and Revolution

Chinese silk workers responded to crises and conflicts in diverse ways, including participating in some of the most intense and notable strike actions in twentieth-century China. During a major strike in 1934, Shanghai silk workers protested wage cuts and other policies that undermined their livelihoods and working conditions. Well organized and highly motivated, they published a newspaper called the "Strike Daily" (*Bagong ribao*), organized pickets and delegates, and presented their demands to factory owners and the Nationalist government, but they encountered only recalcitrance and violence. In an incident known as the March 11 Massacre, striking silk workers clashed with Vietnamese police in Shanghai's French Concession.[1] One woman was killed and ten strikers injured in the two-hour battle, which inspired silk workers in Hangzhou and Huzhou to continue their ongoing strikes and even (in the case of Huzhou) to launch a violent struggle that alarmed the Nationalist leadership.[2]

On April 10, 1934, angered by employers' intransigence and the government's impotence, the striking silk workers surrounded Shanghai's Civic Center and blocked city officials from leaving. They maintained the siege throughout the night in pouring rain and were supported by

1. Perry, *Shanghai on Strike*, 191–92; Meiya Manuscript, 22–25; Zhu Bangxing, *Shanghai chanye*, 153–54.

2. Bloodshed resulted when more than 3,300 Huzhou weavers marched on the county seat of Wuxing on April 2, 1934, and were suppressed. *Huzhou sichou zhi*, 27.

donations of food from local merchants and students. One woman weaver even gave birth that night amidst the crowd surrounding the Civic Center. The next morning, hundreds of police armed with fire hoses, bamboo staves, rifles, and bayonets arrived. After a protracted but uneven battle, the police dispersed the strikers. Over one hundred were injured and thirty arrested. More than ten thousand silk weavers from hundreds of small factories came out in sympathy strikes, but the movement could not be sustained. By April 22, after a fifty-day struggle, the silk workers returned to work, resigned to accept wage reductions and other disadvantageous changes.[3]

As China's modern silk industry developed, distinct groups of silk workers created specific cultures, movements, and forms of association in response to economic and political challenges. Women's participation in the labor movement, sometimes taking the form of union organizing, fostered the development of an active and politically conscious culture of protest among women workers. This chapter describes the silk industry's workforces, labor organizations, and actions in the first half of the twentieth century, highlighting the differences between female filature workers and male silk weavers and contrasting their organizations and tactics, as well as their relationships with their employers and the state.

As discussed in the introduction to this book, historians have struggled to locate a class-conscious labor movement in modern China, and there is widespread disagreement as to the applicability of Marxist class categories to the Chinese context. Objective divisions within the silk industry workforce, such as those based on skill, job, locality, gender, and native place, clearly existed. But such divisions did not always prevent broad-based and unified action among silk workers, who in the late 1940s played a leading role in a very active, powerful, and politically conscious labor movement. The silk industry thus presents an interesting case of emerging class consciousness, albeit one that also highlights the tremendous diversity of Chinese workers. These differences continued after 1949 despite the Communist Party's efforts to foster working-class unity and conformity.

3. Perry, *Shanghai on Strike*, 196–99; Zhu Bangxing, *Shanghai chanye*, 156–61.

Yangzi Delta Silk Workers and the Chinese Labor Movement

Workers in the silk reeling and weaving industries comprised a significant portion of China's industrial workforce in the first half of the twentieth century. Due in part to the volatility of domestic and global silk markets, the lives of even the most privileged silk workers were fraught with insecurity. Nevertheless, life in the textiles industries offered opportunities unavailable in the countryside, especially as earnings from handicraft production declined during the First World War. The capital outlay needed to establish a small weaving workshop was minimal, and these would spring up by the hundreds when supplies were plentiful and market demand encouraged production. When the markets changed, production and employment contracted suddenly, sometimes in just a month or two. Because of these fluctuating conditions, accurate and detailed statistics are generally unavailable. Most surveys conducted by the Social Affairs Bureaus during the Nanjing Decade focused on factories employing thirty or more people, which excluded many silk weaving factories. By some estimates, Shanghai's silk weaving workforce numbered as many as 15,000 in 1936, not including an estimated 2,700 technical and managerial staff.[4] Thousands more were employed in weaving factories in other Jiangnan cities or wove silk at home for various kinds of brokers, agents, and other intermediaries.

As described in the previous chapter, silk filatures in the Jiangnan region exploited a skilled, cheap, and flexible supply of local labor. Filatures employed anywhere from 100 to 1,000 workers, but 500 or 600 was typical. In 1894, one in three of China's estimated 120,000 industrial workers was employed in silk reeling. By 1910, some 90,000 of China's 600,000 industrial employees worked in silk filatures, and in 1933, filature workers comprised about 10 percent of China's 945,000 industrial workers. Of these, 36 percent worked in Shanghai.[5]

The silk reeling workforce was 90 percent female, and before the 1930s about one-fifth of these workers were children. Filatures

4. D. K. Lieu, *Silk Industry of China*, 215–16.

5. Xu Xinwu, *Zhongguo jindai saosi gongye*, 561, 576–77.

employed men mainly as machinists, general laborers, and supervisors. Whereas the male workers enjoyed employment contracts and other benefits, filatures hired women silk reelers on a seasonal basis, which made their situation very insecure. Regardless of whether the work was performed by women, by children, or in some filatures in Shandong and Sichuan by men, working conditions were very difficult. Steam from the cocoon basins filled the workshops and in cold weather contributed to lung infections and other illnesses. Work days at filatures generally lasted ten to thirteen hours, although at some filatures (in Sichuan for example) workers could be on the job as long as fifteen hours a day.[6]

The first stage in the production of silk thread is boiling and beating the cocoons to remove the sericin outer shells and separate the silken filaments. This work was done by children as young as eight years old, whose hands came into frequent contact with boiling water, sometimes in fatal or disfiguring accidents. A foreign observer in Shanghai described the conditions this way:

> Tiny children stood for an eleven-hour day, soaked to the skin in a steamy atmosphere hot even in winter, their fingers blanched to the knuckles and their little bodies swaying from one tired foot to the other, kept at their task by a firm overseer who did not hesitate to beat those whose attention wandered.[7]

The children employed in silk reeling often worked even longer hours than adults, as they were responsible for cleanup once the regular workday was over. Following the enactment of the "Revised Factory Law of China" in 1931, the employment of small children in silk filatures declined and gradually disappeared during the war with Japan.

Silk reeling required constant diligence under difficult conditions. A filature worker had to repair broken filaments quickly to maintain evenness and attend to the basins to remove unraveled cocoons before the chrysalis stained the water. Labor management was brutal, as male

6. Xu Xinwu, *Zhongguo jindai saosi gongye*, 561–64.
7. Hinder, *Life and Labour*, 35–36.

supervisors walked among the filature workers, many of them young girls and teenagers, and disciplined them with harsh language and physical blows. Male supervisors were selected for their severity and rewarded for increased production.[8]

In contrast with the overwhelmingly young and female filature workforce, the silk weaving workforce was mostly made up of adult men and women, and weaving workshops employed very few children. Only eight silk weaving factories surveyed in Shanghai employed children in 1931, and by 1933 only one did so. Male silk weavers were very much a "labor aristocracy"—well paid, autonomous, and well-organized. By 1933, women comprised an estimated 43 percent of China's silk weaving workforce, and by the late 1940s, women made up about half of the industry's workers.[9] The proportion of women was higher in the low-paying preparation jobs such as re-reeling and spooling than among the better-paid weavers who operated the complex, pattern-making looms. Nonetheless, working alongside these well-organized, politically active male weavers provided these women opportunities to participate in the labor movement and the Communist revolution in ways that were impossible for their counterparts in the filatures.

Among the privileged, male weavers working in Shanghai's silk workshops in the 1920s, Elizabeth Perry has identified two distinct cultures. Older artisans were skilled weavers who left rural household employment for urban factory jobs. Hailing from Zhejiang weaving towns, these men were poorly educated and mostly illiterate. On the other hand, young men (and some women) who had at least a primary school education gravitated to the larger, more modern silk factories, such as the Meiya Company. These young workers were highly literate and received training as apprentices.[10] They looked upon factory life as a step up in the world and modeled their dress, customs, and politics on those of urban students their own age. In contrast, the older artisan

8. WMA D2–1–11; Xu Xinwu, *Zhongguo jindai saosi gongye*, 564.

9. D. K. Lieu, *Silk Industry of China*, 217–23.

10. Of these workers, 95 percent of the men and 35 percent of the women could read. Xu Xinwu, *Jindai Jiangnan sizhi gongye*, 304.

weavers viewed factory work as a loss of independence and were more deeply rooted in traditional rural culture.[11]

Silk weavers and filature workers occupied opposite ends of the wage spectrum for textile workers. Between 1930 and 1934, Shanghai filature workers earned an average of 0.41 yuan for an eleven-hour day. Shanghai silk weavers earned more than twice as much, about 1.08 yuan per day.[12] Within the silk weaving industry, however, there was also wide variation. In 1931 male silk workers could earn between 19 and 55 yuan a month, while female workers' wages ranged from 14 to 36 yuan a month. Statistics on wages paid according to job description provide more evidence of gender inequality. For example, in 1930 male power loom weavers were paid an average of .167 yuan per hour, whereas female weavers were paid only .106 yuan per hour. In 1931 these figures were .147 and .108 respectively, in 1932 they were .180 and .124, and in 1933 they were .157 and .126 yuan per hour. By 1934, though, there was a slight reversal: as declining exports suppressed wages, male weavers' wages declined to 0.99 on average, while women weavers' wages only fell to .114 yuan per hour.

This reversal indicates that the larger, more modern factories, which weathered the Great Depression better than the smaller workshops and could offer higher wages, employed a greater proportion of women weavers. Although women remained a small minority among Shanghai's silk weavers, because they comprised a larger percentage of workers in the more successful silk companies, such as Meiya, they did not see their wages decline as precipitously as male weavers in small factories or other women employed in the silk industry. For those who retained their jobs during the Great Depression, daily work hours increased from an average of 10.5 in 1931 to more than eleven in 1933, when nearly two-thirds of Shanghai silk weavers worked eleven to twelve hours a day.[13]

These averaged statistics conceal tremendous diversity in the wage systems adopted in Jiangnan silk weaving factories. Some workers were

11. Perry, *Shanghai on Strike*, 185–88.

12. Honig, *Sisters and Strangers*, 176–77; Perry, *Shanghai on Strike*, 191.

13. D. K. Lieu, *Silk Industry of China*, 219–32. Lieu's statistics are taken from *The Wage Rate of Shanghai Industrial Workers* (1935) by Cai Zhengya of the Shanghai Social Affairs Bureau.

paid according to daily time rates, while others were paid piece-rate wages. Many factories used mixed systems of various types. In some, weavers were paid a time rate for a given quota, with bonuses for exceeding the norm. Other factories paid a standard rate for a quota of cloth produced in a given time. Piece rates for higher or lower productivity were adjusted accordingly. The Meiya Company employed some of the most complex wage standards for silk weavers. Piece rates varied from the lowest for simple taffetas and single crepe fabrics to the highest rates for patterned silks, georgettes, and velvets. Some Meiya weavers' pay scales were twice as high as those of similar weavers in smaller workshops.[14] Silk workers' wages proved difficult to standardize, and wide variation in wage systems and pay rates continued into the Communist period.

Nor were variable wage systems the only aspect of silk industry employment that persisted across the 1949 divide. In the 1920s, under the leadership of General Manager Cai Shengbai, the Meiya Company began to offer its workers a variety of incentives to increase productivity, some of which presaged those of the socialist era. For example, starting in 1927, Meiya held production competitions and rewarded the best weavers with bonuses and public honors. Before the Great Depression, the average monthly wage was fifty to sixty yuan, and the highest-paid weavers could earn eighty to one hundred yuan per month. Under the competition and reward system, weavers with the highest bi-weekly production record were rewarded with an extra two or three yuan, and their names and accomplishments were announced in the company paper. By 1929 the competition system had expanded. Any weaver in a Meiya factory who produced more than one thousand meters in a forty-day period (average daily production of 25.4 meters) received an extra ten yuan. Whoever could exceed this record would then receive fifteen yuan. The top producers' names were embroidered on a red banner to hang in the factory where the outstanding weaver worked, and Meiya factories competed for the right to keep this banner at the end of the year. By this method, Meiya silk weavers' average rate of production reached twenty-six to thirty meters per day. Although Xu Xinwu's 1991 publication claims that "under the capitalist system, this was in fact a

14. Xu Xinwu, *Jindai Jiangnan sizhi gongye*, 340–41.

kind of 'sweat and blood wage system,'"[15] Meiya's young, educated weavers responded positively to the opportunity to earn more for their effort.

As part of Cai Shengbai's managerial philosophy, Meiya provided its employees with many benefits. In addition to room and board, which cost employees 6.50 yuan per month, employees had access to a night school, a social club, and health and hygiene services. The company clinic had its own doctor on staff, and the night school offered one-hour classes in language, literacy, math, singing, and other subjects. In the factories' social clubs, Meiya workers organized performances and used the small library or played chess, cards, or ping pong. Each factory also had a basketball team that competed in inter-factory games. Although these benefits cost the company five thousand yuan annually, the expense was considered worthwhile if it contributed to higher productivity and lower turnover.[16]

The cooperative relationship between labor and management began to change with the economic crisis of the Great Depression. Silk weaving factories throughout the Jiangnan region reduced wages as markets shrank and prices fell, and employment relations changed fundamentally even in large, modern factories like Meiya. From 1931, silk factories in Shanghai began to institute a loom leasing system (*fangliao dingzhi banfa*) to lower costs and reduce conflicts between labor and management. At the Tiancheng Silk Factory, the leasing system was given the grandiose name of "Labor and Capital Cooperation." Under this system, foremen rented looms to weavers at twenty yuan each. The factories supplied the materials and sold the cloth produced. This system provided greater guarantees for the factory owner than the weaver, whose piece-rate wage was subject to market fluctuation while the loom rental fee was fixed by contract.[17]

The implementation of the leasing system at the Meiya Company followed the failed 1934 strike described in the introduction to this chapter and was part of management's retaliatory measures. These included a 30 percent wage reduction and an end to dormitory housing

15. Xu Xinwu, *Jindai Jiangnan sizhi gongye*, 305–6.
16. Xu Xinwu, *Jindai Jiangnan sizhi gongye*, 305–7; Feng, *Cai Shengbai*, 51–54.
17. D. K. Lieu, *Silk Industry of China*, 223.

and subsidized meals. Under the loom leasing system, the Meiya Company leased its factories and looms to management staff, who then rented the looms to individual weavers. This guaranteed the company a minimum income per loom while saving 15–20 percent on operating expenses. Loom leasing furthermore allowed Meiya and other silk factories to avoid direct conflict with weavers, who were becoming increasingly well organized and militant as they saw their wages and benefits erode under the pressures of the global depression.[18] From the point of view of these once-privileged weavers, the loom leasing system was highly exploitative and became an important target during the citywide strikes in Shanghai in 1937.

By that time, Jiangnan silk workers had a long history of organizing. In the 1920s and 1930s, both filature workers and silk weavers played prominent but very different roles in China's growing labor movement. Filature workers were very active in defending their interests, as in a 1911 strike by silk workers in Shanghai's Zhabei District to oppose wage reductions. As S. A. Smith puts it: "Even before a labor movement existed, women silk workers showed a capacity for effective organization, with strikers touring the filatures in a noisy throng to bring out other workers; pickets preventing strikebreaking; representatives coordinating action across different factories; grievances being publicized; and efforts being made to win public support."[19]

One common theme, however, is how vulnerable silk workers' organizations were to outside influence and manipulation from employers, criminal gangs, or political parties. For example, sometimes labor contractors, supervisors, or criminal elements mobilized filature workers for strikes and protests, but their influence more often served employers by preventing walkouts. Therefore, although filature workers went on strike frequently, they rarely succeeded in achieving their goals or establishing autonomous unions.[20]

18. Perry, *Shanghai on Strike*, 200; Xu Xinwu, *Jindai Jiangnan sizhi gongye*, 341–42; Feng, *Cai Shengbai*, 56–59.

19. S. A. Smith, *Like Cattle and Horses*, 56.

20. Between 1895 and 1913, industrial workers in Shanghai went on strike fifty-one times. Fully twenty-six of these strikes occurred in silk filatures. S. A. Smith, *Like Cattle and Horses*, 54. Another source, Zhu Bangxing, *Shanghai chanye*, 190, states that filature workers went on strike at least once a year, mainly over wage issues.

Despite their activism and ingenuity, filature workers' organizations were chronically weak and subject to outside manipulation. The Silk Filatures Women Workers Benevolent Society, established in 1912, was assisted by feminist organizations such as the Chinese Women's Republican Cooperative Society. The union collapsed due to employer resistance, police repression, and filature workers' unwillingness to pay the 0.30 yuan membership fee. The second effort, the Shanghai Women Workers' Association for the Advancement of Industrial Progress, led an all-city strike in 1922 in which nearly twenty thousand silk workers in Zhabei and Xinzha Districts demanded shorter working hours, increased pay, one day off every two weeks, recognition of the union, and protection from abuse and mistreatment at work. Both filature owners and government authorities viewed this large and active movement, with women workers demanding equality and human dignity, as a serious threat and took steps to suppress and redirect it. Although the strike did result in a modest decrease in working hours (the filatures agreed to close a half hour earlier during the summer months), the ease with which employers arrested or co-opted the association's leadership is indicative of the obstacles these workers faced in establishing organizations to protect their interests.[21]

In 1924 some fourteen thousand filature workers joined a strike led by the Shanghai Silk and Cotton Women Workers Association, but the owners bought off the association's leader, a Subei (Northern Jiangsu) woman named Mu Zhiying who had gangland connections. Appealing to native-place ties as well as basic greed, a filature owner from Mu's hometown of Yancheng proposed the formation of an employer-controlled union.[22] Accepting a monthly stipend of three hundred yuan, Mu worked through a network of supervisors to ensure that workers would not walk out or strike. She was so successful that during the May Thirtieth Movement of 1925, filature workers did not join the general strike. Mu Zhiying ruled the bosses' union as a dictator, enjoying the fruits of collaboration and ruthlessly eliminating any competition for leadership. When Gao Yongzhang attempted

21. S. A. Smith, *Like Cattle and Horses*, 65–66, 72, 145–46.
22. S. A. Smith, *Like Cattle and Horses*, 58.

to establish a rival union, the authorities shut it down after just four months.[23]

Nonetheless, Mu's days as leader of the bosses' union were numbered. Wage disputes and strikes were common in the Jiangnan silk industry in the late 1920s. In 1926, for example, Shanghai filatures endured twenty-two strikes involving seventy-three factories and more than thirty thousand people. A strike in June of that year, which both the Communist-led Shanghai General Labor Union and Shanghai women's organizations supported, resulted in reduced hours and an increase of 0.05 yuan to the daily wage.[24] Mu Zhiying sought to take advantage of the pay increase to demand that each worker contribute 0.02 yuan per day to the union. Workers in Hongkou District reacted immediately by striking again to remove Mu's influence. The employers suppressed the strike through police violence and arrests, but fourteen thousand filature workers in Zhabei District also walked out and rallied society to their cause. It seemed Mu Zhiying had become a new source of conflict. The owners removed her from power and closed her office that June. Having accomplished this goal, the silk reelers returned to work on July 1, but other attempts to establish independent and effective filature unions continued to suffer repression and co-optation throughout the Nanjing Decade.[25]

Labor relations were even more contentious in the silk reeling center of Wuxi, where filature owners rarely negotiated in good faith and frequently resorted to violent repression. By the mid-1920s, most of Jiangsu Province's filatures were located in Wuxi, where wages were lower than in Shanghai. In May 1926, more than ten thousand workers from seventeen Wuxi filatures launched a strike for higher wages. Despite the threat of military repression from warlord Sun Chuanfang, the strikers achieved their aims in just ten days.[26] This was due in part

23. Xu Xinwu, *Zhongguo jindai saosi gongye*, 585–88; Perry, *Shanghai on Strike*, 171–75.

24. Zhu Bangxing, *Shanghai chanye*, 190–91.

25. Xu Xinwu, *Zhongguo jindai saosi*, 592–94; Perry, *Shanghai on Strike*, 175–76; S. A. Smith, *Like Cattle and Horses*, 227–28.

26. For documents detailing the 1926 strike in Wuxi see Gao and Yan, *Jindai Wuxi cansiye*, 512–29.

to the ability of Communist organizers to publicize the strike through street demonstrations and written appeals. Other factories and industries in Wuxi quickly rallied in support of the striking filature workers, putting considerable pressure on employers.

The strike forced mill owners to reduce the workday from fourteen to thirteen hours, and to increase the basic wage from 0.45 yuan to 0.50 yuan. These changes were implemented throughout the Wuxi silk reeling industry but were short-lived.[27] The 1927 seizure of power by the Nationalist Party and the "White Terror" in April of that year resulted in the arrest and execution of labor organizers, Communist or not, in most Jiangnan cities. Although some union leaders with Communist sympathies continued organizing under the "Unification Committee," after April 1927 union work in Shanghai filatures was "terrible."[28] Nonetheless, filature workers continued to strike, relying on the same spontaneous and unruly tactics that so intimidated factory owners, the state, and even Communist organizers.

The first major filature strike following the Nationalist takeover of Shanghai was sparked by the death, in March 1928, of male machinist Jiang Axing, who had been injured resisting police efforts to remove him and three other workers fired from the Weilun Filature for attempting to organize a union. Jiang's martyrdom sparked a wave of strikes that lasted months, in which workers protested the handling of his case and demanded wage increases and improved working conditions. By the end of 1928, Shanghai filatures recorded 1.5 million working days lost to strikes and walkouts. In the repressive political climate, however, such activity could not persist, even under the relatively favorable economic conditions of the late 1920s.[29] On November 1, 1929, the Nationalist government promulgated a new union law that banned most existing unions on the grounds that they were controlled by "undesirable elements" and threatened public security. The few existing union organizations in Shanghai filatures were replaced with "yellow" unions controlled by employers. The situation was similar in other

27. Xu Xinwu, *Zhongguo jindai saosi gongye*, 598–99.
28. Perry, *Shanghai on Strike*, 177.
29. Zhu Bangxing, *Shanghai chanye*, 191–92.

parts of the Yangzi Delta, where workers' unions were suppressed or co-opted, their leaders fired or arrested.[30]

Unsurprisingly, the bosses' unions proved ineffective at protecting workers' interests. When filature owners in Wuxi lowered wages in the fall of 1929, the company unions signed agreements accepting wage reductions of 10 percent. Workers again turned to informal means to strike, and the movement spread rapidly throughout the Wuxi silk reeling industry. Despite violent suppression, workers fought back and destroyed the Wuxi Nationalist Party headquarters. But this only brought more severe repression, and police arrested forty filature workers. To gain their release, their comrades were forced to accept a wage reduction and return to work. Just over a year later, workers at Wuxi's Defeng Filature struck to protest another round of wage reductions and layoffs. The strike spread to other filatures, and again the police arrested the leaders. This time, however, sympathy strikes in other industries led to a county-wide general strike that forced the filature owners to restore wages and the police to release arrested leaders.[31]

Bitter about its limited authority and desperate to preserve social order (so conceived), the Nationalist government increasingly sided with employers and suppressed the labor movement with even greater vigor and brutality than had the earlier warlord regimes. Under such repressive conditions, spontaneous action organized through informal networks of small-scale "sisterhoods" was more effective than the responses of formal union organizations with recognized leaders who could be arrested or co-opted. But as the economic environment worsened in the 1930s, there was little that filature workers could do to protect their livelihoods. The global depression hit the Yangzi Delta silk industry especially hard. As early as September 1930, some seventy Shanghai filatures had closed, laying off about twenty-eight thousand workers.[32]

Workers at Wuxi's Yongtai Filature successfully blocked their employer's attempt to intensify labor and reduce wages in the spring of

30. Xu Xinwu, *Zhongguo jindai saosi gongye*, 589, 594–96.

31. Xu Xinwu, *Zhongguo jindai saosi gongye*, 599–600.

32. Honig, *Sisters and Strangers*, 57–78; Honig, "Burning Incense, Pledging Sisterhood," 700–714; Perry, *Shanghai on Strike*, 179–80.

1931, although the struggle turned violent, with police resorting to machine guns and water cannons and filature workers destroying factory property. In 1932, management again attempted to reduce wages, this time by shifting to a piece-rate system. Workers responded by striking, which led to a general strike that was violently suppressed. Fifteen were injured and six arrested in clashes with police. In the end, those arrested were released, but the piece-rate wage system remained in place.[33]

Not all Jiangnan filature strikes were violently suppressed in the 1930s. In Shanghai, filature workers were forced to accept reduced wages after 1930. When international silk markets began to revive in the summer of 1933, workers demanded that wages be restored to earlier levels. Circumventing the officially sponsored union in favor of spontaneous action, the strike began on July 5 at the Zhenfeng Filature and quickly spread to twenty-seven others involving more than twenty thousand employees. On July 10, the strikers returned to work after accepting a settlement drafted by the Social Affairs Bureau that included wages of 0.45 yuan per day. Employers resisted implementing the settlement, however. By 1936, wages continued to lag behind the silk industry's rising fortunes, resulting in another major strike wave that affected nearly all of Shanghai's filatures. The strikers demanded that wages be restored to the level of 0.45 yuan and that the workday be reduced to eleven hours. The filature owners agreed to a lesser wage increase.[34]

Industrial silk weavers were more likely to establish unions than their thread mill counterparts, even if these were no more successful in defending silk weavers' wages, benefits, and working conditions in the 1930s. Male silk weavers in twentieth-century Shanghai had one of the highest strike rates per population of any textile workers in the city. According to Elizabeth Perry, between 1918 and 1940, Shanghai silk weavers launched 20.8 strikes per 1,000 workers as compared with just 2.0 per 1,000 for filature workers. Filature strikes usually involved much larger numbers than weavers' strikes, which averaged

33. Xu Xinwu, *Zhongguo jindai saosi gongye*, 600; Gao and Yan, *Jindai Wuxi cansiye*, 529–36.

34. Zhu Bangxing, *Shanghai chanye*, 192–93.

only 212 participants.[35] Under the desperate conditions of the 1930s, the labor movement among silk weavers grew to become one of the most active and powerful in Shanghai, despite its ultimate failure in the face of economic decline, government suppression, and employer intransigence.

The two types of silk weavers Perry identified—older artisanal weavers and younger recruits to modern factories—exhibited different preferences for organizing and politics. The younger, more educated weavers organized modern-style unions, including male and female members, and often embraced radical politics like the students they emulated in their dress and habits. Older craftsmen preferred more traditional "brotherhoods" and were attracted to secret societies and criminal gangs. The two groups were also employed in different sorts of enterprises with different working conditions. During the Great Depression, however, the circumstances of the more privileged weavers, such as those at Meiya, increasingly came to resemble those of their counterparts employed in small workshops.

Before the Great Depression, weavers in large, modern factories enjoyed high wages and benefits and a relatively cooperative relationship with management. Weavers at Meiya factories responded to production competitions, excellent pay, and benefits by making Meiya into China's leading silk company. By contrast, older, less-educated weavers in the small, scattered workshops in Shanghai and other Jiangnan cities earned lower wages and received none of the benefits enjoyed by Meiya employees. Their lives were far less secure, their jobs dependent on the state of the market. By the late 1920s, Meiya weavers recognized the prosperity their skill and effort had brought the company. Under the influence of a young Communist organizer, He Datong, Meiya weavers in 1927 demanded that the company increase wages, guarantee job security, and accept a union organization. Initially resistant, General Manager Cai Shengbai acceded to these demands after He Datong visited his office carrying a revolver. But shortly after Chiang Kai-shek's seizure of power in April 1927, He Datong was arrested and executed, and

35. Perry, *Shanghai on Strike*, 168.

the union soon collapsed.[36] By 1930, Meiya was requiring its employees to sign a contract that greatly diminished their previous rights and privileges. Two strikes later that year, however, resulted in the restoration of the 1927 agreement, the continuation of bonus payments, and the extension of permanent employment to recently hired temporary workers.

Starting in January 1933, as silk weaving factories began to shut down in response to shrinking markets, silk weavers organized to resist factory closures, and Meiya employees went out on strike to protest wage reductions.[37] With its modern corporate structure, management techniques, and marketing strategies, the Meiya Company was able to weather the depression better than smaller factories. By 1934, Meiya's 1,000 looms comprised fully half of all silk looms operating in Shanghai, but facing declining prices for silk cloth, the company cut wages. A wage reduction of 10 percent in 1933 elicited protests, and a 15 percent cut in 1934 provoked a massive strike by 4,500 Meiya workers.[38]

An important characteristic of the 1934 strike was the high degree of participation by women. Whereas weavers in smaller workshops tended to exclude women from their "brotherhoods," the younger, more radically minded workers at Meiya voiced demands such as equal pay for men and women and paid maternity leave. According to one factory history, at the very moment that the manager of Meiya's Number Nine Factory was assuring Cai Shengbai that his factory would not strike because of the high proportion of women workers, these women, led by Lin Yinnan, joined the strike.[39] Participation in a seasoned and active labor movement such as this surely increased these women workers' confidence in their abilities and recognition of their importance.

36. S. A. Smith, *Like Cattle and Horses*, 124, 216. Elizabeth Perry in *Shanghai on Strike*, 183, recounts that He Datong slipped on a watermelon rind while fleeing police. He was caught and executed.

37. D. K. Lieu, *Silk Industry of China*, 233.

38. Perry, *Shanghai on Strike*, 183–84; Zhu Bangxing, *Shanghai chanye*, 133–35. For detailed accounts of the 1934 strike at Meiya, see Zhu Bangxing, *Shanghai chanye*, 150–68, and Zhang Qi, *Shanghai gongyun jishi*, 13–31.

39. Meiya Manuscript, 19–23.

Faced with a well-organized, disciplined, and inclusive union organization, Meiya management adopted a hard line in the mid-1930s. Although Meiya weavers' wages remained comparatively high, the relative decline in wages and working conditions led them to engage in a series of strikes culminating in the March 11 Massacre in 1934 described above.[40] The Meiya struggle, publicized in the strikers' own paper, not only rallied the support of workers in Shanghai's many small silk weaving workshops, but also encouraged silk workers throughout the region to persevere in strike actions over the following month.

In the midst of this intensifying struggle, Chiang Kai-shek, then leading the fifth "encirclement campaign" against the Communists' Jiangxi Soviet, took a personal interest in the movement. He sent a telegram to the Shanghai Nationalist Party Committee stating:

> At this difficult time for our nation, labor and capital must cooperate. They should accept government and party mediation and must not resort to work slowdowns or strikes in order to raise demands that could lead to a strike wave.[41]

The generalissimo's order did little to abate the strike, but the situation was growing increasingly difficult for these weavers, who had received no income for more than a month and many of whom had become homeless when the company closed its dormitories.[42] Despite the outpouring of sympathy for the strikers (especially from Meiya's smaller competitors), the combination of material deprivation and police suppression brought the strike to an end after fifty days. By April 22 the strikers returned to work resigned to accept wage reductions and other changes to their conditions of employment. The company required all returning employees to register as new workers, which both

40. Perry, *Shanghai on Strike*, 191–92; Meiya Manuscript, 23–25; Zhu Bangxing, *Shanghai chanye*, 153–54.

41. Meiya Manuscript, 30.

42. Zhu Bangxing, *Shanghai chanye*, 156–57; Perry, *Shanghai on Strike*, 198.

eliminated seniority and helped the company to weed out activists, 143 of whom lost their jobs.[43]

It was after the 1934 strike that Meiya began to implement the loom leasing system described above, and weavers took a 30 percent cut to the piece-rate wages they received. The company gradually closed the factory dormitories (and other facilities such as the clinic and basketball team) and increased prices for cafeteria meals. As a result of these changes, Meiya weavers lost many of their privileges. The gap in terms of wages and benefits between the large, modern factories and the smaller workshops diminished.[44]

In early 1935, the Meiya Company reduced work hours from ten to nine hours per day without changing the piece rates paid to weavers. The company also eliminated most subsidies for workers, including paid maternity leave. One of the most significant changes was the elimination of subsidies for "waiting for warp and weft" (*dengjing dengwei*). Ordinarily, if weavers on piece-rate wages had to wait for materials, they would be given a minimal subsidy for their time. The elimination of this subsidy allowed the factory to stop production at any time without providing compensation. In addition, from May to July 1935, Meiya paid its employees half in cash and half in company scrip, which could only be exchanged for bolts of silk. If the weaver could not sell the cloth he received from the factory, his income was reduced by half. Then Meiya reduced work hours again, establishing a three-shift system. By July 1935, production of silk cloth was only 40 percent of 1933 levels.[45]

The situation began to improve in August 1935, as sales and prices revived. However, changes in the structure of the industry and labor relations persisted. Meiya weavers had lost, at least for the time being, their power and privileges. The citywide silk weavers' strikes in 1936 and 1937 focused more on bread-and-butter wage issues than on attempting to address inequalities and conditions of employment. These strikes

43. Meiya Manuscript, 31–39; Perry, *Shanghai on Strike*, 197–99; Zhu Bangxing, *Shanghai chanye*, 158–61.

44. Perry, *Shanghai on Strike*, 200; Meiya Manuscript, 41–43; Zhu Bangxing, *Shanghai chanye*, 166–68.

45. Xu Xinwu, *Jindai Jiangnan sizhi gongye*, 343.

involved far fewer women (except for the strikes at Meiya) and were organized around either the officially sponsored unions or gangster-dominated "brotherhoods." The Communist Party and its affiliated Youth League continued to play a role in some factories, but leftist labor activists were not as prominent as they had been in the 1934 strike.

Affected by global economic depression, Chinese silk production foundered in the 1930s, but by 1936 prices and markets had substantially recovered, and production and employment followed apace. Few of the benefits of recovery accrued to silk workers, however. Filature wages in Wuxi, the dominant silk producing city in the Jiangnan region, remained low even relative to low-paid Shanghai filature workers. Silk weavers were more successful in organizing unions, but their efforts to regain the pay and privileges of the 1920s failed, and their organizations fractured as Nationalists and Communists competed for control of the labor movement.

Due to the recovery of international and domestic markets, as well as the illegal importation of cheap Japanese rayon through North China, silk weaving revived in the Yangzi Delta. By 1937, Shanghai had over five hundred silk weaving factories with a total of seven thousand looms and employing some forty thousand workers.[46] The Meiya Company entered another phase of expansion, establishing a branch in Hangzhou and a silk printing factory in Shanghai.[47] The company furthermore expanded its loom leasing system. In 1934, the proportion of Meiya's product woven on leased looms was only about 20 percent. By 1936 the proportion had increased to about 60 percent.[48] The expansion of loom leasing, along with wage issues and treatment by foremen, were the main factors leading Meiya workers to participate in the twenty-nine strikes in Shanghai's silk weaving industry in 1936. Although numerous, and drawing workers from dozens of silk factories large and small, these actions were usually short-term walkouts lasting only several days.[49]

As Elizabeth Perry has shown in her 1993 book *Shanghai on Strike*, union organizing among Shanghai silk weavers entered a new phase

46. Zhu Bangxing, *Shanghai chanye*, 135.
47. Feng, *Cai Shengbai*, 59.
48. Xu Xinwu, *Jindai Jiangnan sizhi gongye*, 348.
49. Perry, *Shanghai on Strike*, 201; Meiya Manuscript, 50–51.

in late 1936 as Nationalist officials, Communist revolutionaries, and gangsters attempted to manipulate these active and well-organized workers for political and economic ends. Lu Jingshi and Zhu Xuefan, Nationalist-allied labor leaders with connections to Shanghai's dominant criminal organization, the notorious Green Gang, appointed an accomplished labor activist and ally, former Blueshirt Wang Hao, to organize unions among the Shanghai silk weavers. Wang, Lu, and Zhu hoped to use the silk weavers, who had proven their militancy in the 1934 strike, in the power struggle with their political rivals in the Social Affairs Bureau and Nationalist Party organization in Shanghai.[50]

In March 1937 Wang Hao attempted to mobilize Shanghai's tens of thousands of silk factory employees by establishing the Shanghai Silk Weavers Committee for Improved Treatment. By that time, many factory workers had already gone out on strike. More than half of them demanded wage increases and improved benefits, while another fifth protested factories' failure to abide by previous agreements. According to D. K. Lieu, there were a total of seventy-three strikes in the Shanghai silk weaving industry in 1936–37 demanding higher wages, shorter hours, and an end to the loom leasing system.[51] With the establishment of the Committee for Improved Treatment, these dispersed actions were unified under a single umbrella organization, and the strikes intensified.

It soon became apparent, however, that Wang and his allies could not control or contain the silk weavers once they gained an opportunity to organize. Beginning in February 1937, weavers at the Meifeng, Hengfeng, and Jinsheng factories protested the loom rental system and demanded a greater share of increased profits. By mid-March, workers at more than a hundred Shanghai silk weaving factories were out on strike.[52] Not wanting to fall behind, Wang's committee voted to mobilize a citywide strike, which involved more than half of Shanghai's silk weavers and lasted two months. The committee issued a list of forty demands organized under four categories: wages and welfare, fulfillment

50. Perry, *Shanghai on Strike*, 202–3; Meiya Manuscript, 48–49.
51. D. K. Lieu, *Silk Industry of China*, 235.
52. Meiya Manuscript, 50–53.

of labor laws, job security, and equipment and working conditions.[53] Many workers were forced into striking by Wang's Blueshirt-trained pickets in a technique called "factory storming" (*chongchang*), which attempted to bring reluctant silk weavers out to strike and to break through police efforts to prevent the strike from spreading.[54]

To end the strike, the Shanghai Social Affairs Bureau (SAB) made the weavers a generous but impractical offer in the form of "Directive 8476." The directive proposed increasing wages by 10 percent, making Sundays a paid legal holiday, prohibiting unwarranted dismissals and fines, restoring subsidies for waiting for warp and weft, and improving the terms of the loom leasing system. It also required that provisions of the 1929 Factory Law, such as four weeks paid leave for new mothers and compensation for sick or injured workers, be implemented in silk factories.[55] "Directive 8476" was the SAB's strongest effort at promoting progressive labor practices in Shanghai, and Wang Hao's Improvement Committee voted to accept the proposal on April 2. The newly formed Silk Weaving Employers Association rejected the proposal, however, and the SAB was unable to enforce its decision or the law. Led by Cai Shengbai of the Meiya Company, the association adopted a hard line and Cai himself shut down Meiya factories in Shanghai and shipped materials to factories in other cities.[56] The struggle continued, and on April 16, thousands of silk weavers surrounded the Social Affairs Bureau. In Shanghai for medical treatment, and annoyed by daily reports of the silk weavers' actions, Chiang Kai-shek ordered the SAB and local party organs to resolve the situation. On May 14, the police raided the District Four headquarters of the Silk Weavers Union, seizing

53. For the full text of the forty demands, see D. K. Lieu, *Silk Industry of China*, 236–37.

54. Perry, *Shanghai on Strike*, 204.

55. D. K. Lieu, *Silk Industry of China*, 238–39. Under pressure from Chinese socialists and the International Labor Organization (founded in 1919), China drafted very progressive labor legislation, modeled on Japanese factory laws, in 1923 and 1927, but these provisions were not enforced. In 1929 the Nationalist government completed a Labor Code Draft modeled on German social insurance laws, but the Legislative Yuan only enacted certain sections as law. These included the Factory Law and the Labor Union Law of 1929 and the Labor Dispute Resolution Law of 1930. Aiqun Hu, *China's Social Insurance*, 70–81.

56. Zhu Bangxing, *Shanghai chanye*, 176.

documents and arresting those present. These actions only incensed the strikers more, however, and frequent clashes between silk weavers and police continued throughout the month of May.[57]

Fearful that Communist agents would seize control of these militant unions, the Shanghai SAB moved to suppress the strike on June 3, declaring the existing unions illegal, forcing weavers to return to work, and arresting leaders including Wang Hao. Although the silk weavers responded with protests, with more than four thousand walking out on June 9, the tide had already turned against them. In a final effort, some women workers at a Meiya factory initiated a hunger strike. But their movement was already weakened and divided, and the factory owners remained adamant in their resolve not to implement "Directive 8476."[58] After almost three months of struggle, the strike ended with weavers returning to work on June 28. The strike achieved moderate success: parts of "Directive 8476" were finally implemented (a wage increase and a modification of the loom leasing system), and the arrested leaders were released.[59] But the 1937 strike revealed changes in the composition and leadership of the silk workers' movement, as domination of the unions by members of the Green Gang and government agents drew these formerly independent artisans into political conflicts outside their own movement.

At the start of the Japanese invasion in the summer of 1937, Shanghai's silk weavers were divided and disorganized. At the same time, the agents of the Nationalist state found that their attempt to mobilize silk workers for political purposes quickly became entangled in these workers' economic and political struggles. The establishment of a citywide silk weavers' organization created not the bogeyman of a Communist-led labor movement, but the golem of silk factory employees pursuing their own economic interests without regard to the interests of the ruling party. These problems were soon eclipsed, however, as war with Japan dramatically altered the trajectory of modern Chinese history.

57. Perry, *Shanghai on Strike*, 205–6; Meiya Manuscript, 55–57; Zhu Bangxing, *Shanghai chanye*, 176–78.

58. Perry, *Shanghai on Strike*, 206–7; Meiya Manuscript, 57–60; Zhu Bangxing, *Shanghai chanye*, 179–80.

59. D. K. Lieu, *Silk Industry of China*, 239.

Silk Workers at War

The Japanese forces that occupied the most industrialized parts of China from 1938 to 1945 suppressed both economic activity and the labor movement. Mass unemployment and the flight of labor to the countryside resulted in a dispersal of labor's strength and the disruption of organizational networks in the Yangzi Delta. Workers who remained under Japanese occupation labored at the point of a bayonet, and strike activity was greatly restricted. The war also brought important changes in working-class ideology, producing varying degrees of heightened patriotism and class consciousness. Perhaps the most significant development in the wartime labor movement was an increase in Communist influence among silk weavers, both in Shanghai and in smaller Jiangnan cities, even if organizing efforts were driven underground. Filature workers, on the other hand, had little contact with Communist labor organizers until after 1949, but they continued to rely on informal networks and to practice spontaneous action, eventually leading the vanguard in general strikes during the crises of the postwar period. Despite intentions, the Japanese occupation contributed to the Communists' postwar victory by creating a highly politicized and class-conscious labor movement that expanded and intensified during the Chinese Civil War.

As described in chapter 1, the Japanese invasion disrupted the lives and fortunes of China's silk capitalists. The war also brought important changes for workers, whether in occupied or "Free" China. During the war, Yangzi Delta silk workers directly confronted a foreign enemy for the first time. Wartime struggles increased silk workers' sense of nationalism at the same time that widespread unemployment, inflation, and deprivation eroded differences based on skill, gender, occupation, and income. Although there remained important distinctions in the tactics, goals, and ideologies of filature workers and silk weavers, the war brought these groups closer together, with important consequences for the postwar labor movement.

Following Japan's initial invasion and the collapse of production and employment, the situation of silk workers throughout the Yangzi Delta deteriorated quickly. Filature workers and silk weavers in Shanghai's "lonely island" were hard-pressed to find employment given the influx of refugees from the rest of Jiangnan, while those who remained in other locales faced unemployment and declining real wages, as well as bullying, oppression, and worse outrages at the hands of the Japanese military. Alain Roux describes labor actions in Shanghai between 1939 and 1942 as "an impressive revival of labor militancy" in the context of the occupation, but these were very limited compared to the strike waves of the 1920s and the late 1940s. When the Japanese occupation authorities or the Wang Jingwei regime permitted strike actions, these were usually aimed at European employers and were devoid of patriotic content.[60] Factory regulations became stricter, and the occupation authorities responded to any signs of organized resistance with suppression. The Japanese military organized urban workers into unions that were merely fronts for Japanese agents or criminal activities, such as the Association for Worker Welfare (Fuyihui) organized by the Japanese Imperial Navy in 1938. Workers identified as "undesirable elements" were arrested and interrogated, even tortured and executed. In some instances, those who attempted to defend their rights were shot on the spot or buried alive.[61]

Aside from the destruction of war, oppression, unemployment, and poverty, one of the most noticeable wartime developments among industrial workers was the expansion of Communist influence, especially among Shanghai textile workers. One reason for this was the dense concentration of displaced workers in Shanghai's International Settlement and its relatively tolerant political environment, at least before 1942. Although forced to hide their affiliation and downplay their politics, Communists were particularly active in Shanghai's wartime silk weaving industry, where they sought to restore their earlier presence. Extreme repression from the occupation authorities and competition from organizers such as Wang Hao, who collaborated with the Japanese, failed to halt the expansion of Communist influence during the war.[62]

The Communists appealed to urban workers during the occupation in part because of their patriotism. One way the CCP recruited

60. Roux, "From Revenge to Treason," 226–28.

61. Roux, "From Revenge to Treason," 209–28; *Zhejiang gongren yundong shi*, 191–93.

62. Meiya Manuscript, 74–78; Roux, "From Revenge to Treason," 212–15.

new members was through patriotic resistance organizations such as the National Salvation Association. The impression of anti-Japanese resistance proved very appealing, and by late 1938, the Communist Party had established branch organizations at Meiya's Number Four and Number Nine Factories in the Foreign Concessions. Two of the four leading Communist labor organizers operating in Shanghai during the war were silk weavers. Zhang Qi, a leader of the 1934 Meiya strikes, received training at the Lenin Institute in the USSR and became a CCP member in 1936. From 1937 to 1949 he led the labor organizing department of the underground party organization in Shanghai. Fellow silk worker He Zhensheng oversaw general affairs.[63] When Japan seized the Foreign Concessions in December 1941, the Communists were again forced underground. Denied the use of more public tactics such as leafleting and street-corner oration, the Communists could only operate through secret, small-scale meetings, which they infused with a patriotic, anti-imperialist, Marxist ideology.

Another reason for the expansion of Communist influence among urban workers during the war was the emergence of more women labor organizers, many of them trained at YWCA night schools where they first encountered Marxism. Female Communist labor organizers in the cotton and silk industries gave new meaning to traditional working-class "sisterhoods." During the war, these groups served the earlier functions of mutual aid and security, but some of the women were CCP members or sympathizers who introduced women workers to Marxist categories of analysis and, to some extent, Communist ideology. As Elizabeth Perry has emphasized, these familiar groupings "offered a comfortable mode of association,"[64] and women cadres and activists greatly contributed to the expansion of Communist influence among Shanghai textile workers. Small and close-knit "sisterhoods" combined to organize slowdowns and sit-down strikes in Japanese-controlled factories during the occupation.

63. Zhang Qi achieved great success organizing both male and female silk workers according to native-place affinities. He later became director of the Shanghai Federation of Trade Unions from 1949 to 1966, when he was attacked and imprisoned by Red Guards. Perry, *Shanghai on Strike*, 119, 208; Chang Kai, *Zhongguo gongyun*, 761; Li Jiaqi, *Shanghai gongyun*, 814–15.

64. Perry, *Shanghai on Strike*, 209. See also Honig, *Sisters and Strangers*, 209–29.

In the silk mills of occupied Wuxi, these tactics were workers' only means of striking back at their Japanese oppressors, and such actions served to heighten workers' sense of nationalism and their solidarity and identity as members of an oppressed class. Chinese accounts of working conditions under the Japanese occupation typically take the most extreme situations as representative. Japanese labor management was certainly severe in many cases, and there are examples of heinous abuses.[65] But in the silk reeling industry, conditions were not much different than they had been before the war, and were much like thread mills in Japan.

According to Chen Ciyu's impressive history of the Jiangnan silk industry, other than an overall decline in employment and the emergence of rural micro-filatures, there was little change in working conditions and wages in Wuxi's urban filatures. Wages in 1939 were the same as in 1929 (adjusted for inflation), and Wuxi wages remained lower than wages in Shanghai filatures. Silk reelers worked on average 12.5 hours per day, much the same as before the war and similar to filatures in Japan. Chinese filature workers were generally more experienced than their Japanese counterparts because they started working earlier (usually around age twelve) and more often continued working after marriage. Almost two-thirds of Wuxi filature workers had six years' experience or more. Labor recruitment in filatures licensed by the monopolistic CCSC did not change significantly under the occupation. Supervisors were responsible for achieving results in production and had great power over workers—wages, hiring, and firing were all at their discretion. However, supervisors collected no fees from the workers they hired and had no claim to any portion of their wages.[66] The only substantial change was that the higher-level managers were Japanese. There were reports of sexual abuse and rape in filatures under Japanese management,[67] but this, unfortunately, was also nothing new.

65. *Zhejiang gongren yundong shi*, 188–97. For more on Japan's labor practices in occupied Asia, see Ju Zhifen, "Labor Conscription"; Zhuang Jianping, "Japan's Exploitative Labor System"; and Kratoska, *Asian Labor*.

66. Chen Ciyu, *Zhongguo de jixie saosi*, 125–30.

67. *Zhejiang gongren yundong shi*, 191.

Even if working conditions in silk filatures changed little under the occupation, unemployment increased and wartime inflation reduced real wages, trends that worsened with the outbreak of the Pacific War. By May 1942, real wages in Shanghai had fallen to half the level of 1936, and the incomes of most factory workers were insufficient to meet subsistence costs.[68] Another development that contributed to lower wages in CCSC-licensed filatures in Wuxi was the adoption of the Japanese system of bonuses and penalties for attendance and production. "Joint-venture" filatures established an elaborate system to encourage improvements in production, especially to ensure the evenness of the thread produced. Even though these measures were generally unsuccessful in improving quality or consistency, they strengthened supervisors' control over workers' wages.[69]

Within the repressive environment of Japanese-managed factories during the occupation, Jiangnan workers did engage in limited acts of resistance. Those employed in Japanese-controlled filatures and silk weaving factories found ways to resist and undermine production despite their inability to organize openly. Loafing and dawdling (*moyanggong*) were universal practices under the occupation. Whenever the Japanese supervisors or factory guards were absent, Chinese workers sat around chatting. When the Japanese were present, they would work hurriedly to look busy, only to slow down or shut off the machines when the guards had left. Silk weavers throughout northern Zhejiang set up "ventilators" so that a watchman outside the workshop could warn those loafing inside that the Japanese supervisor was returning.[70]

Women workers in Shanghai textile factories organized widespread stealing campaigns to cause losses to Japanese firms. Running the machines at slower speeds, wasting materials, and weaving cloth with defects were all subversive acts through which workers could practice their patriotism and resistance.[71] When the Japanese military attempted to expropriate factories in Hangzhou, workers at the Weicheng Filature joined employees in railroads, electric power, and many

68. Hinder, *Life and Labour*, 45–49; *Zhejiang gongren yundong shi*, 193.
69. Chen Ciyu, *Zhongguo de jixie saosi*, 127–28.
70. *Zhejiang gongren yundong shi*, 196.
71. Honig, *Sisters and Strangers*, 209–29.

other industries to strike in protest. After the CCSC took over the Fuxing Filature in Jiaxing, the whole factory's workforce, numbering more than six hundred workers and staff, "were not willing to be used by them, and left surreptitiously."[72] Presumably, many of these workers found employment in the rural micro-filatures described in chapter 1.

Despite the dangers, Chinese Communist workers attempted to organize silk workers to resist the occupation. Filature workers in Shanghai organized "anti-Japanese rear assistance groups" (*kang Ri houyuantuan*) to provide funds and resources to the resistance.[73] Beginning in 1940, the CCP established branch organizations in silk weaving factories in Huzhou and other Jiangnan cities and even organized some daring strikes. Weavers at Huzhou's Yongchang Silk Factory launched three strikes to demand improvements in wages and benefits, and workers at the Dachang Silk Weaving Factory carried out a struggle to oppose layoffs. Strikes were dangerous because of the threat of retaliation, even execution, but as the occupation authorities' hold began to slip in the later stages of the war, workers' actions grew bolder and more frequent. Silk weavers in Hangzhou launched repeated struggles from April to November 1944, "pleading for higher wages" (*yuqing jiaxin*) to keep up with inflation. As the situation deteriorated for Wang Jingwei's government, there was little he could do but grant local authorities the power to reach a "compromise" in the hope that they could resolve the dispute.[74]

Communist influence among workers in the Yangzi Delta expanded during the war but nonetheless remained quite limited overall. From 1938 to 1939, the number of CCP members in Zhejiang Province increased from just a few thousand to more than twenty thousand.[75] More importantly, however, silk workers' ideologies were transformed during the occupation. Previously, silk workers had little contact with foreign employers and participated less than other workers in anti-imperialist labor struggles such as the May Thirtieth Movement of 1925. Under the occupation, many silk workers experienced the worst

72. *Zhejiang gongren yundong shi*, 194. See also Zhu Xinyu, *Zhejiang sichou shi*, 209.
73. Zhu Bangxing, *Shanghai chanye*, 193.
74. *Zhejiang gongren yundong shi*, 196–97.
75. *Zhejiang gongren yundong shi*, 177–78.

of foreign ownership and management, and in response began to feel a strong sense of anti-imperialist patriotism.[76] Many silk workers (although not all) witnessed their employers collaborating with the Japanese, engaging in speculation and profiteering, and adopting the repressive management techniques of the invaders. These experiences had a radicalizing effect that encouraged further Communist inroads and the spread of Marxist ideology among silk workers. The shared experience of foreign occupation and the wage-leveling effect of wartime inflation created common ground that would later help CCP members successfully organize diverse groups of silk workers from different factories. These workers' newfound unity and radical ideology helped the labor movement to become a powerful force in the years of civil war that followed the Japanese surrender.

Yangzi Delta Silk Workers and the Postwar Labor Movement

As described in chapter 1, the relationship between Chinese capitalists and the postwar Nationalist government was fraught with mistrust and mismanagement, and the Nationalists' policies—deficit spending, inflationary monetary policy, and revenue extraction through exploitative state monopolies—undercut business interests and squandered whatever political capital Chiang Kai-shek's party had won with Japan's surrender. By the end of 1948, the Nationalist government's relationship with China's workers was similarly spoiled. As in the 1930s, the Nationalists sought to control and mobilize industrial workers to eliminate Communist influence through state-sponsored unions and a corporatist approach to labor relations. However, China's postwar government proved unable to meet urban workers' most basic subsistence needs, and failed to control or suppress the labor movement. The collapse of industry and commerce, combined with a highly unpopular civil war and government suppression of workers' protests, created a very active

76. This can be seen as a further evolution of the "class-inflected anti-imperialist nationalism" described in S. A. Smith, *Like Cattle and Horses*, 190–213.

and powerful labor movement in the years before the Communist seizure of power.

By October 1945, an estimated 200,000 to 500,000 out of Shanghai's 800,000 workers were unemployed. More than half of Zhejiang Province's silk factories had gone bankrupt, and only eight of Hangzhou's 140 silk weaving factories were able to continue operations. Within months of Japan's surrender, newly liberated Jiangnan workers voiced their frustration at the absence of tangible "fruits of victory."[77] The first major postwar strikes appeared in Shanghai in the winter of 1945–46. Silk Weavers at the Meiya Company's factories faced a weakened and discredited administration because Cai Shengbai, Meiya's general manager who had ruthlessly suppressed strikers in the 1930s, was a member of the Shanghai Chamber of Commerce during the occupation and was easily denounced as a collaborator. In September, Meiya workers were able to force management to reinstate activists fired before the war and to provide belated severance pay to workers laid off during the occupation.[78] Inspired by the success of the Meiya strikers, in November and December 1945 weavers at other Shanghai silk factories organized a loose alliance of district and factory unions to conduct a forty-day strike for wage increases. Their effort ended with the arrest of the alliance leaders, however. Most Shanghai weavers did not achieve the same success as the Meiya workers.[79]

Despite the Shanghai Garrison's announcement of severe penalties for strikers and the declaration of martial law in November 1945, over the course of the following year the city witnessed more than 1,700 strikes, protests, and other actions.[80] Silk weavers struck again in February 1946, forcing an agreement to increase the basic monthly wage by 130 percent to 1,690 yuan. The agreement also stipulated that wages would be multiplied by a cost of living index so that workers' pay could keep up with inflation—a practice that became government policy in April. Repeated increases in the price of rice, however, as well as unresolved

77. *Zhejiang gongren yundong shi*, 211–13, 217; Pepper, *Civil War in China*, 33, 99; A. Doak Barnett, *China on the Eve*, 74.

78. Xu Xinwu, *Jindai Jiangnan sizhi gongye*, 412–13; Meiya Manuscript, 84.

79. *Zhongyang*, 28 Feb. 1946; Meiya Manuscript, 85–86.

80. Pepper, *Civil War in China*, 33, 99; *Dangdai Zhongguo gongren*, 1:33.

disputes concerning housing, compensation for "waiting for weft and warp," and paid maternity leave, led to intense struggles with employers, the government, and the police in the weeks that followed.[81]

Factory owners viewed the postwar labor movement with growing apprehension. In a statement in *Zhengyan* on April 14, 1946, the Silk Weaving Industry Association complained that workers' tactics, such as surrounding factories for days at a time or running motors and electric lights without working, were detrimental to peaceful negotiations and the industry's recovery. In one incident at the Yongcheng Silk Factory, weavers beat up and kidnapped the factory owner and his wife and held them captive. In another, a worker died while attempting a hunger strike. The factory owners asked, "How can one negotiate with such people?"[82] But Shanghai's silk factory owners also used tough tactics against their employees. On April 16, the owners of the Yuantong Silk Factory announced an end to meal provisions, refused to negotiate with employees, and called police to arrest eight representatives. Wool and cotton workers joined the angry silk weavers so that more than three hundred people surrounded the local police precinct. Police responded with force, killing one striker and injuring many others. A massive demonstration followed on April 18 to demand an adjustment to the basic wage and the release of the "Yuantong Eight." As the struggle continued into May, organizers used the press, plays, songs, and other means to mobilize workers, to make their case to the public, and to put pressure on the government.

On May 10, Zhu Xuefan, director of the Chinese Labor Association (CLA) and one of the most prominent labor leaders in postwar China, spoke to a meeting of silk weavers at Shanghai's Jade Buddha Temple.[83] Zhu expressed support for the silk workers' demands, but called on them to return to work so that he could help them achieve their goals. A nationally respected figure, Zhu convinced the silk weavers to return

81. Meiya Manuscript, 86, 99–100.

82. *Zhengyan*, 14 April 1946.

83. Zhu Xuefan, long-time labor leader, one-time postal worker, and protégé of Green Gang leader Du Yuesheng, served as head of the CLA before the war. After 1945, Zhu's advocacy of CLA autonomy brought him into conflict with Nationalist Party leadership, which attempted to limit his authority by re-establishing the General Labor Unions (GLUs). By the end of 1946, Zhu went over to the Communists and in

to work by May 16. On May 22, union representatives and factory owners signed a twelve-point agreement that included wage increases and back pay dating to February, an eleven-hour workday, four weeks' paid maternity leave, a .50 yuan daily subsidy for "waiting for warp and weft," the restoration of meal provision, and an agreement not to engage in strikes in the future and to handle disputes through legal means.[84]

In order to counteract the effects of inflation on wages, in April 1946 Chiang Kai-shek ordered the introduction of a wage index for industrial workers based on 1936 wage levels adjusted by a cost of living index. This practice began in Shanghai in 1946 but had been implemented in some state-run factories during the war.[85] In February 1947, the government attempted to freeze wages and prices for staples such as rice, wheat, and cooking oil at January levels, but by May market prices again increased by almost 50 percent. The rate of price increases did not accelerate significantly through the summer, but the "general mobilization" for war from July 1947 increased the budget deficit, which fueled China's hyperinflation crisis and exacerbated labor unrest.[86]

To control the resurgent unions and to keep their activities within tolerable bounds, the postwar government encouraged the formation of state-sponsored unions led by loyal Nationalist Party members. In July 1946, the central government issued a "Method for Leading the Workers Movement in the Period of Demobilization," which included appointing "special envoys" and "secretaries" to lead union organizations, as well as mandatory membership in government-sponsored unions for workers in major industries. As early as March 1946, the Shanghai Social Affairs Bureau began to require the formation of unions in enterprises with more than one hundred employees. The SAB encouraged factory-level unions to join citywide industrial unions under the Shanghai General Labor Union, reestablished at the end of 1945 in response to the surge of labor unrest. This was an effort to break up

1948 represented workers in Nationalist-held territories at the CCP's Sixth All-China Labor Congress. Gao Jun, *Zhongguo gongren yundong shi*, 310–12.

84. Meiya Manuscript, 101–3; *Shanghai fangzhi gongren*, 362.

85. Frazier, *Chinese Industrial Workplace*, 67; Howard, *Workers at War*, 134–46.

86. Westad, *Decisive Encounters*, 75, 88; Pepper, *Civil War in China*, 109–12.

district unions, which facilitated sympathy strikes across industries and provided opportunities for Communist infiltration. By the end of August 1946, about half a million Shanghai workers were members of 453 industrial and trade unions (including seventy-four textile unions) under the nominal leadership of the Shanghai GLU.[87]

The stated goals of the government-sponsored unions were to "increase workers' knowledge and ability, develop production, maintain workers' livelihood, and improve working conditions." The union leaders furthermore called on workers in all industries to make allowances for employers' difficulties and to accept wages based on the government's cost of living index. The Nationalist-led unions thus promoted an ideology of labor-capital cooperation claiming that, under the conditions obtaining in China, the existence of classes was simply a form of the "social division of labor." According to this conception, "slowdowns or strikes would not only cause suffering for one or two special classes, but for the whole of the laboring people. Thus, the workers should adopt a spirit of cooperation, set their minds and use their strength to participate in production and build the nation."[88] These statements are strikingly similar to Communist Party rhetoric during and after the Civil War.

The Nationalists' postwar statements concerning labor relations received a sympathetic hearing among some workers, who echoed the appeal for class cooperation. In a letter to the newspaper *Shenbao* dated May 12, 1946, a silk weaver named Chen Qisheng recalled the suffering of the eight-year occupation, as well as his disappointed hopes following China's victory over Japan. However, the weaver also complained that since the reestablishment of the silk weavers' union, there had been so many strikes that most weavers had worked only forty or fifty days in four months. Without wages, he had been forced to accumulate debts of more than thirty thousand yuan, and he feared for his family's survival. Calling for "welfare and democracy for the majority," Chen advocated cooperation among labor, capital, and the state to restore

87. *Zhejiang gongren yundong shi*, 218–19; Pepper, *Civil War in China*, 104–5.

88. *Zhejiang gongren yundong shi*, 220. For similar exhortations in the Chongqing arsenals during the war, see Howard, *Workers at War*.

production and employment.[89] But these goals seemed increasingly unreachable as the year wore on.

As the Civil War intensified and the economy descended into crisis, Jiangnan workers, including hundreds of thousands of unemployed, took to the streets to demand jobs and a living wage. In July 1946, silk weavers in Hangzhou led workers in other industries in a one-week strike, eventually breaking into Nationalist Party headquarters to protest the government's policies. In September, silk weavers launched an industry-wide strike to demand job security, freedom to organize, an eight-hour workday, improvements in workers' living standards, and protections for women workers. The postwar government frequently responded to protests with violent suppression, and strikes usually failed to achieve their goals.[90] As inflation of production costs and commodity prices accelerated through the autumn of 1946, even unions led by loyal Nationalists began to defend workers' interests more aggressively while continuing to appeal for national unity and class cooperation.

Contrary to the claims of both Nationalist and Communist propaganda, most strikes and protests were not organized by agents of the Communist Party. CCP cells in Yangzi Delta cities were very small, and in the late 1940s only about eight hundred Communist labor activists were operating in the entire Jiangnan region, with hundreds of thousands of industrial workers. Communist labor organizers were forced to operate in utmost secrecy and exerted only a limited influence among industrial workers. Shanghai silk weavers were exceptional in the degree of Communist influence in their union organizations in this period.[91]

In contrast with Shanghai silk weavers, there is no evidence of Communist leadership among Jiangnan filature workers. This did not make them any easier for management or the government to control, however, as filature workers' militant actions and reliance on informal networks pressured employers and frustrated government efforts at suppression. As early as July 1946, Jiangnan silk workers began what

89. *Shenbao*, 12 May 1946.
90. *Zhejiang gongren yundong shi*, 222.
91. *Zhejiang gongren yundong shi*, 221.

factory owners called a "regional labor tide" (*quan diqu zhi gongchao*), and employers complained that, far from controlling these workers, the establishment of an official union had strengthened their resolve. Workers' demands included pay increases and safety provisions, which the factory owners pleaded were too difficult and expensive to implement under the circumstances.[92] These circumstances—shortages of raw materials and an inflationary economy—grew worse over the next three years.

In October 1946, some Jiangnan filatures attempted to extend the workday from ten to eleven hours in order to compete with filatures in Japan, which enforced a thirteen-hour workday. Filatures in Hangzhou sought support from the city government to convince the official labor unions to cooperate. But the attempt to enforce an eleven-hour workday at Hangzhou's Weicheng Filature resulted in a work stoppage that soon spread to other filatures in Hangzhou, Wuxi, and Shanghai. Strikers at Weicheng convinced or forced other workers to participate in the strike, even damaging equipment to prevent workers in the cocoon selection workshop from continuing to work. When women workers at Wuxi's Rongsen Filature destroyed the factory gate, cut up silk, and injured staff members, the government union ordered them to return to work by October 30. But these "Red Silk Sisters" ignored the order. Holding an emergency meeting, the filature owners decided to discontinue operations to avoid further losses until the government could resolve the situation.[93]

In the struggle over filature work hours and wages, even Shanghai's official unions supported spontaneous work stoppages on October 4 and 7. In a letter to the Silk Reeling Industry Association, male union official Jiang Weicheng cited both price inflation and the recent "labor tide" in Wuxi in demanding an increase in the basic wage and a more equitable pay scale based on the complexity of work, attendance, and experience. In a second letter dated October 14, Jiang urged the

92. SMA S37-1-17.

93. SMA S37-1-245; *Shenbao*, 30 Sep. 1946, 22 Oct. 1946. The term "Red Silk Sisters" refers to the filature workers' movement in Huzhou, which the Communists claimed as their own. But the term is also applied more broadly to the labor movement among Jiangnan filature workers.

association to respond quickly and to abide by existing laws and the "spirit of sincere cooperation between labor and capital . . . so as to avoid the situation getting out of hand."[94] In response, the association advised the union to negotiate wage adjustments in individual filatures as local conditions varied widely. In regard to increasing the minimum wage, the employers insisted that the Shanghai Labor-Capital Arbitration Committee had already resolved this issue and determined that the basic wage be set at .90 yuan adjusted monthly according to the cost of living index.

The crux of the argument was that real wages were losing ground to inflation and that the measures the filatures adopted were ineffective under these conditions. Another letter from Jiang Weicheng on October 19, 1946, repeated the language of class cooperation while holding out the threat of class conflict. The letter stated that workers had already accepted sacrifices in order to help resolve the industry's crisis and to implement "the spirit of sincere labor-capital cooperation." Claiming that the filature owners enjoyed high profits "derived from the blood and sweat of the workers," Jiang called for additional cost of living subsidies to maintain workers' livelihoods.[95] The issue remained at an impasse until November 24, when silk reelers at Shanghai's Lianyuan Filature stopped work to demand an increase in the basic wage. Workers at Shanghai's other surviving filatures, Dali, Daming, and Hefeng, simultaneously began slowdowns and work stoppages to pressure employers into increasing the basic wage.

At a hastily conveyed meeting, the filature owners argued that the industry suffered from inflated costs, and that the policy of adjusting wages according to the cost of living index was already too great a burden. In a letter to the Social Affairs Bureau, employers demanded that the government investigate the strikers and punish their leaders. The letter stated that due to inadequate supplies of raw materials and fuel, the filatures' situation was desperate and they would soon have no choice but to discontinue operations.[96] That outcome was avoided temporarily through provision of state loans but, as described in

94. SMA S37–1–243.
95. SMA S37–1–243.
96. SMA S37–1–243.

chapter 1, the filatures' business situation continued to deteriorate, which only aggravated labor unrest.

The Nationalists' policy of class cooperation clearly enjoyed some appeal among both workers and employers. It is also evident, however, that the government's goal of labor corporatism, with the state mediating a cooperative relationship between workers and factory owners, foundered on the rocks of worsening inflation and economic crisis. By the end of 1946, unemployment had returned to levels seen a year earlier, with an estimated 250,000 to 300,000 unemployed in Shanghai alone.[97] As the *Wenhuibao* pointed out in January 1947, as long as the civil war and economic crisis continued, labor-capital cooperation was impossible and state mediation could achieve little.[98]

As prices for daily commodities continued to climb, silk workers grew desperate, striking repeatedly throughout 1947. Employers responded by shutting their doors and laying off thousands. In September, Shanghai's Labor-Capital Arbitration Committee brokered an agreement with the assistance of the SAB, the GLU, and the newly formed Shanghai Workers Welfare Committee (Shanghai gongren fuli weiyuanhui) led by Lu Jingshi.[99] According to the agreement, workers accepted pay cuts of 15–20 percent while the factory owners allowed two more rest days each month and a minimal subsidy to cover living expenses during the 1947 strikes. An article publicizing the agreement concluded by expressing the hope that weavers and factory owners would establish a "conference for the promotion of labor-capital compromise" (*laozi xietiao cujin hui*) to strengthen cooperation in overcoming the silk industry's difficulties.[100] But in the face of hyperinflation, there was little hope that cooperation could produce lasting results. Inflation was especially damaging to efforts to mediate labor disputes because any

97. Pepper, *Civil War in China*, 109; Gao Jun, *Zhongguo gongren yundong*, 298–300.

98. *Wenhuibao*, 7 Jan. 1947.

99. Lu Jingshi was a former postal worker who held several posts in Shanghai's labor unions from 1931 until 1949, when he went to Taiwan. A veteran Nationalist labor organizer, he played a leading role in resolving the 1947 silk weavers' strike. Chang Kai, *Zhongguo gongyun*, 768; Perry, *Patrolling the Revolution*, 124–33.

100. *Dongnan ribao*, 29 Oct. 1947.

agreement was likely to become untenable in a matter of weeks as prices outstripped wages.

Even though the Shanghai Labor-Capital Arbitration Committee could not achieve lasting solutions, it did manage to channel worker discontent toward factory owners rather than the government.[101] But as the economy worsened in 1947, workers increasingly directed their ire at the Nationalist Party and its policies. In response, government labor policy shifted toward coercion and repression rather than mediation and compromise. In 1947, Nationalist Party leaders Chen Lifu and Wu Kaixian took control of the Shanghai Workers Welfare Committee from Lu Jingshi.[102] The committee expanded rapidly, establishing branches in hundreds of factories, but many workers remained skeptical of the government's overtures and resisted state control. As one newspaper editor commented to A. Doak Barnett in early 1948, "nobody can really control the unions in Shanghai now."[103]

The engine driving labor unrest was the growing subsistence crisis. By April 1947, several Jiangnan cities faced food shortages. Scarcity was at its worst in Shanghai and Nanjing, where government efforts to control prices were most effective. Because measures to freeze wages were more effective than price controls, food prices continued to increase while wages stagnated. Many urban workers, especially the unemployed, faced starvation.[104] The food crisis led to a wave of strikes and riots in cities including Wuxi, Shaoxing, Shanghai, Hangzhou, Nanjing, and Suzhou, that the police attempted to suppress with violence and intimidation.[105]

In the first two weeks of May 1947, rice prices doubled. On May 4, Shanghai students began demonstrations against hunger and war (a movement that rapidly spread throughout the country) and joined desperate workers in an alliance that terrified the Nationalist government. On May 8, despite the Shanghai mayor's threat that demonstrators would be killed, thousands of Shanghai silk weavers marched in protest.

101. Frazier, *Chinese Industrial Workplace*, 85.
102. *Dongnan ribao*, 29 Oct. 1947.
103. A. Doak Barnett, *China on the Eve*, 77–78.
104. *Zhejiang gongren yundong shi*, 223; Meiya Manuscript, 128–30.
105. Pepper, *Civil War in China*, 110; Moore, *Shanghai Century*, 109.

Breaking through a police cordon, they marched on government offices, shouting demands and distributing leaflets. They were soon joined by power company and postal workers, department store clerks, students, and other urban residents. In the month of May 1947, some 150,000 workers participated in strikes and protests in Shanghai.[106] During the last week of May, the strike movement among Jiangnan textile workers threatened to become a labor insurrection over the issue of basic subsistence and pressured the Nanjing government to agree to a bi-monthly recalculation of the cost of living index. Although this measure provided temporary relief, wages still could not keep pace with inflation, and by December 1947 the cost of living index only amounted to half of average price increases.[107]

With the whole country's industrial workforce angry and marching in the streets, it was clear that the government's labor policy had failed. Labor disputes in Shanghai, including everything from major strikes and protests to letters and petitions, reached a new historic record of 2,538 for 1947.[108] On June 2, 1947, the Ministry of Social Affairs in Nanjing issued a secret order to the Zhejiang Provincial Government, "Points of Attention for Preventing a Strike Wave," that ordered the government-led unions to do everything in their power to prevent and resolve strikes as quickly as possible so as to avoid "socially disruptive behavior." More than a few union leaders sought to demonstrate their loyalty and enthusiasm for Nanjing's policies by producing anti-strike declarations. The Hangzhou GLU's declaration, for example, claimed that strikes were only caused by "disloyal Communists opposed to the interests of the people."[109]

The last expression of the Nationalists' hope of uniting with and leading labor, the Labor Union Act of June 16, 1947 (the fifth revision of the original 1929 law), called for compulsory membership in unions under the leadership of the GLUs and supervised by the social affairs bureaus in each city. But under such desperate circumstances, labor

106. Meiya Manuscript, 131–35; Gao Jun, *Zhongguo gongren yundong*, 302–3.

107. *Zhejiang gongren yundong shi*, 224–28.

108. Pepper, *Civil War in China*, 109, citing statistics published by the Shanghai SAB.

109. *Zhejiang gongren yundong shi*, 229.

unrest could not be contained by legal means.[110] As the military situation turned against the Nationalists in mid-July, the government abandoned even the pretense of partnership with labor and shifted decisively to violent repression. Employers had long criticized the government for being "soft" on labor and the press for being unsympathetic to business. When costs rose and markets shrank in the second half of 1947, factory owners demanded that the government use the police and military to suppress strikers, which led to violent clashes, arrests, beatings, and deaths. But neither police violence nor legal prohibitions deterred desperate workers. In response, the government branded workers' efforts to protect their livelihoods as Communist rebellion and mobilized police, militias, the Guomindang Youth Corps, and paramilitary groups to suppress strikes and protests.[111]

Even these repressive measures were ineffective, however. On July 26, more than 1,700 workers at Hangzhou's Weicheng Silk Filature struck for higher pay and better working conditions, which led to sympathy strikes at Tianzhang and other silk weaving factories. The following month, women laid off from the Zhenfeng Filature surrounded the offices of the Zhejiang Provincial SAB to demand protection of their livelihoods.[112] The provincial government frantically tried to halt the rising tide of labor unrest as society threatened to unravel under the pressures of the economic crisis. By October 1947, cost of living adjustments for filature workers throughout the Jiangnan region had grown to almost 50,000 times the basic wage, which ranged from .82 to .90 yuan per day. Prices continued to rise much faster, however, with the result that a worker's wage might lose half or more of its value in just one month. At an emergency meeting on October 15, members of the Zhejiang branch of the Silk Reeling Industry Association complained that the wage bill was growing too onerous under inflationary pressures and that workers in the larger firms went on strike every month. As more and more filatures discontinued production during the winter of 1947–48, workers' protests shifted from wage

110. A. Doak Barnett, *China on the Eve*, 77; Westad, *Decisive Encounters*, 76–79.

111. SMA C1-1-40, S37-1-243, S37-1-245; *Zhejiang gongren yundong shi*, 230–33; Westad, *Decisive Encounters*, 77; Pepper, *Civil War in China*, 112.

112. *Zhejiang gongren yundong shi*, 231.

issues to demands that filatures reopen and rehire workers, while factory owners appealed to the government to restore social and economic order.[113]

With the Nationalist government adopting increasingly repressive measures, the demands of the labor movement grew more politicized and connected to the political demands of the student movement encapsulated in the slogan "Oppose Hunger, Oppose Civil War." Even the government-led unions could not remain quiescent while facing overwhelming pressure from angry workers. In late 1947 they began to demand wage increases, reduced work hours, and severance pay, and even protested the government's economic policies and the civil war.[114] An Executive Yuan order of August 17, 1948, directed authorities to curb "subversive" activities among students and workers. Mao Sen's secret police made arrests without warrants and conducted summary executions without trial. But under such desperate circumstances, suppression was no more successful than cooptation in curbing workers' actions.[115] According to one Western observer, the recognition that the economic crisis was largely the result of government policy, and that there were stores of food available in the hinterland and in Shanghai warehouses while urbanites faced the threat of starvation, "has helped to create the near-complete demoralization of people of all sorts and the prevailing feeling of cynicism and despair. More people than ever before feel that the present Central Government is approaching the point of complete bankruptcy."[116]

One means of dealing with the problem of inflation outpacing wages was direct provision of goods in lieu of pay. Some factories, businesses, and government offices had implemented direct provision of basic goods during the war, and this practice expanded under the inflationary postwar economy. In an April 1948 letter to the Social Affairs Bureau, the Shanghai Labor-Capital Arbitration Committee recommended that the central government increase the kinds and amounts

113. SMA S37–1–168, S37–1–243.

114. Gao Jun, *Zhongguo gongren yundong*, 301–2.

115. Ezpeleta, *Red Shadows over Shanghai*, 99–100, 140, 150; *Zhejiang gongren yundong shi*, 220.

116. A. Doak Barnett, *China on the Eve*, 82.

of goods provided directly to workers, as well as decrease the purchasing price to work units. This would entail expanding direct provision of goods to more workers and providing them not only with rice, coal, oil, and sugar, but also cloth. The committee made this recommendation to aid the "mutual survival of labor and capital" (*laozi gongcun*). The recommendation claimed that expanding direct provision would help stabilize commodity prices and wages, which would help enterprises to reduce costs.[117]

This practice was very popular among industrial workers, who from late 1948 demanded that employers supply them with rice and oil rather than worthless currency. Dissatisfied with an order from the SAB that the Huisheng Silk Factory should provide employees with an extra ninety-yuan food subsidy, the silk workers organized a slowdown and, claiming that they were unable to purchase rice, broke into and consumed stores of food set aside for the factory's managerial and technical staff. Following negotiations under SAB mediation in November, the two sides reached an agreement that the factory would provide each worker with two and a half *dou* of rice each month.[118] Under Communist rule, this emergency measure to fight inflation became a central aspect of China's *danwei* system of socialist goods provision. As the postwar economic crisis spiraled out of control, however, there was little that could be done. By April of 1949, Shanghai factories were barely able to continue operations and possessed minimal resources to sustain their workers.

The protests and general strikes in cities throughout the Yangzi Delta in late 1948 reveal the depth of China's postwar economic crisis and the extent to which the Nationalist government had lost the support of the Chinese public, including workers and students as well as capitalists, urban professionals, and even many government, union, and military officials. Examining the labor movement on the eve of the Communist takeover also reveals the leading role played by women workers. Women silk workers had engaged in strikes and militant action since the establishment of the republic, often circumventing union organizations established by employers or the state. Women's experiences

117. SMA Q6-7-513.
118. SMA Q6-8-189.

under Japanese occupation fostered their solidarity and militancy, which brought new dynamism to the labor movement in the postwar period. If the women who worked in the silk filatures of the Yangzi Delta were commonly looked down upon as *poxie* (broken shoes), regarded as little better than beggars or prostitutes,[119] then their leading role in the strikes of the late 1940s demonstrates their struggle to change their status and indicates a heightened sense of self-worth and political consciousness. At the very least, women workers were acting on an unprecedented scale and attempting to pursue their collective interests with noticeable effects on the social and political landscape of postwar China.

One of the most prominent issues over which women silk workers struggled with their employers in the postwar era was maternity leave. The Factory Law of 1929 was the Nationalist government's effort to conform to international norms, especially the German model, seen as an alternative to the Soviet model of social insurance. The Nationalists implemented social insurance legislation to pre-empt Communist attempts to rally workers to the revolutionary cause. This concern motivated municipal governments and social affairs bureaus throughout China to demand labor and unemployment insurance in the early 1930s. Among other provisions, the laws enacted in the Republic of China between 1929 and 1935 required eight weeks paid maternity leave, but applied only to factories employing more than thirty persons and utilizing steam, electric, or water power in production. These laws remained in effect after the war with Japan, when the Nationalists attempted to establish a social insurance system according to the provisions of the International Labor Organization Congress of 1944 and British social insurance policies implemented in 1946. Most of these efforts went unrealized, however, as China descended into economic crisis and civil war.[120]

The archives of the Shanghai Social Affairs Bureau include many cases of silk factory owners refusing to pay for workers' maternity leave in violation of existing laws and agreements. In May 1946, the Silk Weavers Union and the factory owners reached an agreement concerning wage adjustments, work hours, rest days, and provision of four

119. Rofel, *Other Modernities*, 72–80.
120. Aiqun Hu, *China's Social Insurance*, 80–101.

weeks paid maternity leave. As the inflationary crisis worsened, however, factory owners sought to avoid paying these subsidies. For example, when prep worker Huang Weili took maternity leave in February 1948, the owner of the Pucheng Silk Factory refused to pay her for the month of work missed; in another case, the owner of the Xinhua Silk Factory refused to pay a month's wages to worker Lu Deyi for maternity leave, despite repeated requests from her union representative.[121]

In both of these cases the employers were eventually made to pay wages for one month of maternity leave, but it could take months to resolve such conflicts. In March 1948 conflicts arose over the issue of whether women who gave birth during the annual Spring Festival vacation, when they were not working, should receive this subsidy. The China Silk Factory, the Fourth District Silk Workers Union, and the SAB reached an agreement in April to the effect that these working mothers should receive four weeks paid leave as usual. The subsidy paid to one worker on April 5, 1948, amounted to three million yuan, by that time sufficient to purchase a simple meal.[122]

When silk workers took leave because of a miscarriage or a birth not carried to term, it could be even more difficult to obtain the wage subsidy to which they were entitled under the May 1946 agreement. In June 1948, a woman worker named Yin Rongqiu brought to the SAB a case against her employer, the Huamei Silk Factory. Yin was in her third month of pregnancy when she had a miscarriage and had to miss work to receive medical treatment. Just as her expenses increased, the factory cut her wages. Although Yin was entitled to a subsidy while she recovered, the factory owner refused, even using humiliating language such as, "Well, I never saw you with a big belly." Yin provided a note from her doctor as evidence (which remains in the archival file), and the issue was resolved.[123] The records of these women's struggles to secure a living wage for themselves and their growing families reveal both the employers' extreme reluctance to add to their ever-increasing wage payments, and women workers' capacity to pursue their own interests despite the political, economic, and social obstacles arrayed against them.

121. SMA Q6-7-242, Q6-8-1516.
122. SMA Q6-7-291.
123. SMA Q6-7-285, Q109-1-1998.

In another example from November 1948, women filature workers in Shanghai increased pressure on the official union by spontaneously electing six representatives to participate in negotiations with management. In a letter dated November 4, the union announced the participation of "women workers' representatives" and demanded an additional month's pay at the October rate in order to make up for losses due to inflation.[124] In another November letter, the worker representatives acknowledged that factory owners had suffered terrible losses due to the Gold Yuan currency fiasco, but also stated that the workers' psychological and material losses were even greater as they struggled to survive without rice or fuel. As Shanghai filatures began to close their doors toward the end of 1948, the unions demanded that employers abide by a law issued earlier in the year forbidding layoffs to protect workers' livelihoods and "social order."[125] There is a sense in these desperate exchanges that the two sides would like to work together and that labor-capital cooperation was an idea that appealed, to some degree, to many workers and employers. But without affordable raw materials, stable markets, or wages that would allow workers to survive, conflict could hardly be avoided.

The situation was similarly desperate in other Yangzi Delta cities. In September 1948, a strike by six thousand filature workers in Hangzhou, nearly all of them women, drew the support of the city's largely male silk weaving workforce as well as workers in other industries. This led to a six-day general strike that resulted in an increase in the cost of living index. Strikes in Hangzhou's filatures the following month saw battles with fire hoses and stones as the city government suppressed the strikers with force, calling out the militia and placing machine-gun posts at factory gates to prevent workers from marching out. The October strikes lasted four days as the filature workers' elected representatives, protected by pickets armed with staves and clubs, conducted negotiations. The Hangzhou filature owners eventually agreed to a 20 percent

124. SMA S37-1-243. Interestingly, Jiang Weicheng, who wrote the letters cited above in October 1946, was retained as provisional chair and his name continued to appear on union missives through the spring of 1949.

125. SMA Q6-8-175.

wage increase.[126] But given the state of the industry and the rate of inflation, there was little that anyone could do to achieve an enduring resolution.

Despite the promise of harsh suppression, on November 17 weavers at Hangzhou's Yong'an Silk Factory led a general strike of more than twenty thousand workers to demand that wages be fixed according to the price of rice. Factory owners complained that the workers "are not concerned with the prohibition on strikes, gather together to destroy the looms and materials, disturb the peace and shake the people's confidence."[127] The factory owners demanded that the authorities order the strikers to return to work and arrest the organizers. By that time, however, the Hangzhou government lacked the ability to suppress the labor movement and simply adjusted the cost of living index once again. The November strikes spread throughout Zhejiang Province, even among the tightly controlled railroad workers, and shook the Nationalist government to the core. Hangzhou declared martial law, and all strike activity was again strictly forbidden. By December these measures were in effect across the whole of Zhejiang Province.

As the Communists' military units approached the Yangzi River in March 1949, the Nationalist government intensified its repressive measures, prohibiting all "reactionary" activities, including strikes. But strikes continued nonetheless, with thousands of textile workers striking in Ningbo in April.[128] As the revolutionary armies crossed the Yangzi, weavers at the Yunfeng Silk Factory in Shanghai were striking to protest non-payment of wages. The factory owner claimed he did not have the resources to meet workers' demands, and he called on the SAB to suppress the illegal strike.[129] By that time, however, the Nationalists were on the run and the Jiangnan population was ready to accept almost any change as a potential improvement on the unbearable status quo.

126. *Zhejiang gongren yundong shi,* 240.
127. *Zhejiang gongren yundong shi,* 241–43.
128. *Zhejiang gongren yundong shi,* 241–43.
129. SMA Q6-7-513, Q6-8-177.

Conclusion

Historians continue to debate the class categories of Chinese society in the twentieth century. Did class "happen," to use E. P. Thompson's phrase?[130] Was there a Chinese bourgeoisie conscious of its historical role? Was there a class-conscious proletariat comprised of workers who organized based on shared experience and ideology? Or were there many working classes, with most workers identifying more with their native place, occupation, or gender? The history of the silk workers' movements described in this chapter could support either formulation, depending on where and when one looks. Certainly, both filature workers and silk weavers were able to organize, act, and pursue their collective interests, albeit in different ways. But there is little evidence of organizing across industries based on working-class ideology until after the War of Resistance.

Both groups of silk workers prospered in the first decades of the twentieth century as Chinese silk exports expanded. By the 1930s and the Great Depression, however, problems in China's silk industry began to undermine the wages and working conditions of even the most privileged silk weavers. These changes in turn produced new strategies and forms of association among female filature workers and male silk weavers. In neither case, however, were workers entirely successful at protecting their status and interests.

During the Nanjing Decade, women workers in Yangzi Delta filatures found spontaneous action more effective than permanent organizations that could be co-opted by employers. Their independence and suspicion of outside influences made them difficult to control. Without support from those in power, however, these workers' actions were violently suppressed. In cases where the strikers were victorious, it was often due to public support in the press and sympathy strikes in other industries. Silk weavers, on the other hand, drew upon both traditional and novel organizations to defend their status as privileged, male artisans. It was mainly threats to that privileged status, such as loom leasing arrangements, that brought silk weavers out on strike in the years preceding the Japanese invasion. Although the silk weavers' movement

130. Thompson, *Making of the English Working Class.*

in Shanghai largely failed to achieve its goals, it nonetheless expanded to include women workers, weavers in small workshops, and filature workers. Changes like these partially eroded the differences between the more privileged workers at companies like Meiya and most silk weavers employed in small workshops. As a result, the strikes in 1937 included a broad segment of Shanghai's silk industry workforce.

The Japanese invasion in 1937 further narrowed the gap between privileged male weavers and other silk workers. Military conflict and the occupiers' policies greatly reduced the production of cocoons, thread, and cloth, and blocked access to international markets. Chinese silk workers and their employers had to choose between remaining in the occupied cities and working under the eye of the occupation, or seeking refuge and employment in rural micro-filatures and weaving workshops. In both cases the devastation and cruelty of the Japanese occupation fostered in many workers a new sense of patriotism and solidarity that continued to grow through the postwar years.

In 1958, Chang Kia-Ngau wrote that in its myopic focus on the military problem, Chiang Kai-shek's government "was curiously blind to the fact that in the long run economic health is a prerequisite of political power." According to Chang, economic instability "finally led to a general loss of confidence in the Nationalist government, and total collapse of political and social morals followed."[131] By 1948 protests over inflation and unemployment had evolved into widespread disaffection with the Nationalist government throughout Chinese society. Inflation depressed wages and increased unemployment, leading to intense conflicts between workers and employers that spilled over into the public arena. Certain elements within the state, especially the social affairs bureaus, were initially sympathetic and supported wage adjustments and job protections. But government efforts to control unions and suppress strikes were too crude and heavy-handed to be effective, and produced suspicion and resentment rather than loyalty and cooperation. The Nationalist Party's lack of an appealing ideology or evidence of sincere support for workers' needs alienated industrial workers and likely did more to encourage workers' interest in Communist revolution than the CCP's propaganda and organizing efforts. Indeed, the more

131. Chang Kia-Ngau, *Inflationary Spiral*, 365.

the politically bankrupt Nationalists condemned the Communists, the greater the revolutionaries' appeal among beleaguered workers.[132]

The postwar years are the clearest (and perhaps the only) period in which historians can find a broad-based and relatively autonomous working-class movement in modern China.[133] One reason for this is that the Japanese occupation and the postwar inflation crisis exerted a leveling effect on wages and standards of living, such that the postwar labor movement exhibited broad solidarity across diverse groups of workers. When the cost of living index was thousands of times the basic wage and wages lost their value after just two weeks, the differences between privileged silk weavers and exploited filature workers diminished.[134] Although different groups of workers maintained their traditions of protest and forms of organization, economic deprivation affected every industry and led to a convergence of interests and tactics that produced the conditions for the possibility of broad working-class solidarity on the eve of the Communist seizure of power.

Women filature workers in Jiangnan cities frequently stood in the vanguard of citywide general strikes that fostered united action and drew together diverse groups of workers. In the strike in Hangzhou that began on July 26, 1947, silk weavers immediately followed the filature workers' lead in striking for an adjustment to the cost of living index. In August 1948, when conditions were even worse, a strike by more than six thousand Hangzhou filature workers not only brought the silk weavers out in a show of solidarity, but incited a citywide general strike that lasted six days and paralyzed production and commerce. Filature workers played a leading role in similar strikes in Nanjing and Wuxi. Of course, some working-class people felt greater affinity for the government or for non-proletarian organizations and identities such as religious or native-place associations. Nonetheless, the frequency of general strikes in the postwar period demonstrates the emergence of a

132. Suzanne Pepper describes the postwar workers' movement as "an increasingly independent labor force that refused, on numerous occasions and in a variety of ways, to comply with the Government's pleas for cooperation and support in its struggle against the Communists." Pepper, *Civil War in China*, 117.

133. For another significant example of working-class consciousness among Chinese workers in the postwar period, see Howard, *Workers at War*, chapter 9.

134. SMA C1-2-12; Howe, *Wage Patterns and Policy*, 46–47.

militant and anti-imperialist class consciousness, conditioned by years of war and economic crisis, among most Jiangnan workers. Women's leadership of these strikes similarly attests to the heightened consciousness and confidence of women workers in postwar China.

Despite intense conflict with employers and the Nationalist government during the civil war, the rhetoric of class cooperation, expressed by both Nationalists and Communists, appealed to many workers. Working-class men and women just as often voiced appeals for class cooperation and mutual benefit as they did radical critiques of existing economic relations. Workers and employers often compromised and cooperated in the face of economic difficulties, but genuine class cooperation based on equality and mutual interest would have to wait for a healthier economy and stronger political leadership more committed to the interests of the working class. When the Communists seized power in the Yangzi Delta, they encountered an emerging class-conscious labor movement, tempered by years of struggle and hardship, that was receptive to the party's message of economic recovery, political equality, and social welfare under the policy of New Democracy.

CHAPTER THREE

New Democracy and Communist Revolution

In the spring of 1949, the Chinese Communists entered the cities of the Yangzi Delta under the banner: "Develop production, make the economy flourish, attend to both public and private interests, and benefit both labor and capital." This slogan expressed both the immediate task of economic restoration and the political theory of "New Democracy." The theory originated in the First United Front with the Nationalists in the 1920s, but Mao Zedong crystallized the concept in his January 1940 essay, "On New Democracy." In the context of Liberation in 1949, "New Democracy" structured the party's responses to the many complex problems they faced after defeating their Nationalist rivals.[1] The economy was in shambles, inflation rampant, business stagnant, and the industrial workforce up in arms over plummeting wages and widespread unemployment. China's Communist revolutionaries included only a small cadre of officials capable of implementing policies to address these issues.[2] As a mainly rural, military and political organization, the CCP had only a limited following among urban

1. For examples of party writings on New Democracy in the early 1950s, see Tang Jianxun, *Xin minzhu zhuyi*; Zhang Jiangming, *Xin minzhu zhuyi jianghua*; and Wei Leshan, *Xin minzhu jiben renshi*.

2. Walder estimates that the CCP had 1.2 million members in August 1945, and 4.5 million members by October 1949, but official cadres numbered only hundreds of thousands. Walder, *China under Mao*, 100.

workers, and most people were unfamiliar with the Communists' goals and policies.

The party's goals in its first months in power were to consolidate Communist Party rule and restore the economy to health, demonstrating the benefits of Communist policies for workers and capitalists. However, the Communists' early policies, which pursued the potentially contradictory goals of liberating Chinese workers while restoring capitalist production, created widely varying outcomes even within the same city or industry. Reorganizing workers into Communist-led unions was a vitally important task for the revolutionary regime, but the unions' roles under Communist Party leadership were extremely difficult, even contradictory. The party utilized union organizations on the one hand to lead and educate workers, but on the other hand to control and discipline them to conform to the party's policies and ideology. This was quite different from what union leaders had been doing during the previous decade—struggling with employers and the state to defend their members' interests—and the demands and conflicts of union work led to widespread dissatisfaction among workers, as well as vacillation and fatigue among union officials.

Shanghai silk weavers' union organizations already had close ties with the Communist Party before 1949, and their relations with their employers, while often conflicted, were relatively equal and respectful. Many silk factory owners had been weavers themselves, and in some cases, such as the Meiya Number Four Factory, both managers and weavers were party members. In contrast, workers in Jiangnan filatures had nothing in common with their employers and no ties to the Communist cadres sent to organize them. Indeed, the shortage of women union cadres continued to plague the CCP's efforts to reach women workers throughout the 1950s. Furthermore, although the party's policy of labor-capital cooperation through party-led institutions was well suited to Shanghai silk weavers, the Communists strongly discouraged the filature workers' traditional tactics of spontaneous protest, direct action, and autonomy. The result was filature unions that were controlled neither by the CCP nor by filature workers, but rather by employers and supervisors who were highly antipathetic to these women's efforts to advance their interests.

The comparison between male silk weavers and female filature workers thus reveals a revolution in which gender, as much as class, conditioned outcomes, often in ways that few actors (especially CCP cadres) were consciously aware of at the time. In this context, gender, like class, industry, and locality, becomes an important axis of analysis that differentiated groups of workers and strongly affected their capacity to take advantage of the opportunities presented by the Communist seizure of power. However, despite the importance of gender for understanding workers' experiences of the revolution and the outcomes of policies such as union organizing and labor-capital cooperation, historians of the Chinese revolution have largely ignored this dimension.

This chapter introduces the complex circumstances and policies that affected employers and workers in the Yangzi Delta silk industry following the Communists' arrival in Jiangnan cities. This included the promotion of "New Democratic" policies in private industry, organizing work among different groups of workers, and efforts to promote labor insurance and workers' welfare, as well as the specific problems the party encountered in reaching and organizing women workers. This sets the stage for the following chapters, which explore these processes in greater detail and examine the intended and unintended consequences of CCP policies.

Winning Hearts and Minds—Liberation and Economic Recovery

In April 1949, Communist forces approached the Yangzi River and the industrial cities of East China. When the Nationalists' capital Nanjing fell on April 23, the People's Liberation Army (PLA) entered the city quietly, without parades or celebration. By the end of April, the Communists had taken Wuxi, and by early May they controlled most of Jiangsu Province. When they entered Hangzhou in Zhejiang Province on May 3, they found Hangzhou residents both relieved that the war had passed them by and fearful of what the conquerors might do next. Over the following weeks, Hangzhou residents were impressed with the Communist troops' honesty and discipline, a pattern repeated throughout China.[3]

Chiang Kai-shek's claim at the end of April that Shanghai would be "defended like Stalingrad" alarmed the city's residents, and those with means fled rather than be caught in a siege. As the front approached, farmers stopped going to the city to sell rice and vegetables, raising the specter of starvation. It is likely that Chiang never intended to make a last stand in Shanghai, however, and on May 8 he sailed for his island fortress on Taiwan.[4] The Communists nonetheless approached Shanghai very cautiously, as they had no desire to damage this political, industrial, and commercial prize.[5] By May 20 the Communists had surrounded Shanghai's airports, and on May 25 the PLA entered the city.[6] A British businessman in Shanghai, Captain W. J. Moore, recorded that the "smart bearing and first-class discipline of the Communist troops as they mounted guard . . . made a great impression on all who saw them."[7] Even Noel Barber, who is otherwise highly critical of the CCP's takeover of Shanghai, records that "everybody remarked . . . on the perfect discipline of the Red Army. Each man was carrying iron rations and was forbidden to buy anything before a proper exchange rate for local currency was proclaimed."[8]

3. James Gao, *Communist Takeover of Hangzhou*, 69–73; Westad, *Decisive Encounters*, 241–44; Hooton, *The Greatest Tumult*, 161.

4. Westad, *Decisive Encounters*, 248–49; Forman, *Blunder in Asia*, 53–54.

5. Ezpeleta, *Red Shadows over Shanghai*, 102.

6. In one of the few battles in the city itself, Nationalist troops holed up in a mint on Suzhou Creek opposite the Shanghai Silk Spinning Factory. Although the silk workers welcomed the red troops at the factory gates, the soldiers decided not to use the factory to attack the enemy so as to avoid damaging it. Instead, they brought heavier artillery to another location to bombard the Nationalist forces, which impressed the factory's workers. Interview with Xu Shancheng, 10 October, 2003. This incident is also described in Yu Jin, *Shanghai*, 2: 962–63.

7. Moore, *Shanghai Century*, 117.

8. Barber, *Fall of Shanghai*, 148. Mariano Ezpeleta reports a similarly favorable impression of the Communists' rural recruits in Shanghai, stating, "To the surprise of many, especially of the foreigners, the behavior of the Red soldiers was exemplary." The soldiers did not disturb traffic, treated residents with respect, invariably refused gifts, and "indulged neither in plunder nor in shooting, in lust or in looting." Ezpeleta, *Red Shadows over Shanghai*, 193–94.

The Communist takeover of the Jiangnan region was largely a military affair rather than a popular uprising, but widespread opposition to the Nationalists and organized support in urban areas helped to minimize further economic disruption, and there was little looting, sabotage, or suspension of services. There are, however, numerous accounts of workers conspiring to hide materials, to remove goods from ships and trucks, or to load trucks with scrap metal instead of valuable machinery.[9] The Communist-led People's Peace Preservation Corps (Renmin baoandui) organized sixty thousand Shanghai workers into "factory protection teams" (*huchangdui*), which maintained order and prevented the removal or damage of equipment, supplies, and finished goods. The Nationalist authorities, attempting to prohibit these organizations, arrested more than two hundred members.[10] Despite having their organization decimated by a wave of arrests in March 1948, Communist silk weavers such as Xu Xijuan (later an official of the Silk Workers Union) also helped to organize factory protection teams. They provided armbands and food for worker-guards and took measures to protect factory equipment from air raids and artillery barrages. At the Meiya Number Four Factory, manager Lin Huiwen was made team chief, and a Communist worker, Ma Liqiang, was made vice-chief.[11]

As a result of these efforts, about half of Shanghai's remaining factories were able to restore production by mid-June, aiding the rapid establishment of Communist administration in Shanghai. Postal service, telephone and telegraph service, electric power, water, and transportation continued uninterrupted or were restored quickly.[12] In contrast with the Nationalists in 1945, the Communists' Military Control Commission (MCC) established detailed regulations for the takeover of government property and carried out extensive education at all

9. SMA C1-2-12; interview with Xu Shancheng, 10 Oct. 2003; Frazier, *Chinese Industrial Workplace*, 98.

10. *Shanghai jiefang*, 141–42.

11. Meiya Manuscript, 147–53; interviews with Lin Huiwen, 6 Apr. 2004, and Qian Binhua, 12 Feb. 2004. On the phenomenon of armed workers in twentieth-century China, see Perry, *Patrolling the Revolution*.

12. Ezpeleta, *Red Shadows over Shanghai*, 192–93; Gaulton, "Political Mobilization in Shanghai," 45.

levels of the military to prevent abuses. Military units were ordered to guard but not remove goods or equipment and to wait for authorized takeover staff to arrive. The MCC assigned offices to military and party organs, avoiding the confusion and corruption that undermined Nationalist "reconversion" efforts in 1945.[13]

The MCC's Reconversion Commission (Jieguan weiyuanhui) assigned specific responsibilities to individual bureaus and cadres. The takeover of the China Sericulture Company, for example, was assigned to the Trade Department under the Finance and Economics Reconversion Commission (Caizheng jingji jieguan weiyuanhui maoyi chu).[14] The Commission appointed Zhu Zuxian, a Nationalist silk industry official, to lead the takeover of the state silk company's offices and subsidiary enterprises and to ensure that all documents, archives, and other materials were preserved and all staff identified and registered. By June 16, Communist Party cadres were in leading positions in all CSC offices and subsidiaries in East China.[15] Lacking experienced administrators, however, and facing a severe shortage of qualified cadres, the CCP found it impossible to staff all government offices with its own people. The party thus retained most government employees, exhorting civil servants to remain at their posts. In Shanghai, only the top Nationalist Party leaders in city government and the police were replaced with Communist Party cadres, and 95 percent of government employees remained at their posts. Retained Nationalist officials continued to handle most government business, with some notable changes such as the near elimination of bribery and corruption.[16]

The Communist takeover of Jiangnan was remarkably peaceful, and won the support of most urban residents, both bourgeois and proletarian. There were also many challenges and difficulties, however. Within a month of the Communist takeover a typhoon and flood struck the Yangzi Delta region, ruining rice fields and sending thousands more refugees into Shanghai. On top of this, from late June the

13. A. Doak Barnett, *China on the Eve*, 340; *Shanghai jiefang*, 31–42, 70–82, 86–87, 105–15, 132–36.

14. *Shanghai jiefang*, 106, 132.

15. *Shanghai sichou zhi*, 94.

16. Barber, *Fall of Shanghai*, 159; Wakeman, "'Cleanup': The New Order in Shanghai," 21–58.

Nationalists began to blockade the mouth of the Yangzi River. Airplanes based in Taiwan and Zhoushan bombed ships bound for Shanghai, disrupting commerce and foreign trade in the region.[17] For several months, air raids frequently targeted Shanghai, destroying the city's main power plant on February 6, 1950. These reminders that the Nationalists had been evicted but not eliminated increased tensions in Shanghai. The Communists continued to establish their rule with little violence, however, and the party was initially cautious about suppressing potential counter-revolutionaries.

The Shanghai MCC's apparent leniency toward known counter-revolutionaries angered and alarmed underground party members, who were anxious to ensure the arrest of Nationalist spies and security agents. Underground Communists and labor activists complained, "The GMD was lenient with traitors, the CCP is lenient with GMD agents" (*Guomindang dui hanjian kuanda, Gongchandang dui tewu kuanda*).[18] The rapid disbanding of the People's Peace Preservation Corps within days of the Communist takeover of Shanghai had a similarly adverse effect on the worker pickets' enthusiasm while emboldening enemy agents.[19] As in subsequent campaigns and purges, it often proved difficult to distinguish between counter-revolutionary agents fomenting unrest among workers and independent labor activists protecting legitimate interests. Tactics attributed to "counter-revolutionaries" in Chinese factories included making excessive demands for wage increases to win over "backward" and "economistic" workers, deceiving "the masses" with demands for "absolute democracy," conspiring with factory owners to take control of the union organizations, and creating conflict among workers through the use of criminal gangs, as well as outright sabotage such as damaging equipment, wasting materials, and arson. The Communist leadership in Shanghai responded by arresting almost 600 suspected enemy agents in the first two days of July 1949, and this kind of suppression expanded during the Korean War.[20]

17. Gaulton, "Political Mobilization in Shanghai," 45. For detailed descriptions of the battle for access to Shanghai, see Moore, *Shanghai Century*.

18. SMA C1-2-12.

19. *Shanghai jiefang*, 51–52, 142; Perry, *Patrolling the Revolution*, 158–60.

20. *Shanghai jiefang*, 142–43; Perry, "Workers' Patrols," 156; SMA C1-2-12.

The shortage of experienced cadres capable of navigating these complex and dangerous waters was a great hindrance to the party's work. Many CCP cadres leading the takeover in Jiangnan cities were North Chinese who were more experienced in guerrilla warfare than economic administration, and these men (and a few women) often failed to understand the complex problems of urban industrial society. There was also considerable mistrust between the party center's "southbound" cadres and underground Communists who had remained in Shanghai.[21] In a July 2, 1949, letter to Minister of Labor Li Lisan, Zhu Junxin stated that newly arrived cadres understood party policy well, but lacked concrete knowledge of the local situation and were prone to "subjectivist" errors. Underground cadres better understood the local situation and workers' needs, but did not have as strong a grasp of party policy. Zhu stated that it would be best if they could work together, and that cooperation had already begun to improve.[22] In cities like Wuxi and Hangzhou, where there was almost no underground CCP organization, the lack of knowledgeable and experienced cadres was an even more severe problem.

If the party's own cadres sometimes found it difficult to comprehend and manage the changing situation, ordinary Chinese citizens were even more uncomprehending. But hope for the future inspired many to make a quick study of the victorious CCP. Shanghai residents generally knew more about Hollywood movies than Marxist theory, and read the tabloids more often than Mao's essays. But urbanites learned the language of the Communist Party remarkably quickly, readily adopting terms like "popular masses" (*renmin dazhong*), "cadre" (*ganbu*), "land reform" (*tugai*), and "liberation" (*jiefang*). New symbols such as the red flag and Mao's image appeared, and some enterprising capitalists even attempted to use these symbols as marketing gimmicks.[23]

In their correspondence with the Communists, Shanghai capitalists showed a remarkable ability to adopt the language of revolution,

21. On the conflict between the party line and "leftists" in the labor movement in Tianjin, see Lieberthal, *Revolution and Tradition*, 40–52.

22. SMA C1-2-12.

23. Gaulton, "Political Mobilization in Shanghai," 48.

referring to themselves as "national capitalists" (*minzu zibenjia*) and demonstrating a strong grasp of the party's policies and ideology. Silk filatures in Shanghai wrote to the new government in May and June of 1949 to request supplies of cocoons, which they feared would not be made available because Shanghai had been "liberated" too late to be included in spring cocoon purchases. Reference to the slogan "develop production and make the economy flourish" in a letter from the Dali Filature dated May 30, 1949, indicates an awareness (and possibly acceptance) of Communist Party policy.[24]

As discussed in chapter 2, non-Communist union representative Jiang Weicheng wrote to Shanghai's filature owners many times between 1946 and 1948 to support silk workers' pleas for a living wage or to protest layoffs or non-payment of wages. In June 1949, he wrote to the CCP authorities responsible for distributing cocoons and continued to use the language of class cooperation and mutual benefit that appears in his earlier letters. Writing on behalf of both filature owners and workers, Jiang used the revolutionaries' own words to request supplies of cocoons. This was not to maintain business and profits but rather to protect the workers' livelihoods:

> Under the Guomindang reactionary regime, the three filatures' employees suffered a serious threat to their spiritual and material well-being. Grateful for Liberation, the whole body of the workers has gladly and resolutely worked to develop production in the silk industry and serve the present restoration of production in Shanghai's other factories. But if these three filatures cannot obtain raw materials, then they cannot begin production, with the result that all the employees' livelihoods will suffer terribly.[25]

Jiang's appeal, making use of terms like "Liberation," received a favorable response a few days later. On June 7 the China Sericulture Company (now under new management) responded to Jiang's letter stating, "Your enthusiasm for production is most welcome, and we are

24. SMA S37-4-2.
25. SMA S37-4-2.

preparing to provide you with effective assistance . . . Please urge your employers to stay in close contact with us to work together to resolve the problem of raw materials."[26] The Communists proved true to their word and during their first year in power made great strides toward economic recovery that would benefit China's urban workers and "national capitalists."

One of the most important ways in which the Communists distinguished themselves from their predecessors and won the support of urbanites was through their successful efforts at fighting inflation. The movement of the front southward and the restoration of rail communications brought immediate relief to Jiangnan cities. By August 1949, wholesale prices in Shanghai were increasing at the casual pace of 13 percent monthly. The Communists introduced a new currency, the Renminbi (RMB) or "people's money," setting the initial conversion rate at 100,000 Gold Yuan to one RMB. The new regime also continued the Nationalists' efforts to centralize the banking system under the People's Bank of China, which became solely responsible for note issues and bond sales. On April 20, 1949, the People's Bank of China introduced the "parity deposit system," which indexed the value of bank deposits to the prices of four basic commodities—rice, wheat, cotton cloth, and coal—reducing the need for consumers to convert money to commodities for fear that the real value of savings would decline. The plan was implemented in Shanghai on June 14, and according to a United Nations study, bank savings grew much faster than prices between July and October.[27] Wage payments were similarly indexed to commodity prices, and the practice of calculating wages in "parity units" (*zheshi danwei*) did more to guarantee workers' livelihoods than had the Nationalists' cost of living index, which increased wages along with prices and exacerbated inflationary pressures.[28]

Like the Nationalists before them, the Communists resorted to police measures to enforce price controls, but they also utilized mass mobilization to prohibit black market trading in silver and foreign

26. SMA S37-4-2.

27. Simkin, "Hyperinflation and Nationalist China," 130; Burdekin and Wang, "Novel End to Big Inflation," 211–29; Riskin, *China's Political Economy*, 42.

28. Moore, *Shanghai Century*, 122–23.

currencies.[29] Even more important for controlling prices, however, was the organization of large state trading companies that effectively manipulated market forces. State trading companies obtained supplies of basic commodities through taxes in kind (rice and wheat), the output of state factories (cotton cloth), or through RMB purchases from private producers. The companies then strategically dumped these goods on the market, forcing prices down and drawing out stockpiles of goods. The profits from state grain trading went to the People's Bank of China and formed the basis for new RMB note issues.[30] Inflation surged again in November 1949, followed by deflation and recession in the spring of 1950, but eventually these policies stabilized prices for most goods. In the twelve months following the Communist takeover of Shanghai, prices in that city increased 200 times, as compared with 78,307 times between January and May 1949. By late 1951, the state directly controlled prices for major producer goods and agricultural commodities such as grain, cotton, tobacco, and silk.[31]

Inflation-fighting measures supported economic recovery, which helped to reduce labor conflicts and promote class cooperation. As costs and prices stabilized by the end of 1949, about two-thirds of Shanghai factories restored production. The expansion of state contracts also helped to restore production and employment in many industries, including silk.[32] In the early 1950s, the CCP presented the system of state-contracted production in private industry as a novel form of "state capitalism" that would move the economy toward socialism. The early state contracting system, however, was not a Communist innovation but was inherited from the Nationalists. Facing the same pressures of inflation, business failure, and unemployment, the Communists initially maintained and expanded the existing system with few changes.

29. On police measures to control prices, see Ezpeleta, *Red Shadows over Shanghai*, 193, and Barber, *Fall of Shanghai*, 160–61. On the anti-silver campaign in Shanghai, see Pepper, *Civil War in China*, 395–96, and SMA C1-2-12.

30. Burdekin and Wang, "Novel End to Big Inflation," 216; Eckstein, *China's Economic Revolution*, 170.

31. Burdekin and Wang, "Novel End to Big Inflation," 211–13; Perkins, *Market Control and Planning*, 31–34; Riskin, *China's Political Economy*, 43, 47.

32. *Jiefanghou Shanghai gongyun*, 23–24, 159.

Recognizing the dire crisis of the Yangzi Delta silk industry, Communist authorities in the Jiangnan region placed great importance on the spring 1949 cocoon harvest. One report stated that "purchasing Jiangnan spring cocoons is a major starting point for the party and the People's Government in launching financial work in the newly liberated areas."[33] To encourage sericulturalists to sell their spring cocoons to state agencies, Xu Xuehan, head of the East China Trade Department, apportioned 90 billion RMB for cocoon purchases and organized sericulture experts to manage the purchasing process. The China Sericulture Company set cocoon prices according to the price of rice, such that each *dan* of fresh cocoons would earn the equivalent of 350 to 423 *sheng* of rice depending on quality, and acquired nearly ten thousand tons of rice to provide to sericulturalists as advance payment. The CSC furthermore purchased filatures' output of raw silk at higher than market prices and offered subsidized loans for cocoon purchases. In the spring of 1949 licensed cocoon *hang* purchased 112,000 *dan* of fresh cocoons, 70–80 percent of which went directly to filatures for state-contracted production. The rest were delivered to the state silk company.[34]

These policies, combined with the end of military conflict in the Yangzi Delta region, resulted in an impressive recovery of silk production. The spring 1950 cocoon harvest almost doubled compared with 1949, and quality improved as well. The 1951 spring cocoon harvest again increased by 20 percent, and the new regime took steps to expand state control over the cocoon harvest.[35] The government purchased only about one-third of the total cocoon crop in 1949, but by 1950 the proportion had risen to more than 90 percent. For the rest of the decade, the government consistently controlled more than three-quarters of the annual cocoon crop throughout the nation, something neither the Japanese nor the Nationalists had achieved.[36]

The Communists also expanded and improved the Nationalists' system of state-contracted production of silk thread in Jiangnan

33. *Shanghai sichou zhi*, 92–93.

34. *Jiangsusheng cansang sichou zhi*, 253; Qian, *Wuxishi sichou gongye*, 469–70.

35. *Wenhuibao*, 17 Sep. 1949, 30 Mar. & 16 Jun. 1950, 25 May 1951; *Dagongbao*, 28 Apr. 1950, 2 Jun. 1950; *Xinwenbao*, 17 May 1950.

36. *Zhongguo sichou tongji*, 437.

filatures. The Huachang Filature in Wuxi, a joint state-private operation under the postwar Nationalist government, was the first to restore operations on July 3, 1949, producing on contract for the CSC. On September 12, the state silk company signed contracts with the nine largest Wuxi filatures, and by the end of the month, thirty-five of Wuxi's filatures had restored production, enabling nearly six thousand employees to return to work. By November, more than fifty filatures had restored production through state contracting, and more than 7,600 workers had returned to work. Shanghai filatures also began to recover in September, when the Dali Filature delivered four hundred *dan* of silk thread to the state silk company.[37]

The CSC required that filatures meet three criteria to qualify for state production contracts. They were required to have a production capacity of at least eighty "sitting" (*zuosaoche*) or fifty "standing" (*lisaoche*) reeling machines, with all necessary auxiliary equipment. The owners had to possess circulating capital sufficient for at least two weeks' operations and the filatures had to be able to achieve production standards of at least half C-grade and half D-grade silk.[38] Production contracts included provision of loans and subsidized fuel, as well as raw materials through "processing and contract reeling" (*jiagong daisao*) and "exchanging silk for cocoons" (*yisi yijian*). The CSC especially promoted the latter method, which attempted to overcome inefficiencies in the earlier loan system through the direct exchange of cocoons for silk thread. Most filatures preferred the earlier practice, however, perhaps because they could receive payment in cash and rice and could benefit from market price increases. By the end of October, dozens of Jiangnan filatures had signed state reeling contracts, but only

37. Qian, *Wuxishi sichou gongye*, 23, 36.

38. Producers of silk thread test each batch of raw (filature) silk to determine its quality. In China quality was assessed using an adapted European system that measured several factors including the evenness of the thread (measured in denier), size deviation, cleanliness, and neatness. The grades for silk thread ranged from the lowest (F, E, and D—barely acceptable for most uses), through C, B, and A, to five grades of the finest thread (2A, 3A, 4A, 5A, and 6A). The standards for state contracting were therefore relatively low. Food and Agriculture, "Silk Reeling and Testing Manual."

a handful had elected to participate in the direct exchange of silk thread for cocoons.[39]

As filatures throughout the Yangzi Delta restored production, tens of thousands of filature workers, some of whom had been unemployed for more than a year, were able to return to work. Every reeling machine engaged in production provided employment for as many as three workers, which went a long way toward earning these workers' support for the Communist Party.[40] By the end of 1949, 98 filatures in Jiangsu Province had restored production, with a total daily output of 4.65 tons of silk thread. The situation was similar in Zhejiang Province.[41] Production continued to improve thereafter, such that total output of silk thread in Wuxi increased seven-and-a-half times from 1949 to 1952.[42]

Prices for silk thread also improved with the cessation of hostilities and the restoration of state contracting. As production expanded in the summer and fall of 1949, silk prices increased relative to the price of rice, although market prices remained insufficient to meet inflated production costs.[43] Between August 1949 and July 1950, the China Sericulture Company steadily increased the purchasing price for high-grade silk to encourage filatures to improve quality. By July 1950, when market prices for silk cloth also began to rise, prices for filature silk had more than doubled compared with the previous year, which promoted further expansion of production.[44]

Under the state contracting system, the CSC paid high prices for filature silk to foster the industry's recovery and maintain employment. In 1949, the state company marketed silk thread domestically at a price equivalent to only 30 percent of its purchasing price. Although this price increased as market prices for silk cloth recovered, by June 1950 the state price of thread sold to weaving factories was still only 66 percent of the purchasing price. As a result, for every *dan* of filature silk

39. Qian, *Wuxishi sichou gongye*, 470; *Wenhuibao*, 22 Oct. 1949, 30 Mar. 1950.

40. *Wenhuibao*, 22 Sep. 1949.

41. *Jiangsusheng cansang sichou zhi*, 253, 257; *Zhejiangsheng sichou zhi*, 25; *Dagongbao*, 2 June 1950.

42. Qian, *Wuxishi sichou gongye*, 473–74.

43. *Wenhuibao*, 22 Sep. 1949; SMA S37-4-4.

44. *Dagongbao*, 17 June 1950; Qian, *Wuxishi sichou gongye*, 472.

sold, the state took a loss of almost 5.4 million RMB.[45] The state thus secured supplies of cocoons, fuel, and working capital for the filatures, and paid for product at higher than market prices, subsidizing the silk industry's recovery until exports could improve. Restoring exports would take some time, however. With the Nationalist navy blockading Shanghai, 1949 was the worst year for exports of silk thread, which totaled only 6,870 *dan*. By the end of 1950, however, the Soviet Union and Eastern Europe were purchasing more than half of Chinese filatures' output, as compared with only 8 percent in 1949.[46]

The situation for Jiangnan silk weaving factories was even bleaker than for filatures in 1949, but despite this the weaving industry initially received much weaker support from the CSC. As prices for silk piece goods dropped to about half the level of production costs, it became impossible for weaving factories to continue operations. By the end of 1949, thirty-eight of Suzhou's eighty-five silk factories had ceased production, and the rest were reduced to operating part time. Thousands of Suzhou weavers were left unemployed.[47] The situation in other Jiangnan cities and towns was similarly dire. Like the filatures, weaving factories faced high production costs and wages, disappearing markets, and a shortage of capital to pay for materials and wages. The blockade also cut off imports of synthetic fibers, and despite an offer from the British-owned Xincheng Machine Factory to establish rayon production in Shanghai, China still had no domestic source of synthetics. Whereas prices for filature silk increased relative to rice, the opposite was true for silk cloth, and it was not until the spring of 1950 that cloth prices began to rise again.

Traditionally, China's silk industry was heavily dependent on exports, but foreign sales of silk had declined during the war. That there was considerable demand for Chinese silk overseas is evidenced by inquiries from interested buyers in India and Cyprus. But the blockade and high production costs restricted cloth exports, and only small amounts were exported through Guangzhou in 1949.[48] With exports

45. *Xinwenbao*, 10 Jul. 1950.
46. *Dagongbao*, 2 Jun. 1950; *Xinwenbao*, 27 Jul. 1951.
47. *Jiangsusheng cansang sichou zhi*, 302–3.
48. SMA S39-4-55.

stifled and domestic sales declining, silk weaving factories faced severe difficulties, and beginning in July 1949 the new government took steps to rescue the industry from imminent collapse. The State Foreign Trade Company's Exports Office and the CSC asked Shanghai silk weaving factories to estimate the amount of product they had in stock, offering to provide them with filature silk in return for cloth.[49]

In late November, more than a year after the Nationalists' tentative experiments with state-contracted silk weaving, the CSC introduced contracts for production of silk cloth. In the first three-month trial period, the state agency supplied qualified silk weaving factories with filature silk and rayon for production of export-quality cloth. Under the contract agreements, factory small groups organized by product type were either to exchange their cloth for supplies of thread (*yichou yisi*) or were contracted to produce cloth for the state company (*jiagong dinghuo*). The CSC agreed to purchase cloth at cost and, in theory, guaranteed weaving factories a profit of 5–8 percent.[50] However, despite contract provisions, such as the requirement that labor relations in factories engaging in state-contracted production be "harmonious," state agencies had little real influence over what happened behind factory doors. Oversight of state production contracts was very loose, and the absence of production and quality standards, as well as the problem of silk producers cheating on government contracts or reselling state-supplied materials, plagued the industry for years to come.

Despite their benefits for business, factory owners had many complaints about state silk weaving contracts. Factories were required to put up product as collateral to receive thread for contract weaving, and owners complained that this practice prevented them from marketing cloth, which exacerbated capital circulation difficulties. Like the Nationalists, the new government was concerned with preventing cheating and misuse of state property.[51] Nonetheless, over the next two years these requirements were relaxed, and contracted silk factories were allowed greater flexibility in obtaining supplies and providing collateral.

49. *Dagongbao*, 30 Jul. & 27 Aug. 1949.

50. *Dagongbao*, 24 Nov. & 1 Dec. 1949; *Xinwenbao*, 23 Nov. 1949; *Wenhuibao*, 23 Nov. 1949; *Shangbao*, 25 Nov. & 3 Dec. 1949.

51. SMA S39-3-1; *Wenhuibao*, 13 May 1950; *Xinwenbao*, 19 May 1950.

Even more common were complaints about the limited amount of state weaving contracts. State-contracted silk weaving in Shanghai amounted to ten thousand bolts by the end of 1949, which was very limited relative to existing capacity. One factory owner compared it to "trying to put out a burning cart of firewood with a cup of water."[52] Total production of silk cloth in Shanghai (both state-contracted and independent) increased from twenty thousand bolts in August 1949 to twenty-four thousand bolts in December, but this was only a fraction of the industry's potential and did little to increase employment.[53] During the winter of 1949–50, the state contracting system expanded to include more of Shanghai's smaller silk weaving factories, but small factories were consistently disadvantaged in obtaining state weaving contracts.

The CCP achieved much headway in its first months in power in Jiangnan. In particular, the party's rapid success in the economic sphere won the support of urbanites of all classes. It was not enough, however, to win the hearts and minds of the Chinese people. The Communists, still a tiny minority in a vast country, needed to educate, organize, and mobilize the population, especially industrial workers. But the party's earliest political education efforts did not reach most industrial workers, as propaganda work was mainly limited to the literate (about 20 percent of the total industrial workforce) and those in state-owned enterprises and the largest private factories. There furthermore remained tens of thousands of unemployed and destitute workers throughout the Jiangnan region. More than two years of economic recovery, mass campaigns, and political struggle were needed before the party could effectively mobilize workers employed in the small, scattered workshops, which represented the majority of Shanghai silk weavers.[54] Even when the party's message did reach industrial workers, this did not necessarily provide effective means of control over privately employed workers, their union organizations, or private manufacturing.

Still, the Communists expected eventually to be able to lead all of China's workers. In the coming years, people of all walks of life would be educated, organized, and mobilized to build and defend New China.

52. SMA S39-4-55.
53. SMA S39-4-44.
54. Gaulton, "Political Mobilization in Shanghai," 50.

Those who did not fit the Communists' conceptions of class and nation, or who actively resisted the party's authority and policies, would be suppressed. In its first year in power, the CCP seemed to most urban residents to be an efficient, well-organized, and dedicated government and army that promised to restore social and economic order out of the chaos of civil war and economic collapse. These accomplishments went a long way toward convincing China's urban workers and capitalists that their situation might improve under Communist rule. But in walking the unexplored and winding path of New Democracy, the CCP needed to tread carefully to win over China's workers while allaying capitalists' fears.

New Democracy in the Yangzi Delta Silk Industry

The party's policies during its first months in power focused on consolidating victory and restoring the economy, and included slogans such as "benefit both labor and capital" (*laozi liangli*). The CCP also conducted a campaign against "leftism" among workers and party cadres to curb excesses such as confiscating employers' property or establishing worker-controlled cooperative enterprises to replace capitalist management. These efforts were part of the party's "New Democratic" revolution, which they contrasted with a "dictatorship of the proletariat" such as the Bolsheviks had established in Russia. According to Mao's theory, New Democracy did not entail abandonment of the proletarian revolution, but rather called for creating the conditions for China's political and economic independence in preparation for a transition to socialism at some point in the future.[55] To begin socialist construction, China first had to develop its economy, especially

55. For Mao's writings on this subject, see Mao Zedong, *Selected Works of Mao Tse-Tung*, vols. 2, 3, and 4 (Beijing: Foreign Languages Press, 1961). The translations of Mao in the public domain can also be found online at https://www.marxists.org/reference/archive/mao/index.htm. The most relevant texts are "On New Democracy" (1940), "On Coalition Government" (1945), "The Present Situation and Our Tasks" (1947), and "On the People's Democratic Dictatorship" (1949).

industry, which necessitated that capitalist forms of production be retained and even promoted "for a long time to come."[56]

Unlike the Bolsheviks' "dictatorship of the proletariat," New Democracy was based on an alliance of all "progressive" classes in Chinese society under a Communist-led "people's democratic dictatorship." Mao conceived of the all-important category of "the people" as an alliance of four classes: workers, peasants, the *petite bourgeoisie*, and China's "national bourgeoisie" (*minzu zichanjieji*). This last group, defined as loyal, patriotic businesspeople, had a particularly important role to play in liberating China from imperialism and economic backwardness. Despite the party's goal of establishing a socialist China, the consensus in the 1940s was that it would be necessary to preserve and protect private business in the course of the New Democratic revolution. For example, in his 1945 speech "On Coalition Government," Mao stated:

> The substitution of a certain degree of capitalist development for the oppression of foreign imperialism and domestic feudalism is not only an advance but an unavoidable process. It benefits the proletariat as well as the bourgeoisie, and the former perhaps more. It is not domestic capitalism but foreign imperialism and domestic feudalism which are superfluous in China today; *indeed, we have too little of capitalism* . . . [I]t will be necessary in the interests of social progress to facilitate the development of the private capitalist sector of the economy . . . [57]

Recognizing the need to utilize the expertise of capitalists, managers, and technical staff in pursuit of economic recovery and industrialization, the new government went to great lengths in the early

56. Before 1953, Mao consistently made this point and used this phrase to emphasize the need for gradual change in China's economy. See for example "Report to the Second National Congress of Workers' and Peasants' Representatives," 23 January 1934.

57. Mao Zedong, *Selected Works*, 3: 283. Emphasis added. See also Mao's 1947 speech "The Present Situation and Our Tasks" in Mao Zedong, *Selected Works*, 4: 157–70.

1950s to convince private businesses to remain in the People's Republic and to continue operations. The CCP moderated workers' demands and supported private businesses financially and materially, as well as assigned representative capitalists prominent positions in political and social institutions.[58] In this way, China's "national capitalists" could make a positive contribution to the New Democratic revolution and the construction of socialism. The theory of New Democracy similarly sought to redefine working-class interests as those of the revolution and the nation, and to win workers' support for the party's developmental goals. The theory of New Democracy can thus be interpreted as an early attempt to redefine class identities in ways that would serve the goal of national economic development and socialist industrialization.

Mao and other CCP leaders agreed that what China needed most in 1949 was stability, economic recovery, and class cooperation more than expropriations and class conflict, at least in the context of urban industry. The Communists' early policy on labor relations was crystallized in the slogan, "benefit both labor and capital." A cartoon published in the *China Monthly Review* in November 1950 illustrates the concept well (fig. 3.1). The cartoon depicts a capitalist and a worker together pushing forward a cart labeled "developing production" on the road of "consultation," using new, modern tires labeled "collective contracts" and "labor laws." Behind them lie discarded and broken wheels labeled "passivity and withdrawal" and "exaggerated leftism."

As Richard Gaulton remarks, this cartoon "would have found favor under the most reactionary regime,"[59] and bears comparison with the Nationalist Party's postwar appeals for class cooperation. The Communists' approach was more successful, however, in part because it included effective steps toward economic recovery and fostered private enterprise, but also because of the party's explicitly pro-labor ideology expressed in policies and regulations to protect workers' interests and enhance their capacity to negotiate with employers.

58. On this topic see Esherick, "The Ye Family in New China," 311–36 and Cochran, "Capitalists Choosing Communist China," 359–85.

59. Gaulton, "Political Mobilization in Shanghai," 53.

Capital casts aside excessive exploitation and labor does away with exaggerated "leftism" to cooperate in developing China's production

FIGURE 3.1. Cartoon appearing in the November 1950 issue of *China Monthly Review* (vol. 119, no. 3).

In the aftermath of dire economic crisis and violent revolutionary upheaval, however, persistent effort was required to get urban workers to accept the party's moderate vision for transforming labor relations. Chairman Mao outlined the specific role of the urban proletariat in China's New Democratic revolution as early as the party's Seventh National Congress in April 1945. Mao praised workers for their "leadership" of the revolutionary struggle, but also emphasized their responsibility for improving production.[60] Nonetheless, as the Communists established themselves in the industrial cities of North China, there was much confusion concerning the policy of "benefiting both labor and

60. Mao Zedong, *Xin minzhuzhuyi jingji*, 5. See also Li Lisan's article "Learn How to Manage Enterprises," where he reminds workers, "The position of master of the

capital." According to one report, in 1947 there were "infringements of capitalists' rights," including physical abuse and seizures of property, in 1,490 enterprises in nine districts in central Hebei. Party and union cadres were often blamed for encouraging such excesses through "leftist errors," for example, incorrectly applying the methods of rural land reform and class struggle to urban industry and the "national bourgeoisie."[61]

In response, the party launched a campaign to oppose "leftist adventurism" (*zuoqing maoxianzhuyi*) in February 1948. A Xinhua editorial announcing the campaign criticized cadres for one-sidedly emphasizing the "immediate and temporary" interests of the working class without regard for the broader goal of restoring and developing the national economy.[62] The editorial was most explicit regarding the need to protect factory equipment and maintain production, and cautioning against demands for wages and benefits that exceeded the capacities of the wartime economy.

By the time this policy was promulgated in East China in the spring of 1949, the party's "south-bound" cadres were well disciplined concerning the need to protect the interests of the bourgeoisie. Many Jiangnan workers, however, viewed the policy of "benefiting both labor and capital" as simply kowtowing to the factory owners, and they resisted the party's moderate line.[63] According to a June 1949 report by the Silk Workers Union:

> On the one hand, many workers were not politically conscious about the meaning of Liberation, and only saw their short-term interests, demanding money from the capitalists as their spoils of the revolution. This greatly affected the unity between workers and capitalists. On the other

---

country is the most glorious position. It is also the position of greatest responsibility." Li Lisan, "Xuehui guanli qiye," 8–9.

61. *Xin gongshang zhengce*, 40. On the Shijiazhuang Incident in 1947, in which armed workers summarily executed local businessmen, see Perry, *Patrolling the Revolution*, 135.

62. *Zhongguo zhigong yundong wenxuan*, 63–64. This part of the editorial was contributed by Mao Zedong himself. See Zhonghua quanguo zonggonghui and Zhonggong Zhongyang wenxuan yanjiushi, *Mao Zedong, Deng Xiaoping*, 32–35.

63. James Gao, *Communist Takeover of Hangzhou*, 119–20.

> hand, capitalists looked only at economics [and also] behaved irresponsibly . . . On the whole, there was little unity or understanding of the New Democratic policy.[64]

Despite CCP warnings to workers and cadres not to seize capitalists' property or engage in struggle against them, factory seizures were common in the ferment of revolution. In such cases the party center blamed labor leaders and underground cadres for encouraging workers' "leftist" attitudes.[65] But the realities of economic crisis and the climate of political revolution nonetheless encouraged many workers to raise economic demands and even to seize property and commit violent acts.[66] Faced with unemployment and life-threatening inflation in the spring of 1949, Jiangnan workers jumped on the opportunity created by the Communist takeover to raise demands concerning job security, wages, and working conditions; their actions were often in conflict with the party's goal of restoring production and economic stability. From May 1949 through the spring of 1950, workers in Shanghai and other cities engaged in strikes, slowdowns, factory occupations, and various forms of harassment and intimidation of employers in one of the most widespread waves of labor unrest in Chinese history.[67] In order to win workers' support and to distinguish themselves from their predecessors in the eyes of China's proletariat, the Communists could not afford to suppress workers' actions, and there is no evidence that they did so in their first months in power despite workers' frequent violations of the party's policy concerning labor relations in industry.[68]

Directives issued in the months following the Communists' takeover of Shanghai attempted to codify the policy of "benefiting both labor and capital" by providing explicit protections for workers and employers. In July 1949, the ACFTU issued the "Provisional Method for Handling Labor-Capital Relations," which emphasized job security

64. SMA C16-2-285.

65. SMA C1-2-7.

66. For examples see *Xin gongshang zhengce*; Pepper, *Civil War in China*, 370–71; Ezpeleta, *Red Shadows over Shanghai*, 196.

67. *Jiefanghou Shanghai gongyun*, 140; Frazier, *Chinese Industrial Workplace*, 101.

68. F. Chen, "Labor Protests," 507.

and stipulated that factories should rehire laid-off workers as soon as production could be restored. Employers were required to maintain at least the wage level before 1949, and to limit wage increases to no more than 50 percent in factories where wages were excessively low and conditions permitted an increase. Workers who were laid off with the approval of the Bureau of Industry and Commerce were to be compensated between one and three months' wages. The "Labor-Capital Relations" directive also called for the establishment of collective contracts, protected workers' right to join unions and to participate in political activities, set standards for welfare provision and injury compensation, and stated that workers who had been fired for participating in revolutionary political activities should be given priority in rehiring.

The directive also protected employers' right to decide issues such as hiring and firing (within the limitations imposed by other laws and regulations) and required workers to maintain labor discipline and to respect factory regulations approved by the union and the Labor Bureau. This provision disallowed the use of violent or destructive tactics or "settling of accounts" and required workers to redress grievances through official channels. The directive furthermore mandated an eight to ten-hour workday, which could be extended to twelve hours if necessary, and mentioned benefits such as overtime pay, equal pay for men and women, maternity leave, labor insurance, and the establishment of factory management committees.[69] At that time, however, these were merely suggestions for factories that had the wherewithal to adopt such measures. In the first year of the revolution, most of these recommendations could not be implemented given the economic difficulties most factories faced.

Another ACFTU document, "Provisional Regulations for the Process of Resolving Labor Disputes," put forward methods for resolving disputes in all state, private, and cooperative enterprises. The document's definition of "labor dispute" was very broad and included any disagreement relating to employment and working conditions, wages, factory regulations, disciplining and firing of employees, and infractions of contracts or agreements brought before the Labor Bureau by either side. (In the first year after Liberation, almost three-quarters of

69. SMA C1-2-7; *Jiefanghou Shanghai gongyun*, 182–86.

such disputes were raised by employers.) Disputes could involve one or all of the workers in a given factory and could take the form of violence and seizures of property, strikes and protests, or petitions to the government. The regulations applied only to disputes that the two sides were unable to resolve independently, which were then brought before the Labor Bureau. The provisional regulations concerning labor disputes established procedures for mediation, as well as the responsibilities of both sides to accept the arbitration committee's decisions and the legal consequences if they did not.[70]

As was the case with many of the Communists' New Democratic policies, the contradictions inherent in labor policy became obvious only as they were put into practice. The conflicting goals of economic recovery and working-class liberation often exacerbated disputes when implemented in industrial enterprises. Although the party officially discouraged violent tactics such as "surroundings," factory occupations, and other actions that could harm production, the party's policies (such as the August 1949 revival of a 1948 Nationalist law prohibiting layoffs) inspired many workers to demand reinstatement, often adopting the very methods the Communists discouraged. The revived regulation provided factory owners some protection by stipulating that employers were not required to rehire workers who had been fired for infractions of the rules or for poor performance. Workers who had already been laid off and accepted severance pay, or who had left of their own accord, were also unable to demand reinstatement. Nor were factories that genuinely could not continue production required to rehire workers, although they had to apply to the Bureau of Industry and Commerce for permission to discontinue production, and the factory union could object. Under the principles of New Democracy, China's leaders preferred workers and employers to address grievances through official (peaceful) channels and discouraged strikes or violence. But in 1949, the CCP exercised only limited influence over urban workers, many of whom continued to resort to earlier, more violent tactics in confrontations with employers.[71]

70. SMA A4-1-11.

71. *Jiefanghou Shanghai gongyun*, 193–94; SMA Q202-1-136.

A letter from labor organizer Mao Qihua to Ma Chungu (who became the director of the Shanghai Labor Bureau) expressed the party's predicament well. Mao stated that many private enterprises in Shanghai had restored production in July and August, but also that recovery was assisted both by government contracts and seasonal increases in demand. For this reason, and because of the need to reduce inflation, it would be inadvisable to encourage across-the-board wage increases in all industries. At the same time, however, Mao stated that "we do not want to dampen the workers' enthusiasm for production."[72]

Mao Qihua made two recommendations. First, the newly established Labor Bureau should create industry-wide standards for bonuses and rewards in order to avoid chaos, disparities, and excessive demands. Second, regulations governing the disposition of profits in private enterprises should be established. On top of the 10 percent set aside for purchases of government bonds, 15 percent of enterprise profits should be invested in improving factory safety and hygiene. Another 10 percent should be deposited in a welfare fund to establish collective facilities such as cafeterias, nurseries, and clubs. Finally, five percent of net profit should be set aside as bonuses for model workers who create new techniques and genuinely contribute to production. He emphasized that bonuses should not be distributed to all workers for two reasons: to preserve their significance as rewards and to avoid universal wage increases.[73]

Provisions like these would be implemented in later years and extended into privately owned factories, but in 1949 they were simply impossible. Communist Party cadres and labor officials had neither the information nor the authority to compel private factory owners to set aside 40 percent of enterprise profits for these purposes.[74] Many enterprises earned no profit at all, and if they did, they were unlikely to share this information with their employees or the government. Not until

72. SMA C1-2-12.

73. SMA C1-2-12.

74. Regulations like these led some contemporary observers to conclude that Chinese businesses were strictly controlled by the Communist Party. (See, for example, Theodore Chen, "Liquidation of Private Business," 81–89.) The gap between stated goals and reality was especially large in this instance, however, and it does not seem that these measures were widely implemented in 1949.

the party had established a presence in individual factories would it be possible to thoroughly investigate enterprise accounts and the disposition of profits. Nonetheless, the regulations issued in the new government's first months went a long way toward allaying workers' concerns and promoting cooperation with employers. Employment regulations, combined with the promise of improved benefits once production was restored, convinced workers that any immediate reductions in benefits and wages were temporary and were in the interest of the enterprise's survival, and that workers would be able to recover what they had conceded once conditions improved.

To mobilize China's "national capitalists" to support the New Democratic deal, the revolutionary regime organized factory owners into associations that could be relied upon to support the party's efforts. The party organized other urbanites into similar institutions such as student associations, labor unions, professional associations, the Communist Youth League, Sino-Soviet friendship societies, and neighborhood committees. Eventually, the party achieved a high degree of control over these organizations and utilized them as extensions of state power. But in 1949, the party leadership was unable to exercise direct supervision over most organizations, even those in which party members played a leading role.

Chinese industrialists and merchants joined "mass organizations" called industry associations (*tongye gonghui*) under the leadership of the Federation of Industry and Commerce at the national and local levels. According to Italian Consul-General Paolo Alberto Rossi, who resided in Shanghai from 1948 to 1952, businesses were compelled to join Communist-led "cooperatives or guilds" to "avoid suppression of their activities." Rossi claims that their main functions were to supervise members' activities to ensure that they operated in accordance with relevant laws and regulations, to inspect account books, and to collect taxes. They also helped to implement the new government's policies and campaigns, especially the drive to purchase government bonds.[75]

Guilds and business associations had a long history in China and had undergone many transformations, most recently under the Japanese occupation and the postwar Nationalist government. Some traditional

75. Rossi, *Communist Conquest of Shanghai*, 61–62.

guilds included both employers and employees, while others were organized around native-place or religious affinities.[76] Traditional business associations usually enjoyed a high degree of autonomy, but in the twentieth century these organizations had a closer, more contentious relationship with state authorities.[77] In 1949, the Communists broke up large interregional business associations and reorganized them on a provincial or municipal basis. For example, the Shanghai Silk Reeling Industry Association, which included hundreds of member filatures throughout the Jiangnan region, was dismantled. New associations were established in Jiangsu and Zhejiang Provinces, with municipal-level associations in major silk centers such as Wuxi.[78] The Shanghai Silk Merchants Association and Silk Reeling Association established a combined organization on March 15, 1950, which included three silk filatures (two private and one state-run), four silk spinning factories (three private and one state-run), and seventy-nine commercial businesses in the city of Shanghai. The new association's governing committee was comprised of representatives of factories and shops, including several government officials from state-run factories.[79]

The Shanghai Silk Weaving Industry Association was not formally established until January 1951. In January 1950, the party authorities had invited leading silk industrialists to form a preparatory committee with Song Baolin, general manager of the Dacheng Silk Weaving Factory,[80] as chairman. There were to be four vice-chairs, including Zhu Zuxian, director of the Shanghai branch of the China Sericulture Company, and Tong Xinbai, general manager of the Meiya Company.[81] According to the constitution of the Shanghai Silk Weaving Industry Association, all members, regardless of factory size or capitalization,

76. Goodman, *Native Place, City, and Nation*.

77. See Wang Xiang, "Cong Yunjin gongsuo dao tieji gonghui," 109–36.

78. SMA S37-4-1.

79. SMA C48-2-31, C48-2-198.

80. Song Baolin was also chairman of the Board of the Dacheng Silk Company, in which he owned a 34 percent share. Song was college-educated and had previously been a factory director at Meiya. He remained as chairman of the Silk Weaving Industry Association until it was dissolved in 1956. SMA S39-4-2, S39-4-83.

81. SMA S39-4-4.

enjoyed the right to elect and be elected as representatives (so long as they were factory owners or authorized administrators of voting age). However, anyone who had been convicted of a crime, had violated the Common Program of the Chinese People's Political Consultative Congress (CPPCC) in word or deed, or engaged in behavior that would damage the credibility of the association was prohibited from serving as a representative. Members also had the right to criticize and make suggestions concerning the viewpoints and methods of the association, and to share in the benefits of its activities.[82]

The association's constitution articulated the organization's main purpose as "uniting and directing the industry under the leadership of the people's government according to the regulations of the Common Program" of the CPPCC, summarized as "attending to both public and private interests, benefiting both labor and capital, and facilitating mutual assistance between city and countryside, and internal and external exchange, with the goal of developing production and making the economy prosper."[83] The association's specific responsibilities included promulgating government policies and the directives and resolutions of the Federation of Industry and Commerce; investigating the industry's situation and offering suggestions to policy-makers; aiding the reform of public-private relations, business relations, and labor relations; mediating disputes; and facilitating the improvement of business management and technology. Members were required to abide by the association's regulations and carry out its resolutions, as well as to provide information on their business operations for statistical reports, and to implement government directives conveyed through the association. The more powerful role of the state in governing private industry through this form of association is indicated by the presence of Zhu Zuxian on its preparatory committee and the inclusion of state-owned silk factories as voting members.[84]

The establishment of organizational influence among employers went a long way toward promoting class cooperation and the press

82. SMA S39-4-11.
83. SMA S39-4-11.
84. SMA S39-4-11.

presented examples of employers and workers cooperating to restore production. Beginning in July 1949, Shanghai's Silk Industry Association, government officials, and union leaders organized meetings to promote class cooperation over class conflict and national interests over revolution. The participants pledged to cooperate to overcome the industry's difficulties, to foil the naval blockade, and to liberate Taiwan as early as possible. The union agreed to accept a basic wage equivalent to four *sheng* of rice, while administrative staff received 3.3 *sheng*.[85] Workers at Song Baolin's Dacheng Silk Weaving Factory agreed to accept wage payments on a less regular basis temporarily so that the factory could avoid taking losses if prices fell.[86] In the face of the blockade, the Meiya Company shifted from producing silk quilt covers for export to producing a cheaper silk-hemp blend for domestic consumption. Because the wage for this cloth was lower than that for quilt covers, this meant a pay cut for Meiya weavers. But the weavers accepted the change so that the factory could continue operations.[87]

In August 1949, in order to help reduce production costs, more than five hundred women workers at Shanghai's Dali Filature agreed to reduce wages from the equivalent of 4.9 *sheng* of rice (which was rather high) to just three *sheng* per day. Other employees, including management, accepted wage reductions of 30–40 percent. Dali workers also agreed to reduce the number of rest days each month from four to two.[88] Labor and management at Dali reached an agreement on August 27, which enabled the factory to restore production when state provision of cocoons began in September. Shortly thereafter, the CSC increased the fee for contract reeling so that filature workers could be guaranteed the equivalent of 3.5 *sheng* of rice per day.[89]

Indicative of changes in labor relations under Communist rule, one of the Silk Weaving Industry Association's earliest tasks was to assist the state in assessing and collecting silk weaving factories' taxes. The silk industry's "democratic appraisal committee" (*minzhu pingyi*

85. *Shangbao*, 29 Jul. 1949; SMA C16-2-287; *Jiefanghou Shanghai laozi guanxi*, 17, 31.

86. *Xinwenbao*, 31 Jul. 1949.

87. *Dagongbao*, 28 Oct. 1949; *Jiefanghou Shanghai laozi guanxi*, 61.

88. *Jiefanghou Shanghai laozi guanxi*, 68–69.

89. *Jiefang ribao*, 31 Aug. 1949; SMA S37-4-2.

weiyuanhui) was elected on March 24, 1950, and organized groups of workers, employers, and accountants to investigate factories' revenues and tax payments. The association's report admits some shortcomings due to lack of experience (mainly insufficient preparation in teaching factory owners how to fill out the forms). But, overall, the work proceeded very smoothly.[90]

An October 1950 report by Shen Fukang, the Meiya management staff and union official in charge of the "*minping*" teams' day-to-day work, stated that most factory owners were cooperative, and some even welcomed assistance with keeping accounts. Unsurprisingly, given the state of domestic silk markets, only twenty-seven of Shanghai's more than three hundred silk weaving factories were found to have under-reported earnings, and most of these were due to unintentional errors. Under-reported earnings totaled more than 117 million yuan RMB, or just 3.2 percent of total reported earnings. Most of the errant factory owners were simply required to pay taxes on unreported income, and only a few were fined.[91] Although the industry's total taxes were originally appraised at 600 million yuan RMB, this was reduced to 200 million in light of the industry's difficulties.[92] This kind of flexibility in applying laws and regulations to private businesses was typical of Chinese Communist practice, and allowed party cadres in Shanghai to begin disciplining the city's capitalists and enforcing the laws while still permitting them the autonomy to persist as private businesses. More importantly, the revolutionary authorities in Shanghai promoted new forms of labor-capital cooperation while improving (although by no means perfecting) their access to information on private businesses.

The success of the Communists' New Democratic policies depended to a large degree on the capacity of employers and workers to cooperate in order to achieve economic recovery under CCP leadership, and union

90. Interview with Shen Fukang, 25 Mar. 2004; SMA S39–4–11, C16–2–287. The report states that because of the large number of small factories, accounting in the silk weaving industry was particularly "backward." Many factories did not keep books properly, or did not keep accounts at all. However, Shen Fukang also told the author that the accounts of small factories were easier to check because they were simpler and more limited in scale.

91. Report by Shen Fukang in SMA C16–2–287.

92. January 1951 report by Song Baolin in SMA S39–4–11.

organizations at all levels played a significant role in this process. Given that the party's organizational and personnel resources varied widely from place to place, efforts to foster cooperation between labor and capital produced divergent results depending on the economic state of the industry and the nature of the workers' organizations in that locality. These kinds of differences strongly influenced the outcomes of CCP policies in the silk cities of the Yangzi Delta.

Shanghai silk weavers, mostly male and located in China's industrial metropolis, belonged to union organizations with strong ties to the CCP, and weavers and employers shared much in common. In contrast, workers in the silk filatures of Shanghai, Wuxi, and other Jiangnan cities did not generally belong to union organizations before 1949, but had marched at the forefront of a very active labor movement during the postwar years of civil war and economic crisis. Under the CCP's New Democratic policies, these women workers frequently found their traditional tactics of direct and sometimes violent action discredited and the new union organizations controlled by their antagonists. Such differences meant that, whereas some workers gained power and benefits through the Communist revolution, others lost what little power they might have exercised previously and faced a revolutionary government that often seemed more sympathetic to their employers' needs than to their own interests.

Organizing Workers in the New Democratic Society—The Shanghai Silk Workers Union and the Wuxi Filatures Union

As the vanguard party of the proletariat, the Communists should have excelled at organizing industrial workers, but in 1949 the Chinese Communist Party's relationship with urban workers fell short of the Marxist-Leninist ideal. Despite its largely rural membership and a shortage of cadres experienced in urban industry, the CCP made considerable progress in recruiting and organizing urban workers in its first years in power. From 1949 to 1952 Communist labor organizers struggled to extend the party's influence among urban workers by promoting the party's ideology, supporting workers' demands and existing union organizations, and establishing new unions. This process was, however, fraught with conflict, and organizers encountered many obstacles, including workers' desire for autonomy from outside influence, the presence of corrupt and even hostile elements in the leadership of many existing unions, and employers' ability to manipulate the unions. Communist labor cadres themselves were often quite inexperienced, and their work fraught with shortcomings. Contrasting two groups of silk workers—the relatively privileged, politically powerful silk weavers in Shanghai and the young, exploited, and fiercely independent filature workers of Wuxi—highlights the difficulties the Communists encountered in their attempts to organize diverse groups of workers. This comparison also reveals the extent to which gender and gender conflict affected the CCP's efforts at organizing workers, a project vital to the revolution's success.

The Chinese Communists' vision of labor unions and the relationship between workers' organizations and the party was influenced by Soviet practices. Since Lenin, trade unions under Communist Party leadership had been conceived both as "mass organizations" representing the interests of industrial workers and as "transmission belts" between the apparatus of the party-state and "the masses" of the proletariat.[93] Many problems arose in union work in the People's Republic of China as a result of this contradictory role; chief among them was the unions' vacillation between promoting the interests of industrial workers and enforcing the policies and goals of the party-state. Although this problem is widely discussed in the literature on labor unions in the PRC,[94] what is less understood is how differences in the labor unions after 1949 influenced the ways in which diverse groups of workers experienced the revolution and Communist rule. As is often the case in modern Chinese history, it is difficult to generalize. Railway

93. Lenin stated in 1920 that the Communist party-state "cannot work without a number of 'transmission belts' running from the vanguard to the mass of the advanced class, and from the latter to the mass of the working people." Lenin, *Collected Works*, 32:21. Stalin in turn described the mass organizations as ensuring Party leadership in all areas, while remaining representative bodies. Stalin, *Problems of Leninism*, 164–68.

94. See, for example, Lee Lai To, *Trade Unions in China*; Howe, *Wage Patterns and Policy*; and Harper, "Party and the Unions."

workers or steel and textile workers in Shanghai had experiences very different from those of coal miners in the northwest or textile workers in Shandong. Similarly, distinct groups of silk workers had very different experiences of Liberation, as did male and female workers, even those within the same factory.

The diversity among Chinese workers in terms of industry, job, gender, and locality greatly complicated the process of organizing and leading China's proletariat. Some unions had a core of Communist activists who came to power in 1949. But the reorganization of existing unions and the rapid formation of new ones, combined with the shortage of experienced party cadres, often resulted in unions that were controlled by labor-gang bosses (*gongtou*), criminal elements, or employers. The most successful unions in the early years of the People's Republic were those that were led by loyal Communists who also had the respect of the rank and file membership—such as Zhang Qi of the Shanghai Silk Workers Union. But even dedicated and responsible labor activists who pursued their constituents' interests could run afoul of the party's policies. Most of the more independent and genuinely representative labor activists were eventually expelled or co-opted as the party worked to subordinate existing union organizations to its control. However, in the period from 1949 through 1951, a few well-established and relatively independent unions, whose goals and interests coincided broadly with those of the Communist Party, were able to win the trust of China's new rulers, provide their members with support and benefits, and negotiate with employers from a much stronger position than was possible under the Nationalists.

Within five days of the military takeover of Shanghai, teams of union cadres and party labor organizers began political and organizational work in the city's factories. The party's goals and methods were similar to those of the postwar Nationalist government: it relied on working-class party members to organize in their own factories, promoted labor-capital cooperation in order to restore the battered economy, and adopted measures to protect jobs and incomes. By January 1950, membership in Shanghai unions ranged from 11 to 15 percent among tobacco and transport workers, to 90 or almost 100 percent in posts and telecommunications, textiles, chemicals, and printing. By June 1950, almost 94 percent of Shanghai's manufacturing workers belonged to unions.[95] Organizers paid particular attention to enrolling women workers. Of China's 568,841 women workers, 398,858 (about 72 percent) had become union members by June 1950.[96] A March 1950 report from Shanghai recorded 205,014 women workers in that city, forming 25.9 percent of the total workforce. By that time, 162,563 Shanghai women had joined unions, comprising 25.4 percent of the city's union members. By November 1950, 94 percent of women workers in Shanghai had joined union organizations.[97]

Despite the high proportion of workers enrolled as union members, nominal Communist leadership of these "mass organizations" did not necessarily indicate effective control or an espousal of Communist ideology on the part of union members. Even with the flood of regulations, instructions, and directives concerning union work issued by the East China Military Control Commission and Shanghai's General Labor Union, in practice it was impossible for the revolutionary authorities to establish direct and effective control over most unions in these early years. The party simply did not have the resources and personnel to exercise more than indirect political leadership over Shanghai's several hundred thousand industrial workers.

The combination of revolution, minimal political control, and economic crisis produced a massive strike wave in the months following the Communist takeover of Shanghai, which continued into the spring of 1950.[98] From June 1949 through April 1950, the Shanghai GLU recorded a total of 8,283 labor disputes, of which 3,847 occurred in the first four months of 1950. More than half of the disputes brought before the Labor Bureau concerned layoffs or demands to return to work, while disputes over wage issues made up another 23 percent of the total. The monthly total of labor disputes of all kinds, including major incidents such as protests, strikes, "surroundings," destruction of property, and factory occupations, as well as less extreme actions like petitions and official complaints, peaked in August 1949 at more than 800, but by

95. *Jiefanghou Shanghai gongyun*, 98, 142–43; SMA C1-1-33.

96. WMA D1-2-6; Andors, *Unfinished Liberation*, 30.

97. SMA C1-2-333.

98. Perry estimates that this was the largest strike wave in Shanghai's history. Perry, "Shanghai's Strike Wave of 1957," 1n3.

November had fallen to 150. Shanghai's silk industry exhibited a similar pattern, reaching a peak of 20 registered disputes in August 1949 (mostly disputes over wages and demands to return to work) and then declining through the end of the year as the situation stabilized. The February Sixth bombing (discussed in chapter 4) then produced a new spike in labor disputes, and the spring of 1950 was described as the "most intense since Liberation" in terms of labor-capital conflict in the city of Shanghai.[99]

Strikes and protests exerted little upward pressure on wages in the year following Shanghai's Liberation due to the party's low-wage policy and the inconsistencies resulting from years of wartime inflation. By 1950, obtaining employment and securing the means of subsistence were still more important for most industrial workers than the face value of money wages. Many of the labor disputes in Shanghai's silk weaving industry arose in response to factory owners discontinuing direct provision of rice and oil in the spring of 1950. Furthermore, years of war and economic crisis had altered the wage structure in the Jiangnan region as wages depended more on the economic health of the industry than objective standards of skill and productivity. Wages in essential consumer industries, especially cotton textiles, were quite high, equivalent to almost five *sheng* of rice. Workers in the tobacco and silk weaving industries received the equivalent of only 3.4 to four *sheng*, while wages in Shanghai's machine-building industries were relatively low, ranging from five *sheng* of rice to just three *sheng*.[100]

By the time the new Shanghai Silk Workers Union was formally established in January 1950, 87 percent of Shanghai's 14,315 silk industry employees had joined.[101] By June more than 97 percent of Shanghai silk workers were union members, including 12,517 production workers (7,647 men and 4,870 women) and 1,449 managerial and technical staff (1,395 men and 54 women). Women comprised about 37 percent of all union members in Shanghai's silk weaving industry at that time.[102] The

99. SMA A4-1-11, C1-2-232.
100. SMA A4-1-11, C1-2-12.
101. SMA C1-1-40.
102. SMA C1-2-75.

unions were organized by districts, in the north, south, and west, with branch organizations in the larger factories. By the end of August there were 32 branch (factory) unions and 37 basic-level committees in factories employing 25 or more people, with another 81 in preparation. In January 1950 Shanghai had 385 officially registered private silk weaving factories and one state-run factory. Of these, 346 employed fewer than 50 workers.[103] Thus, although workers in Shanghai's hundreds of small silk factories were nominally members of the industry union, there was no significant organizational presence in most workplaces.

Some of the newly reorganized unions provided their members significant and immediate benefits. In the year from May 1949 to May 1950, the Shanghai Silk Workers Union provided relief grain to 19,420 silk workers and dependents. The union also organized classes to teach literacy and production skills, and to promote party policy.[104] There remained, however, many problems and conflicts in union work in the early years of the People's Republic. Some groups of workers and their local leaders enjoyed a relatively high degree of autonomy to define and pursue their interests, which could bring them into conflict with the party's New Democratic policies. Many unions were led by elements hostile to, or at least indifferent toward, Communist revolution. Others were dominated by employers and managers. The party's efforts to enforce its policies through union organizations it did not control produced contradictory trends and problems that persisted for many years. These included insufficient consultation with the membership (described as a "lack of democracy"), incomplete understanding of (or outright hostility toward) party policy, passivity, and corruption.[105]

The diverse challenges and potentially contradictory responsibilities that union officials faced made it difficult even for conscientious cadres to attend to their constituents' needs or to repair shortcomings in their work. For example, Article 9 of the Trade Union Law made the unions responsible for maintaining labor discipline and promoting the

103. More than 90 percent of Shanghai factories employed fewer than 25 workers. SMA C16-2-285, C1-1-33, C1-1-190. These statistics do not include an estimated 8,234 unemployed silk workers.

104. SMA C16-2-285, C1-2-15.

105. Harper, "Party and the Unions," 84–119.

policy of developing production, attending to both public and private interests, and benefiting both labor and capital. The unions were charged to oppose acts in violation of state laws or detrimental to production. But this imperative could conflict with the unions' responsibilities to represent and protect their members' interests. In his explanation of this point, Labor Minister Li Lisan emphasized that "the central task of trade union organizations in private enterprises is to increase production. Only in this way will the trade unions be able to take fully into consideration the interests of the working class." At the same time, factory owners were called upon to rely on the workers to improve production, to include them in managerial decisions, and to reform the abusive and oppressive practices of the past.[106]

The conflicts and contradictions in union work created a pattern in which union officials vacillated between a "left" position of supporting whatever workers demanded (criticized as "economism") and a "right" position of emphasizing production at the expense of worker welfare (criticized as "bureaucratism"). An October 1950 meeting of Shanghai union cadres aired several criticisms of union work over the previous year. On the one hand, some union officials were criticized for "forgetting who we are really working for, and who these policies are meant to benefit." On the other hand, the report also criticized cadres who gave in to workers' "unreasonable demands." Because of these contradictory pressures, union cadres wavered in policy implementation, attempting to please everyone and avoid responsibility.[107] The conflicting demands on union cadres and the limited resources available to them led to frustration, passivity, and resignations. For example, one silk factory originally had nine energetic and capable union cadres. But due to layoffs, conflicts, and frustration with official policy, by June 1950 only one cadre remained, and it was difficult for union work to develop.[108]

Despite these challenges, the unions trained thousands of individuals for political, union, and administrative posts in the first year of the People's Republic. By the end of 1950, the Shanghai GLU had trained

106. *Trade Union Law*, 22–23.
107. SMA C1-2-231.
108. SMA C16-2-285.

7,935 people for work in political bureaus, factory administration, technical departments, and union organizations. Only 1,617 of these were production workers, however. The other 6,318 were drawn from the ranks of managerial and technical staff. Of 2,749 newly trained high-level union cadres, only 755 were production workers. Furthermore, only 17 percent of high-level union cadres in Shanghai were women, and the proportion was even lower for full-time union officers.[109] Although the shortage of trained women cadres remained serious, by late 1950 there were already 2,680 women cadres at the basic-level committee and higher, comprising about 20 percent of all union cadres in Shanghai. Of the eighty-three vice-chairs of industry unions, however, only nine were women, and only three of the twenty-five industry-level union chairs were women, despite the high proportion of women workers in Shanghai industry.[110]

These statistics reveal some of the difficulties women workers faced even in industries, such as the Jiangnan filatures, in which most workers were women. Filature workers' traditions of organizing and protesting were very different from those of Shanghai silk weavers and were suppressed under the New Democratic policy of class cooperation. These legacies combined with serious shortcomings in organizing efforts among women workers to produce very different results for Wuxi filature workers as compared with Shanghai silk weavers, or even with women workers in Shanghai's silk filatures.

Wuxi was a smaller city with almost no local Communist cadres, and the unions in Wuxi had fewer resources than their Shanghai counterparts. Furthermore, even if the two branches of the silk industry faced broadly similar market and policy conditions, other aspects of production and factory management, as well as the nature of the relationship between private enterprises and the state, were very different. Wuxi's filature workers thus found that the Communist seizure of power initially did little to remedy the most pressing problems in their lives—oppressive working conditions and exploitation by male supervisors and employers—and these problems persisted after 1949 even in state-run filatures.

109. SMA C1–1–33, C1–2–75, C31–2–15.
110. SMA C1–2–333.

In general, the party cadres sent to organize workers in Wuxi were quite positive about the Communists' reception in that city. As evidence for their optimism, they cited workers' efforts to protect factories on the eve of the Communist takeover, as well as their active assistance in taking over state-run factories after the arrival of Communist forces. By late summer, many Wuxi workers had applied to join the CCP and Communist Youth League, and this was given as proof of their increased "political consciousness" and awareness of being "masters of the country." There were also many problems, however. Union organizers complained that workers' attitudes toward production had not yet returned to "normal." That is, many factory employees had not yet accepted the party's policy of making concessions to employers to help restore production. Wuxi labor officials considered it most important to allay capitalists' fears and to convince them that they could rely on the unions' cooperation.[111] But the unions' mission of "facing production" and mobilizing workers to cooperate with employers proved more problematic in Wuxi's filatures than in Shanghai's silk weaving industry.

The employment situation in Wuxi in the summer of 1949 was most critical, especially for filature workers, some of whom had been out of work for a year or more. The leaders of Wuxi's General Labor Union, however, were reluctant to bring workers together to discuss the wage and employment situation for fear that they would take the opportunity to raise new demands.[112] In contrast with the situation in Shanghai, this reflected a lack of close ties between the union leadership and the rank and file. From May through August 1949, most of Wuxi's filatures, lacking cocoons, cut off from markets, and with prices little more than one-third of production costs, discontinued production and left more than 6,000 people out of work. At the end of August, union representatives met with officials of the Wuxi GLU's Silk Industry Group to address the industry's problems in the context of the policy of "benefiting both labor and capital." To reduce production costs, the union agreed to set wages at 3.28 *sheng* of rice, sufficient to sustain two people. On September 22, the Silk Industry Work Group held a meeting

111. WMA D2-1-10.
112. WMA D2-1-1.

of representatives from all the filatures and organized a "small group" to research and draft a collective agreement. A week later, representatives of the filature owners and the union signed the "Wuxi Filature Industry Labor-Capital Collective Agreement," the first industry-level collective agreement in Jiangsu Province.[113] In October 1949, the CSC adjusted payments for state-contracted production, enabling filatures to increase wages to the equivalent of 3.5 *sheng* of rice. By October 1950, when prices had stabilized, Wuxi began to implement a wage system based on parity units. Filature wages were set at 1.05 Wuxi parity units, equivalent to 4.3 *sheng* of rice.[114]

Workers in Shanghai made similar temporary concessions to preserve their jobs, but the nature of the union organizations and the "worker representatives" negotiating the terms were very different. The leaders of the Shanghai Silk Workers Union were reliably pro-Communist, but they were also relatively independent from both their employers and the party's political leadership. The combination of loyalty to the Communist cause, organizational strength, and an ability to communicate and negotiate with employers enabled the Shanghai Silk Workers Union to pursue its constituents' interests effectively in the early 1950s. In the case of the Wuxi filature industry, however, the new union organizations were dominated by filature owners who had nothing in common with their workers and who controlled the unions through loyal management staff. These employers were frequently able to utilize the party's policy of labor-capital cooperation to suppress workers' efforts to improve working conditions and advance their interests.

The Communists had a strong underground presence in Shanghai and considerable political, administrative, organizational, and economic resources available there. But even with these advantages, the party still could not establish effective leadership of all union organizations in Shanghai until 1952 at the earliest. In smaller cities such as Hangzhou and Wuxi, the situation was even more complex and insecure for

113. *Jiefanghou Shanghai laozi guanxi*, 112–13, 156–58; Qian, *Wuxishi sichou gongye*, 23. For the full text of the agreement, see Qian, *Wuxishi sichou gongye*, 485–87.

114. WMA D2-1-12; Qian, *Wuxishi sichou gongye*, 229.

China's new rulers. Union reports claimed that enemy agents (*tewu*) continued to operate with impunity, even committing acts of sabotage. The effect on production was probably minimal compared with the filatures' supply and marketing problems. But the existence of organizations loyal to the Nationalist Party, as well as "yellow" unions and secret societies, created a "rather complex political situation." Workers in one Wuxi cotton mill, for example, belonged to eight different organizations.[115]

Union organizing efforts in Hangzhou's silk industry faced similar problems. At the Tianzhang Silk Factory, for example, most workers were older, highly skilled, and showed little interest in revolutionary politics. Younger, male workers, who were often unskilled, low-paid, seasonal laborers, were generally enthusiastic about the Communist takeover but voiced immediate demands for wage increases, and few responded to the call to "develop production and make the economy flourish." If the union at the Tianzhang Silk Factory is typical, then the Communists faced great difficulties in establishing politically reliable unions under effective Communist leadership. Of the twelve union members at Tianzhang, only one was a Communist. Five belonged to the Brotherhood Society (Gelaohui), three to the Green Gang, and one had been a Nationalist Party member. The man elected union chair, Xu Dajun, had served the Japanese occupation forces as an intelligence agent.[116]

The shortage of party operatives undermined union organizing efforts in many Jiangnan cities, and the "south-bound" labor cadres sent to Wuxi tended to view the workforce and local labor activists with suspicion. The difficulties the CCP faced in establishing union organizations that Wuxi workers could trust furthermore hindered the party's efforts to win workers' support and promote labor-capital cooperation. One of the main obstacles to overcoming such "thought" problems was the shortage of politically reliable local activists who could understand, accept, and promote the party's policies. Labor cadres in Wuxi organized unemployed workers to report how difficult life could be without a job; this was meant to impress upon those employed

115. WMA D2–1–1.

116. WMA D2–1–1; James Gao, *Communist Takeover of Hangzhou*, 118–19.

the need to help their factories survive by accepting reduced wages and to reassure workers that the new government would make every effort to guarantee their livelihoods, including offering unemployment relief and providing contracts and loans to employers to maintain production and pay wages.[117]

One problem with this approach, however, was that the "activists" on hand were often independent leaders who had emerged from among the filature workers in the postwar labor movement and felt no loyalty toward the Communist Party. In the eyes of Communist labor officials, these home-grown leaders posed the greatest hindrance to getting workers to accept the low-wage policy.[118] Furthermore, the creation of new union organizations often resulted in the removal of the few women who had managed to achieve leadership positions. Their replacement with male supervisors discouraged women silk workers from participating actively in union work and revolutionary politics.[119] Indeed, before 1952 most filature workers saw little evidence in their own lives that they had been "liberated" at all, and felt little affinity with the CCP.

An example from Shanghai's Dali Filature illustrates well the conflict between filature workers' traditions of direct, autonomous action and the Communist Party leadership's process of establishing unions and promoting labor-capital cooperation. In early 1950, workers elected a female colleague, an alleged gang member named Gao Hongdi, to Dali's union committee. In an obviously biased report by union cadres at Dali to the Shanghai GLU's Organization Department, Gao appears as a bold, outspoken, even fierce woman who opposed the union's conciliatory policies and resorted to violence when others did not support her views. When the factory was working out an agreement on wage reductions to maintain production, she undermined the union's efforts by claiming, "Mao Zedong and Chiang Kai-shek are pretty much the same—whoever gives me a higher wage is better."[120] No doubt this statement expressed the feelings of many workers, but it also hindered

117. WMA D2–1–1.
118. WMA D2–1–10.
119. James Gao, *Communist Takeover of Hangzhou*, 119.
120. SMA C1–2–239.

the Party's efforts to convince employees to accept temporary wage reductions so that the filature could continue operations.

When Gao struck one of the management staff during a dispute, the factory (with the union's approval) asked her to leave work temporarily. When she showed up to work anyway, management removed her machine from the workshop. When she saw this, she became furious, striking the other reeling machines with an iron bar and saying, "if there's no work for me, then no one will get any work done!"[121] According to the union report, by destroying three machines and damaging six she brought the whole factory to a halt. Despite such behavior and her alleged record of extortion and violence, however, it took considerable effort for union officials to convince the other women in the factory that she should be replaced. After all, they had elected her, and it seemed wrong to them that the factory administration should be allowed to fire their union representative. By pointing out how Gao's violent behavior sabotaged other workers' livelihoods, however, the union leadership managed to convince them that they should replace her as union representative.[122]

The problem of independent-minded union officials was even greater in Wuxi. The northern cadres sent to organize workers in Wuxi come across in the reports as painfully insecure and even alienated in their position as leaders of the working class. Their reports exhibit, on the one hand, the arrogance of the initiated, and, on the other hand, a degree of fear and mistrust that continued to characterize the relationship between the Communist Party and the working class for years to come. This was typical of the problems that Communist Party cadres encountered in cities throughout China as they attempted simultaneously to restore economic health and represent the interests of the working class.[123]

Union work in Wuxi's filatures exhibited political problems as well. As in Shanghai, the continuing effort to curb the "leftist" excesses of

121. SMA C1–2–239.

122. SMA C1–2–239.

123. WMA D2–1–1, D2–1–10. James Gao, *Communist Takeover of Hangzhou*, 76–79, describes similar conflicts between "southbound" cadres and local people, including an example of collaboration between CCP cadres and silk capitalists at the Yifen Silk Factory in Hangzhou, to the disadvantage of silk workers.

the postwar labor movement confused and discouraged many union representatives. According to a 1953 work report by the Wuxi GLU, after correcting the "leftist" trend in 1949, some union reps became overly cautious (*suoshou suojiao*) and lacked confidence in carrying out union work. This confusion understandably led some to over-emphasize factory owners' interests in carrying out the policy of "benefiting both labor and capital," described as a "rightist" deviation. For example, once production began to recover in late 1950 and early 1951, the unions did not do enough to push employers to restore wages to earlier levels, even though many workers still faced economic difficulties. Similarly, union cadres did not do enough to promote labor insurance in Wuxi filatures, and in some cases they even sided with management in eliminating welfare benefits that had already been granted. Naturally, this led to much dissatisfaction with the unions among filature workers.[124]

One of the main shortcomings of union organizing in Wuxi, from the viewpoint of both the filature workers and the CCP, was that the newly established filature unions were quickly dominated by male supervisors antagonistic to the interests of the women workers they supervised. The Preparatory Committee of the Wuxi GLU was established on May 1, 1949, but it was more than seven months before the GLU itself was formally established on January 13, 1950, and the Preparatory Committee of the Wuxi Textile Workers Union was not established until January 20.[125] In contrast with the Shanghai Silk Workers Union, the organizing process in Wuxi filatures was very much a top-down affair in which Communist labor organizers, most of them male "southbound" cadres without local ties, attempted to reorganize and direct a labor movement that historically had been diffuse, spontaneous, and suspicious of outside influence. Due to cadres' limited experience in organizing urban workers and their lack of ties to the local labor movement, as well as the nature of labor relations in Wuxi silk filatures, Communist efforts to establish new unions met with dissatisfaction and suspicion. To workers, the party and its agents seemed to be colluding with management and focusing solely on economic recovery to the detriment of workers' interests.

124. WMA D2-1-10.
125. WMA D2-1-3.

The problem of employer-dominated unions appeared even in filatures with a relatively strong party presence. The joint state-private Huachang Filature established a union preparatory committee on August 10, 1949. Unlike Wuxi's private filatures, Huachang also established a Communist Party branch organization in September. In early November, a meeting of seven hundred representatives of filature employees established the Wuxi Silk Reeling Industry Union, with Zhang Yuezhen as chair and Huang Rongmei and Gu Bogen as deputy chairs.[126] By December, union organizing had accelerated. The Huachang Filature Union was formally established on December 4 and, within a week, unions were set up in thirty-two filatures that had restored production. By the end of the year, the Wuxi Silk Reeling Industry Union claimed more than 6,200 members, almost 80 percent of Wuxi's 8,000 filature employees. By September 1951, thirty-six of the city's thirty-nine filatures (of which six were state-run or joint state-private enterprises) had established basic-level union organizations. By that time, 10,354 people, or 82.47 percent of Wuxi's 12,555 filature employees, had become union members.[127] The proportion of Wuxi's workers brought into the new union organizations nonetheless fell short of what was achieved in Shanghai a year earlier.

Nor did the Communist Party organization in Wuxi exercise effective leadership over the city's unions. When combined with the drive to organize all industrial employees into unions and the gendered hierarchy of labor relations in Wuxi filatures, the CCP's moderate policy of "benefiting both labor and capital" actually facilitated employer control of the unions. Male managers and shop-floor supervisors who obtained positions as union representatives advanced the factory

126. WMA D2-1-3; Qian, *Wuxishi sichou gongye*, 336. These sources disagree as to whether the organization established was the union or the preparatory committee, and whether it was established on November 1 or 4. They also say almost nothing about these three individuals. Zhang Yuezhen and Huang Rongmei were women workers, and Gu Bogen was a male technician. A Zhang Yuezhen appears as a "March 8 Red Flag Award Winner" for her work as a neighborhood association secretary in Shanghai in 1979; see *Shanghai tong*. Gu became a party member in 1951 and was named a revolutionary martyr in 1958, when he was killed while working during the Great Leap Forward. See *Wuxi ji geming lieshi*.

127. WMA D2-1-3.

owners' interests, as did female supervisors, known as *chetou*, who frequently served as the agents of employers rather than supporting the interests of other women workers.[128] Such persons dominated the filature unions in Wuxi with the result that these unions were ineffective at representing workers' interests.

This calls into question the degree to which the September 1949 "Wuxi Filature Industry Labor-Capital Collective Agreement" to reduce wages was voluntary or even accepted among the rank and file. Representatives from the joint state-private Huachang Filature led the negotiation of the collective contract, but the Campaign for Democratic Reform of the unions in 1951 revealed that management staff and male shop-floor supervisors occupied most of the leadership positions in Huachang's union organization.[129] Most other filature unions in Wuxi were similarly alienated from their membership and served mainly as tools of management controlled by neither the workers nor the Communist Party.

In both state-run and private filatures, male supervisors used threats, intimidation, and manipulation to achieve dominance over the union organizations. At the Huachang Filature, most of the union small groups were dominated by management staff. Male supervisors sought as much as possible to divide, mislead, and control workers by sowing dissent through rumors and misinformation or favoring some workers over others, which made them suspicious of one another. They were also known to bribe activists and union cadres, and they publicly mocked and insulted those they could not bribe so as to undermine their status in the eyes of their fellow workers.[130] All of these phenomena had appeared when filature workers attempted to organize unions in the 1920s, and domination of the unions by managers and supervisors quickly resulted in workers becoming alienated from what were supposedly their own organizations.

128. The *chetou* in Wuxi filatures were similar to the "Number Ones" in British-owned cotton mills in Shanghai, but they were less powerful because of the male supervisors above them. See Honig, *Sisters and Strangers*.

129. WMA D2-1-11.

130. WMA D2-1-11.

Male supervisors also frequently blocked women workers' attempts to participate in political activities. At the Tailun Filature (with 220 workers), a supervisor named Cao Zirong prevented members of the women workers' committee from leaving the factory to attend a meeting, saying, "Workers who go out to attend meetings all have poor skills, those with good skills don't need to go to meetings." A supervisor in the cocoon selection workshop at the China Sericulture Company's Number Five Filature (who was later found to be a "counter-revolutionary") discouraged the workers under his supervision from joining the union, telling them, "Save your union fees and use the money to buy sweets," and closing the doors to prevent anyone from leaving.[131] Experienced at manipulating the young women who worked under them, male shop-floor supervisors were able to win positions of authority in the new revolutionary order—as union representatives, small group heads, and leaders of the workers' pickets. Two supervisors even became party propagandists, gaining the ability to shape party policy to suit whatever purpose they desired.[132] Supervisors' ability to exploit and manipulate the party's political campaigns for their own or the factory's advantage posed a serious threat to the party's relationship with filature workers in the formative years of the PRC.

By placing managers and supervisors in leading positions, filature owners exercised a high degree of control over the unions in their factories.[133] Of the 350 union committee members in Wuxi's 29 filatures with more than 200 employees, 88 were management staff (25.14 percent), 44 were male workers (12.57 percent), another 88 were female supervisors, or *chetou* (25.14 percent), and only 130 were production workers (37.14 percent). The latter were mostly "standing" machine operators or workers in departments other than silk reeling. Very few were "sitting" machine operators, and none were basin workers. Of the 66 union chairs in these 29 filatures, 23 (35 percent) were management staff. Furthermore, many production workers elected to

131. WMA D2-1-9.
132. WMA D2-1-11.
133. Yongtai Manuscript, 35–38.

positions in the union were more loyal to their supervisor-patrons than to their fellow workers.[134]

Controlling the union organizations benefited filature owners. When Labor Bureau officials went to the Xintai Filature to register employees for labor insurance in February 1951, the union chair (a man named Kang Zhengliang, who had his union membership revoked several months later during the Democratic Reform) told them that the filature's employees had decided to refuse labor insurance to help the owner overcome financial difficulties. Factory owners could obstruct workers applying for sick leave or assistance with medical bills by requiring that they fill out five sets of forms. The union chair at the New Guangchang Filature, who was a relative of the owner and infamous for abusing the workers under his supervision, told the employees, "With all your demands, how much has the owner lost? He will have to shut the factory soon, so why don't you all go home and fill your bellies?"[135] This was a perversion of the policy of "benefiting both labor and capital," but given the lack of worker oversight in Wuxi filatures (in contrast with the *minping* teams in Shanghai silk weaving factories), it was easy for those in power to use the policy to play upon workers' fears of unemployment.

The blame for this situation was placed squarely on the leadership of the Silk Reeling Industry Union, which, it was said, had erroneously relied upon management staff to "educate" the workers and had not mobilized the "worker masses."[136] This accords with the assessment that union organizing in Wuxi's silk reeling industry was a top-down process with little input from the rank and file. The problem of employer domination of union organizations was clearly far more serious in Wuxi's silk filatures than in the city's other industries. In the autumn of 1951, only about five percent of Wuxi's basic-level union organizations were controlled by employers citywide, and only about eight percent of all union cadres were considered loyal to management.[137]

134. WMA D2-1-11.
135. WMA D2-1-11.
136. WMA D2-1-11.
137. WMA D2-1-10.

The much higher proportion of filature unions that were dominated by employers and supervisors indicates the degree to which intense and sometimes violent gender conflict impeded class cooperation and exacerbated class conflict in Jiangnan silk filatures. In Shanghai's silk weaving industry, most loom operators were men, and many factory owners had been weavers themselves. Silk weavers often shared with their employers a common language, culture, and background in northern Zhejiang towns, and in some cases both workers and managers belonged to the Communist Party. In contrast, in Wuxi filatures, the divide between male supervisors and young female workers was much greater. The two groups had almost nothing in common, and their relationships were characterized by exploitation, manipulation, abuse, and resentment. There was far more at stake for male supervisors in filature workshops, who stood to lose more of their authority and privileges through the empowerment of women workers than did employers and industrial managers more generally. Communist labor officials in Wuxi, usually male cadres from rural North China with a limited understanding of local conditions, often failed to appreciate the significance of patriarchy and gender relations in their work, a blind spot that significantly impacted how these women experienced the revolution.[138]

Unsurprisingly, the accomplishments of the Wuxi Silk Reeling Industry Union in the first years of the People's Republic reflected the priorities of employers and the revolutionary state more than those of workers. In August 1949, the Wuxi GLU convened a Workers Representative Conference, which adopted a document titled "The Basic Policy of the Wuxi Labor Movement." The union's basic policy was summarized as, "Unite to maintain and transform production and overcome difficulties to achieve the gradual improvement of the

138. James Gao makes this point very well. The few female cadres sent to Hangzhou were the wives of leading south-bound cadres, and they were usually given "feminine" jobs such as working with children and women. As a result, in both Hangzhou and Wuxi leading labor officials were overwhelmingly male and from northern provinces, which adversely affected their ability to understand and lead women workers in Jiangnan filatures. James Gao, *Communist Takeover of Hangzhou*, chapter 7, "Women Cadres," 185–215.

economic situation."[139] A meeting of union cadres on October 19 established a work plan that included recruitment, organizing, and welfare work, as well as a "campaign to practice economy in production," one of the earliest references to the kind of production campaign that would become commonplace during the Korean War. The Wuxi GLU also handled numerous other tasks on behalf of the new government, including mobilizing workers to eliminate speculation in silver dollars and organizing a drive for the purchase of victory bonds beginning on January 6, 1950.[140] Some state-run enterprises, including the joint state-private Huachang Filature, formally established factory management committees, and a few private filatures established labor-capital consultative conferences, which were required according to the Trade Union Law. In practice, however, neither form of "democratic management" (the Chinese Communist term for institutions that included worker participation in factory management) was very widespread or effective in the city's filatures, and later GLU reports describe management practices as abusive, oppressive, and "feudal."

The failure of Wuxi labor cadres to adequately address the main concerns and difficulties of filature workers is representative of more general trends in union work in the early 1950s. Communist labor cadres often found it difficult to reconcile the conflicting priorities of economic recovery and revolutionary transformation or "liberation." Union officials struggled to unite the pursuit of economic recovery with the goal of improving workers' lives. This was especially true when it came to women workers. Despite the CCP leadership's consistent emphasis on women's liberation and the need to attend to the specific needs of women workers, in practice it was difficult for union cadres to address women workers' concerns adequately under the conditions and potentially contradictory policy goals of the early 1950s. Gender, then, was a critical factor that frequently determined how different groups of workers fared in the process of revolution; and the ways in which CCP leaders and party cadres conceived of and represented women's interests often led to misunderstanding or neglect of those interests.

139. WMA D2-1-10.
140. WMA D2-1-3, D2-1-10.

Women, Workers, and Communist Revolution

In the months following Liberation, China's revolutionary leaders worked to establish unions and to get women workers to participate actively in economic recovery and politics. "Woman work," to use Delia Davin's translation of the term "*funü gongzuo*," was supposed to be a vitally important aspect of union work. Getting union cadres to take "woman work" seriously, however, proved difficult, if not impossible. For starters, both male and female union cadres tended to view women as ideologically backward compared with men. Cai Chang, a woman and a national leader in "woman work" in the unions, stated in a 1950 report that it was especially difficult to mobilize Chinese women for union work because they had to defer to their parents or husbands and could not be "their own masters." She stated that it was necessary to carry out education work among women in industry to "raise their consciousness" and eliminate the mentality of "relying on men to carry out union work."[141] Such passivity was thought to be a product of women's double oppression under the old society. Older workers, although praised as "veterans on the production front," were considered "ideologically confused" because they had been raised in "feudal" society. Younger workers, on the other hand, were seen as more active and enthusiastic about politics and union activities. But union reports criticized younger women as vain, liking to "make themselves pretty," and lacking in "character" (*gexing*), such that they feared hardship, did not value labor, and had certain "*petite bourgeois* characteristics."[142] This is but one example of the Communists' penchant for defining anything corrupt, decadent, or feminine as "bourgeois," a prejudice with obvious negative consequences for "woman work" in Chinese unions.

Given prevailing attitudes, it is perhaps unsurprising that many union cadres resisted the CCP leadership's emphasis on "woman work" in party and union policy. An "ACFTU Resolution on Strengthening Union Work Concerning Women Workers" promulgated on September 14, 1950, stated that it was necessary to have dedicated women workers' departments (*nügongbu*) to "prevent the omission of the particular

141. SMA C1-2-333.
142. SMA C1-2-854, C1-2-333.

needs of the broad masses of women workers from ordinary union work." At the same time, China's labor leaders insisted that if "woman work" were left entirely to the women workers' departments, without the involvement of union committees at all levels, then "in practice the women workers' department will become a 'women's union,' dividing the working class into two parts according to sex."[143] The resolution expressed the need for dedicated women workers' departments in municipal and industrial-level unions. Factory-level unions, however, were not necessarily required to establish dedicated departments, and only factories with more than three hundred women workers were required to appoint a full-time cadre for "woman work."

The women workers' departments were expected to ensure attention to women's interests by overseeing the other union departments and checking reports and other documents sent to higher-level union organizations. In the event of neglect of women's issues, the *nügongbu* had the right to offer suggestions and criticisms. There were no procedures established for doing this, however, and union committees frequently ignored the women workers' departments. Many union organizations did not have a full-time cadre devoted to "woman work," and most did not even establish a women workers' department.[144] According to a 1950 report by the Women Workers' Department of the Wuxi GLU, this phenomenon was pervasive and serious throughout China. Where established, women workers' departments were poorly funded and often did not have the resources to address the many pressing problems they discovered.[145]

In assessing the reasons for neglect of women's interests in the unions, reports blamed "the remnants of the feudal ideology of the old society."[146] There were other, more objective impediments to advancing women workers' interests, however. In her 1950 report, Cai Chang argued that if women workers made excessive demands on employers while there was still a large pool of unemployed men, it would incline factory owners not to hire women, whose demands for maternity leave

143. SMA C1-2-333.
144. SMA C1-2-333.
145. WMA D2-1-6.
146. SMA C1-2-334.

and childcare facilities could impose a heavy burden on struggling enterprises.[147] As Phyllis Andors put it, "Factories were reluctant to hire women because of the expense and effort of providing social welfare services that had to be made available; women were used as unskilled laborers who could be shifted from job to job and were most expendable in any contracting labor market situation; women did not receive equal pay for equal work, and educated and experienced women workers were often not promoted."[148]

In keeping with these priorities, a meeting of women cadres in Wuxi textiles mills on March 23, 1950, adopted a resolution that the department's work should "strengthen education concerning practicing economy in production."[149] A report on "woman work" in Wuxi unions six months later described women's main accomplishments of the previous year as "protecting their own factories with the attitude of 'masters' (*zhurenweng*), as well as purchasing government bonds, supporting the army, and launching a campaign to collect signatures for peace."[150] The report also emphasized that there had been many women labor models selected in Wuxi's match industry, cotton textiles, and silk filatures. Many women had received technical training as well as literacy and political education. Some had furthermore received training at Wuxi's Workers Cadre School as part of an effort to address the shortage of qualified (and politically reliable) women labor leaders.

Responding to criticisms of "leftism" and admonishments not to demand too much on behalf of women workers, union cadres frequently went too far in prioritizing class cooperation and improving production to the point of entirely neglecting women workers' interests. This would seem to be another case of the party's vision of women workers diverging greatly from their practical situation, goals, and interests. One of the most prominent criticisms of "woman work" in the unions decried the lack of concern for women workers' health, particularly complications in childbirth. The rate of miscarriages among

147. SMA C1–2–333.
148. Andors, *Unfinished Liberation*, 43.
149. WMA D2–1–3.
150. WMA D2–1–6.

factory workers was very high, even in Shanghai, and several women in that city had died in childbirth over the previous year, including one at the Dali Silk Filature. Women cadres complained that this tragedy was allowed to pass lightly and the union's response was inadequate.[151] A September 1950 report by the Women Workers' Department of the Wuxi GLU stated that the unions had failed to address issues of great concern to women workers, such as working conditions and health care, and that this had diminished their trust in the union organization. The fact that some women had to give birth in their workshops, or even on the street, was an indication of how serious the situation was.[152]

One very important initiative on behalf of working-class women and families in Shanghai was the expansion of childcare facilities. Union organizations in Shanghai improved and expanded existing crèches and nurseries, in many cases making them available to working-class families for the first time. By May 1950, the number of nurseries operated by factories in Shanghai had increased from 36 to 58, with a capacity of 4,353 children, and the number of nursery staff had increased from 204 to 488. By the fall of 1950, factories throughout China had established 1,830 nurseries capable of providing care for 8,917 children.[153] Retraining existing nursery staff and training new childcare workers was the top priority, pursued jointly by the Women's Federation and the unions. By 1952, more than 85 percent of caretakers in Shanghai had received specialized training, with 515 new nursery staff trained and almost five hundred existing staff receiving political education and literacy training as well.[154] By October 1952, Shanghai had 147 nurseries with places for 10,370 children, and the quality of these

151. SMA C1–2–333. By 1952, due in part to the women workers' departments' efforts to promote and make available modern birthing techniques, the number of miscarriages and deaths in childbirth had fallen dramatically. SMA C1–2–854.

152. WMA D2–1–6.

153. *Laodongbao*, 1 Jun. 1950; WMA D1–2–6. Elisabeth Croll reports that, by 1952, the number of nurseries in factories, mines, commercial enterprises, government offices, and schools had increased by twenty-two times over 1949. Croll, *Feminism and Socialism in China*, 247, citing an article, "Mother and Child Care" in *People's China*, 1 Jun. 1953.

154. SMA C1–2–333, C1–2–854.

facilities had also improved dramatically, especially in terms of children's health and nutrition. One report claimed that "these nurseries now at least allow mothers to work peacefully, which has increased production," and provided several examples from Shanghai's cotton textiles factories.[155] Another stated that provision of superior childcare facilities "has also created a healthy foundation for the next generation of builders of socialism."[156]

Despite these accomplishments, however, many problems remained in the provision of healthcare, childcare, and other benefits for women workers.[157] The number of places in childcare facilities for working-class families was chronically insufficient. Providing facilities for ten thousand children in Shanghai by 1952 entailed a significant increase, but even this could not meet the needs of Shanghai's tens of thousands of working-class families. Quality and personnel problems plagued factory nurseries throughout the 1950s. Factories often reassigned trained and professional nursery staff to other work, substituting them with untrained workers from the factory floor. Nursery staff generally worked at least one hour longer than factory workers, often working thirteen-hour days, and there was no standardized pay scale for childcare workers until 1954. Throughout the 1950s there remained a pressing need not only for more nurseries for infants, but also for more boarding schools and neighborhood nurseries for preschool-age children.[158]

The expansion of nurseries for working-class families in Wuxi lagged behind similar projects in Shanghai. By September 1950, the joint state-private Huachang Filature and the China Sericulture Number Two Filature had both set up nurseries for workers' children.[159] The Yongtai Filature established a health clinic and nursery in 1951.[160] By

155. SMA C1-2-333.

156. SMA C1-2-854.

157. For a report on neglect of women's health that resulted in death and disability in a state-run tussah silk filature in Liaoning Province as late as 1955, see "Duidai gongren de elie taidu" (A despicable attitude in the treatment of workers) in *People's Daily*, 22 Jan. 1956.

158. SMA C1-2-854; Croll, *Feminism and Socialism in China*, 248; Davin, *Woman Work*, 110, 182–85; Andors, *Unfinished Liberation*, 43.

159. WMA D1-2-6.

160. Yongtai Manuscript, 36.

1952, there were seventeen nurseries in Wuxi filatures with 136 caretakers capable of providing for 580 children.[161] A June 1952 report on the China Sericulture Number Two Filature's nursery in the *Sunan ribao* described the nursery's five rooms as "brightly painted in white, with fifty little brown cribs."[162] The nursery had only six staff, however, which would have limited the number of places for children to around sixty. A 1953 work report counted a total of twenty-five nurseries in the city, which may have increased Wuxi's total childcare capacity to nearly nine hundred children.[163] But this fell far short of what was needed. Lack of funds was the main constraint, while the limited establishment of women workers' departments in the unions also impeded the expansion of childcare provision.[164] Without facilities to replace women's labor in working class families, the goal of liberating women through factory employment would remain a dead letter.

Another important initiative the women workers' departments pursued in cooperation with other mass organizations was marriage reform. Promulgated May 1, 1950, the Marriage Law was one of the CCP's first major pieces of legislation.[165] The Law provided for freedom of marriage for men and women, prohibited all forms of coercion, arranged marriages, bride purchases, dowries, child betrothal, bigamy, and concubinage, and protected the right of widows to remarry. The law also granted freedom of divorce for both men and women, even in cases where only one party desired divorce, once efforts at mediation and reconciliation had failed.[166] In urban industry, the women workers' departments played a central role in promulgating and implementing the Marriage Law. Divorce became such an important issue for women workers' departments that one woman cadre in Shanghai reported that it was "the main focus of the work of women workers' departments and

161. Qian, *Wuxishi sichou gongye*, 240–41.

162. *Sunan ribao*, 1 Jun. 1952.

163. WMA D2-1-10.

164. *Laodongbao*, 1 Jun. 1950.

165. The Marriage Law has been the subject of considerable research by Western scholars. See Croll, *Feminism and Socialism in China*, 230–38; Ono, *Chinese Women*, 177–84; Davin, *Woman Work*, 84–108; and Diamant, *Revolutionizing the Family*.

166. *Marriage Law of the People's Republic of China*.

union committees."[167] Nonetheless, many middle-aged women workers with children viewed divorce as a threat. Interviews record statements like, "I'm forty-six years old and I have three children. If my husband divorces me, who will want me?" Other married women employed in Shanghai industry expressed similar attitudes toward divorce in union surveys in 1950.[168]

If divorce was the most prominent issue among women workers in Shanghai, child marriage and attendant abuses were more prominent in the Wuxi filatures. At the Yongtai Filature, for example, quite a few of the basin workers were girls from poor families who had been sold as "child daughters-in-law" (*tongyangxi*). Their future in-laws sent them to work in the filatures until they came of age. With the promulgation of the Marriage Law, the women workers' department at Yongtai organized educational meetings and established a Marriage Law Inspection Committee, which soon received a flood of requests for assistance in resolving marriage issues. This work included mediating negotiations to arrange for girls to return to their parents. In one case, a silk reeler named Liu Meidi had been a *tongyangxi* herself and had suffered such abuse at the hands of her husband and mother-in-law that she fled and remarried. Her second husband's family was very poor, however, and she was eventually forced to sell her daughter into the same situation. Discussion of the Marriage Law caused her to recall her own suffering, and through union-organized negotiations she brought her daughter home again.[169]

The Communist Party's efforts to reform marriage practices and promote women's equality encountered fierce opposition. The rise in

167. SMA C1-2-334. The number of divorces in China increased dramatically from 1950 to 1952. The number of divorce cases heard by the courts increased from 186,167 in 1950, to 409,500 in 1951, to 398,243 in the first half of 1952. Of those applying for divorce nearly 75 percent were women, and the proportion was even higher in urban centers like Shanghai. This contrasts with the prevailing prejudices against women who divorced their husbands and the difficulties women faced after divorce. As Ono Kazuko remarks, "For a woman to pursue divorce was virtually high treason against a natural order." Ono, *Chinese Women*, 179–80.

168. SMA C1-2-854.

169. Yongtai Manuscript, 40–41.

divorces resulting from the Marriage Law led some union cadres to refer sarcastically to the women workers' departments as the "divorce departments."[170] Whereas male union cadres might typically pay little attention to "woman work," many actively opposed implementation of the Marriage Law.[171] A 1953 report on the implementation of the law in Wuxi describes "feudal thought" among union cadres as the most important impediment. This is understandable, given the high percentage of male supervisors among filature union officials. In the case of Chen Baozhen, a silk reeler at the Yongtai Filature whose husband (possibly another worker at Yongtai) abused her, the union chair blamed Chen for causing problems and refused to support the women workers' department in helping her. Such cases accumulated at the factory until it became necessary to hold a meeting to "educate" male union cadres at Yongtai. Although the official Yongtai factory history claims great successes in reversing child marriages, the 1953 report states that arranged marriages continued and often resulted in violence and abuse.[172] Clearly, filature unions dominated by male supervisors hostile to the interests of women workers were ineffective at protecting and advancing women's interests.

A 1951 report on "woman work" and marriage reform in the unions points to resistance by union cadres as the greatest impediment:

> Some cadres, when they run into their own problems, do not serve as exemplars and instead violate or distort the Marriage Law, which creates an undesirable influence among the masses . . . [these ways of thinking] ignore the masses' interests, do not show concern for the masses' day-to-day needs, and are a concrete expression of the disease of bureaucratism.[173]

170. SMA C1–2–611.

171. One report by a woman union cadre in Shanghai stated that "male workers and the unions collaborate to ignore women workers' grievances, and the unions unite with male workers to not resolve women workers' problems." SMA C1–2–334.

172. Yongtai Manuscript, 40; WMA D2–1–16.

173. SMA C1–2–611.

The report concludes that despite the seriousness of marriage problems among working-class people, and the party leadership's emphatic support for marriage reform, many union cadres continued to "turn a deaf ear and a blind eye" to women workers' demands when these conflicted with patriarchal traditions and male privilege. Women cadres sought to overcome this kind of opposition by emphasizing the benefits of "woman work" in the unions to the factory's productivity. For example, one report on resistance to marriage reform states, "This situation seriously hinders family harmony and social order, and seriously hinders the project of national economic construction."[174] Union reports emphasized that resolving family and marriage problems increased workers' enthusiasm and diligence, resulting in a "high tide" of production. Some of these women, including Liu Meidi, even achieved the status of advanced producers.[175] A 1950 report from Shanghai claimed that, especially for cases of spousal abuse, once the problem was resolved, women workers "showed progress such as actively participating in union work and resolutely studying literacy and technique."[176]

The campaign to enforce the Marriage Law intensified in the second half of 1951, with Premier Zhou Enlai issuing a "Directive on Investigating the Situation Concerning the Implementation of the Marriage Law" in the *People's Daily* on September 29.[177] The directive was especially critical of cadres who ignored abuses, protected perpetrators, or violated the law themselves; and it called upon party cadres at all levels to lead the courts, police, government agencies, educational institutions, and mass organizations in upholding the law. Despite these efforts, however, the situation had not improved greatly by 1952, and active resistance continued.[178] A 1952 report by the Shanghai GLU Women Workers' Department complained of ongoing resistance, stating, "We have not sufficiently implemented the spirit of the Marriage

174. SMA C1–2–611.
175. Yongtai Manuscript, 40–41.
176. SMA C1–2–334.
177. *People's Daily*, 29 Sep. 1951.
178. Croll, *Feminism and Socialism in China*, 235.

Law, so, at present, there still occur many tragic incidents of suicide or murder due to the lack of freedom in marriage."[179]

Continued resistance to marriage reform stemming from entrenched patriarchy and male chauvinism in the party and unions eventually forced the CCP leadership to modify the campaign. When the party renewed the marriage reform campaign in March 1953, it was weaker and more cautious than earlier efforts. A "State Council Directive Concerning the Thorough Implementation of the Marriage Law" issued February 1, 1953, criticizes the Women's Federation for its "narrow focus" on women's interests and for viewing the Marriage Law exclusively in terms of women's rights.[180] A 1953 program for union work in Wuxi makes no mention of the Marriage Law.[181]

Conclusion

The Chinese Communists accomplished a great deal in their first two years in power. They established their administration throughout China, and most employers and workers joined new, party-led "mass organizations," offering at least nominal support for the party's goals, policies, and ideology. The Communists expanded and improved the system of state-contracted production inherited from the Nationalists while establishing a new currency, reducing inflation, and boosting employment.

Despite its initially limited influence, the CCP quickly won the support of most urban industrial workers. New labor laws protected workers' livelihoods even as the party called on workers to accept short-term sacrifices in exchange for the promise of economic recovery and long-term growth. Nearly all Chinese workers joined the new union

179. SMA C1-2-854. An investigation in 1951 found that there had been more than 10,000 suicides and murders related to marriage issues in East and Central China since the implementation of the law. In the East China region, by 1952 the figure had reached 11,500 and by 1955 it was estimated that there were 70–80,000 such incidents throughout China every year. Ono, *Chinese Women*, 181.

180. Croll, *Feminism and Socialism in China*, 236–38. On the relationship between the Women's Federations and the unions, see Wang Zheng, *Finding Women*, 30–35.

181. WMA D1-1-10.

organizations established after 1949, but their leaders exhibited a wide range of attitudes and capabilities depending on industrial sector, labor relations, historical legacies of labor organizing, and local resources. Some unions, such as the Shanghai Silk Workers Union, achieved impressive gains for their constituents. Other unions, such as the Wuxi Filature Workers Union, became dominated by employers and male supervisors hostile to the party's more liberationist goals. These disparities are readily visible in workers' differential access to welfare provisions and other benefits of the revolution.

The Chinese revolution of 1949 was clearly a gendered process, even if the party's leaders and cadres did not always recognize this. The party's goals and methods, especially encouraging class cooperation through mass organizations such as unions, disadvantaged many workers who were struggling to advance their own interests. The demands of New Democracy discredited and even prohibited filature workers' traditions of action and resistance. The relative neglect of issues of importance to women workers, despite the consistent emphasis on women's liberation in party policy and propaganda, derived from the party's methods and Chinese traditions of patriarchy and male privilege, and this had negative consequences for working-class women. Because of persistent gender prejudice, women continued to be politically, economically, and socially disadvantaged despite the many changes brought about by the Communist revolution. Traditional patriarchy, combined with the party's New Democratic policies, inhibited the revolutionary transformation of labor relations and working conditions in Jiangnan filatures, and for these women workers, liberation remained an elusive goal.

As we will see in the following chapters, the very different ways in which these two groups of workers—Shanghai silk weavers and Wuxi filature workers—experienced the revolution are directly related to their localities, histories, and working conditions, especially the sharply contrasting factory regimes in place. But the divergent experiences of these two groups of workers also derive from gender differences and the party's limited capacity to apply its own critique of gender roles in old China to modern industry. Traditions of male privilege, a filature factory regime based on patriarchal violence and subordination of women workers to male capitalist management, and the hostility of party and union cadres to the goal of women's liberation meant that women filature workers faced great disadvantages in pursuing the benefits of the revolution. In contrast, as the next chapter describes, at least in the early years of the PRC male silk weavers in Shanghai achieved significant progress in participatory management and welfare benefits.

CHAPTER FOUR

"Weavers of Revolution"

From Conflict to Cooperation in the Shanghai Silk Weaving Industry

As their fortunes began to decline in the late 1920s, Shanghai's "weavers of revolution"[1] struggled through a global depression, foreign invasion, an inflationary crisis, civil war, and Communist revolution. By the winter of 1949–50 it seemed that the silk weaving industry's situation could get no worse. If it were not for regulations prohibiting factories from discontinuing production and laying off their workers, most Shanghai weaving workshops would likely have closed their doors. Labor relations were worse than at any time since the strikes and street battles of the 1930s. Finances were in chaos, market demand was vanishing, and raw materials were nearly impossible to obtain even at inflated prices.

The Communist seizure of power alleviated this situation somewhat. The China Sericulture Company provided production contracts for many factories, which helped to ameliorate the intense labor-capital conflict of 1949. The new unions offered some relief for unemployed silk workers, and the CCP's policies fostered the restoration of production and employment in Shanghai's silk industry. But the Nationalist blockade and ongoing economic difficulties, combined with the aerial bombing of the Shanghai Electric Power Company on February 6, 1950, threatened the final demise of this once thriving industry.

1. The title of this chapter is taken from the book by Peter Winn, *Weavers of Revolution*.

Despite such unfavorable conditions, by 1951 Shanghai's silk industry was expanding once again and moving toward recovery. There were several factors at play, including the economic and commercial policies of the revolutionary government, the revival of sericulture in the countryside, and the redirection of exports to the Socialist Bloc countries during the Korean War. One of the most politically significant and intriguing aspects of the silk weaving industry's recovery, however, was the degree of cooperation between workers and employers under the Communist Party's New Democratic policies.

Despite the party's efforts to promote labor-capital cooperation in pursuit of economic recovery, this phenomenon was by no means universal in Chinese industry in the early 1950s. Although the policies promoted (and to some extent implemented) in Yangzi Delta cities were broadly similar, different groups of workers were able to take advantage of these changes to varying degrees. Initiatives such as welfare provision, "democratic management," and the implementation of the 1950 Marriage Law produced different results depending on locality, industry, and gender. Results were influenced by the historical legacies and organizational capacities of different groups of workers, the material and political resources available in different localities, the state of labor relations and the capacity for communication and cooperation between workers and their employers, and finally, the timing of implementation and the strength of production and marketing in a given industry.

For relatively well-organized and well-connected workers such as the Shanghai silk weavers, the combination of revolutionary political power and new institutions for labor-capital cooperation presented an unprecedented opportunity to advance their collective interests. This chapter examines the establishment, accomplishments, and significance of the Shanghai Silk Weaving Industry Labor-Capital Consultative Conference, a novel form of participatory management that greatly benefited both silk workers and their employers as they strove to overcome extreme difficulties in 1950. Shanghai's silk weavers represent the best-case scenario of historically privileged workers who were able to take advantage of the political revolution to advance their interests. But most groups of workers, such as Wuxi's filature workers, had almost no experience with "democratic management" and gained none of the benefits of this revolutionary institution. The consequences of these differences would become an important, if hidden, feature of Chinese state socialism for decades to come.

The February Sixth Bombing and the Expansion of State-Contracted Silk Weaving

During the postwar economic crisis, it was not uncommon for working-class men and women to resort to direct action, including factory occupations, "surroundings," and even kidnapping and violence, to demand redress from their employers. When the Communists seized power in the spring of 1949, their rhetoric and policies promoting labor-capital cooperation reduced conflict to some degree. But even after the establishment of the People's Republic in October, many workers remained skeptical. In Shanghai's silk weaving industry, years of economic crisis had created a very tense and conflicted situation that mere rhetoric could hardly reverse. It took an act of war, the bombing of Shanghai's main electric power plant on February 6, 1950, to motivate workers and employers in this beleaguered industry to abandon the tactics and methods of the recent past and to adopt the New Democratic policy of labor-capital cooperation through the establishment of the city's first industry-level labor-capital consultative conference.

During the winter of 1949–50, Chiang Kai-shek's air force, flying US-supplied bombers, threatened international shipping and coastal cities from bases in Taiwan and the Zhoushan Islands. Between October 1949 and February 1950, Shanghai suffered twenty-six air raids, a striking contrast with the relative lack of violence in the spring of 1949.[2] Although these air raids had little practical effect on the Communists' military position on the mainland, their psychological impact on Shanghai's populace was serious. The blockade and continued vulnerability of China's coastal cities undermined the Communist Party's claims to legitimacy and emboldened its enemies, reminding everyone that the Nationalists could return just as suddenly as they had left.

The February 6, 1950, bombing resulted in the first major industrial damage to Shanghai since 1937. On that day, fourteen B-24 and B-25

2. Xiaoming Zhang, *Red Wings over the Yalu*, 79; *People's Daily*, 4 Mar. 1950.

bombers (possibly with the aid of secret agents sent from Taiwan the previous August)[3] flew four sorties over Shanghai, severely damaging water and electric power facilities, including Shanghai's main power plant, as well as an important shipyard.[4] The bombing resulted in at least five hundred deaths and displaced some fifty thousand refugees.[5] Communist Party Chairman Mao Zedong, in Moscow negotiating a treaty of alliance with the Soviet Union, formally requested Soviet support in the air defense of Shanghai, and on February 13, Stalin ordered the Ministry of Defense to begin preparations to send air force and anti-aircraft troops to China. The Soviet forces arrived with the returning Chairman, and immediately set about the defense of Shanghai.[6] By March, Soviet pilots engaged Nationalist bombers, recording their first kill on March 14. The air war intensified in April, when the Nationalists stationed ten B-25 bombers and thirty P-51 mustangs on the Zhoushan and Daishan Islands. When the new Soviet MiG jets took to the air on April 28, however, the Soviets gained a decisive advantage. By the end of June, the Soviet airmen had secured Shanghai for the Communists.[7]

The most significant consequences of the February Sixth Bombing for Shanghai's workers and factory owners resulted from the destruction of the Shanghai Electric Power Company's main generators, which provided electricity to thousands of factories. Combined with the ongoing blockade, floods, and declining rural purchasing power, as well as reduced inflation and stable prices (which created recession conditions in the spring of 1950), the power plant's destruction severely aggravated Shanghai's economic crisis. Numerous factory closings and mass layoffs left more than 150,000 unemployed by April.[8] The ACFTU mobilized workers throughout China to donate a day's wages for the

3. *People's Daily*, 10 Feb. 1950.

4. *People's Daily*, 9 Feb. 1950 and 6 Mar. 1950.

5. Perry, "Workers' Patrols," 157, 346n71, citing SMA B120-1-69; Zhang Jinping, "Baiwan zhigong," 182–84. Xiaoming Zhang gives a total of more than 1,400 fatalities, citing a 2001 report in *Zhongguo guofang bao* by Jiang Tianran, Chief of Staff of the Shanghai Air Defense Headquarters, established March 1, 1950.

6. *People's Daily*, 17 Feb. 1950.

7. Xiaoming Zhang, *Red Wings over the Yalu*, 79–84. Altogether, between March and October 1950, Soviet pilots flew 238 missions, claiming a total of eight enemy aircraft shot down. See also Hooton, *The Greatest Tumult*, 170–75.

8. Lin Wei, "Shanghai Industry and Commerce," 35.

relief of unemployed workers in Shanghai, and the response was very positive.[9]

Shanghai's silk weaving factories, large and small, almost universally employed electric-powered looms. By eliminating the factories' main source of power, the attack dealt a severe blow to silk producers already suffering from short supplies, lack of circulating capital, and shrinking markets. Factory owners who had little enthusiasm for continuing business but who had been forced to maintain operations due to party policy in 1949 took this opportunity to close their doors and dismiss their employees, claiming, "The Nationalists bombed the power plant! What can we do about it?"[10]

Such claims were of little solace to silk workers threatened with unemployment. In the winter of 1949–50 many Shanghai workers were frightened and angry, afraid they might lose their jobs and wondering if the air raids did not herald the imminent return of Chiang Kai-shek and his army. The crisis led to an upsurge in labor disputes (*laodong jiufen*) over the following months, including protests, strikes, and factory occupations, as well as "surroundings" and petitions. In comparison with the labor unrest of the late 1940s, however, this wave of disputes more often involved dialogue and working through official channels rather than violence. For the year 1950, the Shanghai GLU recorded 9,480 labor disputes involving a total of 819,072 persons. Consistent with historical trends, the number of disputes was very high leading up to the Spring Festival holiday, with 1,231 incidents in January, but it dropped off in February, only to rise again in March and April due to the loss of electric power (see table 4.1). The decline in labor disputes from May through December indicates the effectiveness of the measures adopted to address the crisis.

Fearing for their livelihoods, silk workers not only brought disputes before the Labor Bureau, but also turned to earlier methods the CCP considered illegitimate, such as "surroundings" and factory

9. *People's Daily*, 18 Apr. 1950. For an April 14 letter from the Shanghai GLU to the ACFTU appealing for aid for Shanghai's unemployed, see *People's Daily*, 17 Apr. 1950.

10. SMA C1-2-231.

Table 4.1
Labor disputes in Shanghai, January–December 1950

Month	Number of disputes
January	1,231
February	736
March	1,077
April	1,108
May	826
June	694
July	662
August	820
September	599
October	616
November	654
December	457
Total 1950	9,480

SOURCE: SMA C1–2–232.

occupations, to demand that their employers restore production.[11] Despite the danger of conflict between workers and employers, however, the veteran labor leaders of the Shanghai Silk Workers Union were able to rally support for a program of labor-capital cooperation that would maintain production and employment, protect the interests of factory owners and the livelihoods of workers, and overcome both practical problems and the psychological dangers of fear and discouragement. In a speech to workers at the Xinchang Silk Weaving Factory, a union official exhorted workers not to allow the enemy to succeed in disrupting production and spreading fear. The silk workers, he said, should not give in to terror but should act rationally and think of ways to deal with the "temporary difficulties and limited suffering" caused by the bombing. The union cadre encouraged his audience to think of these

11. "Sizhiye laozi xieshang," 30. See also Frazier, *Chinese Industrial Workplace*, 102–3.

Table 4.2

Production and employment in the Shanghai silk weaving industry, 1950

Month	Number of factories registered	Number of factories operating/shut down	Number of looms operating/shut down	Employment staff/workers	Production (bolts)
January	316	181/135	3,847/1,808	1,319/5,269	25,491
February	357	145/212	1,784/4,184	1,567/5,496	5,000
March	353	74/279	777/5,078	855/5,328	7,275
April	333	67/266	1,147/4,252	844/4,343	7,640
May	347	103/244	1,367/4,268	894/4,078	13,430
June	351	145/206	1,623/3,917	745/3,887	17,550
July	292	155/137	1,639/3,126	761/4,022	18,557
August*	350	180/120	1,922/2,842	832/4,408	21,457
September	359	221/88	2,367/2,573	921/5,309	26,172
October	378	257/70	2,669/2,422	1,061/5,960	34,080
November	397	279/63	2,893/2,240	1,250/6,435	38,932
December	384	290/61	2,999/2,306	1,242/6,314	42,027

*Beginning in August, the number of factories is higher than the total for factories operating and shut down because it also includes those factories that had long since ceased operations and had applied to withdraw from the Silk Industry Association. Source: SMA S39–4–44.

attacks as indication that the enemy was on his last legs and would soon be defeated.[12]

Not all of Shanghai's silk weaving factories lost power after the bombing. The Lou Family's Yunlin Factory was located in the former French Concession, where the power plant remained undamaged.[13] Some of the larger factories, including Meiya and Dacheng, had purchased their own power-generating equipment after the war, when electricity supply was unreliable. The generator at the Meiya Number Four Factory, however, was only sufficient to power twenty looms. Under the union's leadership, the factory worked out an arrangement similar to past practices for "waiting for warp and weft." The factory and the union organized living subsidies and arranged to feed everyone at the factory, and even mobilized personnel for air defense and fire safety.[14]

With electric power rationed first to priority sectors of the economy, the silk weaving industry was expected to make sacrifices. For most Shanghai silk factories, the loss of electric power, combined with the industry's ongoing crisis, was a devastating blow. As table 4.2 shows, production plummeted so that by the end of March, only 74 factories were fully operational, and 279 factories, with a total of 5,078 looms, had shut down. Total production fell from more than 25,000 bolts in January to just 5,000 bolts in February.[15]

Under different political leadership, such a crisis might have resulted in the industry's collapse, causing widespread deprivation and violence. But this was not the case in Shanghai in 1950. Despite the intensification of the silk industry's crisis resulting from the bombing, production recovered quickly and continued to improve. By the end of April, electricity supply had been restored sufficiently to meet the needs of industrial production,[16] a development reflected in silk weaving

12. SMA C16-2-287. State media also channeled the outrage of Shanghai citizens into purchases of government bonds, which skyrocketed after the attack. *People's Daily*, 9 & 16 Feb. 1950.

13. Interview with Lou Erpin and Lou Erzheng, 19 April 2004.

14. Interview with Qian Binhua, 12 Feb. 2004; *People's Daily*, 9 & 13 Feb. 1950.

15. SMA S39-4-44.

16. He Li, "Getting through Difficulties Is Glorious," 31. (Originally published in *People's Daily*, 28 Apr. 1950.)

production statistics. Few factories closed permanently because of the bombing, and by September production exceeded January levels.

If employment and production had not recovered quickly, the February Sixth Bombing might have ended the experiments in state-contracted silk weaving begun the previous November. The industry's recovery was due to several factors, including the rapid restoration of power, the expansion of state contracting, the redirection of exports toward the Socialist Bloc, and the newfound ability of silk workers and employers to cooperate for mutual benefit. By mid-May, the state company had signed contracts with 158 weaving factories, mostly in Shanghai, Wuxi, and Suzhou, to produce a total of 15,655.5 bolts of silk.[17] State contracting provided a more stable source of raw materials and capital than the still-chaotic markets, but the situation remained dire with thousands (about 60 percent of Shanghai silk weavers) unable to find work. Nonetheless, by October, 257 weaving factories had restored production to some degree, and Shanghai's total production of silk cloth for 1950 reached 257,611 bolts utilizing about 80 percent of existing capacity.[18] By the end of the year, Shanghai's silk industry employed more people than it had in January.

Despite the obvious benefits of state-contracted silk weaving, the early contracting system exhibited some persistent shortcomings. An exchange recorded at a meeting of the Silk Weaving Industry Association's "public-private symposium" on July 19, 1950, reveals the conflicts between private producers and the state in the early 1950s. When discussing the policy of taking stores of cloth as collateral for raw materials distributed for state-contracted weaving, several factory owners complained that this policy demonstrated a lack of trust on the part of the state company. Sheng Peisheng, general manager of the Yulin Silk Factory,[19] suggested that better organization and planning were needed to "move in the direction of a socialist society." One of his colleagues

17. *People's Daily*, 22 May 1950.

18. SMA C16-2-285; *Laodongbao*, 26 Oct. 1950; *Xinwenbao*, 9 Jan. 1951.

19. Sheng Peisheng hailed from Hangzhou and was a leader of the Shanghai Silk Industry Association and the Labor-Capital Consultative Conference from their establishment in 1950. In 1951 his factory, Yulin, joined the Second United Factory, which was often cited as a model of labor-capital consultation. By 1951, more than 90 percent of its product was purchased by the CSC. SMA S39-4-4, S39-4-64.

hoped that not all silk factories would be treated like those that had lost the state company's trust for engaging in illegal activities, while another complained that this policy seemed more like "an ambush" than "taking care" of private factories' needs.

In response, the China Sericulture Company representative Zhu Zuxian, also a vice chairman of the Shanghai Silk Industry Association, explained the reasons behind the company's policies in an attempt to allay the factory owners' concerns. He even conceded that current policies might not be necessary. Concerning the issue of taking collateral in the form of product, Zhu said that this was required at the time due to the state of labor relations and state-private relations, but that it could be modified in the future (and these policies were in fact relaxed over the following year). While recognizing factory owners' concerns and hinting at future concessions, however, Zhu also emphasized private factories' dependence on the state company, stating that if silk weaving factories found it too difficult to maintain production under the current circumstances, they were free to apply to the Bureau of Industry and Commerce to shut their doors and lay off their employees.[20]

For the time being, the state company was willing to cooperate with private factories to restore production and employment. As silk production revived in 1950, the state company began to loosen supplies of raw materials and increase contracting and purchasing orders. At the end of October 1950, the CSC announced that it would no longer limit the amount of filature silk and synthetics provided to qualified factories. By March 1951, the CSC allowed any licensed weaving company to purchase raw materials as often as three times a week in units as small as a few pounds. In April, the CSC began to accept cash payment as collateral on contracted supplies, and by the end of July the government had reduced this amount to just 7 percent of value, although some factory owners still complained that this was too high. The extension of the term of state weaving contracts to six months in mid-1951 enabled factories to determine future production plans and needs, which helped to reduce costs.[21]

20. SMA S39-4-31.

21. *Xinwenbao*, 25 Oct. 1950; *Dagongbao*, 24 Jan., 28 Feb. & 7 Aug. 1951; SMA S39-4-62.

On balance, state contracting and purchases of privately produced cloth clearly fostered the silk industry's recovery. Full recovery, however, would depend on renewed exports. Before the war with Japan exports usually comprised about 60 percent of all sales of Chinese silk. After the war, due to inflated production costs, poor quality, competition from synthetic fibers, and a lack of diplomatic initiatives, the Nationalist government was unable to stimulate exports. Domestic demand increased somewhat in late 1949, when sales reached 3.3 billion RMB. Nonetheless, demand for silk cloth, especially expensive high-quality material, declined over the next two years, in some cases to just one-tenth the amount sold in 1949. This was attributed to changes in style of dress as citizens of the PRC began wearing "people's clothing."[22]

As was the case during the postwar economic crisis, the silk industry desperately needed the new government to secure export opportunities. How this was to be accomplished, however, was at first unclear. The Nationalist blockade, American hostility, and competition from nylon and other synthetics in international markets hindered efforts to promote exports of Chinese silk. Even as late as June 1950, the CSC hoped to increase exports to traditional markets in the United States, Europe, and India.[23] As US hostility toward the People's Republic of China grew along with tensions in Korea, this approach was abandoned, and the Communist press urged the silk industry to reduce its "traditional dependence on capitalist markets."[24] In April 1950 foreign trade shifted from Shanghai to the ports of Qingdao and Tianjin in order to avoid the Nationalist blockade. Hong Kong also became a major entrepôt for the PRC's foreign trade.[25]

At the same time, the Soviet Union and the Socialist Bloc countries were quickly becoming an important export market for Chinese silk. As early as June 30, 1949, in his speech titled "On the People's Democratic Dictatorship," Mao Zedong stated that it would be necessary for

22. *Jiefang ribao*, 19 Mar. 1950.

23. *Dagongbao*, 2 Jun. 1950.

24. *Jiefang ribao*, 27 Jul. 1951.

25. He Li, "Getting through Difficulties Is Glorious," 31. On transshipment of Chinese goods through Hong Kong, see Clayton, "Free Trade, Protection and the British Empire."

China to "lean to one side," to ally with the USSR in opposition to US imperialism.[26] At first Soviet aid was meager but welcome. Economic cooperation began in earnest with the signing of the Sino-Soviet Treaty of Friendship, Alliance, and Mutual Assistance on February 14, 1950, which included a loan of 1.2 billion rubles (300 million USD).[27] Over the following year China began to participate in trade shows and exhibitions to attract socialist countries to purchase its products. By the end of 1950, 55.4 percent of Chinese exports of filature silk went to the Soviet Union and Eastern Europe, as compared with only 8 percent in 1949.[28] Chinese silk piece goods were also well received at exhibitions in Hungary and the German Democratic Republic in the spring of 1951, and large orders followed shortly. By August 1951, China had received more orders from socialist countries for georgette, crepe, and satin than it could fill. By September, overseas orders exceeded production levels by 15 percent, and government stores of silk cloth were sold out. In one order, an East German importer purchased 400,000 meters of Suzhou taffeta and complex weaves such as *zhijin* and *guxiangduan*.[29] Under the influence of increased exports to the socialist countries, contract weaving in Shanghai increased more than seven times in 1951 as compared with 1950, with about 80 percent of this product being exported.[30]

In the crisis of 1949–50, state contracting and purchases of privately produced silk cloth by state companies were a vitally important factor in the silk industry's recovery. Although many factory owners had legitimate complaints about the system at the time (and later remember it as a stepping stone on the path to nationalization), it is unlikely that Shanghai's silk weaving industry would have recovered so easily on its own, without government assistance. Nonetheless, the provision of state contracts to private silk factories did not establish a high degree of government control over private silk weaving. Indeed, the complexity of state-private relations and the shortcomings of the dual economy under New Democracy only became apparent with the economy's

26. Mao Zedong, "On the People's Democratic Dictatorship."

27. Meng Xianzhang, *Zhong-Su maoyi shiliao*, 545–46.

28. *Jiefang ribao*, 27 Jul. 1951.

29. *Dagongbao*, 24 Jan. 1951; *Jiangsusheng cansang sichou zhi*, 304; *Jiefang ribao*, 2 Aug. 1951, 12 Sep. 1951, 20 Sep. 1951, 22 Sep. 1951.

30. SMA S39-4-67.

recovery and the expansion of state-contracted production during the Korean War. Perhaps even more remarkable than the silk industry's recovery through partnership with the state company, however, was the shift from conflict to cooperation in labor relations in the Shanghai silk weaving industry, which led the country in establishing a New Democratic basis for labor-capital cooperation.

The Shanghai Silk Industry Labor-Capital Consultative Conference

State contracts and the redirection of exports toward the Soviet Union were undoubtedly of great importance in the recovery of Shanghai's silk weaving industry in 1950. But one of the most unusual and politically significant factors in this process was the unprecedented degree of cooperation between workers and employers. The crisis precipitated by the February Sixth Bombing convinced workers and employers in Shanghai's silk weaving industry of the necessity of cooperating for mutual survival. The Communist Party's policies and institutional arrangements laid the groundwork for such cooperation, and the recent history and characteristics of the silk weaving industry, especially the nature of the union organization, gave these workers certain advantages in cooperating with employers. But the sudden catastrophe forced both silk workers and factory owners to recognize their common predicament and to accept the fact that, if they could not work out some new arrangement to govern labor relations, production, and wages in Shanghai's silk weaving industry, the industry might collapse entirely.

As one report by the Shanghai GLU stated, although the union and the Silk Industry Association had already established a labor relations committee and had managed to resolve some issues concerning wages, there was still much confusion regarding the "spirit, quality, and tasks of labor-capital consultation." After the bombing, however, silk workers and factory owners "realized more strongly the necessity of labor-capital consultation."[31] For many veteran silk producers this entailed a shift in conceptions of labor relations, class conflict, and class

31. "Sizhiye laozi xieshang," 30.

identities. The success of this experiment in class cooperation in a revolutionary context depended less on the leadership of the Communist Party than on the ability of leaders of the Silk Workers Union and the Silk Industry Association for responsible self-governance and compromise. At the very least, by February 1950 the leaders of the Silk Workers Union recognized that it would require cooperation and compromise to begin the long, hard road to recovery from the nadir of its twentieth-century fortunes. The first step in this process was the establishment of a novel institution in keeping with the principles of New Democracy—the Labor-Capital Consultative Conference, or LCCC.

In the weeks following the February Sixth Bombing, the newborn district and factory-level unions found it difficult to respond adequately to the flood of requests for mediation and emergency assistance.[32] What was needed was an industry-level institution that could serve as a forum for conducting negotiations and for resolving disputes openly, fairly, and with concessions on both sides. Without such an institution, deprivation and violence might well result, for despite appeals to the contrary there remained a basic conflict of interest between factory owners and silk weavers that threatened to undermine the party's policy of labor-capital cooperation. If workers were going to accept wage reductions and temporary layoffs to help their employers restore production, they would need some assurance that their long-term interests would be protected.

The Silk Weavers Union began meeting with the Silk Industry Association in March, and by the end of the month the two groups had produced a collective agreement on conditions of production, employment, and dismissal in the silk weaving industry. The agreement set standards that sorted silk weaving factories into three categories according to their prospects for continuing production. Factories that were able to maintain production were to work out arrangements for reduced wages and working hours to help them "break even" (*baoben zigei*). Factories that were unable to continue production but hoped to reopen were to "disperse" (*shusan*) their weavers for a period of three to five months, paying a living stipend of thirty-six parity units per month, with proportionate amounts for prep workers and staff. Finally,

32. SMA C16-2-288.

factories where the situation was considered hopeless could close their doors and lay off their employees after an investigation by the union and the industry association, and approval by the Shanghai Bureau of Industry and Commerce. Laid-off workers were to be compensated with severance pay of one to three months' wages according to existing regulations. This last situation was the most difficult to manage, however, as layoffs required the union's agreement and employees were unlikely to accept layoffs without a struggle.[33]

The March agreement was soon followed by the establishment, on April 17, of the Silk Industry Labor-Capital Consultative Conference (*laozi xieshang huiyi*), the first of its kind in Shanghai. The LCCC, which included both filatures and weaving factories, was an example of "democratic management" (*minzhu guanli*) in private industry.[34] What this entailed, however, bore little resemblance to either liberal democracy or syndicalist worker control. The existing scholarship on "democratic management" in China and the West tends to repeat criticisms of the LCCCs from the mid-fifties with little further examination, and gives the impression that there are no cases in which the LCCCs functioned successfully either to resolve disputes or to improve production.

For example, Mark Frazier devotes only two pages to dismissing the LCCCs as "the failure of labor-management cooperation," and otherwise only discusses them in the context of the Five Antis Campaign.[35] Echoing critics of the 1950s, Frazier mainly faults the LCCCs for not paying enough attention to production. Jackie Sheehan also gives short shrift to the LCCCs, citing newspaper accounts criticizing them as "tools of management," but not attempting to examine the functioning of these institutions in specific industries or enterprises.[36] Lee Lai To, on the other hand, states that the LCCCs did not function very well because factory owners were afraid that workers would use them to raise unreasonable demands.[37] Although, generally speaking, the LCCCs did not

33. "Shanghaishi sizhi gongye," 81–83; SMA S39-4-31, S39-4-1; *Jiefang ribao*, 12 Apr. 1950, *Wenhuibao*, 12 Apr. 1950.

34. On democratic management in state factories, see Cliver, "*Minzhu guanli*," 409–35.

35. Frazier, *Chinese Industrial Workplace*, 110–11.

36. Sheehan, *Chinese Workers*, 19–20, 30–31.

37. Lee Lai To, *Trade Unions in China*, 90, 93, 99.

function as intended, there was clearly far more diversity of outcomes and there were more success stories than one would assume from reading the existing literature on workers and workplaces in the early PRC.

Granted, "democratic management" was criticized and then abandoned throughout Chinese industry after 1954. But before that time, it was one of the main planks of the CCP's efforts to reform private businesses and "bureaucrat capitalist" enterprises of the Nationalist state in line with the principles of New Democracy. The "Directive on Establishing LCCCs in Private Enterprises," written by Labor Minister Li Lisan, stated that the LCCCs' purpose was to "aid labor and capital in private enterprises to consult as to how best to improve production, business, and the treatment of workers."[38] LCCCs were to be established by mutual agreement between the union and management in factories with more than fifty employees, although smaller factories were permitted to establish LCCCs as well. These bodies were to be comprised of an equal number (generally two to six) from each side, with the owner or his representative, the factory manager, and the union chair as *ex officio* members. Employee representatives were to be elected by the workforce, while representatives of the "capital side" were chosen by the factory's owner or board of directors. Meetings were to be held on a regular basis (at least once per month), with emergency meetings called when necessary. The chairmanship of the LCCC alternated between labor and management each meeting. LCCCs were furthermore to be established at the industry level, according to the same procedures, to serve as the second stage of dispute resolution outside the factory. But these were not under the direction of any government organ, such as the Labor Bureau.

Li Lisan's "Directive" stated that the LCCC was "an organ for equitable discussion, and . . . not responsible for enterprise management or administration." This provision protected owners' rights to manage their businesses and their decision-making power concerning product mix, marketing, and finances. Nonetheless, the scope of "equitable discussion" was comprehensive, and included negotiating and implementing collective contracts; planning production and other tasks;

38. Li Lisan, "Directive on Establishing LCCCs," 1. For an English translation, see *Trade Union Law*, 33–38.

improving productivity and quality; improving the organization of production and the allocation of labor; improving technology, methods of operation, technique, and skill level; improving management; implementing changes in factory regulations and wage systems; managing personnel (hiring and firing, promotions and demotions); setting work hours; and overseeing employee welfare including safety, hygiene, workers' health, and issues specifically relating to women workers and minors.[39] Potentially, then, the LCCCs opened for discussion a wide range of issues that had previously been the sole purview of the factory owner and management.

Despite provisions for the election of worker representatives, the LCCC was not necessarily the most "democratic" of bodies. Even where properly elected union officials and employee representatives were sincerely committed to representing the interests of their coworkers, the LCCC was only required to consult with the entire workforce regarding major agreements (such as the collective contract).[40] Other issues, such as the organization of production, work assignments, and hiring and firing, did not necessarily have to come before the whole workforce. Given the unions' problems (described in chapter 3) with "bureaucratism," passivity, alienation from membership, and a tendency to act as "tails of management," these were potentially fatal shortcomings. Indeed, most LCCCs barely functioned and were frequently dominated by the factory owner or his representatives.

One exception to this general rule was Shanghai's Silk Industry LCCC, a successful example of worker participation in management in private industry. There were some impressive examples of functioning factory-level LCCCs in this industry as well. In the context of the crisis of 1950, the industry-level LCCC was a forum, with only limited enforcement powers, established for the purpose of consultation and resolution of disputes. Party leaders had hoped, however, that this body would eventually play a leading role in improving management, technology, and production in the silk industry by transforming labor relations, factory regime, and the nature of cooperation and competition among private silk factories.

39. Li Lisan, "Directive on Establishing LCCCs," 2–4.
40. Li Lisan, "Directive on Establishing LCCCs," 5.

In the main, leaders of the union and the industry association staffed the Silk Industry LCCC. Despite its limited representation of Shanghai's silk workers, however, this institution proved to be a highly effective means of collective bargaining and day-to-day protection of workers' interests during the crisis of 1950. The consultative conference was formed by twenty-two representatives, equally divided between the Silk Workers Union and the Silk Industry Association. Each side took turns chairing the conference. A joint declaration by the two organizations echoed the policies and language of the Communist Party, stating that the LCCC had been established "in order to implement the policy of benefiting both labor and capital, to strengthen labor-capital unity, and to struggle together to overcome the present crisis so as to recover and develop production." The conference would furthermore carry out its work "in the spirit of democratic consultation" and would "assist each factory in handling labor-capital relations well by researching and providing assistance in matters relating to production and welfare."[41] The language of the document demonstrates a strong understanding of CCP policies, emphasizing the goals of restoring production and social order and conceiving of "democracy" as a mechanism for achieving class cooperation through open discussion among representatives considered loyal and responsible both by their constituents and by party authorities.

The most pressing work of the Shanghai Silk Weaving Industry LCCC in its first six weeks was to mediate and resolve disputes according to the principles laid out in the March collective agreement. Of the forty-three disputes brought before the LCCC in April and May 1950, nineteen were resolved with factory owners agreeing to continue production in some fashion. Those factories in difficulty, which necessitated temporary dispersals of the workforce, numbered twelve. An additional five factories faced major difficulties and could not set a specific date for restoring production, and seven discontinued production entirely and dismissed their workers. Most impressive was the LCCC's ability to mediate and protect the interests of both employers and workers, and its relative efficiency in resolving conflicts. As one report pointed out, if these disputes had required the intervention of

41. SMA S39-4-54.

the Labor Bureau, rather than relying on this form of collective consultation, they would likely have dragged on for a long time, threatening both production and workers' livelihoods.[42]

The LCCC played a vital role in helping silk factories to maintain production and provide fair compensation to employees who had to be laid off temporarily or permanently.[43] As a typical example, labor and management at the Dayuan Silk Factory agreed to a plan to reduce production for two months starting on May 21. The factory guaranteed that weavers would receive a wage of at least twenty-six parity units per month, as well as subsidies for rice and other basic necessities. Workers in the preparation department were guaranteed a monthly wage and subsidies proportional to those received by the weavers. If sales income was insufficient to achieve this wage level, the owner would make up the difference. Some factories produced detailed plans as to how much work silk weavers would be guaranteed under reduced production. For example, weavers at Rongcheng worked out an agreement wherein they would each be guaranteed at least five bolts per month. This new institution thus provided a means by which employers and workers could negotiate measures to respond to the crisis while minimizing harm to the enterprise and workers' livelihoods.

For those factories that could not realistically continue production on any scale, the LCCC worked out rules for temporary layoffs or "dispersals," which went a long way toward reducing the threat of unemployment and violence. Appealing to patriotic and revolutionary sentiment, the owner of the Xiexinchun Factory expressed his desire to disperse employees indefinitely "until Taiwan is liberated." Most factories, however, worked out agreements for temporary layoffs of a specific term. For example, the Mofan Silk Factory reached an agreement on April 27, 1950, to disperse the employees for four months with compensation of 144 parity units each. The agreement stated that the factory should be able to restore production once two-thirds of the silk factories in the district had done so. If production could be restored early, then the workers would have to return a portion of the dispersal

42. "Sizhiye laozi xieshang," 31.

43. Unless noted otherwise, the following examples are taken from records of meetings of the Silk Industry LCCC contained in SMA S39-4-31 and S39-4-32.

subsidy on a pro-rated basis. Unemployment remained a possibility, however, and the agreement stated that if production could not be restored by the end of September, then workers would lose their jobs and the factory would pay back wages in the amount of 31.5 parity units per month as severance pay. The agreement protected the owner from further demands by stating that the employees were not permitted to request any additional subsidies, and that rehiring would proceed according to the level of production as negotiated between the factory union and the owner.[44]

Agreements brokered through the LCCC often restricted factory owners' ability to dispose of machinery and other fixed assets. The Mofan Factory agreement stated that the owner had to obtain the union's permission to sell or rent the factory's looms and other equipment. Restrictions on capitalists' ability to dispose of factory assets represented a significant effort to limit the operation of bourgeois property rights and the "law of value" during the silk industry's crisis. But it sometimes proved difficult for the LCCC to enforce such provisions. In a March 1951 incident, the owner of the Dazhong Xingji Factory was found to have rented the factory's equipment to the recently established Dazhong Silk Factory.[45] Although the dispersal agreement stipulated that the original employees should be given priority in hiring once production was restored, Dazhong's shareholders were unwilling to do this. The case was sent to the Labor Bureau for arbitration. In a similar case, when workers at the Shengya Silk Factory sought to return to their jobs in August as agreed, they found that the owner had rented out the factory's machinery without obtaining their permission. The owner claimed that the workers had no right to interfere in his business and the dispute was referred to the Labor Bureau.[46]

Given the silk industry's long-term crisis, the shock of the February Sixth Bombing, and the recession caused by the government's

44. SMA C1-2-231.

45. This enterprise may very well have been a shadow company set up by Dazhong Xingji in order to avoid its responsibilities under the agreement. This possibility is supported by the fact that the new factory employed no workers. SMA S39-4-31.

46. *Laodongbao*, 28 Nov. 1950. Because the archives of the Shanghai Labor Bureau are not yet available to researchers, it is difficult to know how these disputes were resolved.

anti-inflationary policies, factory closures and permanent layoffs were unavoidable in many cases. Existing regulations concerning severance pay, as well as those the LCCC established specifically for the silk industry, required that factories compensate laid-off employees. A typical example is that of the Deji Silk Factory. At the end of May, Deji's owner had claimed that he lacked the means to compensate laid-off workers. Through negotiations at the LCCC in June, however, he was made to comply with the regulations. A portion of the workforce was dispersed for three months with compensation of 108 parity units each. The rest of the workers were laid off, receiving three months' wages and 7.2 *dou* of rice as severance pay.

The collapse of silk production in February 1950 exacerbated not only labor-capital conflict, but also divisions within the working class. Women workers were especially vulnerable to being laid off because of agreements reached through the LCCC to protect the jobs of male weavers. The Silk Workers Union was aware of this problem and took steps to protect women's jobs, but cases involving layoffs of women workers often proved intractable. In at least two such cases, the LCCC had to refer the disputes to the Labor Bureau for resolution. This reveals the extent to which the party's hierarchical conception of class and gender often discriminated against women workers even when such discrimination was officially criticized. Powerful and responsible unions like the Shanghai Silk Workers Union were sometimes able to redress gender inequalities and protect women workers' interests. But as we shall see in chapter 6, inattention to gender conflict in the workplace could disadvantage large groups of women workers, leading to neglect of their interests and producing hostility toward the revolutionary regime.

LCCC agreements for reduced production or temporary dispersals usually set a fixed date by which time production should be restored. Some factories were fortunate. Both the Tiansheng and Hongcheng Factories were able to restore production by the end of May 1950, well in advance of the date set in their respective agreements. After weavers at the Dahe Silk Factory agreed to wage reductions, the factory not only managed to avoid losses, but made a profit of three million yuan. By June 1950, Dahe had restored full production. Most factories were only able to restore production gradually, however. After having dispersed their workers for five months, the Meicheng and Meiyuan Silk Factories went to the LCCC in October 1950 to work out agreements with the weavers to operate twenty looms for no less than eight hours a day. In January 1951, the Dongsheng Silk Factory agreed to restore wages to 85 percent, increasing to 90 percent in February and restoring wages fully by March. This type of arrangement was very common in the first quarter of 1951, and by April of that year most Shanghai silk factories had fully restored work hours, wages, and living subsidies.

Records show that in general, the silk industry's crisis during the spring of 1950 inspired cooperation between the Silk Workers Union and the Silk Industry Association. In many cases, however, silk weaving factories either could not or would not restore production and wages as promised in the original agreement, and such reversals created intense disputes. Some silk factories that had dispersed their employees for a fixed term could have restored production but instead chose to rent out equipment, or to obtain government raw materials and illegally re-contract them to other factories. This amounted to theft of government property that had been supplied with the intention of maintaining production and employment. Even more common were weaving factories that had fully restored production but continued to pay reduced wages that workers had accepted in good faith to aid the factory's recovery.[47] As a result, late 1950 and early 1951 witnessed another surge in wage disputes. The Meicheng and Meiyuan factories took wage disputes to the Labor Bureau in October 1950. In January 1951, the Meiyuan Silk Factory was found to owe wages and subsidized rice from the previous three months. The LCCC managed to resolve this dispute, however, and the factory agreed to provide rice subsidies according to government regulations.

As can be expected from Shanghai's resourceful businessmen in such chaotic times, it sometimes proved difficult to prevent unscrupulous capitalists from circumventing agreements governing labor relations and working conditions. The *Labor Daily* reported in November 1950 that weavers in some silk factories were forced to work fourteen or fifteen hours a day for wages that were one-third to one-half of

47. *Laodongbao*, 28 Nov. 1950.

typical rates of pay, with no benefits or meal subsidies.[48] In most cases, however, employees could bring their complaints to the LCCC, which provided new mechanisms for protecting their interests. With the expansion of state contracting, increased state control over markets, and the growing influence of the unions, employers' ability to violate labor agreements was restricted, but not eliminated.

Sometimes silk workers also found it difficult to abide by the new practices. For over a month, employees at the Hongkang Silk Factory engaged in negotiations to restore production. They had finally reached an agreement when the owner suddenly changed his mind. On April 23, 1950, the angry employees captured him and held him hostage for more than twenty-four hours before the union and Labor Bureau managed to resolve the dispute and reach a new agreement.[49] Although this example demonstrates that labor-capital cooperation sometimes failed to replace earlier methods of struggle, such incidents were much less frequent in 1950 than during the previous three years.

The system of state-contracted production inherited from the Nationalists was another means by which the government could pressure employers to conform to the policy of labor-capital cooperation. "Normal" labor relations, meaning proper treatment of workers and at least nominal participation in management by employee representatives, were stipulated as a requirement for participation in state-contracted silk weaving. The quality of labor relations could, in some cases, determine whether state agencies granted factories production contracts and access to raw materials. Even the amount of finished goods taken as deposit for contracted raw materials depended on the state of labor relations in the factory. State processing contracts included a provision that both the "labor side" and the "capital side" had to sign a guarantee in order to receive a contract. This indirectly created a means by which silk workers could put pressure on their employers, or even directly supervise their performance on state contracts.[50] According to one report, establishing an LCCC was a way for private factories to improve access to loans and production orders. The goal of obtaining state weaving

48. *Laodongbao*, 28 Nov. 1950.
49. SMA C1–2–231.
50. SMA S39–4–57, S39–4–31.

contracts thus motivated workers and employers in many Shanghai silk weaving factories to establish LCCCs by the autumn of 1950.[51]

Following the establishment of the Silk Industry LCCC in April 1950, similar committees were set up in individual factories, beginning with the largest and most modern enterprises. There had been experiments with "democratic management" in the early phase of the Chinese revolution, including efforts to democratize management in Nationalist state-run factories and firms that became employee-managed during the civil war. But in the case of Shanghai's silk weaving industry, the LCCCs were based neither on competitive elections nor syndicalist and collective forms of direct worker control such as appeared in Petrograd during the Russian Revolution or in Madrid in 1936.[52] In keeping with the principles of New Democracy, the new forms of class cooperation preserved capitalist production and private ownership while expanding workers' participation in management.

The Meiya Company, which owned two of Shanghai's largest and most advanced silk weaving factories, established its labor-capital consultative conference on May 1, 1950. Several others, also at large factories with strong, Communist-led union organizations, quickly followed. By June, Tongli, Taicheng, Yongning, Dacheng, Yongda, Hengfeng, Hongchang, and Hongkang (where two months earlier workers had kidnapped their employer) had established LCCCs. By October, almost fifty silk weaving factories and filatures in Shanghai had established factory-level LCCCs.[53]

The Meiya Company's LCCC benefitted from the presence of veteran labor activists, many of them Communists, who both understood the policy of labor-capital cooperation and were willing to stand up to the owners. Within a few months after the February Sixth Bombing, the Meiya Company succeeded in avoiding losses, mainly because the LCCC had convinced workers to accept reduced wages and even dispersals and layoffs. The compensation offered to workers who were laid off permanently was superior to that stipulated in the industry regulations—30 percent of monthly salary for a year, as well as traveling

51. "Zenyang gaohao laozi xieshang," 49.
52. See Avrich, "Bolshevik Revolution and Workers' Control," 47–63.
53. SMA S39-4-44; "Sizhiye laozi xieshang," 34.

expenses. By the end of 1950, the factory had resumed normal operations, and wages had been restored to 90 percent of their original levels. Furthermore, Meiya increased the number of rest days, improved meals for nightshift workers, reached an agreement on annual bonuses, and established a cooperative store.[54]

Most significantly, the Meiya LCCC managed to push through regulations to equalize the pay scales for men and women workers. Women comprised a minority of silk weavers, but made up about half of the industry's total workforce. Although men dominated the union's leadership, the Silk Workers Union nonetheless consistently emphasized women's interests, pushing for gender equality and ensuring women's presence in representative bodies. As in the party's attempts to transform marriage and family relations, however, many union cadres and male silk weavers, particularly in the city's smaller workshops, resisted the union's egalitarian policies.

One report stated that before the Japanese occupation, women silk weavers' wages were generally lower than men's because it was held that women did not know how to repair the looms. (Many men did not seem to have known how to do this either, but the wage difference was based on gender, not on demonstration of skill.) At the Meiya Number Four Silk Weaving Factory, women were not even allowed to learn the skills necessary to repair looms because it was held that if women climbed atop the loom's "dragon head" (the device that set the patterns for complex weaves), they might "bring misfortune" (*chumeitou*) through a kind of spiritual pollution. This form of discrimination was discontinued at Meiya on International Women's Day, March 8,1950. After the Meiya Company LCCC was established in May, it equalized wages for men and women weavers and wrote regulations for equal pay into the industry-level collective contracts. Some men, however, resented these changes, as they felt they were not being compensated appropriately for their skills and their status as heads of household.[55]

54. The information for this section is derived primarily from SMA C1-2-744, interviews with former Meiya Company employee Shen Fukang, and the personal file of Meiya employee Long Jifu from the Meiya Factory Archives. Long Jifu was elected as an employee representative to the Meiya LCCC.

55. SMA C1-2-334.

Through the LCCC, Meiya's management also established regulations for requesting leave time and set up a system for quality control that included standardized bonuses and penalties based on the quality of the finished products. On the production side, labor-capital cooperation ameliorated the abysmal situation in which the factory could not complete its state contracts on time and the rate of defective cloth sometimes reached 100 percent. Although by the end of 1950 about half of the factory's product still contained defects, this was nonetheless a huge improvement. This was achieved in part through the establishment of a production committee responsible for investigating problems and coming up with solutions through consultation among management, production workers, and technical staff.

The Meiya Factory's LCCC also exhibited some problems. A union report on the LCCC stated that management did not pay enough attention to workers' "rationalization suggestions" (*helihua jianyi*). The main difficulty, a common one in Shanghai silk factories, was that the rewards for improvements, such as increasing the diameter of the belt pulley or inventing a technique of spraying with hot water the spools of thread for weaving georgette velvet, were too meager. The practice of designating outstanding workers as "labor models" was not yet widespread, and most private factories did not implement this method of rewarding workers' contributions to production. The union also found that it was much harder to motivate management to cooperate in improving workers' benefits once production had improved than it had been to get their support in persuading workers to make sacrifices during the crisis of 1950.

Both factory owners and workers found other aspects of the LCCCs dissatisfying as well. Just as silk capitalists attempted to circumvent or resist mediation by the LCCC, there were also limits to silk workers' faith in labor-capital cooperation. For example, warp preparation workers at the Shanghai First United Silk Weaving Factory demanded that the factory restore their wages (the highest in the factory) to previous levels. Immediately, and without consulting the factory's union organization, they began to reduce the length of the warp thread, which adversely affected production in the whole factory.[56] It was just

56. SMA S39-4-44.

this kind of disruptive tactic that the LCCC sought to eliminate, but in this case the workers felt that direct action was necessary.

The frustration some workers felt with the Silk Industry LCCC derived from the institution's inherent limitations. The biggest problem was that unlike the China Sericulture Company, which made adherence to the new labor laws a prerequisite for participating in contract weaving, the silk industry's LCCC possessed limited legal authority. Nonetheless, despite its limitations the Silk Industry LCCC accomplished a great deal under very difficult circumstances, and more than 80 percent of the disputes brought before it were resolved within the consultation process. The LCCC referred the remainder to the Labor Bureau for resolution. These were usually the most difficult cases, including disputes over layoffs and restoring wages in which neither side was willing to compromise.

Overall, those involved with the Silk Industry LCCC assessed it quite positively. As early as October 1950, Song Baolin, chairman of the Shanghai Silk Industry Association, announced that labor relations in the silk industry had greatly improved since its establishment. In a January 1951 report, Song claimed that the crisis of the February Sixth Bombing was overcome through cooperation with the union, labor-capital consultation, and protecting the interests of both owners and employees.[57] Song's reports, however, also mention that because the LCCC was so busy settling disputes, the conference members had no time to develop and promote measures to improve production and management.

Beginning in 1951, the Silk Industry LCCC attempted to lead the way in promoting advanced techniques and improved management systems, projects that had been neglected during the crisis of 1950. The LCCC also negotiated an industry-wide collective contract, completed in December 1951, to clarify workers' rights, obligations, and benefits, including important issues like health insurance and maternity leave, while continuing to cleave to the party's emphasis on proletarians' responsibility for improving productivity and labor discipline as "masters of the factory and the nation." The LCCC even achieved a degree of success in these efforts before Socialist Transformation and the merging

57. SMA S39-4-11, S39-4-44.

of the workers' state with enterprise management after 1955 obviated (at least in the eyes of the party leadership) the need for an autonomous and representative institution governing labor relations in Shanghai's silk industry.

Pursuing the Fruits of Revolution—Labor Insurance, Welfare Provision, and the Unions

Shanghai silk workers were divided by gender, with men and women sorted into different jobs or receiving different rates of pay for the same work. Other notable divisions within the Shanghai silk industry included disparities between large, modern factories and small workshops, and between successful, prosperous enterprises and those that continued to struggle financially. Disparities in welfare provision following the Communist seizure of power reflect this diversity. One of the most prominent goals of the revolution was to provide workers benefits such as health care, labor insurance, and improved working conditions. This was a vitally important aspect of the party's relationship with industrial workers, and access to welfare benefits became an important marker of status divisions in China's socialist society from the 1950s.[58] Differential access was closely related to the effectiveness of union organizations, the unions' relationship with the revolutionary state, and labor relations in specific factories, industries, and cities. These disparities also reflect differences in the ability of diverse groups of workers to utilize the laws and institutions of the revolutionary state to advance their interests. The resources, capabilities, and inclinations of factory owners and local officials further conditioned workers' capacity to pursue these goals.

In late February 1951, the central government promulgated new labor insurance regulations that included employment-based provision of medical care, workers' compensation, paid holidays, and maternity leave. However, due to the party's limited capacity to enforce this policy in private industry, especially among struggling factories, many

58. The long-term results of early status divisions within the Chinese working class are detailed in chapter 2 of Walder, *Communist Neo-Traditionalism*, 39–56.

Chinese workers did not immediately gain access to these benefits. The degree to which various groups of workers were able to pursue these goals reflects differences in access to political power, organizational strength, and ability to influence employers.

The benefits granted industrial employees under the February 1951 labor insurance regulations were excellent, at least on paper. But the law also excused a great many employers from having to meet these provisions depending on certain factors, including number of employees and the state of finances in the enterprise. Under the law, expenses for work-related injury and illness were covered in full by the employer, and workers disabled due to work-related injuries were entitled to varying degrees of compensation depending on the severity of the injury. Expenses were paid through the labor insurance fund, an account managed by the factory union to which the employer was required to contribute an amount equal to three percent of the total monthly wage bill. Employers were not permitted to make deductions from employees' wages to pay into the labor insurance fund, and there were strict penalties for employers who tried to circumvent these obligations. The labor insurance regulations also made provisions for pensions and death benefits for employees' families. Maternity benefits included fifty-six days of paid leave with special provisions for miscarriages and difficult births, which were consistent with earlier Nationalist policies.[59]

There were serious limitations, however, as to which workers could gain access to labor insurance. For one thing, the law applied only to enterprises employing more than one hundred workers and staff unless these were transportation, post and telecommunications, or construction units. Other factories, including smaller enterprises or those of a seasonal nature, could implement aspects of the labor insurance regulations by negotiating collective contracts with employers, but this was not required by law.[60] Furthermore, enterprises that were legally

59. *Important Labor Laws*, 13–23.

60. Collective contracts theoretically formed the basis for labor relations, remuneration, and welfare provision in private enterprises throughout China. The ACFTU's "Provisional Method for the Establishment of Labor-Capital Collective Contracts in Private Industrial and Commercial Enterprises," issued in July 1949, provided guidelines to unions and enterprises establishing collective contracts. The

required to implement the labor insurance regulations (i.e., those with more than one hundred employees) but faced financial difficulties could delay implementation after consulting with the factory union committee and receiving the approval of the local labor bureau.[61] The ongoing financial difficulties of Shanghai silk factories made it easy for employers to delay implementing the labor insurance regulations, which were promulgated in Shanghai on February 26, 1951, for a year or more. By the end of the year, only eight Shanghai silk factories provided labor insurance, including Meiya, Dacheng, Yunlin, and the other large factories. Workers in Shanghai's hundreds of small silk weaving factories enjoyed no welfare provisions whatsoever.

Employers had many reasons to avoid implementing labor insurance. One of the greatest difficulties was providing personnel, facilities, and medicines for on-site factory clinics, or obtaining places in designated hospitals for factory employees. As was often the case with CCP initiatives, the goals were progressive, but the resources for fulfilling these goals were lacking. Obtaining medicines, especially expensive imported pharmaceuticals, was one of the greatest impediments to improving workers' access to medical care in 1951.[62]

Even more troublesome, the labor insurance regulations threatened to exacerbate the financial problems of Shanghai's cash-strapped silk factories. Turning the revolution's slogans back on the Communists, factory owners complained that putting this burden on already troubled private silk factories went against the policy of "benefiting both labor and capital." In response, Zhu Zuxian of the China Sericulture Company expressed his commitment to helping factories meet these additional expenses by increasing payments for state-contracted production. In September, Shanghai's largest silk weaving factories sent a joint letter to the CSC requesting additional funding to cover labor insurance

---

first collective contract in Shanghai, signed October 30, 1949, was in the photography industry. Shanghai's silk weaving and dyeing industry, mainly comprised of small workshops, signed an agreement on February 8, 1950. Throughout 1950, most of Shanghai's major industries negotiated collective contracts, which provided a concrete basis for cooperation between workers and employers. *Jiefanghou Shanghai gongyun*, 161, 190–92.

61. *Important Labor Laws*, 11–13.

62. SMA S39-4-53, C1-2-739.

expenses. The state company quickly responded to this letter and agreed to pay for qualified labor insurance expenses in the amount of 5 percent of total wages if factories could provide proof of payment.[63]

Despite these positive developments, most silk workers remained outside the scope of labor insurance provisions. The regulations offered the possibility, however, that workers in smaller enterprises could pursue similar benefits if they could convince their employers to include these in collective contracts. In August 1951, the Shanghai Silk Workers Union took the initiative to expand the scope of labor insurance to include all of its members, not only those covered under official policy. In accordance with Article 3 of the Labor Insurance Regulations, the Silk Workers Union proposed to the LCCC a collective contract that would extend benefits to all Shanghai silk factories. After more than three months of negotiations, the Shanghai Silk Weaving Industry Collective Contract was signed in December, to take effect on January 1, 1952. The collective contract established a ten-hour workday, required full compensation for work-related injuries, and provided 50 percent coverage for non-work-related medical expenses, half wages during medical leave, and forty-two days leave with full pay for expectant mothers. The contract also established standards for production management such as requiring monthly or at least quarterly production plans, and set industry-wide standards for the compensation and term of apprenticeships.[64]

The timing of the collective contract was unfortunate, however. During the chaotic spring of 1952, when the Five Antis Campaign raged throughout Chinese industry, there was little oversight of the contract's implementation, and many silk factories simply ignored its provisions, such as the ten-hour workday. This was due not only to employers' reluctance, but also to workers' fears that reduced hours would mean reduced income. Few factories implemented the requisite production plans or made any effort to standardize the industry's "chaotic" wage system. Indeed, wide variations in wage systems and rates of pay continued for years, even after the Socialist Transformation. Even some basic safety provisions, such as a ban on cigarette smoking in silk

63. SMA S39-4-62.

64. *Laodongbao*, 29 Dec. 1951.

weaving factories, were frequently ignored.[65] This indicates that many of the provisions of the first collective contract reflected the concerns of the leadership of the Silk Workers Union more than those of the rank and file.

When the first collective contract expired in June 1952, the LCCC negotiated a new contract, which sought to remedy some of the shortcomings of the first contract by, for example, expanding welfare benefits and attempting to link benefits to improvements in production. Unsurprisingly, given the frenzied nature of production during the Korean War, as well as the more "disciplined" union organization that emerged from the wartime campaigns, the new contract strongly emphasized production, even incorporating the party's "Campaign to Increase Production and Practice Economy" among the contract's provisions.[66]

Because factory union representatives had been criticized for not discussing the first contract widely with the rank and file, preparations for the second contract included extensive canvassing of opinions and inclusion of new provisions. Under the 1952 contract, silk weavers were given one day off each week regardless of the shift system in place in their factories. Silk weavers were also paid full wages for official holidays as opposed to half wages, as had been the practice previously. Maternity leave was extended to fifty-six days with full pay. The new contract also expanded workers' medical and accident coverage in line with the state's labor insurance regulations.[67] Finally, it included provisions to protect workers' livelihoods, guaranteeing that wages would not be reduced under the ten-hour workday and requiring factory owners to retain employees and existing factory regulations and practices even if they transferred ownership to another business.

For the party leadership, the primary goal of establishing labor insurance and democratic management was to improve production. The silk industry's June 1952 contract thus attempted to establish clear standards for productivity and quality, and called for cooperation between unions and management in creating production plans, maintaining

65. SMA C1-2-530, C1-2-739.
66. SMA C1-2-739.
67. SMA C1-2-739.

labor discipline, launching labor competitions, and establishing a Soviet-style "territorial responsibility system" and quality inspection system. The contract also called upon the unions to promote advanced techniques and encourage "rationalization suggestions" (without, however, specifying how such innovations should be rewarded). The contract defined "labor discipline" as respecting the contract, seriously engaging in production, coming to work on time, caring for machinery and conserving on raw materials, and not smoking in prohibited areas. Interestingly, "labor discipline" also included "accepting the leadership and direction of management staff on the foundation of democratic management," a provision that had become necessary due to the shift away from class cooperation during the Five Antis Campaign.[68]

The Five Antis Campaign delayed negotiation of the new contract, which was not completed until the end of October 1952. The contract remained in effect from October 1952 until the end of March 1953, but it is unclear just how widely the new provisions were implemented. According to a report by the Shanghai GLU from the end of 1952, the collective contract in the silk weaving industry was successful in "correctly shifting capitalists' negative attitude toward production to a positive attitude following the Five Antis Campaign, and guiding the worker masses to pour their enthusiasm for the Five Antis struggle into production."[69] Other successful outcomes the report attributed to the collective contract were also related to production, including the proliferation of "rationalization suggestions," encouraging union cadres to "face production," and impressing upon workers that long-term improvements in living conditions depended on increased productivity.[70] But many of the specific provisions of the contract relating to production, such as the requirement that factories create monthly or quarterly production plans, were implemented haphazardly if at all.

The collective contract was expanded in 1953 through negotiations at the Silk Industry LCCC, which reached agreements on means to increase apprentices' subsidies and improve meals for nightshift workers.

68. SMA C1-2-530, C1-2-739.
69. SMA C1-2-654.
70. SMA C1-2-654.

The LCCC also resolved that large factories with enough resources should establish nurseries and workers' dormitories. Implementation of these additional provisions was delayed until the end of 1953 due to the industry's difficulties in the first half of that year. But the provision of labor insurance and other benefits steadily expanded through the industry's "socialist transformation" in 1956 to include more and more of Shanghai's small silk weaving factories. This was due mainly to the combined efforts of the union and the industry association in the LCCC.[71]

Continuing inequalities in the provision of welfare benefits following the Communist seizure of power highlight the diversity of experiences among different groups of Chinese workers. In the case of the Shanghai silk weaving industry, the union organization took the initiative to expand the scope of labor insurance to include all silk workers, not only those covered by the official policy. In contrast, the Wuxi filature union showed little interest in expanding coverage among the city's silk workers. Given the size of most filatures, most Wuxi silk workers should have enjoyed access to medical care following the promulgation of the labor insurance provisions in February 1951. It was not until July, however, that the city's Textiles Union began to organize training for union cadres in the "policies, significance, and content" of the labor insurance provisions. Upon returning to their own factories, the cadres' main activities seem to have been to conduct "propaganda and education" to compare life under the "old" and "new" societies to "raise the masses' political consciousness" and further motivate efforts in production.[72]

In practice, most filature owners ignored these provisions or claimed that they did not have the resources to implement them. Although twenty-six of Wuxi's thirty-nine filatures nominally had clinics or dedicated hospitals that their employees could use, thirteen had no provisions for workers' healthcare at all. Filature healthcare facilities were generally of poor quality, and furthermore reveal the extent to which prejudices against women workers continued unabated. Many of the doctors employed in factory clinics looked down on filature workers and did not treat them responsibly. Medical staff at the Ruilun Filature, with almost five hundred employees, frequently misdiagnosed ill

71. SMA S39-4-5.
72. Qian, *Wuxishi sichou gongye*, 239, 337.

unmarried workers as pregnant, or diagnosed pregnant workers as suffering from illness.[73] This shows that even when labor insurance provisions were implemented, they did not always meet workers' needs effectively.

For those with access, labor insurance could be a great benefit; and even for those without access, it indicated the Communist Party's commitment to improving the lives of China's industrial workers in the long term.[74] The process of registering workers for labor insurance also enabled the Communist Party to identify and attract the most active and loyal workers to its ranks. However, the Communist Party's labor insurance policies also frequently created or reinforced status divisions within the working class, especially those based on gender, industrial sector, and locality.[75] Despite efforts by the party and unions to implement labor-capital cooperation, welfare benefits, and gender equality, existing practices and prejudices were often strong enough to resist these efforts, and existing power relations remained unchanged for years. Indeed, the emphasis on capitalists' rights under New Democracy often reinforced existing prejudices and power relations or created new ways in which men could preserve their privileges vis-à-vis women.

By 1953, most workers in silk weaving factories and filatures enjoyed some degree of labor insurance benefits.[76] However, the majority of industrial workers were, by that time, also increasingly subject to the demands and discipline of the Communist Party, which exercised its power not only through the organs of the state and the instruments of the public media, but also through the workers' "own" organizations—the unions. As a result, while workers' earlier strategies for pursuing their interests—strikes, walkouts, and more violent actions—were de-legitimized, even the new strategies of collective bargaining and cooperating with employers through institutions for democratic management grew less

73. WMA D2-1-9.

74. Even some of the Communists' harshest critics agree. See Ong, *Labor Problems in Communist China*, 78–80.

75. On the importance of welfare benefits for China's "neo-traditional" system of industrial management, and the effects of enterprise welfare systems on status divisions among workers, see Walder, *Communist Neo-Traditionalism*, 28–84.

76. SMA S39-4-53.

effective as the priorities of the party-state shifted and its organizational dominance of the labor movement increased.

Conclusion

Shanghai's Silk Industry Labor-Capital Consultative Conference was not only the first of its kind, but it was also relatively successful compared to other experiments with "democratic management" in revolutionary China. The industry-level LCCC did not eliminate conflict in Shanghai's silk weaving industry completely, but this novel institution contributed immensely to getting workers and employers to reach compromises and protect livelihoods. By the end of 1950, the silk weaving industry was on the road to recovery thanks to the combination of labor-capital cooperation and state-contracted weaving for export. There remained, however, many entrenched problems in this context, such as the tendency to discriminate against women workers in layoffs, wages, and welfare provision.

Disparities in the effectiveness of "democratic management" and welfare provision reveal persistent prejudices against women workers in Chinese society. There was also a wide divergence in conditions in different localities and different sectors of the economy. Shanghai silk weavers, whose union organization was well-connected and committed to improving conditions for all silk workers (men and women in large and small factories), achieved substantially better benefits than their counterparts in the Wuxi thread mills. But even within the Shanghai silk weaving industry there were wide disparities. The factory-level LCCCs were more successful in the large, modern, and resource-rich factories like Meiya, which enjoyed not only material and financial resources but also political connections and experienced personnel. This was not the case for the more numerous small workshops, which usually lacked the resources needed to implement either "democratic management" or labor insurance. Despite the efforts of the Silk Workers Union, a great many silk workers did not gain access to welfare benefits for years following the promulgation of the labor insurance provisions, mostly because of the small size and limited resources of the factories where they worked.

Nonetheless, some obvious improvements in silk production and working conditions did result from the successful cooperation of labor and capital. By the end of 1951 it seemed that private silk weaving might enjoy a bright future under state assistance and direction. The Shanghai Silk Industry Association, the China Sericulture Company, and the Silk Workers Union together made plans to expand production by 30 percent in 1952, increasing the number of looms and workers employed by 22 percent. There were also plans to increase the amount of profit offered to contracted factories by 60 percent, to an average of about 8 percent of total sales, and to increase outlays for labor insurance by 6–8 percent.[77] At that point it looked as though the experiment of New Democracy had saved the silk industry from disaster by introducing new forms of labor relations and bringing real benefits to workers and employers. The outbreak of war in Korea, however, altered this trajectory, and the campaigns the Communist Party launched during the war years, which are the subject of the next chapter, brought significant changes to the industry. Ultimately, the shortcomings of the system of state-contracted production and labor-capital cooperation under New Democracy could not be overcome without radically transforming class relations in Chinese industry.

77. SMA S39–4–64, S39–4–68; *Laodongbao*, 8 Dec. 1951, 7 Aug. 1951.

CHAPTER FIVE

Creating a Campaign Society

Mass Mobilization during the Korean War

Within a year or two of the Communist seizure of power in 1949, most Chinese citizens had experienced mass political campaigns, the party's preferred method of mobilizing society to pursue its policy goals. Mass campaigns addressed a host of problems, from reforming currency to popularizing the new Marriage Law.[1] Whether struggling against undesirable behavior, opposing enemies both real and potential, or mobilizing workers to "increase production and practice economy," mass campaigns became a ubiquitous feature of Chinese society by the mid-1950s.[2] Mass campaigns in the early PRC, however, were neither as widespread nor as effective as one might conclude after reading Communist propaganda or Western accounts of "thought control" in "Red China."[3]

State-contracted production and the mass campaigns of the early 1950s facilitated economic recovery and called for the removal of large numbers of "enemies" from society and the workplace; at the same

1. John Gardner wrote that the "implementation of policy by means of mass mobilization is one of the most distinctive features of the Chinese Communist political process." Gardner, "Wu-fan Campaign," 477.

2. Examples of social science literature on mass campaigns in the PRC include Cell, *Revolution at Work*; Alan Liu, *Communications and National Integration*; Bennett, *Yundong*; Whyte, *Small Groups and Political Rituals*; and Frederick Yu, "Campaigns, Communications, and Development."

3. See, for example, the 1952 book by Hunter, *Brain-Washing in Red China*.

time, they promoted a heightened understanding of the Communist Party's goals and ideology and strengthened the party's organizational presence in society. By mobilizing the Chinese populace in pursuit of the party's goals, as opposed to implementing policy through a civil bureaucracy or police state, mass campaigns inevitably produced many results that party leaders neither intended nor welcomed. Although it is difficult to gauge the extent to which mass campaigns genuinely succeeded in transforming individuals' "political consciousness," urban residents adapted quickly to the new paradigm. They adopted the new political discourse and were often able to reconcile campaign goals with their own interests. Those who excelled at this found new opportunities for advancement as activists, labor models, union cadres, and party members.

At the same time, workers' earlier strategies for advancing collective interests, such as direct action in labor disputes, reliance on traditional forms of association, and the mobilization of personal networks of patronage and affinity, became less effective as the revolutionary government's campaigns and legislation encouraged new modes of behavior. Opponents of the party's policies nonetheless found opportunities to manipulate these campaigns for their own purposes, or successfully blocked or diverted the party's efforts at revolutionary transformation. Furthermore, as proponents of state economic administration discovered, mass mobilization in production campaigns had deleterious effects on economic planning and Soviet-style "scientific management," as these two approaches to economic development often proved incompatible in practice.

The scope of state involvement in silk production and marketing expanded dramatically during the first year of the Korean War, from 1950 to 1951, and the wartime campaigns affected filature workers and silk weavers differently. The varying fortunes of silk thread mill workers and industrial silk weavers in the early years of the Chinese revolution stemmed from differences in the characteristics of the two groups of workers (especially gender and political affiliation), in their traditions of labor organizing, and in the nature of the factory regimes in place. But as mass mobilization and production campaigns reached into more workplaces in more cities over the course of the 1950s, the political contexts and power relations in which the two groups of workers existed became increasingly similar.

By means of mass campaigns during the Korean War, the Communist party-state extended its ideological and organizational influence into many privately owned factories for the first time. But in the summer and autumn of 1950, as New China mobilized for war with the United States in Korea, the party's hegemony was incomplete, and there remained considerable room for diversity, resistance, and cooptation. Developments such as union reform and implementation of labor insurance in the two branches of the silk industry in this period depended on the timing, scope, and nature of contemporaneous mass campaigns as much as the nature of the workforce, recent history, and factory regime. The achievements of the Shanghai Silk Workers Union, described in chapter 4, developed in the relatively open and flexible context of 1950–51. Democratic Reform of the unions and improvements of working conditions in Wuxi's filatures did not begin until late 1951, in the context of political campaigns to mobilize workers to increase production and eliminate political enemies, and the results differed substantially from those achieved by Shanghai silk weavers. This chapter details the party's efforts at mass mobilization during the Korean War and the creation of a campaign society, establishing the context in which the revolution finally came to the silk filatures of the Yangzi Delta, described in chapter 6.

Campaigns to Mobilize Labor and Capital during the Korean War

The Korean War enabled the Chinese Communist Party to advance the projects of state formation, social revolution, and economic development by harnessing an upwelling of patriotic fervor and renewed confidence in the Chinese nation.[4] Following reports of Chinese

4. For more background on China's involvement in the Korean War, see Chen Jian, *China's Road to the Korean War* and *Sino-Soviet Alliance*. See also Spurr, *Enter the Dragon*, and Whiting, *China Crosses the Yalu*.

victories in the winter of 1950–51, the war became a powerful rallying point that enabled the party to expand its base of support. The party appealed to patriotism to push forward campaigns to restore and develop the economy, to root out counter-revolutionaries, and to amass capital for the war effort in the form of "donations" from businesses, unions, and individuals.

The retaking of Pyongyang in December 1950 and Seoul in January 1951 coincided with the first "high tide" of the Campaign to Resist America and Aid Korea (*Kang Mei yuan Chao yundong*).[5] In the early months of 1951, the campaign focused on "propaganda and education" (*xuanchuan jiaoyu*), in other words, disseminating information about the war and promoting anti-American sentiment. Recruitment of young students and workers for the military cadre schools was also a priority.[6] These early campaigns, however, exacerbated some existing problems and created new ones that the party-state addressed by means of further campaigns in the winter of 1951–52.

Industrial workers and their employers were among the first targeted by revolutionary propaganda in 1949, and they were also the first mobilized to support the war effort in 1950. As early as November 1950, Shanghai's labor unions and prominent businessmen made statements in the press patriotically supporting the war effort and pledging to improve production and stabilize prices.[7] At that point, however, the party still lacked sufficient resources to conduct effective propaganda work among most Shanghai workers. Operating through existing party cells and networks, as well as printed materials, the party's propaganda network in urban industry was mainly concentrated among literate, male workers or those employed in large, state-run enterprises. Most

5. The Chinese government responded to US intervention in Korea by mobilizing a propaganda campaign and organizing protests and rallies to oppose the US action from July 1950. Liao Kai-lung, *From Yenan to Peking*, 134–36.

6. More than 100,000 students and 12,490 workers in East China signed up for the military cadre schools. In Zhejiang Province, in the first recruitment drive alone, more than 17,000 students signed up. *People's Daily*, 1 May 1951; *Ba kang Mei yuan Chao yundong*, 77, 89–90, 106–7. According to a 1952 report by the Women Workers Department of the Shanghai GLU, 1,524 young working-class women in Shanghai entered the military cadre schools during the war. SMA C1-2-854.

7. *People's Daily*, 6 Nov. 1950.

workers—the illiterate, those employed in private industry and handicrafts, the unemployed, most women, and even many union cadres—had little or no exposure to the party's propaganda. As Richard Gaulton puts it, "A large percentage of Shanghai's people—those for whose benefit the revolution had been carried out—had to be reached by indirect, unsystematic methods if they were to be reached at all."[8]

The wartime campaigns were, to some degree, successful in achieving the leadership's goals, but inevitably there were also failures, misreporting, manipulation, and unintended outcomes. The CCP had governed China's major cities for barely a year when the country went to war in Korea, and its administrative and propaganda organs had only begun to penetrate society. Wartime mobilization extended the regime's reach through organization, recruitment, propaganda, and intelligence gathering. But this did not always translate into effective influence, and many people interpreted the campaigns in their own way, manipulated the movement for their own ends, or simply pretended to comply while ignoring the campaign's demands in practice. Production campaigns in the Yangzi Delta silk industry were typical of those in private industry generally. There was an impressive upsurge in patriotic fervor and support for the Communist Party following the victories of the Chinese People's Volunteer Army, and silk factories were able to achieve their quotas for "donations" to the war effort. But patriotic fervor did not translate into increased productivity or conformity with either industry standards or the political ideals promoted in campaign propaganda.

One of the first measures of the wartime campaigns, the "patriotic agreements" or "compacts" (*aiguo gongyue*), first appeared in Beijing in November 1950 and were promoted throughout the country by March 1951.[9] These were supposed to be the foundation for the "patriotic production competitions" intended to mobilize China's workers. The leaders of the campaign, however, complained in the press that the

8. Gaulton, "Political Mobilization in Shanghai," 51–52.

9. The first "patriotic agreement" was signed by business associations and unions in Beijing on November 7, 1950. It included only five articles with rather vague provisions to support the war in Korea, to uphold the law, and to struggle to improve production. Liao Gailong, *Aiguo yundong lunji*, 99–100.

implementation of "patriotic agreements" was not widespread and that the agreements were not taken seriously. Organizers responded with repeated efforts to "expand and deepen" the campaign, urging all Chinese citizens to establish "patriotic agreements," to launch "patriotic production competitions," and to participate in demonstrations protesting the US invasion of Korea.[10]

Despite such efforts, as late as May 1951, most factories in the Jiangnan region had not established "patriotic agreements." Where factories did create agreements, they were usually not carried out in any systematic way, and often amounted simply to listening to some speeches, shouting some slogans, pledging to work hard and support the troops, and then returning to business as usual. Even the response of the party's own cadres was lukewarm. The Chinese People's Committee to Resist America and Aid Korea (*Zhongguo renmin kang Mei yuan Chao weiyuanhui*), the national committee responsible for the "patriotic campaigns," was especially critical of local leaders' lack of enthusiasm.[11] Even if these reports are exaggerated for rhetorical purposes, they reveal the party's frustration at efforts to mobilize the "masses," or even their own cadres, despite the advantage of a relatively popular and patriotic wartime campaign.

A *People's Daily* editorial on June 2, 1951, called for "patriotic agreements" to be practical and specific in nature, as well as voluntary and drafted through "democratic discussion." The editorial stated, "Only if everyone genuinely feels that the agreement is their own creation can it be carried out effectively and with benefit to the unit and the nation."[12] The "patriotic agreements" were often neither voluntary nor "democratic," however, and in many instances, factory workers were compelled to sign an agreement they had no part in creating.[13]

This was certainly the case for young women in the Wuxi filatures. Conflict between female filature workers and male supervisors in the Jiangnan silk industry did not disappear with the establishment of the People's Republic. On the contrary, conflicts continued through

10. *Ba kang Mei yuan Chao yundong*, 10.
11. *Ba kang Mei yuan Chao yundong*, 88, 90, 94–95, 112.
12. *People's Daily*, 2 Jun. 1951; *Guanche zhixing*, 11–16.
13. *People's Daily*, 15 Aug. 1951.

the campaigns of the early 1950s in ways that alienated many workers from the Communist Party's politics. After 1949, male supervisors in Wuxi's thread mills maintained their dominance over filature workers and frequently held positions as union officials or propagandists, which enabled them to manipulate the campaigns for their own benefit. For example, in early 1951, supervisors at the Huachang Filature in Wuxi used the campaign to establish "patriotic agreements" to force workers to accept extended work hours, stricter production norms, and reduced wages. Demands from the leaders of the Campaign to Resist America and Aid Korea that the "agreements" be more specific and practical provided an opportunity for filature supervisors to intensify their control over the workforce through documents that had the weight of the ruling party's "patriotic campaigns" behind them.[14]

The implementation of "patriotic agreements" fell short of leaders' expectations in other ways as well. As late as August 1951, nearly half of all Shanghai employees had never signed a "patriotic agreement." By October, the proportion of enterprises that had established "patriotic agreements" was still reported as "more than fifty percent," and the majority of those drafted were still vague and formalistic.[15] One workshop created a "patriotic labor agreement" simply by taking the existing "labor agreement" and adding the word "patriotic" without altering the content. By the end of 1951, only ten out of more than two hundred Shanghai silk factories had established detailed "patriotic agreements."[16] The campaign also produced opportunities for official corruption and embezzlement of citizens' donations.[17] One highly critical newspaper report went so far as to state that "the problems discovered in this investigation of patriotic agreements in Shanghai are nothing less than the thought and work-style problems of Shanghai's current leaders."[18]

14. WMA D2-1-10.

15. Liao Gailong, *Aiguo yundong lunji*, 100, reports that by October, more than sixty thousand enterprises in Shanghai had established "patriotic agreements," which would indicate that only about half of all sizeable enterprises in Shanghai had done this.

16. SMA C1-2-524.

17. *People's Daily*, 10 Nov. 1951, 1 Mar. 1952; *Jiefang ribao*, 18 Jan. 1952.

18. *People's Daily*, 10 Oct. 1951.

An important goal of the "patriotic campaigns" in the second half of 1951 was transforming the "great upsurge of patriotic fervor" into a force for improving production and stimulating the economy. The Campaign to Increase Production and Practice Economy, which included patriotic agreements, production competitions, and the designation of labor models, mobilized industrial workers to improve productivity and contribute the savings to support the war. A detailed set of instructions published in the *People's Daily* on June 13, 1951, called on the unions to "correctly lead the campaign to increase production and make donations," emphasizing that the goal of the current campaign was not only to make donations for the purchase of war machines, but to transform the patriotic upsurge into a sustainable means of improving production throughout the still-recovering economy.[19]

The newspapers publicized the RMB prices for specific war machines: fighter plane, 1.5 billion; bomber, 5 billion; tank, 2.5 billion; heavy artillery, 900 million; anti-aircraft artillery, 800 million.[20] Those contributing could request that their funds go toward purchasing a specific type of armament, and some factories even had planes named after them. For example, the Tianyi Printing and Dyeing Works in Shanghai, with over four hundred employees, donated a "*Tianyi hao*" fighter plane with the surplus produced after six months.[21] Records of meetings of the Shanghai Silk Industry Association's executive committee in the summer of 1951 reveal that the Federation of Industry and Commerce had assigned a "donations" quota for the city's silk industry.[22] The amount that each factory was expected to donate was decided

19. *People's Daily*, 13 Jun. 1951.

20. *People's Daily*, 23 Feb. 1952. According to statistics from December 31, 1951, the Chinese people had donated a total of more than five trillion RMB in the previous six months. Given this spectacular success, and the fact that victory still had not been achieved, the leadership decided to continue the campaign. The Shanghai Silk Weaving Industry was asked to donate another two fighter planes. SMA S39-4-2. By June 1952, total donations reached over 5.5 trillion yuan, exceeding the original goal by 17 percent, and the campaign leaders announced that these funds had contributed decisively to the ability of the Chinese People's Volunteer Army to inflict heavy losses on the enemy. Wen-hui Chen, *Wartime "Mass" Campaigns*, 72–73.

21. *Guanche zhixing*, 2–9; SMA C1-2-194.

22. Shanghai's private businesses as a whole were asked to donate the equivalent of 240 fighter planes, or 360 billion yuan.

through discussion among the association members and was based on business turnover in each factory. Factories had some flexibility as to how to achieve their quota. In general, silk weaving factories were required to donate at least 2 percent of the payments received for state-contracted weaving and no less than 1 percent of total business income.[23] The factory unions were responsible for mobilizing workers to donate wages, bonuses, and savings, as well as to provide voluntary labor for digging air-raid shelters or caring for the families of military personnel. Shanghai workers fulfilled their quota of donating fifty fighter planes (seventy-five billion yuan) by August 1951.[24]

Wuxi's unions ultimately donated a total of 8.6 billion yuan, surpassing the original goal of donating the equivalent of five fighter planes (7.5 billion yuan). The Wuxi silk reeling industry collectively donated 1.5 billion yuan (the equivalent of one fighter plane) of which only 288 million came from increased productivity and economizing efforts.[25] This indicates that "donations" mainly came in the form of wages and factory profits rather than surpluses achieved through improvements that reduced production costs. The government's hope, however, was that the campaign would lead to increased productivity and "surplus profit" to be divided among the government, the factory owners, and the employees.[26] The campaign's leaders did not want people to simply "dig into their pockets," but rather to utilize slack production potential, reduce waste, lower costs, and develop new techniques to improve production. Although campaign leaders praised workers and factory owners for their "warmth and enthusiasm," they

23. SMA S39-4-1, S39-4-2.

24. SMA C1-1-513.

25. Yongtai Manuscript, 39; WMA D2-1-10.

26. The Shanghai Silk Weaving Industry LCCC negotiated agreements concerning the division of "surplus profits" during the war in Korea. The proportions varied from factory to factory, but in general, 60–80 percent of net profit was donated to the state in the name of the entire enterprise. The remaining 20–40 percent was divided between the collective welfare fund (usually 10–15 percent), profits (10–20 percent), individual bonuses, and aid to soldiers' families. Factory owners could also donate a portion of their share of the profits in their own name, and might need to do this in order to fulfill their portion of the industry's quota. SMA C1-2-194, C1-1-65.

also criticized these kinds of donations for not "fostering consciousness or linking up with production."[27]

CCP leaders put great stock in mobilizational techniques as a means of improving industrial production. Production competitions, later called "socialist competitions," were based on Soviet practices and methods developed during the party's years in Yan'an,[28] as well as earlier methods used by capitalist employers such as the production competitions at the Meiya silk weaving factories in the 1920s. Most "patriotic agreements" called for "patriotic production competitions" as the means to increase productivity.[29] The "patriotic agreement" of the Shanghai Silk Weaving Industry Association specifically pledged to identify and promote positive models for enterprise management and planning, to improve product quality and eliminate speculation, and to ensure that state contracts were completed properly and taxes paid on time. The factory owners' representatives also pledged to contribute voluntary labor, to suppress "counter-revolutionaries," and to "consolidate the unity of labor and capital."[30] As was the case in the rest of China, however, most of these provisions amounted to empty verbiage that was ignored in practice. Persistent problems, especially unsystematic enterprise management, chaotic accounting, poor product quality, and cheating on government contracts became even more serious by the end of the war.

Despite their perceived potential and later prevalence, the wartime "socialist competitions" were initially very limited, especially in private factories. According to statistics published by the ACFTU in February 1951, by that time only 2,065 state and private enterprises and 1.66 million employees had participated in labor competitions nationwide.[31] By March 1951, only seventy-four enterprises in southern Jiangsu Province and only the ten largest factories in Hangzhou had launched production competitions. Another report claimed that the number of

27. SMA C1-2-194, C1-2-524, C1-1-65.

28. Miin-ling Yu, "Labor Is Glorious," 231. Sheridan, "Emulation of Heroes," 47–50, notes similarities with the emulation of exemplars in the Confucian tradition.

29. Liao Kai-lung, *From Yenan to Peking*, 113–14. See also Wen-hui Chen, *Wartime "Mass" Campaigns*, 17–18; Gaulton, "Political Mobilization in Shanghai," 59–60.

30. SMA S39-4-1.

31. *People's Daily*, 23 Feb. 1951.

East China workers nominally participating in "patriotic production competitions" had reached 290,000 by that time, and that in Hangzhou, more than 20,000 workers had done so by mid-April.[32] By July 1951, over two million factory workers, miners, transport workers, medical workers, educators, shop assistants, and other employees, staff, and government officials had participated in some form of production competition.[33] But these statistics likely include a great deal of formalistic compliance that produced few tangible improvements.

In Shanghai, production competitions began on a small scale during the "Red May" of 1950, almost exclusively in state-run factories. One of the few silk factories to implement production competitions even on a small scale was the Shanghai State Silk Spinning Factory, which organized a competition in one of its weaving workshops. By the end of the year, only about 10 percent of Shanghai factories employing more than three hundred workers had organized competitions. Before July 1951, production competitions were organized only in the very largest silk weaving factories, and there is no evidence to suggest that most of the smaller silk factories engaged in anything like the flags-and-gongs campaigns in other factories and industries. Shanghai union officials attributed this to the fact that the Silk Industry LCCC was still too busy resolving labor disputes, and they also blamed union cadres "lagging behind the masses who are demanding labor competitions."[34] But this was also due to the lack of a Communist Party presence in most silk weaving factories and the party-state's limited influence over factory-level union organizations. Even as late as 1952 very few Shanghai silk weavers had any experience with production competitions, as the party's mobilizational efforts simply failed to reach most workshops.

Another reason given for the limited scope of production competitions in 1950 was concern on the part of union cadres, employers, and state administrators that the competitions would disrupt production. One union cadre in a Shanghai dyeing and weaving factory claimed that they could not hold production competitions there "because they

32. *Ba kang Mei yuan Chao yundong*, 107, 111–12.

33. Wen-hui Chen, *Wartime "Mass" Campaigns*, 41.

34. SMA C1-2-194.

would produce ruined cloth." Older workers compared the production competitions to Japanese efforts to intensify labor during the war, and warned younger workers, "If you young fellows work so fast, you will break these old bones of ours!"[35] But factory workers were not permitted to confront the Communist Party leadership with the kinds of collective slow-down tactics used against the "Japanese devils." Older workers who could not adapt to the stepped-up pace of the production campaigns soon found themselves falling behind.

The labor competitions promoted as part of the Campaign to Increase Production and Practice Economy emphasized collective effort and self-sacrifice for the good of the nation and the revolution, but also offered individual rewards and prestige. The war in Korea provided a vehicle for promoting the concept of revolutionary self-sacrifice as a defining characteristic of "proletarian consciousness." Industrial workers, constantly reminded of how their efforts contributed to victories on the battlefield, were urged to identify with soldiers giving their lives for the nation. Production competitions acquired their own military vocabulary, which produced "an intense, militarized atmosphere in the workplace."[36] Leaders exhorted industrial workers with slogans like "Every additional unit of production adds to our strength in defending peace" and "Factories are our battlefields, machinery is our weapon."[37]

Silk weavers, too, heard militaristic slogans such as "Eliminating one defective product is like destroying one of the enemy" and "One loom is equal to a cannon; a shuttle is equal to a gun."[38] Silk workers were reminded of how their efforts contributed to national economic construction with statements like "One ton of filature silk can be exchanged for eighty-seven tons of steel. Five hundred tons of filature silk can lay a railway line. One bolt of silk can be exchanged for one ton of gasoline. If we produce substandard silk cloth in the factory, what then of the steel, the railway, the gasoline?"[39] An article in Shanghai's

35. SMA C1-2-194.
36. Gaulton, "Political Mobilization in Shanghai," 60.
37. *Guanche zhixing*, 22–23; *Jiefang ribao*, 15 Sep. 1951.
38. *Shanghai gongren kang Mei yuan Chao.*
39. SMA S39-4-73.

Labor Daily in December 1951 claimed that if the silk reeling industry could conserve just five *jin* of cocoons per *dan* of raw silk produced, in one year the industry could save enough to purchase twelve airplanes or construct three new filatures equipped with the most advanced machinery.[40]

Material rewards in the form of cash bonuses or prizes also played an important role in motivating workers. Although the party's leaders warned against "economism" and expressed a preference for inexpensive ideological incentives, groups and individuals who exceeded norms received bonus pay as well as prizes such as fountain pens, watches, and radios. By the fall of 1951, however, party leaders complained that factory administrations relied too much on material incentives and not enough on "raising workers' consciousness," with the result that the production drive could not be sustained once bonuses were distributed. Campaign leaders maintained that material rewards should merely supplement the political education work of party organizations "so as to foster and sustain the workers' enthusiasm and creativity."[41] The most important aspect of this was persuading industrial workers that their interests were identical to those of the "workers' state" and "the people." Material rewards alone could not cultivate the desired form of "class consciousness."[42] The conflict between these two approaches to motivating industrial workers intensified during the First Five-Year Plan (1953–57) as party propagandists persistently sought to redefine working-class interests as those of the party-state and to identify contrary views as "backward," "economistic," "bourgeois," and "individualistic." This project aimed for nothing less than the construction of a "class consciousness" that was patriotic, statist, and self-sacrificing, reflecting the Communist vision of how true proletarians should think about their work.

40. *Laodongbao*, 26 Dec. 1951. Miin-ling Yu, "Labor Is Glorious," 237, comments that in comparison with the postwar USSR, Chinese production campaigns focused more on conserving raw materials.

41. *People's Daily*, 22 Sep. 1951. Bonuses were also used irrationally. In one coal mine in Shandong Province, it was found that the value of the gifts offered workers for over-quota production exceeded that of the surplus produced.

42. Miin-ling Yu, "Labor Is Glorious," 239.

The identification and reward of "labor models" (*laodong mofan*) was an important aspect of the production competitions and central to the goal of raising workers' "political consciousness."[43] But the designation of "model workers" (*mofangong*) during the campaigns of the Korean War suffered from the same shortcomings as the production competitions. In Chinese Communist theory and practice, "model workers" could serve as vehicles for promoting advanced techniques and work methods, as well as exemplars of the proper proletarian attitude toward labor. Labor models were rewarded with bonuses and other material prizes, but more importantly received honor, prestige, and, potentially, influence and access to political power.[44] Becoming a model worker was a potential path for workers' personal advancement, as labor models were frequently selected for party membership or promoted to administrative positions. As with the "patriotic production competitions," however, the earliest labor models were mainly found in state-run enterprises, and the scope of implementation was very limited. Difficulties in defining norms and standards, and issues like cheating, favoritism, and jealousy from coworkers, also impeded the identification and reward of labor models.[45]

The Shanghai GLU expressed the goal that production competitions would produce "a large cadre of labor heroes not only in state enterprises but also in private enterprises." Communist union leaders hoped that these exemplars of the "new attitude" toward labor would struggle against "backward and economistic ideas," which they contrasted with "a reasonable reward system in production competitions."[46] Launched in August 1950, the national labor model program expanded very slowly. Almost all of the municipal, provincial, and national-level labor models honored in 1950 were employed in state-run or joint state-private factories. Of the 673 Shanghai workers designated as municipal-level labor

43. On women labor models in rural Shaanxi Province, see Hershatter, *Gender of Memory*, 210–35.

44. See, for example, the career of Qingdao textiles worker Hao Jianxu, a famous model worker in the 1950s, who rose to the position of vice-minister of textiles and a member of the CPPCC. Miin-ling Yu, "Labor Is Glorious," 238–43.

45. Miin-ling Yu, "Labor Is Glorious," 249.

46. SMA C1-2-194.

models in 1950 (of whom fifteen were recognized as national-level labor models), the majority worked in state-run enterprises or the largest private factories with close ties to the state (such as the Shenxin system of cotton mills). Only 219 worked in private enterprises.[47]

Only four Shanghai silk workers, all of them employed at the Shanghai State Silk Spinning Factory, were honored as municipal-level model workers in 1950—Liu Fupei, Wang Baosheng, Wang Arong, and Qian Xiaomei (the only woman).[48] The characteristics they had in common exemplify the qualities expected of model proletarians in the early 1950s. None of them could be considered "young workers," the youngest being Qian Xiaomei who was nearly forty. All of them had experienced the occupation and postwar economic crisis, which they could contrast with the revolutionary present. While union leaders claimed this experience produced the "heightened political consciousness" necessary for outstanding work, only Qian Xiaomei showed an interest in political activism. A more prominent distinguishing feature among these and other early labor models was their dedication to and pride in their work, as well as a proprietary sense of taking care of "their" factory that was no doubt enhanced following the Communist takeover, but was also likely a product of long tenure. Finally, all of them showed a willingness to share their skills and experience to help others improve their work.

In 1951 more model workers were identified in private factories, but the scope was still very limited. That year twenty-five men and women in Shanghai's silk industry achieved status as municipal-level labor models. One extraordinary silk weaver, a woman named Liu Cuizhen, whose achievements at Shanghai's state-run silk weaving factory were publicized in the press, did not produce a single defect in the twenty-one months from February 1950 to November 1951. Another woman weaver, at the private Fufeng Silk Factory, increased productivity

47. SMA C1–1–114. Only seventy-one of these honored Shanghai proletarians were women. A report by the Shanghai GLU's Women Workers Department stated that far more would have to be done in terms of establishing childcare facilities, providing education and technical training, and promoting women's status generally to eliminate impediments to women's achieving labor model status. SMA C1–2–333.

48. SMA C1–2–217, C1–2–221, C1–2–222; *Shanghai fangzhi gongye zhi*, 834. Liu Fupei was the only national-level labor model in the history of the Shanghai silk industry.

from five bolts per month to seven. Overall, labor productivity in the silk weaving industry increased by more than 10 percent in the second half of 1951.[49]

For the most part, however, the wartime production campaigns created a burst of energy that was not sustained and did not translate into lasting improvements. Often, existing wage and bonus systems and management methods inhibited production competitions and the designation of labor models, and many privately employed workers viewed these as just another means of intensifying exploitation. The additional financial burden of "donations" inspired some factory owners to engage in cheating and deception (which were usually easier than making real improvements in production), and union cadres frequently colluded in this.[50] Some factory owners took advantage of increased production to line their own pockets, leading workers to complain that "we increase production and the boss gets rich" (*zengjia shengchan, laoban facai*) or "now the boss is getting rich on 'donations'" (*laoban xianzai yao fa juanxian cai*).[51] Factories were also criticized for "blindly" launching competitions without adequate preparation, planning, and discussion among the workers.[52]

A June 1951 report by the Shanghai GLU's Production Department stated that the main task in organizing competitions was setting production norms to "lay an initial foundation for future production . . . and economic accounting."[53] But difficulties in setting clear production norms and collecting accurate statistics on workers' performance proved to be a great impediment.[54] Ideally, the Chinese Communists hoped to emulate Soviet-style management practices, which emphasized objective standards and "scientific" management, promoted advanced

49. *Laodongbao*, 7 Aug., 5 Nov. & 8 Dec. 1951.

50. For examples of employer resistance and cheating on state silk contracts in 1951, see SMA S39-4-27, C1-2-194, C1-2-527.

51. SMA C1-2-524.

52. *People's Daily*, 23 Feb. 1951.

53. SMA C1-2-194.

54. One report stated that though there were likely many potential labor models in private silk factories, without accurate statistics there was no way to identify them. Because of the difficulties involved and the other pressing demands on their time, neither employers nor union cadres were very enthusiastic. SMA C1-1-65.

techniques, and relied on a system of individual responsibility for production tasks.[55] These goals proved impossible to achieve in practice, however, even in state-run enterprises managed by loyal and competent cadres. The irony is that the method adopted to achieve these goals—patriotic production competitions—frequently undermined attempts at systematizing production on a more rational basis.[56]

Statistical systems in most Chinese factories in 1950 were very primitive, and most managers and workers had only a vague idea of how to set appropriate production norms. This was particularly true of the Shanghai silk weaving industry, dispersed in hundreds of small-scale workshops. Standards for daily output and wages for different varieties of cloth varied from factory to factory, as did norms like utilization of raw materials or quality standards such as the number of defects permitted. Even measurements such as the standard length of a bolt of gold georgette varied considerably.[57] Well into 1952, silk factory owners, silk workers, and state representatives wrestled with the problems of standardizing production norms and wages, which persisted even after socialization in 1956.

Conflict over norms and standards is common to all forms of industrial production, but is particularly prominent in efforts to implement "scientific" management and centralized planning. The CCP's attempt during the Korean War to use political mobilization to improve factory production frequently impeded the technical organization of production. China's political leaders realized this contradiction only gradually (if ever), and initially viewed "patriotic production competitions" as a way of mobilizing workers to participate in the process of setting higher production norms and increasing productivity. However, it was difficult to determine baseline norms for rewarding improvements,

55. On "scientific management" in the USSR see Lieberstein, "Technology, Work, and Sociology"; S. A. Smith, "Taylorism Rules OK?"; Sochor, "Soviet Taylorism Revisited."

56. Schurmann, *Ideology and Organization*, 236.

57. SMA S39-4-29, S39-4-1. In October 1952, the Shanghai Silk Industry Association attempted to establish industry-wide standards for thirteen priority varieties of silk cloth, but they received little cooperation or assistance from either the CSC or factory owners. And although the association promulgated these standards, most factories made no effort to implement them.

and this difficulty remained one of the greatest impediments to production competitions and the designation of labor models. Political mobilization only exacerbated the problem by encouraging workers to pursue gross output targets and ignore most other production standards.[58]

In the context of the silk industry, appropriate norms and accurate statistics were necessary to determine who (if anyone) had "won" the competitions by producing the highest quality product. But given the lack of industry-wide standards, as well as wide variations in production requirements, factory managers and silk weavers usually had only a vague idea concerning norms for output, quality, and use of raw materials. Setting norms according to accurate data was more feasible in the larger silk weaving factories that employed middle management professionals and technicians. When launching its production campaign in the fall of 1951, the Dacheng Silk Weaving Factory organized a team of twenty-two technical staff and weavers to collect data on all aspects of production. This team alone was larger than the entire workforce of many Shanghai weaving factories. In some factories, workers were able to establish statistical systems to record their own achievements, which heightened their awareness of ways they could improve. For example, recording the weight of waste silk produced in the prep departments of weaving factories made prep workers aware of this problem and helped to reduce waste.[59] In most cases, however, the ideal of developing production based on accurate norms, which would then be exceeded by politically inspired workers, remained an elusive goal for years to come.

Because of the difficulties in collecting statistical data and assessing performance, many factories tended to favor "egalitarianism" in the distribution of bonuses and other rewards. This practice, however, conflicted with the philosophy of providing individual incentives for those who exceeded norms and promoting outstanding "models" for other workers to emulate. This created confusion and dissatisfaction in the distribution of rewards. The union organization at Shanghai's Meiya

58. On the conflict between "scientific management" and political mobilization campaigns in Chinese industry, see Schurmann, *Ideology and Organization*, 231–35. He uses the terms "technical" and "human" integration.

59. SMA C1-2-527.

Silk Weaving Factory collected more than ten million yuan in production bonuses, but cadres did not know how to distribute these funds and had to appeal to higher-level organizations for instructions.[60]

Production competitions during the Korean War appeared earlier and were more widespread in the filatures of the Yangzi Delta than in the region's silk weaving factories. In this context, however, factory owners and supervisors manipulated campaigns to "heighten workers' political consciousness" as a way of maintaining control. Like Shanghai silk weavers, Wuxi filature workers were told to "make the factory a battlefield, make the machinery a weapon," and to "sweat a bit more to help the Volunteer Army bleed a bit less."[61] They too were reminded how the silk thread they produced helped to import the steel, oil, and machinery needed to develop the Chinese economy.[62]

One of the most striking achievements during the wartime campaigns, recognized at the highest levels of government, was the production of high-quality silk at the joint state-private Huachang Silk Filature in Wuxi. In January 1951, workers at Huachang produced five *liang* of AAAA grade silk on "standing" reeling machines, and five *liang* of AAA grade silk on "sitting" reeling machines. No Chinese filature had produced thread of such high quality since before the Japanese invasion in 1937. According to the Shanghai Commodity Inspection Bureau, 53 percent of the filature's product in January 1951 was AA grade or higher. On February 20, the factory reported this feat to ACFTU chair Liu Shaoqi and Chairman Mao Zedong. Liu sent a letter of congratulations to the factory's employees (fig. 5.1), and the filature subsequently received several visits from state officials, including Marshall Zhu De. During the spring of 1951, the CSC's Number Two Factory and the Ruilun Filature in Wuxi, as well as Hangzhou's state-run Chongyu Filature, also produced AAAA grade silk.[63]

By April 1951, 1,406 small groups and 18,493 individual workers had (at least nominally) participated in production competitions in Wuxi

60. SMA C1–2–527.

61. WMA D2–1–10; *People's Daily*, 23 Feb. 1951.

62. *Laodongbao*, 26 Dec. 1951.

63. WMA D2–1–10; Qian, *Wuxishi sichou gongye*, 23, 468; *Jiefang ribao*, 27 Jul. 1951; *Laodongbao*, 5 Nov. 1951; *People's Daily*, 17 Mar. 1951; *Hangzhou sichou zhi*, 17.

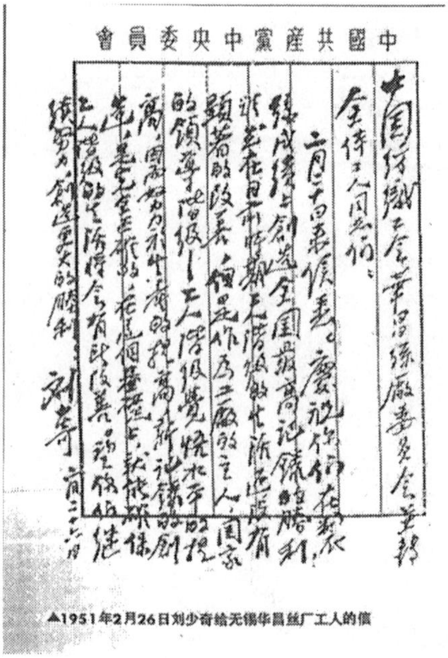
中國共產黨中央委員會

▲1951年2月26日刘少奇给无锡华昌丝厂工人的信

FIGURE 5.1. Letter from ACFTU Chair Liu Shaoqi to the union committee of the Huachang Filature in Wuxi. In Qian, *Wuxishi sichou gongye zhi*, 468.

factories,[64] and the Campaign to Increase Production and Practice Economy expanded in fits and starts through the end of the decade, culminating in the quixotic efforts of the Great Leap Forward. Nonetheless, a 1954 union report stated that production competitions were still quite limited and often consisted of a burst of sloganeering and intensified effort without significant improvements in management or production systems. Union and party cadres were still not paying sufficient attention, and only nine out of the city's (then) thirteen filatures had even implemented production competitions.[65]

The results were similarly mixed regarding efforts to reward and promote model workers in Wuxi's filatures. The designation of labor models potentially offered many benefits to women workers, if only the system could be implemented fairly.[66] A union report from 1953 stated

64. WMA D2-1-10.

65. WMA B17-2-6.

66. In 1950 only four Wuxi filature workers were honored as municipal-level model workers. One was Zhu Qiuhua of the joint state-private Huachang

that Wuxi had produced a total of 627 labor models between 1949 and 1953, as well as two model workshops, thirty-seven model small groups, and eighty-one "advanced producer" small groups.[67] In 1952, a total of nineteen employees at the Yongtai Filature were designated as factory-level labor models. Li Fengying, Zhou Qizhen, and other model silk reelers developed ways to reduce the amount of cocoons used in production so that, on average, each worker could save the equivalent of 5,000 yuan in raw materials each day. Li Fengying, the leader of this group, was selected in August 1952 to attend the international meeting of the world textile union in Berlin. On the way, she passed through Moscow to celebrate the thirty-fifth anniversary of the October Revolution and was honored with the opportunity to meet revolutionary leader Comrade Joseph Stalin.[68]

Although women were a small minority among the early labor models, they were among the most highly praised and publicized in the press.[69] Becoming a labor model was a potential path to personal advancement for many women, one that had not existed in the old society. The labor model program was by no means free of gender discrimination, patronage, or favoritism, but, at least in theory, it was based on objective standards that any man or woman with the necessary skills and determination could achieve. Because most silk factories lacked accurate statistical and record-keeping systems, however, it was difficult to determine whether workers had achieved any significant improvements. Even when workers' accomplishments were measurable, it was not always possible to reward and promote individuals, nor was it obvious that improvements necessarily resulted from individual effort, let alone "political consciousness."

Party propaganda attributed the achievements in production of silk thread in the first months of 1951 to Communist Party leadership, the "patriotic production campaigns," and filature workers' increased enthusiasm for production after Liberation. But these were dubious

---

Filature. The other three all worked in state-run or joint state-private factories. WMA D2-1-7.

67. WMA D2-1-10.

68. Yongtai Manuscript, 41; Qian, *Wuxishi sichou gongye*, 338.

69. Tina Chen, "Female Icons," 268.

claims under the circumstances. The union organization at the joint state-private Huachang Filature remained under the control of management, and the filature's party organization was very weak. Most importantly, there was no attempt to reform the abusive "feudal" management system by which male supervisors dominated women workers. It is difficult, then, to accept explanations of Huachang's accomplishment in terms of "liberating" the creative energies of the working class or of workers' and managers' "heightened political consciousness." On the contrary, the quality improvements achieved in January 1951 would seem to be the product of improved cocoon supplies, economic stability, and increased demand—positive trends that existed within the same brutal management system practiced in Jiangnan filatures for decades.[70] Indeed, during the Democratic Reform Campaign in the fall of 1951, it was found that the quality standards achieved in January could not be sustained because of the shortcomings and injustices of the existing factory regime.

In the same month that Huachang workers produced AAAA grade silk for the first time in fourteen years, almost half of the filature's workers were fined for falling short of production standards. This did little to inspire further efforts. According to a Wuxi GLU report, the arbitrary system of bonuses and fines at Huachang "suppressed the masses' creativity and activism, and because of this, the achievement of producing AAAA grade silk could not be consolidated or surpassed."[71] The same situation appeared at the Number Two Filature and the Ruilun Filature, which also found that they could not sustain long-term production of AAAA grade silk.[72]

By the end of 1951, the production campaigns coincided with improvements in Jiangnan silk production, even if they cannot be credited for all of them. Whereas in 1949, only 17 percent of Jiangnan filature silk achieved grade B or higher, by 1950, 55 percent reached this quality standard, and by 1951, the proportion of high-quality silk was 65 percent. Average daily per-capita output in silk filatures increased from 20 *liang*

70. On improvements in sericulture since 1949, and on the bumper cocoon crop of 1951, see *Zhongguo fangzhi*, 10 Aug. 1951.

71. WMA D2-1-11.

72. WMA D2-1-12, D2-1-10.

in 1949 to 30 *liang* or even as much as 40–57 *liang* in exceptional cases. Efficiency improved as well, and the average amount of dried cocoons needed to produce one *dan* of raw silk fell from 4.2 *dan* to 4 *dan* or even as little as 3.5 *dan*. Shanghai's Dali Filature managed to use less than one ton of coal per *dan* of silk produced. Production costs were reduced by 60 percent, and quality improved such that more than half of the filature's silk reached grade B or higher.[73]

Despite the filatures' increased production of A and B grade silk, much of this product contained imperfections, and the rate of defective silk remained high. In 1950, defective silk comprised 10.85 percent of total annual production. In 1951, the proportion was 15.01 percent, and in 1952, Wuxi filatures produced 137,791 kg of defective silk, comprising 18.39 percent of total production. Total losses caused by defective product amounted to 16.2 billion yuan, enough to purchase 2,035 new "standing" reeling machines.[74] Although there were some impressive improvements in production of silk thread during the early 1950s, ongoing problems with product quality reveal the limitations of the Communist Party's mass mobilization approach to improving industrial production. Even more important, if the improvements of 1951 were to be sustained based on workers' patriotism and "heightened political consciousness," then the brutal and exploitative management system in place in Yangzi Delta filatures would have to change.

Mass mobilization campaigns and production competitions also produced mixed results for state-contracted manufacturing and exports, which increased dramatically between 1950 and 1952. These two efforts—political mobilization and state-contracted production—often worked at cross-purposes and are representative of the contradictions contained in many Communist Party initiatives of the 1950s. It was crucial that these efforts succeed, however, as silk became a vitally important export product during the Korean War. Indeed, it is likely that the revival of exports and expansion of state-contracted production contributed more to improvements in silk production during the war than did the contemporaneous "patriotic production campaigns."

73. *Laodongbao*, 5 Nov. 1951; *Dagongbao*, 7 April, 27 July & 26 Dec. 1951.
74. Qian, *Wuxishi sichou gongye*, 474.

Table 5.1
Employment, wages, and production in Shanghai's silk weaving industry, 1949–54

Year	Total employees/ production workers	Total wages (mill. RMB)	Total production (10,000 meters)
1949	8,830/7,130	n.d.	1,195
1950	6,995/5,303	49,664	1,095
1951	7,664/6,414	59,396	1,433
1952	9,283/7,561	70,086	1,826
1953	9,641/7,912	78,603	1,687
1954	n.d.	n.d.	2,363

SOURCE: S39–4–44 and *Xin Shanghai gongye tongji.*

Following China's entry into the Korean War in October 1950, the United States led the imposition of an economic embargo on China, and by 1951 the United States had banned all trade with the PRC. The US-led embargo organized under the United Nations' "China Committee" in 1952 was far more comprehensive than similar restrictions imposed on trade with the Soviet Union, because it sought to deprive China not only of military equipment but also of the means to industrialize and develop its economy. The result was a strengthening of trade and aid relations between China and the Soviet Union.[75] The Soviet Union and its Eastern European satellites were prepared to purchase Chinese silk at above-market prices in exchange for ruble credits, foreign currency, military hardware, and advanced industrial equipment that could support a Communist China. In April 1951, the Ministry of Foreign Trade removed all export tariffs on silk cloth and allowed private silk brokers to export their goods independently, mostly through Hong Kong.[76] The results for production and employment in Shanghai's silk weaving industry were impressive (table 5.1).

By 1952, total production of silk cloth in Shanghai had reached 90 percent of existing capacity. The proportion of silk production

75. Engel, "Fat and Thin Communists," 445–74; Mustanduno, *Economic Containment*; Cain, "US-Led Trade Embargo," 33–54; and Clayton, "Free Trade, Protection and the British Empire."

76. SMA S39–4–67.

Table 5.2
Production and state contracting for the first six months of 1951 and 1952

	1951	1952
Number of factories	350–59	343–45
Number of looms	4,928–5,080	4,708–4,840
Number in operation	2,281–2,603	2,929–2,675
Bolts produced	172,308	148,360
Delivered to CSC	25,835	94,276
Independently sold	138,023	51,666
Quilt covers produced	92,439	158,681
Delivered to CSC	0	96,422
Independently sold	92,343	42,900

SOURCE: SMA S39-4-68.

contracted to the state also increased dramatically from late 1951, as the data show (table 5.2).

Silk was an especially important export product and source of foreign exchange for China during the Korean War, amounting to about 30 percent by value of total exports from the city of Shanghai before 1953. More than 90 percent of China's silk exports passed through Shanghai. Nationally, in 1951 and 1952, silk comprised more than 95 percent of textile exports by value and was the top foreign exchange earner per production cost among textile products. In 1950, Chinese silk exports earned the equivalent of 21 million US dollars, and exports of silk cloth increased 30–50 percent annually over the next four years. By 1954, the amount of foreign exchange earned by silk exports had reached 61 million US dollars (table 5.3).

At first, Chinese silk cost more than Japanese or French silk and was generally of poorer quality. Nonetheless, the Soviet government preferred to purchase Chinese silk in order to aid its political and military ally and because it enjoyed favorable terms of trade with China. As production efficiency improved and costs fell, by 1952 Chinese prices reached levels comparable to those of Japanese products. Quality problems continued to plague the silk weaving industry for years thereafter, but in the early 1950s Chinese producers were able to reduce costs and improve production to the point that socialist countries were no longer

Table 5.3
Silk export statistics, 1950–54

Year	1950	1951	1952	1953	1954
Total value of exports (mill. USD)	552	757	823	1,022	1,146
Exports from Shanghai (mill. USD)	104.32	99.62	118.66	183.29	274.04
Total value of silk exports (mill. USD)	21	31	41	55	61
Silk exports from Shanghai (mill. USD)	nd	nd	nd	48.41	55.46
Exports of silk cloth (mill. meters)	8.21	13.95	17.38	20.36	29.42
Silk exports as proportion of total textile exports (%)	80.8	96.9	95.4	68.8	61.6
Silk exports as proportion of total value of exports (%)	3.8	4.0	5.0	5.3	5.3

SOURCE: *China Silk Statistics.*

subsidizing Chinese silk production but were making relatively equitable exchanges. The expansion of exports during the Korean War was a great boon to beleaguered silk producers. However, the world socialist economy's capacity to absorb Chinese silk was not unlimited. By mid-1952, state weaving contracts were reduced by about 15 percent, threatening to renew the industry's crisis.[77]

During the Korean War, the proportion of silk thread produced on contract to the state expanded even more rapidly than that of silk cloth. By 1951, all of Wuxi's filatures were producing on contract for the China Sericulture Company, which in cooperation with the Jiangsu Provincial Foreign Trade Company operated the most complete monopoly in silk products in the industry's history. By 1952, all private filatures in Jiangsu Province were producing entirely on contract for the CSC. In the same year, the proportion of state-contracted production in Shanghai filatures reached 98.62 percent, but in the silk weaving industry was only 50 percent. By 1954, all production in Shanghai filatures and silk

77. SMA S39-4-6.

spinning factories was contracted to the state, while there remained a high proportion of independent production and marketing in the city's silk weaving industry.[78]

The Communist system of state-contracted production in silk weaving was relatively successful compared with its previous incarnation under the Nationalists, but there nonetheless remained many problems. In March 1951 factory owners were still reporting shortages, especially of synthetic fibers, as well as delays in receiving raw materials from the state silk company.[79] Even more problematic, factory owners complained that as much as 70 percent of the filature silk they received from the CSC was substandard. The Yumin Silk Factory had to discard 215 pounds of filature silk received on contract because of mildew. Tong Xinbai, general manager of the Meiya Company and a vice chairman of the Silk Industry Association, complained repeatedly about the lack of responsibility on the part of the filatures, who, under the state contracting system, were accountable only to the state company and not to the end users of their products. Factory owners also said that payments for state contracts failed to keep up with equipment depreciation and labor costs such as annual bonuses, paid vacations, meal subsidies, and labor insurance.[80] In the absence of direct market exchanges, however, silk producers could only report problems to a bureaucratic entity that was less than responsive to their needs.

Despite many shortcomings, the wartime production campaigns contributed to restoring China's economy, developing production, increasing state revenues, and to some extent "raising the political consciousness" of workers and employers. Nonetheless, the limited scope of the campaigns and their mediocre results in improving productivity disappointed many in the party's leadership. Although the campaigns were credited with some remarkable accomplishments, these could be attributed to more mundane factors, such as improved supplies and the restoration of exports. Most Chinese workers responded positively to

78. Qian, *Wuxishi sichou gongye*, 30–31; *Jiangsusheng cansang sichou zhi*, 253; *Shanghai sichouzhi*, 95; SMA C48-2-1252.

79. SMA S39-4-67. In the early 1950s China was importing synthetics from Czechoslovakia and Hungary, but the quality of these products was considered inferior to Italian and Japanese synthetics.

80. SMA S39-4-29, S39-4-62.

the call to increase production and make donations to support the war, but at the same time the factories often neglected other goals such as reducing waste, lowering costs, and improving product quality.

The production campaigns furthermore revealed or created many new problems, exposing the scope of official corruption and difficulties in the relationships between state agencies and private businesses. Closer cooperation between the government and private enterprises through state contracting produced many opportunities for corruption and cheating, while all the old tricks of the wartime and postwar economy—tax evasion, bribery, misuse of materials, and profiteering—continued and even worsened during the Korean War. Although the CSC recognized several private factories as "model contract weaving factories," the state company also had to censure factories for "not paying sufficient attention to processing tasks, misusing state-supplied raw materials, selling contracted products on the black market, and other outdated bad habits of speculation and profiteering."[81] Local and central party leaders responded with a series of campaigns from the autumn of 1951 through the summer of 1952 to expose, punish, and reform these undesirable practices. The new campaigns identified wayward capitalists as "enemies" on a par with "counter-revolutionaries," and deserving of similar treatment.

Enemitizing Campaigns of the Korean War

The CCP's wartime production campaigns were more heavily publicized and directly affected more people than some of its other well-known campaigns. But other wartime political campaigns, especially those that sought to identify and eliminate various kinds of "enemies" in Chinese society, probably had a greater influence on popular politics in the early 1950s. In its first months in power, the Communist Party was remarkably lenient toward its enemies, often to the dismay of underground activists who hoped for more decisive action. With the outbreak of war in Korea in June 1950, however, efforts to suppress

81. *Laodongbao*, 7 Aug. 1951.

active and potential opposition intensified, eventually becoming the Campaign to Suppress Counter-Revolutionaries (*Zhenya fan geming yundong*).[82]

Drawing upon earlier rectification campaigns from the party's Yan'an days, this was the first of a series of "enemitizing" campaigns, which defined certain behaviors, political alignments, and social groups as "enemies" of the revolutionary national community defined as "the people." Just as the land reform campaigns targeted landlords as enemies of the people to be liquidated, the wartime campaigns from 1950 to 1952 mobilized the party, the police, the unions, and "the masses" to expose and attack urban "enemies" of the revolution, including Nationalist agents and spies, corrupt officials, unfeeling bureaucrats, criminals, and cheating capitalists. In order for production to develop further and the war effort to succeed it would be necessary to reform these people's thought and behavior, and to excise this cancer from the body politic. In pursuit of these goals, "enemitizing" campaigns like the Campaign to Suppress Counter-Revolutionaries were fairly successful at rooting out and discouraging actual and potential enemies of the revolutionary state.[83] Like the "patriotic production campaigns," however, these enemy-targeting campaigns often did not develop according to the leadership's directives or failed to achieve their (frequently ambiguous) goals. They not only met with resistance, but also provided opportunities for groups and individuals to subvert or manipulate the campaigns in pursuit of interests and issues not included in the original directives.

According to statistics on the Campaign to Suppress Counter-Revolutionaries from ten industrial unions in Shanghai, 233,458 workers participated in 2,712 "public trial meetings" (*gongshen dahui*), and the authorities received a total of 4,673 anonymous denunciations, many of them sent by groups of workers. It was estimated that 40 to 45 percent

82. For two recent works on the politics of suppression in the early PRC, see Dutton, *Policing Chinese Politics*, and Aminda Smith, *Thought Reform and China's Dangerous Classes*.

83. On the Campaign to Suppress Counter-Revolutionaries, see Yang Kuisong, "Reconsidering the Campaign to Suppress Counterrevolutionaries," 102–21, and Strauss, "Paternalist Terror," 80–105.

of the city's total employees directly participated in public meetings and denunciations.[84] The campaign culminated in mass arrests at the end of April 1951. In a series of coordinated actions, some 8,500 alleged counter-revolutionaries were arrested, about one-third of whom (2,748) were seized on factory premises. By May 5, more than 9,000 individuals had been arrested in Shanghai.[85] By September, arrests totaled 6,077 just in Shanghai factories and enterprises. Out of a total 5,909 Shanghai silk workers, there were only fourteen arrests. The campaign thus directly affected only a very small minority of Shanghai workers. However, the fact that, over the course of the entire campaign, arrests were made in 81 percent of state-run textiles factories, 83 percent of private cotton mills, and 37 percent of private silk weaving factories meant that a great many workers directly witnessed arrests or participated in struggle meetings and denunciations.[86]

China's "national capitalists" were generally protected from mass campaigns before the Five Antis Campaign in early 1952, but some members of the bourgeoisie came under attack earlier for collaboration with the Japanese or Nationalists. In the Yangzi Delta silk industry, the Campaign to Suppress Counter-Revolutionaries saw the confiscation of only a few private factories. On May 29, 1951, the owner of Wuxi's Dingchang Filature, Qian Fenggao, was found to have "engaged in production for the enemy," and the filature was confiscated. The filature reopened shortly thereafter, jointly operated by the municipal and provincial governments. Only two other Wuxi filatures were confiscated during the campaign—Hongfeng on June 18 and Runkang on June 27. Most silk production remained in private hands, however, and for the most part, the factory owners continued their operations unmolested.[87]

Due to ambiguity in identifying "counter-revolutionaries" and the devolution of authority to worker-deputies, many errors and injustices

84. SMA C1–1–28. This document also provides examples of individuals informing on family members as models for emulation.

85. Perry, *Patrolling the Revolution*, 171; Li Jiaqi, *Shanghai gongyun*, 419.

86. SMA S39–4–12, C1–1–28, C1–1–73. By far the highest proportion of arrests among Shanghai textile workers was in the wool industry, where almost 1 percent (0.979%) of 7,250 employees in privately owned factories were arrested.

87. Qian, *Wuxishi sichou gongye*, 171, 337, 473.

were committed during the campaign. In many cases, those accused were not in fact active opponents of the revolution but were individuals, such as labor gang bosses and abusive supervisors, whom workers detested and considered "counter-revolutionary" according to their own standards.[88] Rather than dampen workers' enthusiasm and weaken their support, the authorities usually accepted such accusations. Campaign leaders recognized that when known "enemies of the working class" were not arrested, it could produce widespread "dissatisfaction with the unions and the public security organs."[89]

In some factories, over-zealous union cadres demoted or denied labor insurance to entire categories of employees such as the female supervisors in Shanghai cotton mills known as "Number Ones." There were also cases of administrative cadres using the campaign to reduce excess staff and "simplify personnel," which not only cost the individuals their jobs but also saddled them with an abhorrent and irremovable political label. In factories where there had been an intense underground struggle before the revolution, the campaign produced a "settling of accounts" with those who had cooperated too closely with the old regime.[90]

An example from the Meiya Number Four Silk Factory reveals how the climate of fear and mistrust could affect underground Communists. A silk weaver named Long Jifu had joined the party in 1937 and during the occupation was active in Shanghai and rural Zhejiang, as well as Hong Kong. When he returned to Shanghai in 1945, he continued working at Meiya and participated in underground party activities, helping to organize strikes in 1947. Because his contact had been killed in 1946, however, he lost touch with the party for two years. When the Communists seized Shanghai in 1949, he was told that his membership had lapsed. Long, however, had believed that he was a party member in

88. See, for example, Frazier, *Chinese Industrial Workplace*, 120.

89. SMA C1-1-28.

90. Perry, *Patrolling the Revolution*, 170, 175, finds that the Campaign to Suppress Counter-Revolutionaries encouraged underground activists to reveal themselves, now that the party was acting decisively to eliminate those who had been a threat to them before. At the same time, the campaign put intense pressure on underground activists who might have joined Nationalist organizations to protect themselves, perhaps even on the orders of party leaders.

good standing and had been doing party work. As political repression intensified from 1950, his reapplication for membership was repeatedly denied despite letters of support from established party members who knew him. It appears that there were also some personal conflicts involved, but Long was clearly a victim of the party's mistrust of its own urban activists. He was not readmitted to the party until 1987.[91]

Investigations also brought to light examples of union leaders abusing their authority to eliminate personal enemies, which understandably had an adverse effect on "the internal unity of the working class."[92] Despite prohibitions against physical violence, there were also cases in which the accused was forced to kneel or be stripped of their clothes in "struggle meetings," and other incidents of abuse. Typically, the party leadership sought to correct such "leftist errors" and excessive zeal without dampening the masses' enthusiasm. A November 1951 Shanghai GLU report criticized union cadres and workers who "did not clearly distinguish among thought, life, and work-style problems, and who did not strictly distinguish between backward elements and counter-revolutionaries."[93] A union report on the arrests of April and May 1951 stated that there were "too many people categorized as serious counter-revolutionaries." A survey of 35,820 employees in seventy-two factories carrying out "democratic reform" in the fall of 1951 found that 384, about 1 percent, had been categorized as "serious counter-revolutionaries," but officials considered even this small proportion too high upon examining individual cases. Among 24,860 employees in twenty-eight Shanghai textile factories, almost 5 percent had been categorized as "serious counter-revolutionaries." The report considered this percentage much too high and a terrible injustice.[94]

Workers' responses to the Campaign to Suppress Counter-Revolutionaries ranged from jubilation to trepidation. Many experienced the campaign either as an act of revolutionary revenge or as a necessary evil that would ultimately enhance their sense of security

91. Personal file of Long Jifu, Meiya Factory Archives.
92. SMA C1-1-28.
93. SMA C1-1-28.
94. SMA C1-1-73.

and liberation.[95] At the same time, it was an event that increased fear, anxiety, and uncertainty. The ambiguity of the category "counter-revolutionary" raised fears that anyone could be found guilty for past associations such as having served as a union picket under Nationalist rule. Some workers likened the Communists' use of terror in the workplace to the actions of the Nationalists.[96] Factory workers may have been grateful that known enemies were removed, but there must also have been some concern as to who might be targeted next or how easily one might run afoul of the revolutionary authorities and their agents.

As an example of the Chinese Communists' use of mass mobilization techniques, the Campaign to Suppress Counter-Revolutionaries was very different from the police purges under Stalin in the Soviet Union's Great Terror of the late 1930s. In China, the party-state sought to gain the active cooperation of the majority in the suppression of a minority. This approach resulted in many injustices, but it served the purpose of involving the population in the policies and aims of the party-state. As a result, the authority to use coercion to suppress counter-revolutionaries was dispersed more widely in society than was the case in Stalin's Great Terror. The CCP introduced not only the worker pickets, but ordinary factory workers and even previously powerless persons such as old women and young girls, to the new weapons of denunciation and struggle.

A related campaign that grew out of efforts to suppress counter-revolutionaries among the working class, a precursor to the Three Antis and Five Antis Campaigns, was the Democratic Reform Campaign, conducted mainly within union organizations. As a mass mobilization campaign, Democratic Reform (*minzhu gaige*), carried out nationwide in the fall of 1951, should be distinguished from experiments with "democratic management" (*minzhu guanli*) in state and private

95. For reports of positive responses to arrests in Shanghai cotton mills, see SMA C1-1-28.

96. Perry, *Patrolling the Revolution*, 171–72. Perry also reports widespread resentment toward the worker pickets, who began to serve as political enforcers, getting people to attend meetings and participate in the campaigns of 1951. In a few cases, the pickets even helped factory administrations to conduct bodily searches, a powerful symbol of workers' oppression under the old regime (SMA C1-1-60).

industry, such as the labor-capital consultative conferences.[97] The Democratic Reform Campaign mainly sought to purge union and party organizations of "undesirable elements," including criminals, secret societies, religious sectarians, and Nationalist Party loyalists, but also labor gang bosses, foremen, and agents of the bourgeoisie.[98] A Xinhua editorial of August 20, 1951, stated that the campaign aimed to eliminate "feudal" elements "who politically oppress and economically exploit and defraud" workers.[99] In the Shanghai textiles industry, for example, the campaign targeted "Number Ones," female shop-floor bosses who dominated and exploited mill workers. If exploitative labor bosses and workshop supervisors were not suitable targets for "suppression of counter-revolutionaries," they were decidedly "undemocratic" and required removal from positions of responsibility.[100]

Even more important for most of the population were the problems of illegal activities among China's "national bourgeoisie" and corruption among union and government officials. By the winter of 1951–52, the "patriotic campaigns" to increase production, practice economy, and make donations to the war effort temporarily took a backseat to the Three Antis and Five Antis Campaigns. The Three Antis Campaign (*Sanfan yundong*) developed in the fall of 1951 in response to mounting criticisms in letters to the *People's Daily* and by top party leaders of the corruption, bureaucracy, and lavish lifestyles of some party, government, and union cadres.[101] In late November, Chairman Mao issued a set of instructions to party cadres at all levels in which appeared the first reference to the "three antis," described as corruption, waste, and bureaucratism.

97. See Cliver, "*Minzhu guanli.*"

98. Brugger, *Democracy and Organisation*, 90–111; Fletcher, *Workers and Commissars*, 30–31.

99. Quoted in Sheehan, *Chinese Workers*, 40. The process of how the campaign worked to remove people from positions of responsibility is described in detail in chapter 6.

100. Sheehan, *Chinese Workers*, 37–41. On the Democratic Reform Campaign at the Shenxin Number Six Mill, see Frazier, *Chinese Industrial Workplace*, 117–19.

101. *People's Daily*, 7 & 28 Nov. 1951.

The campaign was officially launched on December 1, 1951, with the publication of a Central Committee resolution calling for a campaign to oppose corruption, waste, and bureaucratism in government work, but also to resist "the corrosion of the party by the bourgeoisie."[102] A CPPCC directive at the end of the month explicitly linked the new campaign to the patriotic production drive and stated, "If we do not curb and overcome this kind of serious phenomenon, then it will corrode our newborn government organizations." The directive also blamed the influence and practices of "degenerate and decadent bourgeois" and "reactionary Guomindang" for the corruption that had become so prevalent among Communist Party cadres.[103] On January 20, 1952, Marshall Ye Jianying, Governor of Guangdong Province, presented the problem in the starkest terms, stating that official corruption had resulted in the People's Government becoming "divorced from the interests of the people." Ye stated: "For two years the leading cadres have been enjoying officialdom and bureaucratism while there is no democracy for the common people. The people are severely oppressed, and dare not express their opinions to the higher authorities." Ye also stated that "the influences of the urban bourgeoisie are particularly damaging to the party members, who had been long accustomed to country life; and this is true even among cadres of long standing."[104]

The first to be targeted in the Three Antis Campaign were usually officials retained from the old regime, many of whom could be found guilty of one form or another of "corruption, waste or bureaucratism."[105] Under the policy of leniency for those who confessed and cooperated, only the worst offenders were removed from office, and there were very few arrests of either retained officials or Communist Party cadres.[106] Outrage at rampant corruption produced a flood of

102. Wang Chaobin, *Sanfan shilu*, 45–46, 50, 52; Sheng, "Mao Zedong and the Three-Anti Campaign," 56–80.

103. *Fantanwu, fanlangfei, fanguanliaozhuyi*, 1–2.

104. *Nanfang ribao*, 23 Jan. 1952.

105. Gardner, "Wu-fan Campaign," 493.

106. According to State Council regulations concerning penalties for official corruption approved in March 1952, for cases involving less than ten million yuan,

denunciations and revelations as campaign committees received hundreds of thousands of accusations, informants' reports, and confessions. Wang Chaobin reports that individuals informed on officials as highly placed as county chiefs and department heads, who were required to make public self-criticisms and to engage in "remedial study" (*buke*). Although the campaign also targeted waste and bureaucratism, it was the struggle against official corruption that received the most enthusiastic response from ordinary Chinese citizens.[107] The Three Antis Campaign was embraced by activists within the party and government, often young southerners newly recruited to the party, who were especially ruthless in hunting down corrupt "big tigers" among veteran cadres from the north.[108]

The Three Antis Campaign called for mass mobilization, but this was mainly limited to accusations and denunciation letters, and there were far fewer mass struggle meetings than in the Democratic Reform Campaign or the Five Antis Campaign. In many cases, powerful officials suppressed those who attempted to struggle against them. Some officials were even able to turn the campaign against corruption into a campaign against "anti-party behavior" by condemning their critics as "counter-revolutionaries" and mobilizing their own supporters.[109] Party cadres may have been willing to mobilize "the masses" against "counter-revolutionaries" and capitalists, but were less sanguine about inviting mass criticism of themselves and their comrades.

In combination with the campaigns focused on Democratic Reform and Suppression of Counter-Revolutionaries, the Three Antis Campaign dramatically affected union organizations. Nearly half of

---

offenders would be subject to one year of imprisonment, probation, or reform through labor, and could possibly face revocation of party membership, demotion, demerit, warnings, and other administrative penalties. More serious cases carried mandatory prison or labor reform sentences, or even the death penalty. Supplementary provisions in April established the legal basis for punishing cases of corruption and recovering stolen funds, and also stated that punishment could be made retroactive dating back to the founding of the People's Republic on October 1, 1949. *People's Daily*, 12 Mar. & 22 Apr. 1952. The full texts of all relevant directives and legislation are provided in Wang Chaobin, *Sanfan shilu*, 194–217.

107. Wang Chaobin, *Sanfan shilu*, 194, 219–20.

108. Lin Yilan, *Soushan dahu*, 1–2.

109. Willy Kraus, *Economic Development and Social Change*, 40.

all union cadres in Wuxi were found to be problematic, either colluding with employers in some fashion, engaging in corruption or graft, or possessing a "poor work style and muddled ideology."[110] In the Shanghai GLU, the Three Antis Campaign focused on the Unemployed Workers Economic Relief Committee, which was rife with corruption. A January 1952 report stated that members or employees of the committee had embezzled more than 37 million yuan and 17,490 *jin* (8,745 kg) of relief rice. A later report stated that a total of 589.12 million yuan had been stolen from unemployment relief funds, of which 64 percent was recovered during the campaign. Four party members on the committee were found to have engaged in serious corruption involving theft of relief funds or blackmailing women for sexual favors. The most serious case involved a party member who used his position to blackmail capitalists into giving him silver, furniture, and other bribes.[111]

In the Shanghai unions, the Three Antis Campaign pulled in a total of 4,827 officials guilty of at least one of the "three antis." Of these, 32 percent were found guilty of corruption through misuse of public funds, bribery, illegal sale of state property, and false purchasing orders. Although only 1,560 union cadres were found guilty of corruption, 2,922 (45 percent) were removed from their posts, a result that can be viewed as a continuation and expansion of the Democratic Reform Campaign. The proportion varied widely from industry to industry. In textiles, only 28 percent of union cadres were replaced, as compared with more than 50 percent in metalworking and light industry.[112] The campaigns of 1951–52 thus resulted in considerable "new blood" entering the union organizations. One February 1952 article stated, "In the violent struggle to beat the 'tigers,' a great many 'tiger beating braves' have already distinguished themselves."[113] In Shanghai, a special school was established to prepare campaign activists for party membership, and six hundred workers were promoted to positions in factory administration.[114]

110. WMA D2-1-10.
111. SMA C1-2-695, C1-1-73.
112. SMA C1-2-695, C1-2-808.
113. Lin Yilan, *Soushan dahu*, 3.
114. *People's Daily*, 18 Apr. & 30 Jun. 1952.

The campaigns of 1951–52 also revealed that many workers who had been honored previously as labor models were in fact unworthy, or even "counter-revolutionary." The January 1952 issue of *People's China* reported that, as of July 1951, 60,644 Chinese workers had attained the status of labor model nationwide.[115] During the Three Antis, however, many were found to have achieved this status through deception or favoritism as "running dogs" of the capitalists. Of Shanghai's 673 municipal-level labor models honored in 1950, ninety-four were found to have engaged in corruption or otherwise "degenerated" by 1952, and thirty-nine were exposed as "corrupt elements." Two had become capitalists while twenty-five were denounced as "counter-revolutionaries" during the suppression campaign and Democratic Reform.[116]

As was the case with the CCP's other campaigns, the Three Antis Campaign did not entirely succeed in achieving its goals. Although opportunities for corruption were greatly reduced, waste and incompetence continued, and "bureaucratism" proved especially difficult to eliminate. Persistent problems in government and the unions led to the launching of a "New Three Antis" Campaign from January 1953, which targeted "bureaucratism, commandism, and violating laws and discipline."[117] Intended as a relatively mild reform of cadres' work style, in some cities (such as Hangzhou) the New Three Antis became a bitter intra-party struggle, including public denunciations of party cadres who had stifled criticism during the earlier Three Antis.[118]

From the beginning of the Three Antis Campaign, leaders cited bourgeois influence as a more prominent cause of corruption than bureaucratism, and as time went on more and more of the blame for official corruption was shifted onto the "national capitalists" in what became the Five Antis Campaign.[119] There was obviously some relationship between private business and official corruption. But given the power relations involved, it is often difficult to tell who was

115. *People's China*, vol. IV, no. 1, 1 Jan. 1952, 4.

116. SMA C1-1-114.

117. SMA C1-2-914.

118. James Gao, *Communist Takeover of Hangzhou*, 179–82.

119. As expressed in Wen-hui Chen, *Wartime "Mass" Campaigns*, 54–55, "From the very beginning the Communists blamed the city bourgeois for corrupting the good old Communists."

corrupting whom.[120] Tax evasion, speculation, and other forms of economic manipulation on the margins of the state and private sectors created endless opportunities for illegality, while the increasing dominance (and sometimes incompetence) of state organs in all aspects of economic life, combined with the onerous exactions of wartime donations, created systemic incentives for corrupt business practices beyond simple greed.

In the winter of 1951–52, the Communist Party leadership grew increasingly vitriolic in its attacks on China's capitalists and mobilized the populace, especially industrial and commercial workers, against the bourgeoisie. In a January 1952 speech, Vice Premier Bo Yibo went so far as to state that the Three Antis Campaign was nothing less than a "counter-attack against the frenzied attack on the working class and the Chinese Communist Party carried out by the bourgeoisie over the past three years." Bo condemned these "attacks" in the strongest terms, calling them "counter-revolutionary" and "reactionary" and describing the struggle against bourgeois influence as a "serious class struggle."[121] Public propaganda attacked China's "national bourgeoisie," calling them "vile enemies of the state" and "criminal counter-revolutionaries," who were bound to resist most strenuously so as to carry out their nefarious, anti-party plans. The authors do not seem to have considered that the innocent might resist just as strongly, even stating that "if they do not surrender voluntarily, they should be captured" like tigers.[122]

There probably was a great deal of malfeasance and illegality among China's capitalists in 1951. For one thing, Chinese capitalists had for many years resorted to bribing officials, evading taxes, and making backdoor deals to survive in China's war-ravaged economy. The economic structures of New Democracy inspired few changes in this regard, and most businesses continued to pursue profit as they had

120. As one contemporary observer noted, "the greatest corruption took place in government and Party agencies that dealt with economic matters and had closest contacts with commercial and industrial circles." A. Doak Barnett, *Communist China*, 139. For a detailed treatment of a prominent case of tax evasion, bribery, and corruption involving silk merchants and tax officials in the city of Changzhou, Jiangsu Province, see Wang Chaobin, *Sanfan shilu*, 128–35.

121. Bo, "Wei shenrude," 8–10.

122. Lin Yilan, *Soushan dahu*, 9–13.

done in the past, now with the added burdens of "donations," increased taxes, and factory welfare funds. Responding to the incentives of the hybrid economy, Chinese businesses continued to engage in a variety of schemes and dodges to increase revenues and survive in a rapidly changing context.

Growing out of the Three Antis Campaign in the winter of 1951, the Five Antis Campaign (*Wufan yundong*) in the spring of 1952 was a form of controlled class warfare aimed at reforming the business practices of China's "national bourgeoisie" without eliminating the capitalists as a class. The campaign sought to eliminate the "five poisons"—bribery of government workers, tax evasion, theft of government property, cheating on government contracts, and stealing state economic information for private speculation. These were far more complex problems than party ideologues imagined, for they were not only legacies of China's war-torn economy, but were also rational (if illegal) responses to the structural incentives of the mixed economy.[123] Communist Party officials, however, usually attributed these problems not to contradictions inherent in the New Democratic economy but to "the 'evil' essence of capitalism."[124] In the eyes of these Marxists, such practices were the product of individual immorality and greed rather than structural economic incentives.

The Communists' claim that the Five Antis was a "counterattack" against the "frenzied attack of the bourgeoisie" also seems contrived in light of archival sources. Nor do claims that the campaign was the next step in the process of achieving state control over private industry provide adequate explanation for the campaign's goals and consequences.[125]

123. Gardner, "Wu-fan Campaign," 492, states that the "belief that the new regime would be neither willing nor able to exercise strict control over the bourgeoisie must have encouraged many industrialists and businessmen to continue to behave as they had done under the Nationalists, and to indulge in various corrupt practices which were an accepted part of urban life before the Communist takeover." In other words, in a context that continued to pose great challenges, capitalists continued time-tested survival strategies.

124. Bennis So, "Abolition of Private Ownership," 695.

125. Richman, *Industrial Society in Communist China*, 896, claims that "one of [the campaign's] real chief aims was to speed up the transformation of private enterprises into joint private-state and pure state ownership." But the evidence from case studies does not lend itself to such a linear and pre-determined conclusion.

More than anything, the campaign was an attempt to make China's private merchants and industrialists abide by the laws and regulations governing private business to benefit both the national economy and state revenues.[126]

Furthermore, the fact that the party leaders chose to launch a mass campaign rather than suppress illegal business practices by legal/juridical means reveals both the limited reach of the party-state and the Communists' belief in the transformative power of mobilization campaigns. Juridical methods were less attractive both because the Communists did not trust the existing legal/judicial establishment[127] and because a juridical approach provided less flexibility. A mass campaign would allow the leadership to exercise a policy of "leniency" and to protect those capitalists who were cooperative and valuable while treating harshly those who resisted or who owned assets the state hoped to expropriate immediately.

Equally important was the transformative aspect of participation in mass campaigns, both for "the masses" of privately employed workers and for the "enemitized" capitalists themselves. A campaign against private employers could raise (and redefine) the "class consciousness" of workers in private enterprises and (it was hoped) extend the party's organizational apparatus into this sector of the working class, building on the advances achieved through the production campaigns and Democratic Reform Campaign. The mobilizational approach also allowed local authorities to account for the tremendous diversity of private businesses in China, to protect local businesses from disruption, or to avoid expropriating complex or failing industries.[128]

126. Ecklund, "Protracted Expropriation of Private Business," 239, aptly states that this "show of force, while destroying any hope of 'business as usual' under the Communists, fell far short of outright confiscation." He suggests that the campaign was designed "to instill in businessmen a healthy respect for the new regime but at the same time to leave the door open for continued operations in the private sector."

127. Taire, *Shanghai Episode*. For an interesting historical discussion of law in the early People's Republic of China, see Cohen, "Reflections on the Criminal Process," 323–55.

128. On the flexibility afforded China's leaders through the use of a mass mobilization approach to reforming China's capitalists, see Gardner, "Wu-fan Campaign," 535–39, and James Gao, *Communist Takeover of Hangzhou*, 172–79.

In the case of Shanghai's silk weaving industry, the combination of state contracting and factories' financial difficulties produced incentives and opportunities for factory owners to engage in tax evasion, cheating on government contracts, and misuse of state-supplied materials. A weaving workshop might operate only two or three looms but report five or seven, selling the excess thread supply on the black market. There were many other dodges and scams factory owners adopted to increase their meager profits under state contracting.[129] In September 1951, before the official launch of the Five Antis Campaign, Zhang Huirong, the owner of the Jiuji Silk Weaving Factory in Shanghai, admitted to having used half of the filature silk provided by the state company to produce cloth for private sale. This was considered "theft of state property," and Zhang was made to write a self-criticism, which was distributed among the members of the Silk Industry Association as a warning.[130]

Similar practices, such as passing off mixed batches of filature silk as high-quality silk or altering the inspection certificates for farmers' cocoons to suppress prices, were prevalent in Jiangnan silk reeling filatures, and represent a continuation of filatures' practices in the 1930s. The efforts of private factory owners to protect their profit margins also fueled corruption. Xue Zukang, the owner of Wuxi's Yongtai Filature, fostered "a group of loyal running dogs" in government organs including the State Sericulture Management Bureau, the East China Branch of the CSC, and the Southern Jiangsu Sericulture Company.[131] Xue and other Wuxi filature owners also continued their attempts to dominate and control the union organizations, using tactics such as treating cadres to gifts, meals, and trips on Lake Tai, loaning money, bribery, and procuring the favors of women. During the Five Antis Campaign, these were cited as examples of the "frenzied attack of the bourgeoisie," which "caused much dissatisfaction toward the unions, the government, and state companies among the workers."[132]

129. *Xinwenbao*, 6 & 24 Oct. 1950.
130. SMA S39-4-62.
131. Yongtai Manuscript, 38, 41–42; Qian, *Wuxishi sichou gongye*, 474.
132. WMA D2-1-10.

In January 1952, industry associations in Chinese cities began to establish committees to organize the campaign and accept their members' confessions.[133] The Shanghai Silk Industry Association organized its own "Four Antis" Committee[134] on January 24 to study the ongoing Three Antis Campaign, to consider the role capitalists had played in producing such problems, and to confess their crimes to one another. These early confessions usually mentioned only minor offenses and sought to explain or excuse potential transgressions. But the ambiguity of the campaign's goals and guidelines, combined with the threat of "enemitization," produced fear and uncertainty among China's business class. Capitalists' confessions to the Silk Industry Association included exposure of questionable relationships with state silk officials, many of whom had been colleagues and coworkers only months earlier, regardless of whether they had done anything illegal.[135]

In February, silk merchants and industrialists in Wuxi participated in a series of twenty-three meetings organized by the city's Federation of Industry and Commerce. These were not "struggle meetings" like those that proliferated in the later stages of the Five Antis, but were an example of the business community's self-policing. In these meetings, Wuxi silk merchants confessed numerous crimes to one another, including keeping false accounts, tax evasion, destruction of evidence, concealing funds, and selling silk thread for "excessive profits." Several silk merchants admitted to having bribed Comrade Shi Zhuer of the Tax Bureau to avoid paying taxes totaling more than five billion yuan.[136] Further investigations revealed that before 1949 most filatures bribed officials of the Commodity Inspection Bureau (most of whom were still on the job in 1952). Relationships with government officials

133. A. Doak Barnett, *Communist China*, 145; Gardner, "Wu-fan Campaign," 505–6.

134. At first there were only four "antis": bribery, fraud, excessive profits, and tax evasion. By February, "excessive profits" was replaced with "theft of government property," and the addition of "stealing state economic information for private gain" made it "five antis." SMA S39-4-1.

135. SMA S39-4-113.

136. WMA D5-2-200. In another case, Zhu Lingshuang of Wuxi's Hengyuan Silk Factory stated that he had attempted to bribe Hua Shaoyun of the Tax Bureau, but that Comrade Hua had refused.

were one of the resources that helped factory owners to survive the turmoil of the previous decade, but from 1952, the new government took steps to break down these relationships and to block strategies for advancing business interests that fueled official corruption.

By February 1952, the Five Antis Campaign was in full swing in Yangzi Delta cities. Teams of propagandists mobilized employees, distributed propaganda materials, investigated the owners of factories and shops, and organized workers to criticize their employers. On February 20, the Shanghai GLU reported that it had already received some 210,000 denunciations from workers. Many businessmen saw the situation worsening and attempted to flee, or they resisted by intimidating their employees through factory closures, lockouts, threats, abuse, and spreading rumors.

Regulations issued by the Shanghai People's Government prohibited such tactics and attempted to discourage unauthorized investigations of individual capitalists by workers, as well as physical abuse, torture, and theft.[137] Despite these prohibitions, workers often revived the violent tactics of the past. In one case in June 1952, one or more workers at Shanghai's Jianye Silk Factory struck and injured the owner, a representative on the industry LCCC named Hu Tingkun. The offenders were prosecuted according to the law but were let off lightly. The LCCC investigation also decided that labor relations at Jianye were not "normal," and officials admonished Hu (in his hospital bed) to focus on production and to enact reforms to address the problem. The Silk Industry Association also took the opportunity to protest the treatment of factory owners during the campaign generally and to request specific instructions from the Labor Bureau as to what "reforms" should be implemented.[138]

Vitriolic propaganda concerning capitalists' economic banditry and the "frenzied attacks of the bourgeoisie" during the previous months fanned the flames of class conflict and unleashed the outrage and hostility of Shanghai workers upon the "national bourgeoisie." During the Five Antis Campaign, meetings of labor-capital consultative conferences often devolved into shouting matches as workers learned

137. Gardner, "Wu-fan Campaign," 507–8, 513–17.
138. SMA S39-4-2.

that while they had accepted reduced wages and benefits to help enterprises recover and make donations to the war effort, the factory owner had derived illicit profits by cheating on government contracts. Factory owners often did this in order to meet the rising costs of maintaining their employees.[139]

By March, Jiangnan capitalists had been attending meetings, listening to broadcasts, and confessing their "crimes" for more than two months. It must have come as some surprise, therefore, when Shanghai Mayor Chen Yi announced the official launching of the Five Antis Campaign on March 25. He outlined the principle of "leniency for those who confessed and severity for those who resisted," urging all Shanghai capitalists to confess their crimes. At the same time, Mayor Chen sought to reassure Shanghai's capitalists by emphasizing that the Five Antis Campaign would differ from land reform in that the bourgeoisie was not to be eliminated as a class, that production and commerce should be maintained, and that the government would assist businesses that encountered difficulties by giving them production contracts, purchasing their products, and providing loans.[140]

By April 21, with more than fifty thousand workers and management staff organized into investigation teams, the campaign was, as John Gardner put it, "actually 'penetrating' factories, enterprises, and shops about which it already had gained some degree of knowledge."[141] The investigation teams took charge of the campaign, checked factory accounts, and mobilized the employees to "speak bitterness" and denounce factory owners. Investigators especially pressured senior managers and accountants to reveal what they knew of their employers' business dealings, and mobilized businessmen's families to convince them to confess. Capitalists who had already confessed were organized

139. Liu Changshen, long-time labor leader and chair of the Shanghai GLU, described it in these terms: "In the past, employers had a bad attitude toward workers; now workers are reversing roles." Frazier, *Chinese Industrial Workplace*, 116, citing *Zhongguo zibenzhuyi shehuizhuyi gaizao*, 1: 151–54. As A. Doak Barnett noted, however, "the terror to which [capitalists] were subjected was largely psychological; there was very little physical violence in this campaign." A. Doak Barnett, *Communist China*, 146.

140. Gardner, "Wu-fan Campaign," 517–18; Wen-hui Chen, *Wartime "Mass" Campaigns*, 62, 65–66.

141. Gardner, "Wu-fan Campaign," 517.

into "Merit Achieving Teams" to convince their fellows to do likewise, and by early May there were more than two thousand such teams in Shanghai alone.[142] Investigations led to "mass struggle meetings" to announce findings and to compel business owners to make public confessions. As A. Doak Barnett has pointed out, "it was essential that the businessmen confirm and accept the verdicts by their confessions."[143] This served to undermine capitalists' authority within their own factories and to break down relationships between employers and employees. It also disrupted the networks between businessmen and government officials and within the business community that provided the social framework for illegal practices.

The experiences of China's businesspeople during the Five Antis Campaign varied widely, even within the Yangzi Delta silk industry. Because Cai Shengbai, the general manager of the Meiya Silk Company who was notorious for his suppression of strikers in the 1930s, had already fled to Hong Kong, Meiya workers were denied an effective target for struggle. The "capital-side representative" at Meiya, Tong Xinbai, only owned a half share in the company and was well regarded by most of the workers. The struggle against him was purely a formality involving public acknowledgment of the "leading role of the working class," and Tong was not subject to harsh criticism or struggle.[144] At the family-run Yunlin Silk Factory, however, the Five Antis Campaign brought intense struggle. Given his strong personality and sense of himself as a legitimate businessman, the factory's manager, Lou Erpin, did not submit meekly to criticisms or confess to "crimes" when he genuinely felt that he had done nothing wrong. Mr. Lou's "lack of cooperation" resulted in harsh treatment from the leader of the campaign, a former weaver who had left Yunlin to join the Communists after the war and later returned to the factory as a party member and labor organizer.[145]

142. SMA C1-2-1654; Wen-hui Chen, *Wartime "Mass" Campaigns*, 62–66; Gardner, "Wu-fan Campaign," 518–20.

143. Barnett, *Communist China*, 148–49.

144. SMA S39-4-4; Interviews with Shen Fukang, 19 Nov. 2003, and Qian Binhua, 12 Feb. 2004.

145. Mr. Lou and his brother stated that their experiences during the Five Antis Campaign were too painful to discuss in detail. Interview with Lou Erpin and Lou Erzheng, 19 Apr. 2004.

Overall, the Five Antis Campaign does not seem to have been especially severe in most Shanghai silk weaving factories. Although there were many examples of owners cheating on government contracts and misusing state-supplied materials, most of these cases were handled through the Silk Industry Association, and there was far less of the kind of public struggle meetings in Shanghai's small silk factories than was common in the city's larger and more prominent firms.[146] By contrast, the campaign was quite intense in some of the silk filatures in Wuxi. The struggle at the Yongtai Filature played out in a series of thirteen small and three large "struggle meetings" beginning in late March 1952. At first the owner, Xue Zukang, managed to keep his senior managers loyal, telling them, "If I have [committed the] five poisons, then you managers are also partly to blame," and some even secretly sent him copies of their watered-down denunciations. In one case, a manager's daughter convinced him to cooperate with the campaign and expose his employer's crimes. Through a combination of public meetings (to hear workers' accusations) and private appeals (to reassure staff members that they would be better off cooperating with the campaign), more and more accountants and technical staff proved willing to reveal Xue's illegal business dealings. Xue Zukang continued to resist and ignored accusations and calls for him to confess, but it became impossible for him to manage the factory effectively. Every time he walked into the workshops the women workers shouted out, "Warn Xue Zukang he must thoroughly confess! This is his only way out!" Others pasted up paper strips with the slogan "Xue Zukang! Quickly and thoroughly confess! We don't need you to manage production." Faced with such criticism, as well as evidence of his illicit dealings brought forward by his closest associates, Xue eventually confessed to a long list of crimes large and small.[147]

On April 30, the *Liberation Daily* announced "basic victory in the 'Five Antis' campaign in Shanghai."[148] The majority of working-class

146. For silk factory owners' confessions during the Five Antis Campaign, see SMA S39-4-113.

147. Yongtai Manuscript, 42–43.

148. Gardner, "Wu-fan Campaign," 522. On the conclusion of the campaign in Beijing, the restoration of private production, and efforts to restore labor-capital unity, see *People's Daily*, 3 Jun. 1952.

people in Shanghai had been drawn into the struggle, and reports claimed that 80 percent of workers and shop assistants had taken part in mass struggle meetings and heard public confessions by employers.[149] Most of the capitalists who confessed received lenient punishments and were forced to pay fines and back taxes. There were very few arrests or confiscations of property, and only a handful of capitalists committed suicide because of the pressures of the campaign.[150]

The penalties assigned to silk capitalists by the end of the campaign varied widely. Only five of Wuxi's thirty-nine filature owners were found to be in violation of the law. The rest were either "law-abiding" or "basically law-abiding."[151] Xue Zukang was found to have illegally acquired a total of more than two billion yuan (Old Renminbi)[152] in the previous three years. Because of the "completeness" of his confession, however, as well as the importance of the Yongtai Filature to the city's silk reeling industry, Xue was treated leniently. Aside from having Xue repay his "illegal earnings" in installments, the Wuxi Increase Production and Practice Economy Committee categorized Yongtai as "basically law-abiding" despite Xue's attempts to resist during the campaign.[153]

Of the thirty-two members of the Shanghai Silk Industry Association's executive committee, fifteen were found either to have committed no errors or to be "basically law-abiding," and thirteen were found to be "semi-law-abiding." Two were arrested for nonpayment of taxes and placed "under surveillance by the masses," which amounted to house or work arrest. Two others were representatives of state enterprises and not subject to the campaign. Almost all of them (twenty-eight) were required to make pecuniary recompense in the form of fines, back taxes, or "illegal earnings" returned to the government.

149. A. Doak Barnett, *Communist China*, 150.

150. For horror stories and similar anecdotes from the Five Antis, see Taire, *Shanghai Episode*.

151. WMA D5-2-204.

152. The numbers associated with monetary values in the PRC in the early 1950s are astronomical because of the lingering influence of inflation. In 1955, the central government initiated a currency reform and issued new RMB equivalent to ten thousand "Old Renminbi." Cheng Chu-yüan, *Communist China's Economy*, 104.

153. Yongtai Manuscript, 43.

Total payments amounted to more than 6.3 billion yuan (Old Renminbi). Of this, more than 5 billion was imposed on the Lou family's Yunlin Silk Factory, indicating that Yunlin was treated very harshly. This probably had less to do with any actual "crimes" than with Lou Erpin's "attitude" toward the campaign and unwillingness to collaborate in his own demise. Other factories' payments ranged from 1,731,725 yuan for Zhao Zifu of the Jiudashengji Silk Factory, which had been found to be "basically law-abiding," to 489,076,090 yuan for the joint owners of the Shanghai Second United Silk Weaving Factory, which was only "semi-law-abiding."

The penalties for some "basically law-abiding" factories, such as the owners of Yongda and Shanghai First United, who had to pay more than thirty million yuan each, were sometimes higher than for factories designated as "semi-law-abiding," such as the Hongchang Factory, which only had to pay just over one million yuan.[154] This demonstrates the ways in which the policy of "leniency" interacted with revenue-extracting goals to produce fines that were, more or less, "whatever the market would bear."[155] Although the campaign certainly cost China's "national bourgeoisie" financially and in terms of status and prestige, it had other, more far-reaching results that were both unintended and unwelcome, products not of Communist Party leadership and political education, but of workers' efforts to pursue their interests in the context of a complex and chaotic mass campaign.

Factory owners were not entirely powerless in the face of this campaign and sought to protect themselves in a variety of ways. Some factory owners responded with what officials described as the "three stops"—halting wage payments, suspending the provision of meals, and ceasing production—although such actions were prohibited.[156]

154. SMA S39-4-4.

155. As Barnett puts it, almost all businessmen "suffered financially, roughly according to their ability to pay." A. Doak Barnett, *Communist China*, 140–41. For statistics on the penalties imposed on capitalists following the campaign in Shanghai, see Gardner, "Wu-fan Campaign," 522–23. For Hangzhou, see James Gao, *Communist Takeover of Hangzhou*, 171–72. For the whole of China, see Richman, *Industrial Society in Communist China*, 896.

156. A. Doak Barnett, *Communist China*, 147–48; Frazier, *Chinese Industrial Workplace*, 123.

Campaign leaders also complained of "blind wage increases" as capitalists attempted to win their employees' support and shield themselves from mass criticism. It is difficult to distinguish, however, between employers' efforts to protect themselves and employees' attempts to manipulate the campaign to advance their own interests. The opportunity to struggle against employers inevitably involved demands for higher pay and benefits that factory owners were in no position to refuse.

A union report from Wuxi claimed that the Five Antis Campaign had taken labor relations to a "new stage" but also admitted that there were many "deviations," including workers using their newfound influence over employers to arbitrarily demand wage increases and other benefits.[157] A report by the Shanghai GLU mentioned that wage issues became the focus of many disputes during the campaign, especially in smaller factories. Excessively low wages, inter-factory disparities, rewards for advanced producers, the treatment of apprentices, and disparities between men and women or between old and new workers were all points of contention during the Five Antis.[158] Although the China Sericulture Company set standards for wage calculations in July 1952, which the Silk Industry Association and the union approved, enforcement proved difficult. In October, disputes over wage standards appeared even in "backbone" enterprises (advanced, reliable factories with strong, loyal union organizations) such as Meiya, Yongda, Second United, and Yongyuan.[159]

A November 1952 report indicated that wage disparities among workers producing the same types of cloth continued despite the CSC standards, most likely because some silk workers were able to extort higher wages by pressuring their employers. Weavers frequently complained that wages were too low, but factory owners were constrained by the level of payments for state contracting, which were not easily adjusted. Such disparities not only caused problems for state planners and factory owners, but also created conflicts among workers.[160] Despite efforts to control the "class struggle," the leaders of the Five Antis

157. WMA D2-1-10.
158. SMA C1-2-739.
159. SMA S39-4-29.
160. SMA C1-2-739.

Campaign faced the recurring problems of "economism" and "leftism" among workers and even among party and union cadres. Wuxi union leaders criticized basic-level cadres for acceding to workers' demands for increased wages and benefits that "hindered the circulation of capital, causing employers to become passive and affecting production."[161]

In a speech on October 31, 1952, Song Baolin, chairman of the Shanghai Silk Industry Association, criticized Shanghai's silk factory owners, saying, "Many capitalists cannot pass the test (*jingbuqi kaoyan*) and do not uphold their administrative responsibilities. They meekly increase wages causing difficulties for their enterprises." He then announced that the China Sericulture Company had made arrangements for a union symposium to exchange opinions on the problem of excessive wage increases resulting from the campaign.[162] At another meeting that October, the Silk Industry Association discussed the issue of labor disputes and requested that the Labor Bureau take a hand in resolving these issues and "strengthening labor-capital relations." The Association also requested that the Shanghai Textiles Union hold monthly meetings of the LCCC to help resolve disputes over wages and similar issues.[163] Clearly, many Shanghai silk weavers and other workers were able to pursue their economic goals with some success despite opposition from the authorities.

By the time the Korean War ground to an uneasy end and China embarked upon its First Five-Year Plan in 1953, working conditions had changed significantly as compared with 1949. Inflation was under control, the bourgeoisie had been chastised and disciplined, production and employment expanded dramatically, and most Chinese workers were organized in unions under at least nominal Communist Party leadership. As a result of the wartime campaigns, especially the extension of "production competitions" into private industry, the lives of Chinese workers began to converge with regard to workers' welfare

161. WMA D2-1-10. Mark Frazier reports that, in Guangzhou, party and union cadres frequently supported workers' demands for increased wages in violation of official policy. Frazier, *Chinese Industrial Workplace*, 122, 126.

162. SMA S39-4-29.

163. SMA S39-4-1.

provisions. The conditions under which they labored had also become politicized and militarized.

Conclusion

If the CCP's primary goals following its seizure of power were to promote economic recovery through labor-capital cooperation and to establish Communist Party rule under New Democracy, these priorities began to shift with the outbreak of the Korean War in 1950. Despite the climate of fear and insecurity it engendered, hostilities with the United States also helped the Communists to enhance their legitimacy and authority in Chinese society. By means of propaganda and mass campaigns, the party promoted an upsurge in patriotism and political consciousness that, it hoped, would translate into increased productivity in industry and greater activism in politics and society. It was difficult, however, for party propagandists' messages to reach everyone, and even when the message was received, it was often misunderstood or misinterpreted.[164]

One feature of the relationship between the Yangzi Delta silk industry and the state during the Korean War was the expansion of state-contracted production of both thread and cloth. The wartime campaigns, however, especially the "patriotic production competitions," not only proved to be limited in terms of their success and reach, they also frequently disrupted production and the fulfillment of state contracts in unpredictable ways. Furthermore, the "enemitizing" campaigns of the Korean War, including the Campaign to Suppress Counter-Revolutionaries and the Three Antis and Five Antis Campaigns, while aiding the consolidation of Communist Party rule, contributed to a climate of fear and mistrust.

By 1952, the Chinese people had been mobilized to improve production, to contribute to national defense through donations and voluntary labor, and to root out enemies of the revolution. Although the official policies of New Democracy concerning private business and

164. For examples of popular misunderstanding (intentional and otherwise) of CCP policies and propaganda, see Diamant and Feng, "First National Critique," 1–37, and S. A. Smith, "Talking Toads and Chinless Ghosts," 405–27.

capitalist production did not change dramatically during this period, politics and society were becoming more restrictive, and the range of options available to both workers and their employers was beginning to narrow. Exactly what means and methods China would adopt to construct socialism remained unclear. Nonetheless, as mass mobilization and production campaigns extended even deeper into the Chinese economy and factories, the environment for both privileged silk weavers and Wuxi filature workers was converging on a workplace governed by Communist Party ideology and a politicized, militarized, mobilizational factory regime.

The next chapter examines the experiences of filature workers during the early 1950s, the period of New Democracy and the Korean War. In contrast with the Shanghai silk weavers, especially those in the large, modern companies like Meiya, the young women who worked in the silk thread mills in cities like Wuxi saw few immediate changes after 1949. On the contrary, most continued to suffer under an abusive factory regime that suppressed workers' aspirations and exploited the party's policies and campaigns through the fall of 1951 and even beyond.

CHAPTER SIX

"Women of the Silk"

Class, Gender, and the State in the Wuxi Filatures

In the first two years of the revolution, Shanghai silk weavers won substantial benefits, including job security, a greater role in factory management, and welfare benefits, while restoring and expanding production and exports. This victory had as much to do with these workers' actions and characteristics as with the Communists' policies and ideology. Shanghai silk weavers possessed capable union leadership with strong connections to the CCP and sufficient autonomy to pursue their constituents' interests effectively. Their effective union leadership, combined with the relatively small scale of operations of the silk weaving industry and a shared culture of working-class masculinity, contributed to their success in restoring production, implementing democratic management, and providing labor insurance.

Other groups of workers did not benefit from the Communist seizure of power in the same way as these privileged Shanghai proletarians. Workers in construction and transportation, coal miners, textile workers in factories outside of the metropolises of Shanghai and Tianjin, and filature workers throughout the Jiangnan region encountered many obstacles in their struggle for liberation. In thread mills in the cities of Hangzhou, Huzhou, and Wuxi, "women of the silk"[1] had little or no access to the fruits of the revolution enjoyed by Shanghai silk weavers or even their counterparts in Shanghai's filatures. For

1. Gail Tsukiyama's book *Women of the Silk* inspired the title of this chapter.

many women working in Wuxi's filatures, China's "Liberation" might as well have happened in another country.

The conditions and characteristics of workers in Jiangnan filatures were very different from those in Shanghai weaving factories. Having learned how easy it was for employers to co-opt their leaders in the 1920s, filature workers had not attempted to organize unions for decades. These workers traditionally relied on spontaneous action including wildcat strikes, walkouts, factory seizures, and even wrecking, organizing on the spur of the moment through informal networks rather than permanent union organizations whose leaders could be bought off or arrested. There were almost no Communists among these young, female workers, so they did not enjoy any of the patronage or connections to power that the Shanghai Silk Workers Union possessed after 1949. The factory regime in silk filatures was also not based on a common culture or even "scientific" management or Fordism, but rather patriarchal despotism that Communist authorities referred to as "feudal." The young women who worked in silk reeling filatures shared almost nothing in common with their employers or the older, male supervisors who managed the workshops. The filature factory regime employed the most brutal methods, including physical beatings and patriarchal surveillance, to discipline workers and reduce costs.

If workers employed in Shanghai's three filatures benefitted from their affiliation with the Shanghai Silk Workers Union, as well as the political and economic resources available in the great metropolis, their counterparts in Wuxi and other smaller Jiangnan cities had no such advantageous alliances or resources. Compared with Shanghai, Wuxi's political leadership was deficient, and neither administrators in state-run filatures nor officials of the Wuxi Labor Bureau took effective measures to improve working conditions and labor relations in the silk industry. The story is more complicated than to say that male workers benefitted while female workers did not, but the political leadership in Wuxi obviously ignored the gendered dimension of capitalist exploitation and the role of male violence in managing the female filature workforce. Communist labor officials and factory administrators did nothing to reform these aspects of the filature factory regime until silk reeler Shen Gendi was beaten to death by her supervisor in August 1951, more than two years after the Communists seized power in the region.

Deficiencies in the work of labor cadres who neglected to reform these abhorrent working conditions meant that Jiangnan filature workers did not see the same changes and benefits in the first two years of the revolution as did the Shanghai silk weavers described in chapter 4. On the contrary, intense oppression and gender-inflected conflict exacerbated labor disputes and complicated the politics of class cooperation and class struggle for filature workers in the early 1950s. The ability of employers and male supervisors to dominate the unions established under Communist auspices, and even to manipulate the message coming from the party's propaganda organs, denied women filature workers the support they needed in their struggle for liberation. The diversity of outcomes in this instance cannot be attributed to political ideology or government policy. Instead we must look to local factors—political leadership (or lack thereof), the characteristics of the industry and the factory regime, the gendered dimension of labor relations, and the specific historical context of the early 1950s—to comprehend the experiences of Jiangnan filature workers in the Chinese revolution. The comparison between Wuxi filature workers and Shanghai silk weavers reveals the complexity of China's Communist-led revolution, as well as the dangers inherent in drawing general conclusions about the Chinese working class or the 1949 revolution.

Working Conditions and the Factory Regime in the Wuxi Filatures

In most major Jiangnan cities, as in Shanghai, the Communists' top priorities in their first months in power were securing the party's authority, restoring production, controlling inflation, and organizing the populace. One way they went about tackling these problems was by establishing industry associations and labor unions. The silk industry's postwar crisis resulted in a massive decline in production and widespread unemployment as tens of thousands of silk reelers were laid off throughout the Yangzi Delta. Historically suspicious of formal union organizations, Jiangnan silk reelers nonetheless managed to put tremendous pressure on employers and the state through spontaneous action, often marching in the vanguard of general strikes in 1947–48, as described in chapter 2. Under worsening economic conditions, however, they achieved few practical gains in protecting their jobs and incomes. Soaring production costs, declining supplies of cocoons and fuel, and shrinking markets exacerbated labor unrest as Communist troops arrived in Jiangnan cities in the spring of 1949.

Although the Yangzi Delta's silk reeling and weaving industries both faced disastrous economic conditions in the late 1940s, silk reeling filatures were more closely tied to the state in 1949 than were weaving factories, a result of both the Japanese occupation and the Nationalist government's postwar policies. But despite closer government involvement in Jiangnan silk production, and in contrast with Shanghai silk weavers, filature workers saw few improvements in welfare, working conditions, or labor relations in the first two years of Communist rule. Aside from the increasing proportion of production contracted to the state, and the presence of CCP cadres in some of the state-run and joint state-private filatures, work in the thread mills remained largely unchanged after Liberation. Even when significant improvements began to appear in the summer of 1952, these were not the result of actions taken by the filature workers' own leaders and organizations, but of campaigns led by the party and the unions. Except for some union initiatives to provide hygiene education and to establish two nurseries, the CCP's policies of New Democratic revolution and Liberation produced only minimal changes in management practices and welfare benefits in the Wuxi filatures. This was due mainly to the domination of the filatures' union organizations by employers and the men who served them as supervisors and enforcers on the factory floor.

The shortage of capital resources and the difficulty of upgrading equipment in the Wuxi filatures were two important factors that impeded improvements in working conditions and the technology of production. The filatures' equipment was generally outdated and in need of replacement, a project frustrated for more than a decade by war and economic crisis. By 1951, the older, less efficient "sitting" reeling machines (*zuosaoche*) still comprised about 70 percent of all equipment in Wuxi's silk reeling industry, and some filatures even continued to use primitive hand-powered "tiger" reeling machines.[2] Naturally, these conditions could not be changed overnight. But the Wuxi filature industry did not even establish its Committee for the Improvement of Silk Filature Equipment until March 1951. The committee achieved some initial improvements, retiring 736 "sitting" reeling machines and replacing these with 618 "standing" reeling machines (*lisaoche*). The committee and the unions also trained 1,163 workers to use the new machines.[3] But these changes mainly affected the few state-run filatures, and it took several more years to bring the city's silk reeling technology up to date.

Many other aspects of the filatures' infamously poor working conditions that could have been improved relatively easily also remained unchanged. Leaving aside for the moment the filatures' brutal management practices, the physical conditions in silk filatures also saw little or no improvement before 1952. Bathroom facilities were very limited, with hundreds of workers using a single toilet. The women's toilet at the Yizhong Filature was simply a primitive tent by the side of the road, and male supervisors strictly controlled access to it. Only eight Wuxi filatures had cafeterias, and although the larger filatures provided relatively decent dormitories, the smaller filatures' dormitories were very crowded. In some cases, ten or twenty workers lived in one room, which was often poorly ventilated and infested with vermin. Most of the buildings were old and crumbling, and some structures had become dangerously unstable. Some filatures were so decrepit that when it rained, workers had to hold umbrellas while operating their machines. The problem of temperature regulation was also very serious. During the summertime, workshop temperatures routinely exceeded the legal maximum of 94 degrees Fahrenheit, reaching 98 or even 115 degrees. But many filatures

2. Qian, *Wuxishi sichou gongye*, 474; WMA D2-1-11. The more advanced "standing" machines (*lisaoche*) were better suited to using high-quality cocoons and produced thread at least one grade higher than "sitting" machines. Productivity was also higher, as two operators of a "standing" reeling machine could handle twenty threads, while a "sitting" machine's single operator could only handle six. The "sitting" machines also required a basin worker to beat the cocoons by hand. The "standing" machines used about 10 percent less cocoons (by weight) to produce the same amount of thread.

3. Qian, *Wuxishi sichou gongye*, 337.

did not even have thermometers installed, and management was generally disinclined to comply with state safety regulations.[4]

Most of the sixty-two boilers in use in Wuxi filatures were old and in poor condition, and only about two-thirds of them had safety shut-off valves. Moving machinery was usually exposed, with no shields covering the gears and belts. If a belt in the power transfer equipment above the reeling machines broke, it could fall on the workers below, causing serious injury. Electrical power equipment was similarly unprotected, and fire safety equipment was limited. The Xinlun Filature, with over two hundred employees, had only one fire extinguisher, and that was kept in the accounting office.

Work hours in Wuxi filatures were not excessive by today's sweatshop standards but nonetheless exceeded the target eight- to ten-hour workday. Most filatures (85 percent) operated on a ten-and-a-half-hour workday, with a few operating eleven to eleven and a half hours per day. Filature owners adopted various tricks to extend work hours further. Although the working day was supposed to start at six o'clock a.m., management at the Xintai and Dachang Filatures would set the factory clocks ahead by fifteen or thirty minutes. Rest breaks were only ten to fifteen minutes, and some filatures did not allow rest breaks at all. At the Zengxing Filature, workers were allowed only a ten-minute break each day in which to eat and use the bathroom. Nor was it easy for filature workers to take sick leave. When a worker at the Xinlun Filature became ill and requested leave, her supervisor refused, saying, "I'll spend three months' wages to buy you a coffin, how's that?"[5]

The wage system in Wuxi filatures was also problematic. In October 1950, government regulations set the average daily wage for a "sitting" machine operator at 1.05 Wuxi parity units, theoretically enough for three people, including the worker herself, to subsist on. "Standing" machine operators earned a bit more, about 1.25 parity units on average, because their work was more demanding and their productivity higher. The wages of the basin workers (called *pengong*), the girls who beat the boiling cocoons, were officially set at about two-thirds of a "sitting" machine operator's wage, but most only earned one-third of this wage,

4. WMA D2-1-10, D2-1-11.
5. WMA D2-1-11.

Table 6.1

Production results and earnings of four silk reelers at the Yongtai Filature, March and June 1951

		March 1951			
Yongtai average	80.69	Standard 20—22	328.1	20.42	
Name	Evenness (threads per 25.4 mm)	Thickness (denier)	Materials (*jin*)	Production (*jin*)	Wages (parity units)
Guo Huifen	80.79	+2	330.8	20.66	1.047
Mu Hedi	82.74	+44	333.9	20.76	1.142
Zhang Ajin	84.24	+33	330.9	20.41	1.160
Sang Qinxian	79.08	+41	314.9	20.85	1.055
		June 1951			
Yongtai average	82.52	Standard 20—22	292.0	30.71	
Name	Evenness	Thickness	Materials	Production	Wages (parity units)
Guo Huifen	78.34	+5	291.5	30.81	.943
Mu Hedi	82.79	+6	296.0	30.05	1.042
Zhang Ajin	84.62	+9	291.7	30.86	1.125
Sang Qinxian	81.02	+22	293.3	30.34	1.017

SOURCE: WMA D2-1-12.*

* The original table from which this is translated does not include units because these would be so well known to workers in the silk industry. The units provided here are standard international units as described in Food and Agriculture, "Silk Reeling and Testing Manual" available online. Evenness is measured using a panel light board to count the number of threads or filaments per 25.4 mm of yarn or raw silk. Thickness is measured in denier, which is the number of grams of silk thread per ten km. Materials refers to the amount of dried cocoons (by weight in *jin*) used in producing the listed amount of raw silk produced (also given in *jin*). China used different means of measuring the qualities of silk thread at different times, so it is uncertain if these are the correct units, but the trend is the same regardless—workers are improving the quality of the thread produced but are earning less wages.

about 0.336 parity units. Many filature workers earned less than the standard minimum wage.

Under the system of bonuses and penalties introduced during the Japanese occupation, called the "point picking system" (*caidianzhi*), peculiar to the silk reeling industry, points were added or deducted from workers' wages each day depending on four criteria: total output per day, productivity per unit of cocoons, and the evenness and thickness of the thread produced. Even if this seems reasonable on the surface, in practice the system was arbitrary and irrational. Aside from the thickness of the thread, for which there existed international standards, there were no fixed standards for evenness, productivity, or output. Instead, most filatures simply used the average achieved by the whole filature, which varied from day to day, as the standard against which each worker's product was measured. As a result, even if a silk reeler steadily increased her productivity, on any given day she might fall behind the filature's average and thus earn less.[6] This opaque and arbitrary remuneration system made filature workers' earnings highly unstable. One worker complained, "Even we don't know how [the standards] are calculated. We only know that each day when the managers report the results, some are fined and some receive bonuses."[7]

A comparison of production results and earnings for four silk reelers at the Yongtai Filature in March and June of 1951 demonstrates the system's shortcomings (see table 6.1). The example of Sang Qinxian is especially instructive. Although most of her production results improved between March and June (other than thickness, which was still not very close to standard), her wages dropped by 3.6 percent because the standards had changed. Furthermore, because the system of bonuses and fines was based on average production throughout the filature, "bonuses" were taken from other workers' wages in the form of penalties. Total wages remained the same, and managers found ways to shift things even more in the filature's favor. On average, total fines imposed were higher than the bonuses paid. For example, at the Zhengfeng Filature with its 681 employees, in the first half of July 1951 bonuses to silk reelers totaled 40.572 parity units, while penalties totaled 50.644

6. WMA D2-1-12.
7. WMA D2-1-11.

parity units, earning the owner ten parity units in saved wages, equivalent to about one hundred thousand yuan.[8] The owner of the Dexin Filature, which did not begin production until after May 1951, was said to check the production results recorded on the blackboard each day and recalculate them so that fines exceeded bonuses by as much as eight times.[9]

This system did little to encourage silk reelers to improve quality or conserve raw materials. In 1950, the silk produced in Wuxi filatures averaged grade C or D. In 1951, for various reasons, including perhaps the inspiration provided by the "patriotic production competitions," average quality improved to grade B or even A. But silk reelers' wages remained the same because the production norms also increased.[10] Because workers had little incentive or opportunity to improve production methods, high-quality cocoons, which could have been used to produce A grade silk, only produced B or even C grade silk. The complexities of silk reeling and the interaction of cocoon quality, production equipment, workers' skill, weather, and other factors complicated efforts to set clear standards for production. Nonetheless, the system in effect in Wuxi filatures in 1951 still fell short of what was possible and desirable under the circumstances.

As early as 1950, Wuxi's state-run filatures attempted to improve the wage system by setting clear standards for productivity and quality and offering bonuses of 30 percent to workers who exceeded standards. This initially produced positive results. But due to resistance by Wuxi's silk capitalists, who made up the majority in the industry association and begrudged the additional expense (estimated at more than two million yuan per month), the new system was soon abandoned. Even when filatures set clear standards and offered rewards to outstanding producers, as was the case at the CSC's Number Two Filature and the Yongtai Filature, standards were set so high that almost no one could achieve them. As a result, in 1951, not a single worker at the Number Two Filature received a bonus.[11]

8. WMA D2-1-9.
9. WMA D2-1-11.
10. WMA D2-1-12.
11. WMA D2-1-12.

Most filatures furthermore implemented a highly differentiated wage system that advantaged male workers. Even when men and women did the same work, they were paid at unequal rates. For example, male packaging workers at the state-run Number Two Filature were paid 30 percent more than women doing the same work. Management staff and male workers were paid monthly salaries and enjoyed dormitories and meal subsidies that were not withheld from their wages, while women had these benefits taken out of their paychecks. Furthermore, male workers' monthly wages did not change depending on the filature's production situation, while female silk reelers' wages were vulnerable to seasonal fluctuations.[12] Silk reelers comprised the majority of filature workers. Their work required the greatest skill and effort and directly affected the filatures' business. Nonetheless, these women earned less than even the most peripheral male workers, and their basic wages were subject to many adjustments. According to statistics from March 1951, even general laborers (*zagong*) in the filatures, who were usually men, earned 80–100 percent more than female silk reelers. With the unions dominated by management, the problem of wage inequality was even more intractable in the Wuxi filatures than in Shanghai's silk weaving industry, and there were few attempts to address these disparities before 1952.

Perhaps improvements in welfare, working conditions, and the wage system would have come earlier to Wuxi's filatures if these workers' union organizations had been more capable of representing workers' interests and negotiating with employers from a position of strength, as was the case in the Shanghai silk weaving industry. But as an unintended consequence of the Communists' rapid establishment of unions in 1949, women workers in Jiangnan filatures found their position weakened vis-à-vis their employers. One reason was that the strategies silk reelers had previously adopted to pursue their interests were prohibited in the context of class cooperation and "benefiting both labor and capital." The theory of New Democracy discouraged direct action in favor of negotiation and compromise through state-sponsored unions. Yet Wuxi filature workers found that the new union organizations were, like silk reelers' unions in the 1920s, co-opted by

12. WMA D2-1-12.

employers and male supervisors who successfully resisted attempts to advance workers' interests or overthrow the supervisors' hegemony on the shop floor. This situation lasted until a series of campaigns in 1951–52, beginning with Democratic Reform and continuing through the Five Antis Campaign, targeted these issues and established a new organizational and political context.

With unions dominated by capitalist employers and male supervisors, it is no surprise that these organizations implemented only those aspects of the party's program that benefitted filature management, while neglecting the reforms and goals most important to these workers. If the Communists were successful in promoting "labor-capital cooperation," which benefitted workers like Shanghai's silk weavers, this policy proved detrimental to Wuxi's filature workers. These workers saw some improvements in their family and married lives, as well as limited improvements in access to medical care and childcare facilities in the first two years of the revolution. But the fundamental reforms that were needed to truly "liberate" these workers were slow to come. The party-state was most successful in mobilizing filature workers to increase production and improve quality, because this goal matched the needs of filature owners more than the goal of improving working conditions or establishing "democratic management." Even so, the oppressive factory regime and the chaotic and arbitrary wage system remained unchanged and hindered efforts to mobilize workers to improve production during the Korean War.

The Democratic Reform Campaign in the Wuxi Filatures

Between 1949 and 1951, the Communist Party's campaigns, especially the "patriotic production competitions" of the Korean War, became a prominent aspect of life in the Jiangnan silk industry. Other than these growing efforts at political mobilization by the new ruling party, however, little else had changed in Wuxi filatures in the two years since Liberation. One of the most significant continuities with the past was the persistence of brutal and inhumane management practices, even in state-run filatures taken over by the revolutionary government in

1949. Party authorities came to recognize that the so-called "feudal" management system in place at the Huachang Filature, as well as the "point picking system" of assigning wages, bonuses, and penalties, inhibited the sustained production of AAAA grade silk. Patriotic exhortations, it seemed, were not enough. Systemic reform to address poor working conditions and improve labor relations was needed as well.

Despite the party's ideological commitment to improving workers' lives and liberating women, when party cadres attempted to implement policy in specific local contexts, they often misunderstood or overlooked important aspects of workers' lives, with the result that the outcomes of policy implementation were neither what the Communist authorities had hoped for, nor what women workers desired. In the case of Wuxi's silk mills, municipal labor cadres had only a vague understanding of the oppression and brutality carried out by male shop-floor supervisors, such that when they took steps to improve management methods and working conditions as part of Democratic Reform in the autumn of 1951, many filature workers were disappointed with the results, much as they had been with the unions established in 1949. What appeared to Communist Party cadres as a backward and "feudal" system of class relations was experienced by women workers as gender oppression and exploitation. For these women workers, the struggle for respect and dignity *as women* was just as important to the process of making filatures worthwhile, dignified, and humane places to work as were the Communists' concepts of class conflict, "feudal" society, and economic development.

One report from 1951 excused the continuation of the filatures' "feudal" management system by stating that the leaders of the Wuxi GLU had been focused on the city's cotton mills.[13] This does not explain, however, why the filatures' brutal factory regime remained in place in state-run filatures after 1949. The official union history of the Yongtai Filature, which for several months in 1950 was managed by agents of the party-state, similarly confessed that "after Liberation the feudal management system still seriously restricted the worker masses'

13. WMA D2-1-11.

enthusiasm for labor, caused the workers physical and mental suffering, and the foremens' arrogance was still fearsome."[14]

Under the existing management system, male supervisors (*guanche*) ruled the silk reeling workshops with an iron hand, or more accurately with a wooden stick. They were the lowest level of management staff, responsible for directly supervising production. They also appointed *chetou* from among the silk reelers, usually rewarding loyal clients. These women sat at the end of each row of machines and assisted the supervisors in monitoring the other workers. Silk reelers were further divided into those operating "standing" and "sitting" machines. The former operated more advanced equipment, were paid more, and often looked down on those who operated the "sitting" machines. Both supervisors and the machine operators disciplined and abused the youngest girls, the "basin workers" who boiled and beat the cocoons to prepare them for reeling.

In contrast with the Shanghai silk weaving industry, which led the establishment of institutions for democratic management in that city, Wuxi filatures rarely established labor-capital consultative conferences (LCCCs), even though these were required by law. And even when organs for "democratic management" were created, they were usually dominated by management and did not function as intended. For example, while under state management in 1949, the Huachang Filature established a factory management committee.[15] This supposedly representative body, however, produced no meaningful changes in management practices. The newly established unions were largely under the control of managerial staff, working conditions remained miserable, and shop-floor supervisors continued to utilize the most abusive and divisive practices to control filature workers. Similarly, despite having been under state management for nine months (from September 1949 to June 1950), the Yongtai Filature did not establish any organs for "democratic management." The filature established an LCCC in December 1950, six months after the filature reverted to private ownership, but the committee's work focused on complying with the party's "patriotic campaigns." Two of the main "accomplishments" of the Yongtai

14. Yongtai Manuscript, 37.
15. Qian, *Wuxishi sichou gongye*, 336, 468.

LCCC were to set tasks for the "campaign to increase production and practice economy" and to produce a plan for making contributions to the war effort. The "consultative conference" made no changes to the filature's working conditions or management practices.

Over the course of 1951, the Yongtai LCCC achieved some modest improvements in employee welfare. According to a factory history written in 1959, procedures for requesting leave were improved, meals were provided for "standing" reeling machine operators,[16] and a health clinic and a nursery were established, so that all of these issues were reported to be "resolved reasonably." Nonetheless, the owner, Xue Zukang, successfully resisted many suggestions for changes raised at the LCCC. For example, although the LCCC was supposed to be chaired by the owner and the union representative on a rotating basis, Xue consistently managed to delay meetings that he did not chair. When the union raised the issue of improving safety equipment and increasing the number of fire extinguishers at the filature, the owner delayed implementation by claiming that the filature could not afford the expense. Xue also resisted the union's demand (and Labor Bureau policy) that new workers should be hired from unemployed filature workers registered with the Wuxi Labor Bureau.[17]

When "democratic reform" finally came to the Wuxi filatures, the process was initiated and controlled by the municipal GLU and was combined with other campaigns during the Korean War. As a result, the changes effected in Wuxi filatures reflected the goals and priorities of the party-state more than the concerns of filature workers. This is not to say that no benefits resulted from these reforms. There were great improvements in working conditions, labor relations, and worker welfare in 1951 and 1952. However, unlike the situation in Shanghai silk weaving factories in 1950, the "democratization" of factory management in Wuxi, carried out in the context of wartime mobilization and "enemitizing" campaigns, was carefully orchestrated by party cadres

16. Filatures often provided meals to "standing" machine workers, whose productivity was higher. A greater problem was differential treatment of "sitting" and "standing" machine operators.

17. Yongtai Manuscript, 36. For more on Xue's efforts to block or control the union at Yongtai, see chapter 5.

to achieve narrow goals set by municipal and national party leaders. The results disappointed those who imagined "democratization" as a "second Liberation."

The Democratic Reform Campaign in the fall of 1951 was a nationwide effort to remove counter-revolutionaries and other undesirable elements (including criminal organizations, religious sects, and independent labor leaders) from China's socialist unions.[18] As described in chapter 3, the combination of the policy of "benefiting both labor and capital" and the gendered hierarchy of labor relations in Wuxi filatures enabled employers to control filature unions in 1949. In the course of Democratic Reform in 1951, it became apparent that management staff and male shop-floor supervisors occupied most leadership positions in the unions. According to one report, the "great majority of unions were dominated by management staff, directly or indirectly controlled by the capitalists, and could not protect workers' interests."[19] By September 1951, eleven filature unions were considered to be controlled by management, and only eight could be called anything but company unions. At the small Hefeng Filature, which employed a total of sixty-seven workers and eight staff, the union committee was comprised of four management staff and only three production workers. The union chair was furthermore known to be a "disciple" of the general manager. At the Zhengfeng Filature, the union chair was the general manager's mistress, demonstrating that even when production workers obtained leading positions in the union organizations, this did not necessarily mean they represented their fellow workers' interests.[20]

Democratic Reform in the Wuxi filatures took the form of "abolishing the feudal management system" (*feichu fengjian guanli zhidu*) as well as reforming the unions. But the campaign was closely tied to the contemporaneous Campaign to Suppress Counter-Revolutionaries. The abusive shop-floor supervisors who were the main targets of "democratic reform" were also often suspected of being Nationalist loyalists or anti-Communist elements. At the state-run Number Five Filature, for example, eighteen supervisors and other male employees had been

18. Sheehan, *Chinese Workers*, 34–41.
19. WMA D2–1–11.
20. WMA D2–1–11.

members of "reactionary organizations" or "foreign organizations," and several of them were later labeled as "counter-revolutionaries."[21] In this instance, there was a strong correlation between the target of the party's campaign and the most immediately oppressive forces in filature workers' lives, although this was not always the case.

Male shop-floor supervisors frequently possessed little in the way of technical skills, but were valued for their ability and willingness to manage silk reelers using the most barbaric and brutal means. Abuses ranged from shouting, insults, and vicious sarcasm to beatings and physical abuse. Although the practice of beating filature workers was officially banned after the Communist takeover, it nonetheless continued in most filatures, including those operated by the government. One supervisor at the Hongfeng Xiecheng Filature used a bamboo rod to "discipline" production workers. Two supervisors at the CSC's Number Five Filature adopted the practice of hanging skeins of silk from the ears of silk reelers whose work was not up to standards, humiliating them in front of the rest of the workers. At the Xintai Filature, at least one or two workers each day would be insulted and humiliated so badly that they would be brought to tears.[22]

Harassment, demanding sexual favors, and even rape were also common in Wuxi silk filatures. A supervisor at the Yizhong Filature named Chen Lihua was a union cadre at the factory. Chen was notorious for taking advantage of women workers at Yizhong, including raping the daughter of one silk reeler in late 1950 after getting her alone on the pretext of shopping for Spring Festival. Another of his victims became pregnant, but Chen ignored her pleas for aid. He also took advantage of workers in financial difficulties to demand sexual favors.[23] Some supervisors used lascivious behavior to create divisions among the women workers. Even if a supervisor's attentions were unwelcome, simply being subject to them could draw criticism and disdain from other workers. Such practices could have a deleterious effect on production and created divisions among the workers, but managers used them to maintain control.

21. WMA D2-1-11.
22. WMA D2-1-11.
23. WMA D2-1-9.

The "feudal management system" was not only brutal and inhumane but also arbitrary and inefficient. In this system, shop-floor supervisors had the power to fine and even fire workers. Although regulations established after the Communist takeover removed this power, management practices did not change quickly. Some supervisors continued to punish workers by denying them work for a month or even kicking them out of the factory.[24] Shop-floor supervisors also controlled the "point picking system" and used this power to punish and reward workers. One supervisor at the Hongfeng Xiecheng Filature treated pretty workers well, even if they could not produce high-quality silk. But he would record lower results and even insult and fine workers he did not find physically attractive. As was common in many factories throughout China, supervisors also demanded gifts from workers seeking employment or trying to improve their position by upgrading to a "standing" machine.[25] Gifts could include favors such as shopping or mending clothes. One supervisor at the CSC's Number Two Filature even demanded fifty thousand yuan from one woman for giving her a job at the filature. Women workers might also be compelled to provide sexual favors to get the best jobs.[26]

The "basin workers," who comprised almost 30 percent of the filature industry's workforce, suffered at the bottom of this vicious pecking order. Their ages ranged from nine to eighteen, although most were thirteen to seventeen years of age. Despite the promulgation of very progressive labor laws, Liberation did little to improve the famously difficult situation of these child workers, and conditions in some filatures even worsened. Basin workers generally worked about thirty or forty minutes more each day than silk reelers, and spent their entire day standing over vats of boiling cocoons, their hands frequently coming into contact with 180-degree water.[27] Not only did their health suffer from miserable working conditions, they were also subject to abuse from both supervisors and reeling machine operators. At the Hetai Filature, in just one month there were 330 incidents of supervisors or other

24. Yongtai Manuscript, 37.
25. Honig, *Sisters and Strangers*, 62–66.
26. WMA D2-1-11.
27. WMA D2-1-12.

workers striking basin workers. The union chair at the Yongchangxin Filature struck basin workers fifty-seven times in just six days. Furthermore, just as the supervisors demanded favors from silk reeling workers, the silk reelers demanded that the juvenile basin workers help them prepare for work, cook rice, and even wash their clothes.[28]

Observers suggested several reasons why silk reeling workers abused the basin workers who assisted them. One reason was "tradition." Many silk reelers had started out as basin workers and had suffered the same abuse as young girls. Perversely, it thus seemed proper to them to continue this treatment. Some said, "If you don't beat them, they won't grow up" (*bu da, bu chengren*). Often these basin workers had been introduced into the filature by their parents, who knew someone who worked there. Thus, they could not complain to their parents for fear of receiving a beating at home as well as at work. The main reason why these young, powerless girls suffered abuse at the hands of other workers, however, was the filature wage system. Since October 1950, the daily wage for silk reelers was set at 1.05 Wuxi parity units, but under the "point picking" bonus and penalty system actual wages could be much less. In extreme cases, silk reelers could lose a whole day's wages. Some silk reelers took out their anger and frustration on the basin workers, blaming them for defects in the thread and beating them.[29]

The primary goal of the Democratic Reform Campaign was to eliminate the influence of employers, labor gang bosses, "counterrevolutionaries," and secret societies in union organizations nationwide. But the immediate impetus for the campaign in the Wuxi filatures was the death of a woman worker named Shen Gendi at the CSC's Number Five Filature—a state-run factory—on August 27, 1951. Shen died in hospital after receiving a vicious beating by the filature's general supervisor, a man named Shi Rongzhao. The *Sunan ribao* reported the incident, which provoked widespread anger among filature workers throughout the region.[30]

28. WMA D2-1-11.
29. WMA D2-1-9, D2-1-12.
30. Qian, *Wuxishi sichou gongye*, 337–38; Yongtai Manuscript, 37.

In the past, this kind of incident might have led to a mass walkout and protests by filature workers. In this instance, however, the government and the unions seized the initiative and responded quickly to manage the crisis. The Wuxi GLU immediately sent a work team to the filature to investigate the incident. By August 30, a work team began organizing the campaign at the Yongtai Filature.[31] Within days, the GLU sent work teams to several key filatures to co-opt workers' spontaneous action. On September 7, the Southern Jiangsu Administrative Office (*xingzheng gongshu*) and Labor Bureau held a mass meeting to discuss the incident and the measures the government was adopting, including sentencing Shi Rongzhao to two years in prison.[32]

Before launching the campaign, the Wuxi GLU set as its goals to "abolish the barbaric feudal management system, and actively establish a new democratic management system step by step," as well as to purify the union organizations by removing undesirable elements and strengthening working-class unity. These measures, it was hoped, would improve labor relations, laying the foundation for future advances in production. Wuxi labor cadres' approach to implementing management reform reveals a great deal about their methods, ideology, and attitudes toward filature workers. Preparations for the campaign read like a battle plan, emphasizing top-down direction, mobilizing "the masses" in a controlled way, and focusing on strategic "key points."[33] For example, the union's plan began with "concentrating forces" in two "typical" factories, the Number Five Filature and the Yongtai Filature. Only after testing the waters in these two factories was the campaign expanded to the whole industry. Instructions for union cadres similarly demonstrate how carefully controlled the process was.[34] On the one hand, union cadres were admonished to avoid "throwing cold water on the worker masses' enthusiasm." On the other hand, once "the masses" had been mobilized, the union cadres had to ensure that discussions and criticisms cleaved closely to official policy to avoid raising

31. Yongtai Manuscript, 37.

32. Qian, *Wuxishi sichou gongye*, 338.

33. WMA D2-1-11.

34. Sheehan, *Chinese Workers*, 39–40, also emphasizes this characteristic of the Democratic Reform Campaign.

any "irrelevant" issues or struggling against factory owners, who were not the targets of the movement. But, as was the case in other mass campaigns, efforts to control the scope and direction of Democratic Reform often failed in the face of workers' demands and interests.[35]

Union work teams began by holding small group discussions to learn about the situation in each filature and to identify potential activists and targets for criticism. Each work team furthermore conducted a thorough investigation of union cadres' political attitudes and the degree to which state factory administrators accepted the ideology of "relying on the working class." In this way, the union leaders hoped (echoing the writings of Chairman Mao) to "draw a clear distinction between the enemy and ourselves."[36]

The work teams strictly delineated the goals and scope of reform. "Democratization" was to be based on "educating" factory employees, establishing a new basis for unity within the factories, and reforming, rather than eliminating, deviant managers. Typically, the methods included "criticism and self-criticism" followed by confessions and the removal from union posts of those found guilty of abusive practices or "undemocratic" attitudes. The most serious offenders had their union membership revoked, and anyone deemed a "counter-revolutionary" was referred to the People's Government for prosecution. It was thus assumed from the start that "counter-revolutionaries" existed in Wuxi filatures and that abusive management practices arose from the incorrect class standpoint of some supervisors rather than the factory regime or the filatures' gendered hierarchy.

A preliminary planning report for the joint state-private Huachang Filature exemplified the party and the GLU's priorities in carrying out the Democratic Reform Campaign, as well as the perceived link between "counter-revolutionary" activity and the "feudal" management system. Despite the filature's impressive accomplishments during the production campaign, the abuses found in other Wuxi filatures

35. Frazier, *Chinese Industrial Workplace*, 122, mentions that the campaign in Guangzhou, in which some 618 individuals were targeted for criticism in fifty factories, not only attacked undesirable elements in the unions, but also opened up "unanticipated workplace issues." Workers in privately owned knitting mills in Guangzhou, for example, took advantage of the campaign to demand higher wages.

36. WMA D2-1-11.

continued at Huachang in 1951, from the arbitrary fining and firing of workers to beatings, verbal abuse, and sexual exploitation. Managers and shop-floor supervisors dominated and manipulated the union organizations by rewarding workers who were loyal to them and punishing those who resisted.

The leaders of the Democratic Reform Campaign, however, emphasized the mentalities and activities of "counter-revolutionaries" rather than gender conflict or problems inherent in the filatures' management system. The report stated that "reactionary organizations" at Huachang had mainly relied on outside organizers and were thus not systematically established or well-organized. Despite a "democratic investigation" in 1950 (probably to check the political backgrounds of employees at the factory), "counter-revolutionaries" continued to operate, and shop-floor supervisors successfully resisted reform through threats, intimidation, and punishment. Even after the arrival of the Democratic Reform work team in September 1951, there were three incidents of sabotage at Huachang, and during the campaign itself one supervisor was reported to have reminded workers, "You can voice opinions until the sun comes up, but it is still I who will supervise you."[37]

What the campaign organizers identified as a conflict between proletarians and "counter-revolutionaries," however, was more likely a manifestation of conflict between male supervisors attempting to preserve their authority and women workers attempting to overthrow a hated oppressor and assert their rights and interests. Labeling abusive supervisors as "counter-revolutionaries" obscured the gendered dimension of conflict at the filature because it represented male abuse and oppression of women as a political act motivated by defiance of the revolutionary regime. There was a clear disconnect between the Communist Party's goals in mobilizing workers, and women workers' aspirations for dignity and fair treatment.

The Democratic Reform Campaign in Wuxi's filatures lasted one month. The first phase, from September 1 to 5, focused on the two "key point" filatures—the Number Five Filature and the Yongtai Filature. Group discussions began by organizing workers to read and discuss reports on the death of Shen Gendi, and filature employees were

37. WMA D2–1–11.

encouraged to relate Shen's death to conditions in their own factories. The second phase lasted from September 6 to 15, and consisted of four main activities. The first was a meeting of activists from filatures throughout the city to collect "typical" accusations and denunciations. The next step was to carry out propaganda work using these materials to expose the evils of the "feudal management system." The third set of activities included holding small group meetings in the city's filatures to collect materials for use in the fourth kind of action—mass accusation meetings in which key offenders were publicly accused and criticized. The individuals accused in these meetings were to be dealt with according to the severity of their offenses based on the principle of "strongly supporting the masses in a timely fashion." Although these activities provided opportunities for filature workers to express their complaints and concerns, the fact that Wuxi's labor cadres exercised careful control at every stage restricted the scope of complaints workers could raise.

The third phase lasted from September 16 to 22, and involved purging the union organizations. This consisted of holding meetings of new activists identified during the previous two weeks' activities and "thoroughly reforming" the unions through criticism and self-criticism in order to achieve "stronger unity among the masses of workers." Finally, the newly reformed union organizations were to discuss how to establish a more "democratic" management system.[38] Considering that this was the ostensible purpose of the campaign, it is surprising to see it included in the union's plans in such an offhand way. The campaign's limited achievements in terms of reforming managerial systems in Wuxi filatures, as opposed to identifying allies and enemies of the revolutionary regime in the workforce, reveal the gap between the campaign's purported goals and the methods adopted.

The most detailed report available on the process and results of Democratic Reform in Wuxi filatures comes from the Huachang Filature, which was exceptional in some ways but all too typical in others. Huachang was established as a joint state-private enterprise immediately following the Communist takeover and was the first Wuxi filature to restore production in July 1949. Unusual among Wuxi filatures, Huachang had a Communist Party branch organization by September

38. WMA D2-1-11.

1949; it was also one of the first filatures to establish a union organization. By October 1951, Huachang had 557 employees. These included 485 women workers (87 percent), 32 male workers (5.7 percent), 22 management staff (3.9 percent), and 11 shop-floor supervisors (1.97 percent). Of these employees, 530, or 95 percent, joined the union, which boasted 121 cadres. Huachang also had 45 Communist Youth League members and 16 Communist Party members (of whom three were party cadres assigned to the factory after the takeover). Given the party's relatively strong presence in the filature, union organizing work proceeded smoothly, and the filature also established a women workers' committee and a worker militia.[39]

The Democratic Reform work team sent to the Huachang Filature first organized small group discussions and larger meetings to explain the campaign. To some extent, however, they had to rely upon and work closely with the existing organizations in the filature, which were dominated by the same male supervisors who were the targets of the campaign. To overcome this impediment, the work team also established direct relationships with women workers. This included learning more about production tasks at the factory, studying the records of past results in production, and helping workers to resolve some immediate difficulties such as installing electric lights in the cocoon sorting room and repairing the paths around the filature.[40]

Although the oppressive nature of the factory regime in silk filatures was obvious to the women employed in them, it initially proved difficult for the work team to mobilize Huachang workers to participate in the campaign. Many workers were understandably skeptical toward the possibility of reforming a system that had proved so resilient in the two years since Liberation. One woman was recorded as saying, "At the most, democratic reform will be just like the democratic investigation [of 1950] . . . calling on the supervisors to make a little self-criticism, and then we will just continue to live under their thumb."[41]

Despite these initial obstacles, the campaign progressed from collecting materials and speaking with individuals, to holding small

39. WMA D2-1-9.
40. WMA D2-1-11.
41. WMA D2-1-11.

group discussions, to organizing mass meetings. The campaign organizers started with the "sitting" machine operators, who were more blatantly oppressed and thus easier to mobilize. The circumstances of "standing" machine operators were, relatively speaking, not so bad, as the supervisors generally did not beat or insult them as much. Thus, they did not initially see the campaign as relevant to their situation. The work team's remedy for this problem was to organize meetings to "speak bitterness" about the past and present, and to convince the "standing" machine operators that the management system could and should be reformed. Some of the most effective techniques were circulating cartoons and broadcasting accusations, partly because less than 20 percent of filature workers could read.

Once the "standing" machine operators realized that the campaign was serious and might have a chance of succeeding, they became more willing to join the other workers in speaking out and criticizing their supervisors. The work team's exposure of what happened to a worker named Zhou Yuxian went a long way toward convincing these workers to participate actively in the campaign. Zhou, a "standing" machine operator, had been an early activist at Huachang and after Liberation had joined the Communist Youth League. As she became increasingly active in the union, the supervisors sought to turn her by taking her for outings on rest days and using other means to influence her. Zhou proved easily seduced by these overtures and increasingly became a tool of management. Because male supervisors were constantly stopping by her work station to chat, the other workers began calling her "Railway Station" (*huochezhan*). By exposing the methods supervisors used to divide workers and corrupt their potential leaders, much as happened to the filature workers' unions in the 1920s, the work team encouraged the "standing" machine operators' outrage and criticism of the supervisors. Eventually, even the male workers at the filature, mostly machinists and porters, joined the growing effort to isolate and criticize the shop-floor supervisors.[42]

Finding themselves on the defensive, the supervisors' attitudes began to change. Those who had not committed many serious abuses assumed that they would eventually be fired, demoted, or punished

42. WMA D2-1-11.

with hard labor. Some of the worst offenders, however, resorted to underhanded means to threaten or eliminate their accusers. One supervisor named Chen Xizhang told workers, "I am not an enemy agent (*tewu*), so I can't be fired. Be sure that you say only good things about me," implying that he would still be around to take revenge on anyone who criticized him. Some supervisors sought to expand their network of clients by adjusting workers' production records or lending them money. Others spread rumors to discredit their accusers. When the work team discovered such attempts, they exposed the individual and removed him from his post as a picket brigade or union small group leader by holding a spontaneous election and encouraging the union members to elect someone else in his place.[43]

Through these efforts, the filature workers grew more willing to speak out against abusive supervisors. The next step was to criticize the management system, referred to as "the old system" (*jiu zhidu*), although no new system existed yet. These meetings helped senior managers and technical staff understand the goals of reform and their place in it. Once they came to understand that the campaign was aimed at the shop-floor supervisors and the management system as a whole, not at senior management or the owner, they too were willing to participate. Finally, the supervisors were encouraged to criticize themselves and one another, exposing their own abusive behavior. This served to isolate the worst offenders and prepared the way for the final stage of "democratic reform," the convening of a mass struggle or accusation meeting (*shuoli douzheng dahui* or *kongsu dahui*).

The work team made careful preparations for the meeting, including selecting suitable targets for criticism, gathering evidence, preparing accusers to say the right things, and making preliminary decisions as to how to handle each case so that punishments could be announced at the meeting.[44] The mass struggle meeting was not a trial. There was no defense, and the outcome was predetermined. The purpose was to

43. WMA D2-1-11. Frazier, *Chinese Industrial Workplace*, 118, describes how a "Number One" at the Shenxin Number Six Textiles Mill in Shanghai instructed her subordinates as to how she should be criticized and punished during the Democratic Reform Campaign, telling them that they were to force her to sweep the floors so that she could avoid the more strenuous work of tending the spinning machines.

44. WMA D2-1-11.

make examples of the worst offenders and to involve the filature's employees in condemning and punishing them, with the aim of raising workers' "political and class consciousness" and demonstrating the party's concern for workers' interests (even if it had taken two years). Nonetheless, there is no record of any discussion of the gender hierarchy on which this abusive factory regime was based.

In the end, seven individuals, all men, most of them shop-floor supervisors, became the targets of mass struggle meetings at the Huachang Filature. Two were supervisors in the "sitting" reeling department (Chen Xizhang and Zhao Xiangchu), two were supervisors in the "standing" reeling department (Yang Wenxin, a known "counterrevolutionary," and Shen Qinshu), one worked in the finishing and re-reeling department (Wu Tingxi, who was also a suspected "counterrevolutionary"), and two were male workers (Fan Wenqin and Mo Hegen, who was a suspected "enemy agent").

Chen Xizhang was the first to be struggled against because he was notorious for beating, insulting, and manipulating workers, and he had also attempted to resist the campaign. At this struggle meeting, the silk reelers vented their fury against him with shouts and insults. Because of the work team's careful preparation efforts, the employees were well-primed and the content of accusations and other speeches was "generally in accordance with policy."[45] Such meetings were highly emotional events, with silk reelers getting on stage to denounce the accused and eager voices in the audience doing likewise. Participants became angry and emotional, many shouting their accusations with tears streaming down their faces. Some held their hands up for a long time waiting to speak and became upset if not given the opportunity to do so. At a similar meeting at the Yongtai Filature, a woman named Ni Suzhen took the stage and recounted how her supervisor, Yang Zhehong, had persecuted her to the point that she wanted to kill herself. Both Ni and her fellow workers were moved to angry tears.[46]

45. WMA D2-1-11.

46. Yongtai Manuscript, 37. The process in the Wuxi filatures exactly matches that described by Frazier in the Shenxin Number Six Textile Mill in Shanghai. At Shenxin, cadres even tabulated figures on the number of workers crying and the intensity of emotion. Frazier, *Chinese Industrial Workplace*, 118. This may indicate that the campaign organizers intentionally manipulated sentiment to get workers

The mass meeting to struggle against Chen Xizhang was followed by meetings in individual workshops over the following two nights to handle the cases of Shen Qinshu, Zhao Xiangchu, Mo Hegen, and Fan Wenqin. These men's self-criticisms were not very satisfying for most workers, however, and there was also no public announcement of how they would be punished. Dissatisfied workers demanded another mass struggle meeting, but it was not allowed. The small group meetings provided more opportunities for nuance and the expression of alternative views of "democratic reform," even if these meetings had the potential to undermine class unity. During the struggle session against Zhao Xiangchu, two workers who had benefitted from Zhao's patronage spoke up in his defense. Their support for Zhao outraged the rest of the workers at the meeting, who demanded that the two be excluded from participating. The work team could only accede to their wishes, and only when Zhao's supporters had been removed was the group satisfied.[47]

The cases of the two worst "counter-revolutionaries" at Huachang, Wu Tingxi and Yang Wenxin, were dealt with in a final mass struggle meeting. By this time, because the crowd was already well practiced and fully united, including not only male and female employees but also those supervisors who had already been struggled against, Wu and Yang were thoroughly exposed and isolated, made pariahs even by their fellow supervisors. It must have been a terrifying experience for them, but intoxicatingly powerful and satisfying for many in the crowd. Wu Tingxi, reportedly a fair-faced but cruel and vicious individual, had severely mistreated the workers under his supervision, and when he came before the crowd the atmosphere was one of intense anger, grief, and outrage. Perhaps to avoid having this outrage directed against themselves, the leadership accepted the crowd's demands concerning Wu's punishment. He was stripped of his membership in the union and worker pickets and fired from his position as supervisor. The workers' mood after the meeting was described as jubilant.[48] In contrast, before the struggle session against Yang Wenxin, the work team

emotionally involved in the campaign, although such a tactic had the potential to backfire if results did not match expectations.

47. WMA D2–1–11.

48. WMA D2–1–11.

leaders admonished the Huachang employees against "leftist" tendencies, which seemed to have spoiled their mood. Although people participated in struggling against Yang, they did not do so with the same enthusiasm they had displayed earlier. It may also be the case, however, that Yang's "counter-revolutionary" associations did not greatly concern most Huachang workers, perhaps because they did not perceive his abuses in the factory as terribly severe.

The final phase of Democratic Reform at Huachang entailed encouraging confessions and self-criticisms among the production workers and requiring every worker to "clarify his or her history" (*jiaoqing lishi*) before registering for labor insurance.[49] As described in chapter 3, registration for labor insurance served several important political purposes. The first step in this process in Wuxi's filatures was to use the foundation established by the campaign against the "old management system" to criticize the Nationalist government, which was blamed for just about everything wrong with Chinese society and industry. The target of criticism thus shifted from the filature's supervisors and factory regime (which remained largely intact) to the "Nationalist Party reactionary clique" (*Guomindang fandongpai*) and comparing past suffering and exploitation with the progress achieved since Liberation.[50]

One important goal that registering workers for labor insurance accomplished was the repudiation of the quasi-religious millenarian society called the Yiguandao. The Yiguandao society, based on a hierarchy of "altars" with an organizational influence in many Chinese cities and in the countryside, had been subject to Communist suppression in North China as early as January 1949.[51] The Communists condemned the Yiguandao as a "counter-revolutionary" organization, part of the old "reactionary order," and as a superstitious cult that deceived and exploited laboring people. In April 1951, in combination with the

49. It is unclear why this was not done several months earlier when the labor insurance provisions were first promulgated. Huachang workers were certainly eligible, and the delay indicates that the party–state representatives at Huachang were either negligent or too distracted by factory finances to implement the Labor Insurance Law.

50. WMA D2-1-11.

51. Lieberthal, *Revolution and Tradition*, 108–18; DuBois, *Sacred Village*; Jordan and Overmyer, *Flying Phoenix*.

Campaign to Suppress Counter-Revolutionaries, the CCP launched a concerted effort to eliminate the Yiguandao in Wuxi. At the Huachang Filature this campaign included not only propaganda meetings, accusation meetings, and confessions by Yiguandao leaders, but also efforts to "recover" funds and property that the Yiguandao hierarchy had collected from rank-and-file believers. This provided a material incentive for people to repudiate the Yiguandao, undermining the society's support and ultimately eliminating the sect.

The April campaign seems to have missed many adherents at the Huachang Filature. Whereas the campaign against the sect the previous spring had discovered twenty-three Yiguandao adherents at the filature, during the "clarification of histories" it was discovered that there were really thirty-seven. In addition to ordinary workers, there were also two Communist Party members, four Youth League members, and several activists who had also been members of the sect. Following the Democratic Reform Campaign, the GLU work team organized meetings at which workers signed their names to statements that they had been hoodwinked by the sect and pledged to never participate in such activities again. Because "clarifying one's history" was a prerequisite for receiving labor insurance benefits, this provided an added incentive for workers to publicly reject the Yiguandao and other pre-revolutionary allegiances.[52]

In general, filature workers' responses to the Democratic Reform Campaign (and especially provision of labor insurance) were positive. Given the filatures' abusive management practices, it comes as no surprise that people welcomed the opportunity for reform. The actual results achieved in the Wuxi filatures, however, often fell short of workers' expectations, even if the campaign managed to achieve most of the party's goals. The work team at Huachang reported a great many achievements resulting from the campaign. The most important, of course, was overthrowing the "feudal authority" of the shop-floor supervisors, as well as eliminating (to some degree) their influence through networks of patronage. Democratic Reform was also thought to have raised workers' "political and class consciousness," as manifested in their willingness to speak out against their oppressors. The work team

52. WMA D2-1-11.

furthermore felt that their efforts had successfully linked the "old management system" to the Nationalist Party's reactionary regime in the minds of the workers, although, of course, this system was in no way the creation of Chiang Kai-shek's government.

The enthusiasm for struggling against abusive supervisors in the Wuxi filatures carried over into production in the winter of 1951–52. Ostensibly because they had developed a sense of responsibility and proprietorship as "masters of the factory," silk reelers were more careful about clearing their work stations of lint and stray threads. They were also willing to help one another by spraying the silk filaments with water or tying off broken threads. More importantly, silk reelers came to realize how little the supervisors contributed to production. One worker in the re-reeling department was recorded as saying, "In the past, Wu Tingxi boasted that 'without me you couldn't handle production.' Now let him come and see. We are getting along fine without him."[53]

Democratic Reform did not necessarily make Wuxi filature workers more receptive to the party's political ideology. One report on the post-campaign situation in the Yongtai Filature stated that the enthusiasm of the "masses" began to "cool down" soon after the campaign was completed in late September. In the final stage of reform, discussing the political import of labor insurance provision, women filature workers did not speak up or even pay much attention in meetings. Some preferred to knit or chat with one another rather than listen to the speeches, which caused the union cadres great consternation.[54] The response to the union's political education classes was even more disappointing, and union cadres increasingly adopted a passive attitude toward their work, waiting until they could be replaced in the next election.

The report by the work team at the Huachang Filature stated that the Democratic Reform Campaign had provided great benefits for the

53. WMA D2-1-11.

54. In contrast, the official union history of the Yongtai Filature (written in 1959) stated that, following the mass struggle meetings, Yongtai workers applauded and shouted, "Long live the Chinese Communist Party!" and "Long live Chairman Mao!" Yongtai Manuscript, 37.

party and union leadership, such as giving them a much better understanding of social and political relations within the filature, which would help to improve union work in the future. The struggle meetings also uncovered valuable information concerning "counter-revolutionary" activities, demonstrating the intelligence benefits of the "mass line." Furthermore, whereas there had previously been just over forty activists in the filature, mostly among "standing" machine operators, by the conclusion of the campaign there were 126, and these were distributed more evenly throughout the factory.

Even more important, the workshop-level union organizations were no longer dominated by management staff, but were led by newly identified activists drawn from among the production workers. There is little evidence, however, of direct and democratic worker control over the factory-level or industry-level unions. On the contrary, the report stated that one result of the campaign was that it had enhanced the party's capacity to lead and direct union work around core policy issues.[55] "Bureaucratism" and "subjectivism" thus remained serious problems in union work, and the union was no more independent of the filature's administration than it had been before. Democratic Reform at Huachang enhanced workers' capacity to express and advance their interests to some extent, but there is little reason to conclude, as the report did, that the women workers of Huachang had truly become "masters of the factory."

The excited and appreciative mood at Huachang following the campaign quickly soured when it was discovered that, because a new management system was not yet established, most of the men targeted during the previous days' struggle sessions were back on the job. Chen Xizhang, Zhao Xiangchu, and Shen Qinshu were all "temporarily" returned to their previous positions as shop-floor supervisors. "The masses" were naturally outraged and expressed their dissatisfaction in no uncertain terms. Even Wu Tingxi and Yang Wenxin, who were supposed to have been returned to their home villages, were still living in the dormitory and eating the filature's food, which some workers clearly felt was too good for these men. The fact that Fan Wenqin's case had not yet been decided also dissatisfied many workers. This situation, the

55. WMA D2–1–11.

report stated, demonstrated the need for quick resolution of such cases once "the masses' emotions had been aroused."[56] Treatment of the targets of Democratic Reform at the Yongtai Filature was similarly lenient. Supervisor Yang Zhehong, reviled for his persecution of women workers at the factory, and supervisor Xue Baoyan were simply demoted and had their salaries reduced. Only one supervisor, Dan Yuanjia, was "purged" (*qingxi*) because he expressed no remorse or desire to reform.[57]

The most striking shortcoming of the Democratic Reform Campaign in the Wuxi filatures is that there was very little change in filatures' management systems, a fact which receives almost no mention in the Huachang work team's report. Only on the report's last page, listing "remaining problems," does the issue come up: "After the abolishment of the supervisory system, there is an urgent need for a new system, as well as suitable new personnel and a clearly defined responsibility system. Only then can production develop smoothly." Aside from remedying the worst abuses, there is no evidence that a system of "democratic management" was ever implemented at Huachang.[58] This is not to say that there were no improvements in filature management practices. Many managers' attitudes changed, and supervisors were more restrained than in the past and reduced the use of heavy-handed tactics to discipline workers. But the "old management system" remained largely intact, and the idea that workers were the "masters of the factory" was not manifested in any thorough-going systemic changes.

One indication of the limitations of Democratic Reform in empowering filature workers is the section on "remaining problems" in union work contained in a 1953 report by the Wuxi GLU. It mentions that the unions still have not done enough to oversee factory administrations and capitalists in improving management systems since September 1951. Nor does the campaign seem to have eliminated employers' ability

56. WMA D2-1-11.

57. Yongtai Manuscript, 37.

58. In regard to the Shenxin Number Six Textile Mill, Frazier, *Chinese Industrial Workplace*, 118–19, states: "Neither classified reports about the campaign nor documents published for propaganda purposes claim that the Number One 'system' was eliminated, as some workers had demanded prior to the campaign. Despite the broad and unprecedented mobilization of workers in this campaign, many pre-1949 labor supervisors managed to survive a campaign in which they were the targets."

to influence and control the unions in many factories. At least until the Five Antis Campaign of 1952, employers continued to use bribery and favoritism, conspired to get their cronies appointed as union cadres, and usurped the leadership of factory-level unions. The report claimed that capitalists went by the maxim, "Controlling the union chair and the workers' affairs cadre is like controlling the law, and any problem can be resolved."[59]

Even more shocking, the report stated that despite the supposed abolishment of "feudal management systems" in Wuxi filatures, the abusive practices of the past did not disappear entirely, indicating that supervisors in some filatures continued to use physical violence to control workers. Thus, although the "democratization" of management and the union organizations in the Wuxi filatures ameliorated the abuse of female filature workers by male supervisors, management systems were not fundamentally altered. In the end, the Democratic Reform Campaign did more to bring the unions under Communist Party control, thereby enhancing the party's ability to mobilize workers for political and production campaigns, than it did to represent workers' interests effectively.

The fact that long-awaited improvements in working conditions in Wuxi's filatures were initiated not by autonomous unions controlled by women workers, but rather by city labor cadres who felt little sense of urgency to take on this task, demonstrates the nature of the filature unions after Democratic Reform. That it took more than two years, and the death of a young woman, for Wuxi's labor cadres to take any action to improve filature working conditions reveals the gap between Wuxi's Communist Party leadership and these neglected proletarians. Filature workers did not gain the power to initiate improvements in welfare and working conditions on their own, and the "workers' state" belatedly took action on their behalf. Following the Five Antis Campaign in the spring of 1952, the Wuxi Municipal People's Government initiated improvements in filature working conditions that at least partially overcame decades of decay and neglect.

The improvements in filature working conditions were particularly impressive, especially considering how bad the situation had been before 1952. Many filatures were dilapidated and rundown, threatening

59. WMA D2-1-10.

workers' health and safety, and accidents were common. The factory buildings of the Dachang Filature, for example, let in the wind and rain. The floors were always wet, hygiene facilities were substandard, and the factory's structural supports were rotten and unstable. On the morning of December 30, 1951, Dachang's main production workshop collapsed, seriously injuring five workers. The New Yongtai Filature (which was no longer new by that time) also collapsed in 1951. At the Xintai Filature, workers in one reeling workshop had to use supports to prop up a wall that leaned in more than a meter at the top. Although Xintai had four hundred women workers, there was no bathhouse for them to use. Temperatures in the re-reeling workshop of the Dachang Filature could reach 110 degrees Fahrenheit. Heat and humidity affected not only workers' health but also the quality of the silk produced. Although the city government passed legislation in 1950 stating that work should stop when the temperature in filature workshops reached 94 degrees, the law was not enforced.[60]

In September 1951, the first All-China Labor Protection Work Conference in Beijing passed the "Draft Provisional Regulations on Factory Safety and Hygiene." But it was not until the spring of 1952 that these regulations filtered down to Wuxi filature workshops. During and after the Five Antis Campaign, most Wuxi factories repaired or upgraded their boilers and other machinery, attempted to bring workshop temperatures within legal norms, and improved safety and hygiene facilities. The newly reformed labor unions oversaw these tasks and led some two thousand filature employees to carry out safety inspections. Temperatures in the re-reeling workshop of the joint state-private Huachang Filature could reach 110 degrees on hot days because of the lack of insulation, but management would not allow workers to open windows for fear that it would adversely affect the drying silk. In April 1952, however, the factory established a production improvement research small group. By the end of the month they had insulated the workshop with thick cloth and opened the windows, which lowered the average temperature by five degrees without increasing the humidity. The silk dried properly, and its color was not affected.[61]

60. Qian, *Wuxishi sichou gongye*, 248–49.
61. WMA D2-1-10; Qian, *Wuxishi sichou gongye*, 249.

From May 16 through the end of June, the Wuxi Municipal People's Government organized the city's state-run and private filatures to stop production and carry out an industry-wide renovation of filature facilities. The main goals were to lower temperatures in filature workshops, to renovate some of the rundown factory buildings, and to upgrade the production equipment. The project was funded with a government loan of 7.6 billion yuan (Old Renminbi) divided among twenty-six private filatures. More than thirty Wuxi filatures, state and private, installed insulation to keep out the heat and insulated hot water pipes and cocoon basins with asbestos.[62] Many filatures installed ventilation apertures and some even installed powered fans and air conditioning equipment. These measures lowered workshop temperatures by two to five degrees Fahrenheit on average, and in some cases as much as ten degrees Fahrenheit.

There are indications, however, that inspection and supervision of measures to improve working conditions were less effective in Wuxi's silk filatures than in other industries. In July 1953, the Wuxi Textile Union and Filature Workers Union, along with the city's Labor Bureau, organized a Filature Labor Agreement Inspection Group and carried out inspections at twelve of the city's filatures. The group mainly inspected filatures' implementation of the "labor protection agreements" established during the Five Antis Campaign. These agreements contained a "distribute cocoons and shut down machines" (*peijian tingche*) condition. When indoor temperatures reached 94 degrees, the materials prep workshops were supposed to stop boiling cocoons. The cocoons that had already been prepared were to be distributed evenly among the reeling workshops so that they would all stop production at the same time. Some filatures, such as Zengxing, Qixin, and Hengda, were found to violate this inconvenient regulation routinely, continuing production even when the temperature exceeded regulations. Extreme temperatures and cases of heat exhaustion and fainting thus continued in the summer of 1953.

Inspections also revealed that measures to protect against cold in winter were insufficient. Between November 1952 and January 1953, the

62. It was unknown at the time that asbestos, an excellent insulation and fireproofing material, also causes lung cancer when inhaled as small particles.

Yongtai Filature reported 1,215 incidents of respiratory illness. The state-run Number Two Filature had 905 incidents in the same period.[63] The All-China Textiles Union issued a notice on preventing illness during the winter months, and Wuxi filatures adopted measures such as providing heavy coats for women workers at the filatures' exits. But ongoing problems with temperature regulation and unhealthy working conditions indicate that employee oversight remained limited.

A Wuxi GLU work report from 1953 confirms this impression, stating that despite considerable progress, safety and working conditions were still less than ideal, nor had there been sufficient effort to study and prevent work-related illnesses. This was attributed to the capitalists' mentality of "only attaching importance to machinery, not to people." But the report also criticized the unions for not doing enough to improve health and safety, even where such improvements were feasible.[64]

During the downtime for renovations in the summer of 1952, the Wuxi unions organized filature workers to engage in study, a welcome opportunity and relief from the strain and monotony of filature work. This was part of an ongoing campaign to eliminate illiteracy among the city's filature workers, most of whom had been employed (or even married) from an early age and had never had the opportunity to attend school. Through union literacy classes, filature workers received forty-two days of intensive training, in which time they supposedly learned 2,200 characters and could read a newspaper. This claim is doubtful, however, given the amount of time it takes most school children to learn to read Chinese. A 1955 union investigation into education levels in Wuxi filatures found that 11,433, or 78 percent of filature workers, remained illiterate or semi-literate. Nonetheless, it was an encouraging

63. Qian, *Wuxishi sichou gongye*, 249–51.

64. WMA D2-1-10. Conditions in state-run filatures were no better, even in 1954, when a woman worker at a tussah filature in Dalian, Liaoning Province, Zhu Baoshan, died of tuberculosis because she was not permitted to take enough time off from work to recover. The same report mentions that another worker at the filature, Sun Guixiu, had a miscarriage and was permanently disabled as a result of the factory administrators' focus on production to the exclusion of workers' welfare. *People's Daily*, 22 Jan. 1956. The description of conditions in the filature's childcare facility is so awful as to be unbelievable.

start. More than 8,500 filature workers received some form of literacy or technical training during this period, which ended with a celebration on July 9, 1952. Four Wuxi workers, including a young woman named Zhu Xingdi who worked at the Huachang Filature, were accepted as students at People's University in Beijing the following month. This was the first time a Wuxi filature worker had been able to attend college, and more of Wuxi's young women followed Zhu's example in later years.[65]

Literacy education in Wuxi in 1952 was part of a nationwide initiative to improve worker education and train industrial workers in technical and administrative skills, grooming a new generation of working-class managers and technicians who would presumably be grateful and loyal to the party for the opportunity.[66] In Wuxi, a total of 21,241 workers in all industries attended union-organized classes by the end of 1952. Of these, 2,758 earned middle school diplomas, 1,086 received technical training, and 293 participated in rapid literacy training classes. Many of these workers went on to teach others as educational opportunities continued to expand.[67]

Conclusion

The experiences of the young women who worked in the Jiangnan thread mills bear little resemblance to those of the privileged, well-organized, and relatively autonomous silk weavers in Shanghai. The former saw little or no change in their day-to-day working lives in the first years of the PRC, while the latter were at the forefront of working-class gains following the Communist seizure of power. Gender is not the only characteristic that distinguishes these two groups of workers from one another. Many women working in Shanghai's silk industry benefitted from their union's accomplishments alongside their male colleagues. The most significant aspect of the gendered division of labor in the Yangzi Delta silk industry is that the factory regime in Jiangnan filatures used patriarchal violence to control a young, female workforce. In contrast, male silk weavers shared with their male employers

65. Qian, *Wuxishi sichou gongye*, 254–55.
66. SMA C1-1-73. See also Harper, "Trade Union Cultivation."
67. WMA D2-1-10.

and managers not only a common dialect and background, but also a working-class culture of masculinity that allowed more honest and productive dialogue between labor and management than was the case in the filatures of Wuxi.

Even when the authorities of the party-state were moved to address the injustices of the filature factory regime following Shen Gendi's violent death in September 1951, the results of their efforts, achieved through the Democratic Reform Campaign, were disappointing in many ways. "Feudal" management methods persisted in some of Wuxi's silk mills, and it was difficult to see how factory management had been "democratized" in any meaningful way. The context of the Korean War and the ongoing Campaign to Suppress Counter-Revolutionaries helped to ensure that democratic reform served the needs of the party-state more than those of the filature workers. These young women might very well have worked toward different goals if they had been masters of their own movement.

By 1953, most filature workers had seen undeniable improvements, including safety measures and concern for workers' health. It is significant, however, that these benefits did not come about as the result of initiatives on the part of the filature workers' union or an autonomous movement among the rank and file. They were granted by the authorities of the party-state, both at the center in Beijing and in the local government of Wuxi. Neither the establishment of filature union organizations nor the Democratic Reform Campaign had enabled these working-class women to take control of their own lives and set their own priorities for revolution and reform in the way that Shanghai silk weavers had already been able to do.

In contrast with the "labor aristocrats" in Shanghai's silk weaving factories, Communist vanguardism and traditional Chinese patriarchy conceived of the young women workers in Jiangnan filatures as child-like people whose consciousness needed to be raised so that they could recognize where their interests really lay. Although conceptions of gender roles and women's status were changing in a variety of ways throughout China during the revolution, the government's emphasis on working-class and women's liberation could only go so far in achieving these goals when other policy initiatives, such as labor-capital cooperation, economic recovery, and the elimination of "enemies" in society took precedence. Without effective organizations of their own, and without political resources to utilize in the struggle for change, there was little filature workers could do to achieve, or even express, their goals and priorities for themselves.

As the next chapter shows, during the First Five-Year Plan, industrial workers' most pressing and immediate needs and interests took a backseat as the party accelerated the Chinese people toward its vision of state-led industrialization. Throughout the 1950s and 1960s, the party repeatedly called on workers to participate in production competitions and other campaigns based on their "class consciousness," and to demonstrate their loyalty and activism by increasing their efforts in production. Some individuals found new opportunities to advance their interests by such means, becoming labor models and party members. But by the end of the decade, China's "national capitalists" and industrial workers, whether privileged male silk weavers or neglected female filature workers, had few options available to them other than depending on their Communist leaders, working hard, and hoping for a better future.

CHAPTER SEVEN

The Socialist Transformation of the Yangzi Delta Silk Industry

The developmental path of China's modern silk industry was fraught with crisis and difficulty. Despite broadly similar economic and political conditions, the two branches of the silk industry—thread filatures and weaving workshops—developed very different factory regimes, business strategies, and relations with workers and governments. The comparison presented in this book demonstrates that silk workers' experiences in China's Communist-led revolution also varied dramatically. However, the Communist Party's policies for labor and industry gradually brought the circumstances of filature workers and silk weavers closer together. Even as early as 1951, the conditions of silk weaving and filature work began to converge through the implementation of "patriotic production campaigns" and the related "labor model" program. The First Five-Year Plan (launched in 1953) and the "socialist transformation" of 1955–56 continued this trend as factory management, labor organizing, and state-society relations changed under CCP hegemony.

Production campaigns and party leadership were not the only new aspects of factory life in the 1950s. The party's policies also brought improvements in working conditions and welfare benefits under the *danwei* system of state-run industry. Workers in state-run factories enjoyed an "iron rice bowl" and impressive benefits, so long as they conformed to the party's expectations. Not all workers made this transition to socialist employment, however. The desperate economic situation following the Great Leap Forward of 1958–61 gave rise to new categories of workers based on an urban-rural hierarchy enforced through the PRC's "household registration" (*hukou*) system. In the collapse of industry following the "Leap," many silk workers, and some capitalists, were "sent down" to the countryside, and were only allowed to return to urban industry as temporary or contract workers in the 1960s.

This chapter first examines the results of CCP policy toward urban industry following the Five Antis Campaign in 1952. Second, it examines the roles of China's silk capitalists and their employees in the rapid socialization of Chinese industry and commerce in 1955–56. Looking beyond the conference rooms of Zhongnanhai and the pages of the *People's Daily*, this chapter details the process of "socialist transformation" in the Yangzi Delta silk industry. The socialization of privately owned factories enabled the party-state to enforce its policies and campaigns more effectively in individual enterprises. The process was driven, however, not only by Communist ambition, but by the demands of workers employed in private industry, and by the responses of Chinese capitalists to policy statements like the 1953 "General Line for the Transition to Socialism." As was often the case with CCP initiatives, the results were surprising. Workers anticipated that "socialization" would bring improved benefits and greater influence over management, but instead they faced dictatorial state administrators and efforts to intensify labor. Silk capitalists hoped that "socialization" would help to overcome the industry's many difficulties, and that their status as capitalist pariahs would end. Instead, they found themselves marginalized in their own enterprises and repeatedly targeted as members of an "enemy" class.

Workers, Capitalists, and the State after the Five Antis Campaign

In 1965, A. Doak Barnett described the 1952 Five Antis Campaign as the "indirect or disguised socialization of private enterprise" and claimed that following the campaign, the party-state exercised "enough control over private industry and trade as a whole to apply state planning in various degrees and forms to the entire economy."[1] Historians of the early PRC have echoed Barnett's claims,[2] but there is little evidence to support the theory that the Communist party-state was capable of integrating private firms into the nascent planned economy in 1952. Most planning organs were not established until 1954, and it is difficult to see how the party-state could ever achieve precise bureaucratic control over China's diverse and dynamic economy.[3] In general, the Maoist economy exhibited little in the way of economic planning. Market institutions, worn from years of war, mismanagement, and economic crisis, were never fully replaced with planning mechanisms, and the resulting economy was less a "planned" economy than an "unplanned" economy.[4]

Much of what happens in revolutions is unplanned, although both the revolutionaries and their detractors like to imagine that things play out according to plan and consistent with ideology. Party hacks credit the revolution's leaders with near-omniscient strategy, and the party's line with impossible consistency. When foreign critics and observers repeat claims about the perspicacity and subtle genius of party leaders like Mao, it can become part of the mythological canon of world revolution. For example, in his 1982 publication, *The Messiah and the Mandarins*, Dennis Bloodworth, Far East Correspondent for *The Observer* from 1956 to 1981, wrote that Mao "is supposed to have said" that getting the capitalists to submit to socialization was like "getting a cat to eat chili." "Rub the chili into the cat's ass, and when it begins to burn,

1. A. Doak Barnett, *Communist China*, 143, 162.

2. See, for example, James Gao, *Communist Takeover of Hangzhou*, 172; Gardner, "Wu-fan Campaign," 523–26; Lieberthal, *Revolution and Tradition*, 170–72.

3. Choh-ming Li, *Economic Development of Communist China*, 6–7, emphasizes that in 1952, China's Communist-led government was "not as yet in a position to absorb all private enterprises into the public sector" and that the economic downturn created by the Five Antis Campaign motivated the government to take measures to revive private production and trade "not for the sake of the private interests but for the health of the economy as a whole."

4. The application of the term "unplanned economy" to the Maoist era grew out of a discussion with Kajima Jun and Feng Xiaocai at the World Economic History Conference in Kyoto in 2015 and applies to the Maoist economy of the early PRC. It differs from the use of "unplanned" to refer to economies based on healthy market institutions.

the cat will lick it off, and be glad you let it."[5] This repeats a story, almost certainly apocryphal, about Mao, Zhou Enlai, and Liu Shaoqi discussing how to get a cat to eat hot chili peppers that may have been a popular joke in the 1950s. It certainly seems to express what many capitalists must have felt.

The context in which Bloodworth heard this story is unclear from his book, but it is written into his description of the nationalization of private industry and commerce in the "socialist transformation" of 1956. A popular textbook in modern Chinese history that was first published in 1991 and is now in its fifth edition, *Modernization and Revolution in China*, cites Bloodworth's book and repeats the claim that Mao compared the process of socialization to making a cat eat chili. The later work, however, places this story in the context of the Five Antis Campaign of 1952.[6] A 1997 work, citing *Modernization and Revolution in China*, also connects this story to the Five Antis and repeats the claim that "harassment and pressure were so great that one businessman after another gave up his or her business and surrendered to the government" in 1952.[7] This narrative of socialization, however, is inaccurate and misleading, as is the anecdote that implies that the process from 1949 to 1956 developed smoothly according to Mao's subtle if insidious plan.

If the Five Antis Campaign did not achieve the socialization of private industry, what did it accomplish? In the summer of 1952, China's leaders announced that the Five Antis Campaign had achieved "basic victory." As described in chapter 5, most capitalists were identified as "basically law-abiding" and treated leniently. The fines were heavy, and many factory owners went into debt to repay "illegal earnings" or back taxes,[8] but the party-state did not expropriate their enterprises, and instead went to great lengths to resuscitate private business following the campaign. Nor did the Five Antis Campaign attempt to define specific class categories in urban China, as was the case in rural

5. Bloodworth, *Messiah and Mandarins*, 111.

6. Grasso, *Modernization and Revolution*, 142.

7. Malik, *Chinese Entrepreneurs*, 7–8.

8. For a discussion of the financial forces at work in the "socialist transformation," see Feng, "Rushing toward Socialism," 240–358.

land reform.[9] Nonetheless, the campaign emphasized capitalists' "dual nature" and potential disloyalty to the revolution, and educated their employees about class differences between workers and capitalists. Following the campaign, China's "national bourgeoisie" was no longer identified as part of "the people," but rather as an "enemitized" pariah class, a mistrusted but still useful social group that would be subjected to continuous "reform" over the following two and a half decades.[10]

For the most part, China's capitalists responded to rhetorical (and sometimes physical) abuse during the Five Antis Campaign with passivity and withdrawal. Factory owners showed little enthusiasm for managing their factories, often abdicating their authority and conceding whatever their employees demanded. Confronting capitalists' passivity and workers' "economism" (demanding higher wages and benefits from beleaguered employers), in late 1952 CCP cadres throughout China directed workers away from class struggle and back onto the path of "facing production" and "benefiting both labor and capital." There was no immediate talk of nationalization or state management, to say nothing of direct worker control or cooperative enterprise.[11]

Employee management temporarily proliferated during the Five Antis Campaign as workers and staff attempted to maintain production in their employers' absence, but CCP leaders were no more enthusiastic about employee takeovers in 1952 than they had been in 1949, and there is no indication that the party encouraged workers to take over private enterprises.[12] Worker supervision, through LCCCs or similar provisions for "democratic management," preserved capitalist

9. Richard Kraus notes that "precise and universal class identification was not an integral aspect of the movement." Richard Kraus, *Class Conflict in Chinese Socialism*, 24.

10. Feng, "Shenfen, yishi yu zhengzhi," 32–38.

11. Sheehan, *Chinese Workers*, 41–44.

12. Barnett claims that the state encouraged internal takeovers of private businesses by staff members and workers during the Five Antis, giving one example of a retail business in Shanghai. A. Doak Barnett, *Communist China*, 165–66. But it is now clear that party authorities encouraged the restoration of capitalist management after the campaign and there are very few examples of worker takeovers of private enterprises. For the model example of the Zhenhua Electrical Wire Factory in Tianjin, see *People's Daily*, 15 Jun. 1952.

ownership and merely tasked the unions with ensuring the fulfillment of state contracts. In a May 19, 1952, report, Shanghai GLU chair Liu Changsheng[13] emphasized the need for unions in private enterprises to "face production" and stated that the best way to overcome "tense" labor relations and prevent recurrence of the "five poisons" was the revival of "democratic management." Liu admitted that although the Common Program and the Labor Union Law had provisions for workers' participation in management, these were rarely put into practice. He nonetheless claimed that establishing factory committees like the LCCCs would advance labor-capital unity and resolve issues in the "public-private relationship" by overseeing capitalists' fulfillment of state contracts, management of raw materials, and payment of taxes. Liu also emphasized, however, that worker supervision should not extend to the factory owner's property rights, managerial authority, or control over personnel assignments (including wages).[14] Liu's vision thus represents a return to "New Democracy" rather than appropriation by workers or the state following the Five Antis Campaign.

Before 1952, "democratic management" in Shanghai's silk weaving industry was mainly limited to the largest factories or those with an existing core of CCP members. According to factory owners' responses to a survey conducted by the Industry Association, almost sixty factories had established organs for worker participation in management before April 1952.[15] Following the Five Antis Campaign, LCCCs and production committees expanded, and reports from November 1952 list dozens of silk factories establishing committees for "democratic management." Although these no doubt functioned imperfectly, their expansion indicates that at least some workers gained greater influence over factory affairs following the campaign.[16]

13. Liu Changsheng was a leather worker and underground Communist organizer in Shanghai during and after the Japanese occupation. After the establishment of the PRC, he served as vice-chairman of the ACFTU. He was a member of the Eighth Central Committee of the CCP from 1954 until his death in 1967. Perry, *Shanghai on Strike*, 253.

14. SMA C1–1–73.

15. SMA S39–4–6.

16. SMA C1–2–754; S39–4–29.

The expansion of worker supervision and "democratic management" did not, however, produce the hoped-for improvements in production and fulfillment of state contracts. For one thing, the revived rhetoric of harmonious labor relations failed to restore capitalists' confidence in the United Front or enable them to manage their businesses effectively. Union reports from late 1952 complain that factory owners no longer managed their enterprises actively and left responsibility for production tasks to the unions. Union cadres at the Mofan Silk Factory reported that the owner frequently went out to gamble and did not come to work. When the union reps requested a meeting to discuss the state of production, he simply ignored them. He was later sentenced to one and a half years in prison for non-payment of taxes and selling cloth contracted to the state.[17] Union reports also described employers' "passive resistance," simply showing up for work but not attempting to manage anything. Lou Erpin, of the Yunlin Silk Factory, stated that after the Five Antis Campaign, he sometimes did not go to the factory at all. Labor discipline problems, including absenteeism, neglect of production norms, and insubordination, proliferated in the second half of 1952.[18]

Nor could the unions manage workers effectively in the post-Five-Antis economy. The return to "labor-capital cooperation" placed a heavy burden on inexperienced union cadres, many of whom had been promoted for their political zeal and ability to struggle with employers rather than their expertise in production planning or accounting.[19] A union report from Wuxi blamed shortcomings in factory management on "leftist" union cadres who interfered with employers' business and personnel decisions. In some factories, the owner needed the union's permission to utilize enterprise funds, which adversely affected his "enthusiasm for business management."[20] An investigation of factory unions in Wuxi at the end of 1952 found that most cadres lacked experience and had difficulty navigating the party's convoluted line.

17. SMA S39-4-5, C1-1-1637.

18. Interview with Lou Erpin and Lou Erzheng, 19 Apr. 2004.

19. Harper, "Trade Union Cultivation," 144; John Lewis, *Leadership in Communist China*, 108.

20. WMA D2-1-10.

Union cadres furthermore received frequent criticism from other workers, which left them discouraged and eager to be replaced in the next election. For many filature employees, union work was less appealing than focusing on production, becoming a labor model, and "getting the chance to meet Chairman Mao."[21]

Union cadres in Shanghai's silk weaving industry faced similar challenges. Although there were experienced officers staffing the citywide union, the quality of cadres in Shanghai's numerous small factories was generally poor, and most had only a vague understanding of policy. Weavers in small factories frequently had a poor opinion of their unions, which impeded these cadres' efforts to mobilize workers to improve production.[22] In 1953, labor discipline problems such as a disregard for safety regulations, lax work habits, absenteeism, and failure to care for tools and equipment undermined efforts to increase production, conserve raw materials, and improve management systems.[23]

The breakdown of labor discipline also affected state-run factories as workers sought relief from campaign fatigue and pressure to "increase production and practice economy." Managers in private factories hardly dared to direct workers for fear of being identified as "running dogs" of the capitalists, and administrators of state-run enterprises faced similar resistance.[24] Employers were pessimistic and demoralized, financial management had collapsed, and costs and wastage remained high. Despite the goal of worker supervision and exhortations to "unite with capitalists to carry out production," the situation following the Five Antis Campaign was more often one in which no one took responsibility for managing production.

The collapse of managerial authority adversely affected product output and quality, and a November 1952 Shanghai GLU report picked out the silk weaving industry as especially problematic. At Song Baolin's factory, Dacheng, the rate of defects for *liuxiang* spun silk cloth reached

21. WMA D2-1-16.

22. SMA C1-1-1637.

23. SMA S39-4-27, S39-4-75.

24. Frazier, *Chinese Industrial Workplace*, 126–27; Bennis So, "Abolition of Private Ownership," 700.

76.8 percent. Quality problems adversely affected China's trade with the Soviet Union. In 1952, China was only able to deliver half the agreed amounts of AA soft satin and shameuse (embroidered silk), and only 20 percent of the cloth delivered achieved quality standards. Poor product quality and high costs made it difficult for exporters to compete in international markets.[25]

Such difficulties prompted industry leaders to call for direct state management of private silk weaving, but government authorities showed no desire to administer this complex and troubled industry. Rather than establishing state management of silk factories, the government encouraged private producers to improve management systems and become financially self-reliant. In 1953 state authorities even reduced the proportion of product contracted to state companies, another indication that there was little interest in "socializing" silk factories in the aftermath of the Five Antis Campaign.

Estimates of the proportion of private production contracted to the state after the Five Antis Campaign vary. George Ecklund claims that by 1953, "the state was purchasing or marketing 63 percent of the gross output of private factories."[26] Bennis So found that state processing and purchasing orders accounted for 81.5 percent of the turnover of private businesses between March and June 1952, with an average of 56.04 percent for the whole of 1952.[27] Following the Five Antis Campaign, the proportion of private production contracted to the state exceeded that produced independently, but the expansion of state contracting in 1952 was less dramatic than in the previous three years and was not sustained.

Even after the campaign there remained considerable diversity in private factories' relationships with state companies. In the silk weaving industry, state authorities *reduced* production contracts in the year following the Five Antis. By contrast, Shanghai silk filatures were producing entirely for the state by 1952, which continued through the industry's nationalization in 1954–55. By the end of 1952, Shanghai's silk weaving industry was more dependent on state contracts than ever

25. SMA C1-2-739; B83-2-1348, S39-4-67.
26. Ecklund, "Protracted Expropriation of Private Business," 240–42.
27. Bennis So, "Abolition of Private Ownership," 693–95.

before, with 86.51 percent of production contracted to the CSC.[28] Although payments from state contracts comprised silk factories' main source of revenue, many found it difficult to earn a profit. The Silk Industry Association warned, "Our only hope is to maintain the current contracting situation and not reduce it." At the end of March 1953, however, the Shanghai Silk Weaving Industry Association announced that its members should "make thought preparation" (*zuo sixiang zhunbei*) to expand independent production and marketing as state contracts diminished.[29]

Exports of silk to the Soviet Union and Socialist Bloc increased rapidly during the Korean War, but by the war's end in July 1953, these markets were glutted with Chinese silk and the CSC's surplus inventory amounted to more than three billion yuan. China and the Soviet Union were furthermore negotiating a new trade agreement, and the CSC could not set quotas for production contracts until this was completed. In response to this unplanned fluctuation in the supposedly planned economy, the state company reduced cocoon purchasing prices to discourage sericulture, cut back filature production, reduced supplies of synthetic fibers, and required private weaving factories to rely on shrinking domestic markets and independent sales. The number of Shanghai silk factories producing on contract for the state fell from 122 to just thirty-five. Overall output of silk cloth in 1953 declined by almost 10 percent compared with 1952, and the proportion contracted to the state fell to just 56.88 percent, a decrease of 34 percent (see table 7.1).[30]

The reduction in state contracts exacerbated the silk weaving industry's financial difficulties. Many factories had installed new equipment in response to expanding state purchases the previous year, and the state company's reduction plan elicited immediate protests. One factory owner compared the "blindness" of the market to that of the "plan" stating, "[you say that] we are blind—it turns out you are blind too!"[31] Despite factory owners' pleas, however, the CSC reduced its plan for production of silk cloth by more than 4,000 bolts in the first quarter of

28. SMA S39-4-44; *Shanghai sichou zhi*, 235.
29. SMA S39-4-6.
30. SMA S39-4-44, S39-4-5; *Shanghai sichou zhi*, 235.
31. SMA S39-4-27.

Table 7.1
State-contracted silk weaving as a proportion of GVIO (mill. RMB), 1950–1953

Year	Total GVIO (mill. RMB)	Contracted to CSC (mill. RMB)	Proportion of total output (%)
1950	257,225	75,206	29
1951	391,944	99,511	25
1952	532,958	439,685	82
1953	573,239	315,296	55

SOURCE: SMA S39-4-44.*

* *Shanghai sichouzhi*, 235, gives somewhat different statistics for the proportion of total output contracted to the state in these years, but the overall trend is the same: 25.51% for 1950, 45.56% for 1951, 86.51% for 1953, and 56.88% for 1954.

1953. In the second quarter, the CSC planned to further reduce the amount of contracted silk by 20,000 bolts to just 55,000. This led to a wave of labor disputes (sixty-three in total), of which 90 percent concerned wage reductions or non-payment of wages and bonuses.[32] Nonetheless, these changes also provided an opportunity for labor-capital cooperation in the face of adversity, much like the February Sixth Bombing in 1950. By June 1953, more than ten silk weaving factories had drafted "labor-capital production agreements" to weather the crisis by improving product quality and reducing costs, demonstrating the kind of close cooperation between factory owners and union officials that was possible even after the Five Antis. That same month, however, the CSC again reduced the amount of contracted silk by more than one-third as compared with May, and state-contracted weaving comprised only 21.4 percent of total production of silk cloth in the third quarter of 1953. As a result, twenty-six factories went out of business and laid off their workers, giving rise to another round of labor disputes.[33]

The CSC provided some relief in the form of reduced prices for nylon thread and assistance in promoting domestic sales.[34] Under the circumstances, however, it was difficult for silk producers to revert to

32. SMA S39-4-6, S39-4-27.
33. SMA S39-4-5, S39-4-27, S39-4-2, S39-4-6, S39-4-44.
34. SMA S39-4-44, S39-4-27.

"independent production and sales." Competition for new markets in Xinjiang led to a price war, and prices for double-sided satin and gold velvet fell below production costs. To make matters worse, the CSC lowered state purchasing prices for thirty-seven types of cloth. Echoing their earlier pleas to the postwar Nationalist government, factory owners demanded that the CSC restore purchasing prices, set prices according to actual costs, and promote Chinese silk in international markets. Although the state company restored prices for some products, this did not address the problems of reduced contracts and stagnant exports.[35]

By the time the state silk company restored weaving contracts at the end of 1953, factory owners had successfully adapted and were starting to turn a profit as exports revived and independent sales on domestic markets became more viable. In July 1953, Zhu Zuxian of the China Sericulture Company made a report to the Silk Industry Association on a trade mission to the Soviet Union. He reported that roughly 20 percent of Soviet silk garments were produced using Chinese cloth. Curtains on cars and airplanes were made of spun silk cloth. Linings for women's coats used Chinese georgette, which was also used for blouses. In August, Shanghai silk producers were asked to provide examples of their best products for an upcoming exhibition of silk products organized by the Sino-Soviet Friendship Association. In May 1954, an agreement on Soviet development aid, to be repaid with exports of Chinese goods, further advanced the revival of silk exports to the Soviet Union.[36] Closer ties and Soviet support for China's First Five-Year Plan increased opportunities for trade, which benefitted the silk industry as it had in 1950. Exports to countries in Asia, Europe, the Middle East, and the Americas (excepting the United States and its "satellites") also expanded. With the revival of exports and higher prices for silk on domestic markets, most silk weaving factories earned a profit by the end of 1953. Overall business turnover increased 38 percent as compared with 1952, while the proportion of business income from state contracts fell 35 percent.[37]

35. SMA S39-4-1, S39-4-2, S39-4-27.

36. SMA S39-4-27; Meng Xianzhang, *Zhong-Su maoyi shiliao*, 570–74; Eckstein, *Economic Growth and Foreign Trade*, 91–116, 145–82.

37. SMA S39-4-2, S39-4-44, S39-4-5, S39-4-6.

As silk cloth became more profitable from late 1953, the state company reinstituted contract weaving. The number of factories producing on contract for the China Sericulture Company[38] expanded from a low of thirty-five in July to forty-eight in August and steadily increased thereafter. As export demand revived, the CSC compelled factories to sell stores of export-quality cloth. With domestic demand for silk cloth rising in December in advance of Spring Festival, mandatory state purchases elicited a chorus of resistance.[39] The 1953 retreat from state contracting was, however, the last gasp of the market economy as far as Shanghai's silk weaving industry was concerned. By December, more than 80 percent of silk cloth was contracted to or purchased by state companies and (according to a Silk Industry Association report) the industry had "set out upon the path of state capitalism."[40]

During the temporary retreat from state contracting in 1953, many phenomena of the earlier economy, including the "five poisons," reappeared. The forced return to independent sales in 1953 encouraged illegality such as reselling state-supplied materials and selling cloth at prices higher than those set by the state—oddly referred to as "speculation" (*touji*). Some reports claim that the "five poisons" may have been even worse than before the Five Antis Campaign, prompting a "New Five Antis" Campaign in 1953.[41] Party leaders and state administrators hoped that "worker supervision" would ensure that capitalists did not violate the terms of their contracts or engage in illegal activities. Employees at the Chengchang Silk Factory, for example, exposed the factory owner's misuse of state-supplied materials in 1954. He was fined a total of 2.8 million yuan (Old Renminbi), which could not have improved the factory's financial situation.[42] Union reports from Wuxi filatures mention offenses such as concealing enterprise funds, purchasing private

38. On October 27, 1953, the China Sericulture Company (Zhongguo cansi gongsi) changed its name to the China Silk Company (Zhongguo sichou gongsi) and moved its headquarters from Shanghai to Beijing. Wang Zhuangmu et al., *Xin Zhongguo sichou dashiji*, 19. For consistency this chapter uses China Sericulture Company or CSC.

39. SMA S39-4-5, S39-4-44.

40. SMA S39-4-5.

41. SMA S39-4-29, C1-2-914.

42. SMA C1-1-1637.

houses, taking excessive salaries, and wasting funds by engaging in a "degenerate lifestyle."[43]

Even when employees reported their employers' illegal activities, however, state authorities often failed to respond, and union cadres grew discouraged when their reports did not elicit any action. For these reasons, in most small factories, neither union cadres nor workers were very enthusiastic about supervising their employers. Although workers at the Wanli Silk Factory considered the owner "good for nothing," they believed his days were numbered and did not bother to supervise him. Most silk workers were not concerned with ensuring that their employers complied with state policies. As long as they received their wages on time, along with meal subsidies and other benefits, workers were unlikely to supervise capitalists' activities too carefully—an unintended form of labor-capital cooperation. Workers at the small Hesheng Factory supported the owners' poor opinion of state-contracted production, saying, "Why bother to engage in production when we only make an ounce of rice or a single penny?" By 1954, silk workers had little interest in "increasing production and practicing economy" and adopted a passive attitude, waiting to see what the impending "socialist transformation" would bring.[44]

One of the problems that silk workers hoped state management could resolve was the "chaotic" wage system in Jiangnan silk factories. In 1954, average wages in silk weaving factories ranged from 562,000 yuan to 907,000 yuan (Old Renminbi), and even within the same factory there were wide disparities. Wages at Shanghai's Second United Factory ranged from 295,000 yuan to 2.34 million yuan. Workers also complained of large gaps between weavers and prep workers and between men and women workers, and few believed these problems could be resolved under capitalist ownership.[45] The tendency to wait for the state takeover impeded attempts to resolve wage issues and rationalize management systems in the years leading up to the "socialist transformation." Workers hoped to gain the benefits of employment in socialist

43. WMA D5-2-224, D5-2-226.
44. SMA C1-1-1637.
45. SMA C16-2-107, S39-4-75, S39-4-1.

factories, while many capitalist employers looked forward to socialization as a way out of their difficulties.

The Five Antis Campaign resulted in a degree of worker supervision in some industries but fell far short of worker control.[46] The growing hegemony of the revolutionary state, however, meant that Chinese workers increasingly faced not harrowed and humiliated capitalists, but a powerful party apparatus that controlled the means of production and the means of subsistence for the majority of workers. The role of the state in the national economy expanded dramatically during the First Five-Year Plan (1953–57) as China attempted, with only limited success, to establish a Soviet-style economic planning bureaucracy. As markets dwindled and most consumer goods became rationed, industrial workers grew increasingly dependent on their places of employment for survival. Party administrators criticized dissenting workers as "backward," "economistic," and even "bourgeois." Squeezed between their employees' demands for socialist benefits and the requirements of the expanding state-run economy, many capitalists decided long before the party leadership that it was time to accelerate the pace of "socialist transformation."

The "Transition to Socialism" in the Yangzi Delta Silk Industry

One of the most important moments in the shift from reviving private businesses after the Five Antis Campaign to pursuing the socialist transformation of private industry and commerce three years later was the publication of the "General Line for the Transition to Socialism" in October 1953. If the Five Antis Campaign was the party's short-term response to the problems of the New Democratic economy, the "General Line" was presented as a long-term solution to those problems—a Chinese path to socialism that would bring industrialization and prosperity for the Chinese people.

46. For a definition and thoughtful discussion of "worker control" in modern industry, see Montgomery, *Workers' Control in America*.

In August 1953 Chairman Mao issued a directive that summarized the "General Line," expressing the uneasy consensus among party leaders that recent events and current conditions required progressing from the compromise arrangements of New Democracy toward a fully socialist economy:

> The time between the founding of the People's Republic of China and the basic completion of socialist transformation is a period of transition. The Party's general line or general task for the transition period is basically to accomplish the country's industrialization and the socialist transformation of agriculture, handicrafts, and capitalist industry and commerce *over a fairly long period of time*. This general line should be the beacon illuminating all our work, and wherever we deviate from it, we shall make Right or "Left" mistakes.[47]

A *People's Daily* editorial on October 1, 1953, introduced the "General Line" to the public and explained its purpose and significance. Regarding the transformation of the capitalist economy, the editorial stated that the policy was to "continue to carry out the transformation of private industry and commerce [and] correctly give play to the role of individual farming, handicrafts, and private industry and commerce; to guarantee the steady increase of the socialist proportion of the national economy [and] to guarantee gradually raising the level of the people's material and cultural life on the foundation of developing production."[48] Thus, the "General Line" entailed a continuation of the party's goals as expressed in the Common Program and other documents and did not signal a radical shift in policy. Official statements emphasized the gradual pace of reform and the need to maintain private production for many years to come. If it had not been obvious to workers, capitalists, and state cadres previously, the "General Line" eliminated any doubts that China's future was socialist.

A popular trend in recent scholarship has been to talk about the "Stalinization" of China under Mao. Usually this refers to the

47. Mao Zedong, *Mao Zedong wenji*, 6: 316. Emphasis added.
48. *People's Daily*, 1 Oct. 1953.

concentration of power in the hands of the supreme leader—the "cult of personality"—as well as the attempt to establish a Soviet-style planned economy in the People's Republic in the 1950s.[49] We now know that the Soviet planned economy never worked the way it was intended and that the "plan" was a legal fiction that every economic actor in the country routinely violated in order to achieve their assigned quotas under the plan.[50] Soviet and Chinese Communist leaders may have aspired to possess total political, economic, and social control, but no leader achieved this in practice, and central economic planning was even less developed in the PRC than in the USSR. Andrew Walder comments that although the planned economy was the most obviously "Stalinist" aspect of the People's Republic, by the end of the 1950s the CCP had abandoned the Soviet model in favor of a typically Maoist mobilization regime and "politics in command" to pursue economic development.[51]

Previous scholarship on China's "socialist transformation" has focused on the central leadership and the spectacular events of the "socialist high tide" in January 1956. Adopting the view from the center, however, has generally inclined scholars to neglect the details of the process in specific industries and localities.[52] This is regrettable, because the process was important and defined China's unique path to socialism. In China, the socialization or nationalization of private industry was completed not by outright expropriation but through "joint state-private mergers" and the policy of "buying out" (*shumai*) factory owners—compensating former capitalists for assets contributed to the joint enterprise.[53] This approach created enterprises that were incorporated under government agencies or state companies, but many former owners remained in managerial positions and received compensation in the form of "fixed dividends" (*dingxi*).

49. See, for example, Hua-yu Li, *Economic Stalinization of China*, 113–15; Meliksetov and Pantsov, "Stalinization of the People's Republic," 198–233.

50. This truth is readily apparent in Stalin-era memoirs like Andreev-Khomiakov, *Bitter Waters*.

51. Walder, *China under Mao*, 82, 98.

52. One exception is Kathrin Sears's 1985 dissertation, "Shanghai's Textile Capitalists."

53. Bennis So, "Abolition of Private Ownership," 684.

As the comparison of silk filatures and weaving factories in this book demonstrates, the process varied considerably across geographical regions and industries. Because of their size and production function, silk filatures previously had close ties to state banks and companies like the CSC under both Nationalists and Communists. Silk filatures were integrated into the state-run economy earlier and more smoothly than the hundreds of small silk workshops in Jiangnan cities. It appears that neither the Shanghai Municipal Government nor the China Sericulture Company was eager to take over the administration of private silk weaving. Just as the process of "Liberation" was different for filature workers and silk weavers, so too was the "socialist transformation" different in the two industries.

The First Five-Year Plan (1953–57) was China's attempt to implement a Soviet-style planned economy on a national scale. However, China did not establish statistics and planning systems until 1954 or 1955,[54] and the process of extending government control over China's complex and diverse economy, especially the private sector, was fraught with complications. In 1953, the state and private sectors of the Chinese economy had both expanded compared with 1952, by 33.7 percent and 18.5 percent respectively. If state-contracted production in private firms is included, "state capitalism" increased by 39 percent in 1953.[55] Following the promulgation of the "General Line" in October, the expansion of the state and "state capitalist" sectors of the economy accelerated. Markets for most agricultural products were eliminated beginning in November 1953, and many consumer goods were distributed through a rationing system. Other commodities, including grain, edible oil, cotton cloth, tea, tobacco, bamboo, timber, cocoons, and silk thread, were not rationed but came under a system of "unified purchasing" by state companies.[56]

Because the First Five-Year Plan called for the "vigorous development of silk production," provincial and local governments throughout

54. The national plan was not formally completed until February 1955 and was not published until July. Donnithorne, *China's Economic System*, 457–58.

55. Hsia, *Economic Planning in Communist China*, 79.

56. Choh-ming Li, *Economic Development of Communist China*, 22–23.

the Yangzi Delta worked to improve sericulture.[57] By 1952, state agencies handled almost the entire cocoon harvest, something that neither the Japanese occupation forces nor the Nationalists had achieved. Of a total of 241,700 tons of cocoons produced in Jiangsu Province in 1952, the state purchased 228,600 tons (95 percent), all of which were supplied to Jiangsu filatures for contract reeling. By 1953 the Jiangsu Provincial Government claimed that sericulture and silk reeling had "entered into unified planned management" under provincial administration.[58] By 1954, Jiangnan silk filatures were receiving their entire supply of cocoons from state companies, which also handled all filature products, even cocoon remnants. By the end of 1955, all Yangzi Delta silk filatures and weaving factories obtained supplies of raw materials exclusively from state agencies. Silk weaving factories continued to market a portion of their product independently in 1954, but by 1955 only hand-woven cloth could be sold privately, and only through CSC-licensed merchants.[59] The next step would be to bring private silk production under direct government administration.

The "socialist transformation" of China's capitalist businesses was a formidable task given the small scale and scattered geography of most private enterprises. In 1955, private enterprises in Shanghai (which employed some 400,000 workers and accounted for more than half of total production in that city) numbered 26,000, of which more than 90 percent had fewer than twenty-five employees.[60] Developments since 1949, however, had made it increasingly difficult for capitalists to manage their businesses effectively. If anti-capitalist campaigns like the Five Antis were not enough, problems in supplies, marketing, finances, labor discipline, and the vicissitudes of the state contracting system inclined

57. See, for example, the *People's Daily* editorial, "Vigorously Develop Silk Production" (7 Jan. 1955), which called for increased production to recover to prewar levels by 1962.

58. *Jiangsusheng cansang sichou zhi*, 257–58.

59. SMA C48-2-1252, B170-1-142; *Zhejiangsheng sichou zhi*, 27–30. The proportion of private production contracted to or purchased by state companies throughout the Chinese economy amounted to 62 percent in 1953, increasing to 79 percent in 1954, and 82 percent in 1955. Perkins, *Market Control and Planning*, 14.

60. *Dagongbao*, 23 Dec. 1955.

many capitalists to look forward to the day when the state would simply take over their businesses.

Because of this situation, the owners of private firms played a surprising role in accelerating the "socialist transformation."[61] As Bennis So puts it, "Even though it was generally understood that the transformation was rapidly completed in 1956 because of Mao's further 'leftward' shift and the Party mobilization, it was also a rational choice for the capitalists to strip off their valueless capitalist integument as soon as possible."[62] By 1953, one of the few options available to Chinese capitalists was to embrace socialization and demonstrate enthusiastic compliance to make a place for themselves in the new socialist order.

The "General Line for the Transition to Socialism" adopted joint state-private enterprises (*gongsi heying qiye*) as the means of transforming private industry and commerce. Li Weihan,[63] the leading party official in charge of United Front work, introduced the policy to the business community in a speech to the All-China Congress of the Federation of Industry and Commerce on October 27, 1953. Li made it clear that the private sector would be integrated, gradually but thoroughly, into the developing socialist economy.[64] In theory, the process would take about fifteen years and would be completed by 1968, but in fact the pace accelerated more quickly than the party leadership anticipated.

Li Weihan's speech was based on his report to the Central Committee the previous May, which focused on state-contracted production and joint state-private enterprises as the means of harnessing the economic dynamism of the private sector while gradually bringing private production and commerce under state leadership and planning. Li did not use the term "transformation" (*gaizao*) in the May report, but recommended that "state capitalism" should be adopted as the means of achieving China's economic goals. In the autumn of 1953,

61. For more on this topic, see Cliver, "Surviving Socialism," 139–64.

62. Bennis So, "Abolition of Private Ownership," 701–2.

63. Li Weihan was an early member of the CCP and close comrade of Mao Zedong. He served as president of the Central Party School and as a member of both the CPPCC and the Politburo of the CCP Central Committee, but was removed from his posts in 1967. He died in 1984. *New York Times*, 13 Aug. 1984.

64. For this speech, see Li Weihan, *Tongyi zhanxian wenti*, 64–80. For an English translation, see *Current Background* 267, 15 Nov. 1953.

however, joint state-private enterprises were still few and far between, with no more than 1,000 throughout China employing a total of 270,000 people and producing a mere 5.7 percent of the nation's industrial output.[65] Nonetheless, over the following two years this form of "state capitalism," which could trace its origins to various forms of cooperation between government and private interests under the Qing dynasty and Nationalist government, became accepted as a form of "socialist" enterprise.

The State Council promulgated its "Provisional Regulations on Joint State-Private Industrial Enterprises" in September 1954, defining a joint enterprise as a firm that "works with state investments or another mixed state-private enterprise and stands under the common direction of capitalists and state-appointed functionaries."[66] Following the merger, the socialist or state side would "play the leading role," integrating enterprises into the emerging planned economy, following the policy of "buying out" to compensate capitalists. Initially based on a portion (around 25 percent) of the enterprise's annual profits, in 1956 the compensation policy was changed to "fixed dividend" (*dingxi*) payments of 5 percent annually based on the assessed value of the former owners' shares.[67]

The "Provisional Regulations" also stipulated that joint enterprises should continue to employ all current personnel, including former capitalists, and should introduce "in appropriate form a system of management in which workers' representatives will take part." The provisions for worker participation in management were very vague, however, and there was little distinction between labor relations in state-run and joint state-private enterprises.[68] With the shift away from

65. Riskin, *China's Political Economy*, 95–96.

66. Chao Kuo-chun, *Economic Planning and Organization*, 1:72–75.

67. Chao Kuo-chun, *Economic Planning and Organization*, 1:24–25. Reflecting the small scale of most private businesses, in about 80 percent of Shanghai firms the private share was assessed at two thousand yuan or less, which provided annual dividends of just one hundred yuan—very meager compensation indeed. Most dividend payments were discontinued by 1966. Ecklund, "Protracted Expropriation of Private Business," 242–46; Richman, *Industrial Society in Communist China*, 897–98.

68. SMA C1-2-1296; Chao Kuo-chun, *Economic Planning and Organization*, 1:74–75.

"democratic management" in state enterprises after 1953, and the tendency for state-appointed managers to emphasize production requirements over workers' rights and benefits, workers in joint factories potentially lost a great deal of autonomy and influence under state administration. No longer enjoying the right to "supervise" management, workers in joint state-private enterprises were just as subject to state agents' authority as their former employers were.

By the end of 1954, the proportion of industrial output produced in joint state-private enterprises had more than doubled to 12.3 percent of China's Gross Value of Industrial Output (GVIO). But fewer than one thousand new joint enterprises were established, and these were mainly large-scale firms in heavy industry and transportation. Socialization proceeded even more slowly through most of 1955, when the proportion of industrial output produced in joint enterprises increased to 16.1 percent of the national total. Joint state-private mergers suddenly expanded toward the end of 1955, however, culminating in the "socialist high tide" of January 1956. In less than four months, nearly all remaining private production and commerce came under at least nominal state management, and joint state-private enterprises' share of GVIO expanded to 30 percent in 1956.[69]

Overall, in the Yangzi Delta silk industry very few new joint enterprises were established between 1949 and 1954, and these were mostly limited to silk filatures expropriated from "counter-revolutionaries" in 1951–52. Even after the promulgation of the State Council's "Provisional Regulations" in September 1954, the process was slow, and only a few of the larger filatures were "transformed." In Shanghai's silk weaving industry, no new joint state-private factories were established before the entire industry was "socialized" in December 1955.

After the publication of the "General Line" in October 1953, the Wuxi Municipal People's Government immediately announced plans to expand joint state-private operations in the city's silk reeling industry. The first step was to establish a Textile Management Bureau, including a Silk Reeling Industry Department to administer the anticipated expansion of state-run filatures. It was not until a year later, however,

69. Ecklund, "Protracted Expropriation of Private Business," 243; Riskin, *China's Political Economy*, 95–96.

in October 1954, that the first filatures (Yongtai and Meixin) were approved for joint operations, and by the end of 1954 only one other joint state-private filature was established.[70] The "socialist transformation" did not spread to other Wuxi filatures until August 1955, when the silk reeling industry became the first in the city to initiate industry-wide mergers as the path to "socialization." The Ruilun, Zengxing, and Dalong Filatures were the first to combine operations on an experimental basis, and on August 22, the three factories formed the Wuxi Number One Joint State-Private Filature. No new joint filatures were established during the following two months, however, until the city's seventeen remaining filatures were combined to form five new filatures in November. On December 3, they were approved *en masse* for joint operations.[71]

One goal of merging filatures before socialization was to concentrate Wuxi's advanced "standing" reeling machines in large filatures to operate on a system of day and night shifts. The Zengxing and Dalong Filatures were merged with the Ruilun Filature because Ruilun possessed the more modern "standing" reeling machines and enjoyed healthy finances. Dalong, in contrast, had no assets, and the owner had fled during the Five Antis Campaign, leaving management of the factory to a union-led production maintenance committee. The resulting Wuxi Number One Joint State-Private Filature planned to run 158 "standing" reeling machines in two nine-hour shifts employing a total of 1,026 personnel, with all workers and staff retaining their original positions and wages.[72]

At a symposium of Wuxi filature owners on November 7, 1955, Gao Jingyue, former owner of the Zengxing Filature, described his experiences with the merger and expressed his commitment to the "socialist transformation." According to Gao, in the two months following the merger, quality and productivity improved and costs fell. The merger created many problems for filature workers, however, especially in terms of adjusting to the new location and two-shift system. Nonetheless, Mr. Gao claimed that factory management had gone from a state

70. Qian, *Wuxishi sichou gongye*, 23, 338–40; Yongtai Manuscript, 48–50.
71. Qian, *Wuxishi sichou gongye*, 23, 338–40.
72. WMA D5-2-232.

of "chaos" to one run according to regular procedures and planning. He attributed this to the "direct leadership of the state representative and the supervision of the working class." At one point, Gao even gushed, "The spiritual joy we have felt as a result of achieving joint operations through the merger is really indescribable."[73] Whether this statement was sincere or not is impossible to know.

Throughout his speech, Mr. Gao emphasized the importance of carrying out mergers to prepare for joint state-private operations. In the case of Ruilin, Zengxing, and Dalong, it was sixty-three days from the merger to the state's approval of joint state-private operations. During this time, the new enterprise carried out the work of appraising assets, retraining workers and staff, and constructing new facilities. In most cases, however, the entire process was compressed into less than a month's time. Facing the growing pressure of the "socialist high tide," the Wuxi Federation of Industry and Commerce moved quickly to "transform" the city's filatures in October and November 1955, despite not having completed the prerequisite mergers.[74]

The process of "socialist transformation" in the Wuxi filatures was similar to that of other major producer goods industries like steel and machine building. By contrast, Shanghai's silk weaving industry was complex, dispersed, and fraught with conflict. If the process of "socialist transformation" in the Wuxi filatures seemed rushed and chaotic, in the Shanghai silk weaving industry, officials seemed unwilling to take decisive action, which frustrated both workers and capitalists. State cadres, union officials, and Silk Industry Association leaders constantly harped on the need for silk weaving factories to establish "scientific systems of management," especially recording systems to better assess costs and materials usage. Although some factories made improvements in production of high-priority types of cloth and were able to reduce costs and wastage in 1953, most failed to achieve significant progress.[75] Having failed in their efforts to promote industrywide standards and quality control procedures, the Silk Weaving Industry Unified Standards Inspection Corps grew so frustrated that they requested

73. WMA D5-2-232.
74. WMA D5-2-232.
75. SMA S39-4-5, S39-4-81, C1-2-1192, C1-1-1637.

stronger leadership from the state company. From late 1953, Industry Association leaders persistently advocated for state administration as a means of improving factory management, overcoming supply problems, improving quality, and ameliorating financial difficulties and labor discipline problems.[76]

Party authorities repeatedly told factory owners that they must improve their attitude toward labor, examine their shortcomings, and go down to the workshops to "rely on the thought of the working class" to improve production.[77] Many of the industry's problems, however, derived not from capitalists' shortcomings, but from flaws in the "state capitalist" economy. Frequent changes of policy and product mix wasted valuable time and resources.[78] The CSC exported the best filature silk and supplied weaving factories with only the lowest grades, which were unsuited to production of high-quality cloth. Reports by factory owners and union representatives in 1955 continually complain about insufficient and deficient thread supplies and other problems, which no amount of political propaganda could overcome.[79]

Silk capitalists had little incentive to invest time and money in improving management systems since the "General Line" clearly stated that private firms would be merged with the state-run economy, even if this would take "a fairly long period of time." Quality inspection systems and factory regulations, such as penalties for absenteeism, reading or sleeping on the job, or smoking in the factory, depended on workers respecting managerial authority. After the Five Antis Campaign, it was extremely difficult for private employers to enforce quality standards or labor discipline without support from the state company. For their part, most workers, like their employers, were simply looking forward to the day when the state would take over the factory and they could enjoy the much-publicized benefits of socialism.

The leaders of the Shanghai Silk Weaving Industry Association, in cooperation with municipal authorities, began drafting plans for factory mergers and the "socialist transformation" of Shanghai's silk

76. SMA S39-4-1, S39-4-2, S39-4-5, S39-4-27.
77. SMA S39-4-75.
78. SMA S39-4-74, S39-4-76, S39-4-110.
79. SMA S39-4-84, C1-2-1670.

industry as early as January 1954.[80] The plans categorized Shanghai silk weaving factories into three groups according to their readiness for joint state-private operations and suggested that, as in the Wuxi filatures, many small factories would first have to be combined into large enterprises before they could be "transformed."[81] As it turned out, however, the "socialist transformation" of Shanghai's silk factories proceeded with hardly any preparations at all.

The limited expansion of joint state-private silk weaving before the end of 1955 had less to do with factory owners' reluctance or resistance than with the industry's difficulties and the lack of preparation by the state company and the municipal government. Many Shanghai silk factories began to apply for joint state-private status in the months following the promulgation of the "General Line." The Meiya Company submitted an application on January 18, 1954, followed by applications from the Futian Weaving Company in May and the Second United Silk Weaving Factory in June. By the end of 1954, nineteen out of Shanghai's more than two hundred silk factories had applied for joint state-private mergers, but none were approved.[82]

The applications reveal much about factory owners' expectations and vision of the socialist future, including references to the "leading role of the state in the economy," as well as the advantages that modern, well-managed, and well-equipped firms could contribute to socialist silk weaving and the development of the national economy. The Meiya Company's application emphasized that production had steadily improved and that labor relations in Meiya factories were "normal." Over the previous four years, the company had achieved financial solvency and worked hard to "satisfy the people's needs and accumulate capital for the nation."[83] Furthermore, because the state company already owned shares in Meiya, there would be no need for further government investment. The general manager of the Meiya Company, Cai Shengbai, had already fled to Hong Kong, so there was no reason to delay socialization. On the contrary, the members of the board of directors welcomed state

80. SMA A66-1-18-1, A66-1-18-15, B123-2-1195.

81. SMA S39-4-5.

82. SMA S38-4-23.

83. SMA B133-2-10.

management of Meiya's operations throughout China and emphasized the benefits the company could provide China's socialist economy.

Many of the early applications to establish joint state-private silk weaving factories emphasized the difficulties of private ownership in a socialist economy. This referred not only to problems in supplies and finances, but also to conflicts with workers. The owners of the Second United Factory stated that "because workers' consciousness has been raised, they are dissatisfied with production relations in the capitalist factory, which inhibit their enthusiasm and creativity."[84] In other words, both factory owners and their employees were ready for state authorities to take charge instead of repeating criticisms of the "capitalist mentality" or "backward and chaotic" management.

The factory owners who actively pursued joint state-private operations before 1955 were influential and well connected, and many of them were officers of the Industry Association. Given the strong incentives to apply and the poor prospects for thriving as a capitalist firm in socialist China, however, why did fewer than 10 percent of Shanghai silk factories apply for mergers before November 1955? One reason is that despite the obvious political and economic pressures, it was still unclear to many capitalists precisely what the socialist future might hold for them. Larger factory owners might aspire to a high-ranking position in the socialist silk industry, but small factory owners had few hopes for top management positions. Many expressed concerns that they would not be able to "qualify" for joint state-private operations or that they would suffer criticism from party cadres because of problems in their factories.[85]

Once it became clear, however, that all private factories would be socialized regardless of their inefficiencies, finances, or problematic labor relations, factory owners rushed to jump on the socialization bandwagon. Following Chairman Mao's meeting with Shanghai capitalists in October 1955, and directives concerning joint state-private mergers issued the same month, capitalists throughout China flooded municipal governments with applications for joint state-private mergers. Between August and December 1955, eight industries completed the

84. SMA B133-2-10.
85. SMA S39-4-110.

"socialist transformation" nationwide, including silk reeling and weaving.[86] According to the Silk Industry Association's report for the fourth quarter of 1955, factory owners were increasingly anxious to join the "socialist high tide," repeatedly asking why Shanghai's silk weaving industry had not yet been approved for socialization. These capitalists clearly saw how the ground was shifting and did not want to lag behind, but the Shanghai government's response was less than enthusiastic.[87]

By November 20, 1955, 231 private silk weaving factories had applied for mergers and only fourteen had not yet submitted applications. Silk factory owners demanded that they be granted joint state-private status as soon as possible, but none of these applications received approval.[88] A November report from the Silk Industry Association stated that members were "universally enthusiastic" about state-private mergers, especially owners of small factories in financial difficulties who feared they might be left behind or simply allowed to go bankrupt. Many factory owners welcomed the prospect of a state takeover and viewed socialization as the solution to their managerial and financial difficulties. Most factory owners were constantly seeking raw materials or loans, or trying to collect payment for work contracted to the state company, and many hoped that better integration with the state-run economy would resolve these long-standing problems. With joint state-private administration, these would become the concern of Communist administrators, who presumably would be better able to manage workers under a socialist economy. As the application from First United put it, China's capitalists recognized that it would be necessary to take the socialist road "in order to have a bright and happy future."[89]

86. The other seven industries were woolen and cotton textiles, hemp weaving, cigarette rolling, paper making, enamelware, and flour and rice milling. By the end of October, twenty-one Shanghai industries—including cotton and wool textiles, cigarette factories, candy factories, flourmills, shipyards, steel plants, and machine building and electronics factories—had all completed the "transition to socialism." SMA C1–1–170.

87. SMA S39–4–74.

88. SMA S39–4–83.

89. SMA S39–4–110.

By November 1955, it was clear that the future was socialist, but there was still much uncertainty about how this transition would be accomplished. For example, the owner of the Meiwen Factory wondered whether it would be possible for him to sell off the factory's antiquated silk reeling equipment, unused for years, before socialization. A common concern was the employment of capitalists' family members and their livelihoods. For the most part, however, the consensus was that the Silk Industry Association should push for the socialization of all factories sooner rather than later. Even the owner of the Yunlin Silk Factory, Lou Erpin, never very keen on "state capitalism," advocated handling applications in groups to "get it over with." Concerns that they would have to take on the financial burdens of smaller factories if mergers were carried out before socialization also inclined the owners of larger factories to advocate for broad socialization first, with individual mergers to follow later.[90]

The applications of private silk factories that had been accumulating in the offices of the Shanghai Federation of Industry and Commerce over the previous two months were finally consolidated in the form of a whole-industry application for joint state-private operations submitted by the Shanghai Silk Industry Association on December 12, 1955. The one-page application simply stated that the owners of the association's member factories felt "unparalleled joy" at the prospect of socialization and joined together to request that the entire industry be permitted to enter joint state-private operations "so as to further accept socialist transformation" and to "contribute their energies to work for the nation's socialist construction."[91] The Shanghai Textiles Bureau and the Shanghai Committee of the CCP approved the application on December 19, and an industry that had remained largely in private hands since 1949 became "socialist" at one stroke.

A press release the following day announced that more than 370 Shanghai factories engaged in various aspects of silk production had "won approval" for joint state-private status. The press release stated that more than 90 percent of Shanghai's silk production was for the export market and that silk was responsible for earning "a large amount

90. SMA S39-4-110.

91. SMA S38-4-22, C48-2-1153.

of foreign exchange for the nation." The industry was still plagued with problems, including high rates of defective cloth, poor management systems, and high production costs, but the press release stated that through socialization "all of these problems can gradually be resolved."[92]

The "Socialist High Tide" and Its Aftermath

The "socialist high tide" of January 1956 was the most spectacular and visible part of the socialization process, but it produced few immediate changes. The rapidity of the "transformation" surprised everyone, including central party leaders.[93] CCP Chairman Mao Zedong, Premier Zhou Enlai, Vice Premier Chen Yun, and Shanghai Mayor Chen Yi met with Shanghai's leading business owners in October 1955 to mobilize capitalists and cadres for the "socialist transformation." In this context, the leaders of Shanghai's business community enthusiastically expressed their desire to speed up the process "lest the national bourgeoisie lag behind in the progress toward socialism."[94] In December 1955, when Chairman Mao announced the stepped-up goal of realizing the "socialist transformation" of Chinese industry and commerce by the end of 1957, provincial and municipal governments confirmed this target date and began to draw up plans.

The Shanghai Party Committee's initial plan was to convert 80 percent of the city's private enterprises (based on production value) into joint state-private enterprises in 1956, to reach 90 percent by the end of 1957.[95] But with local officials and factory owners primed and ready to demonstrate their compliance with party policy, even the Chairman's optimistic targets were quickly overtaken. On December 21, the

92. SMA S38-4-23.

93. On the surprise (and delight) of top leaders such as Mao Zedong at the "socialist high tide" and the unexpected rapidity of the "socialist transformation," see Gao Huamin, *Gongheguo nianlun 1955*, 222–34.

94. MacFarquhar, *Origins of the Cultural Revolution*, 2: 19–22. See also *Zhongguo zibenzhuyi shehuizhuyi gaizao.*

95. "Overall Planning of Transformation of Private Industry and Commerce throughout Country," NCNA, 1 Jan. 1956, trans. in SCMP 1210, 18 Jan. 1956: 19; SMA C1-1-170.

Beijing Party Committee issued a plan to complete the transition to socialism by the end of 1956. Imitating the rate-busting mentality of factory production competitions, party committees in Wuhan and other cities quickly proposed similar targets. Beijing soon over-fulfilled its target, however, and all private industry and commerce in the capital was incorporated (superficially) into joint state-private enterprises in the first ten days of January. In the spirit of "socialist competition" other cities attempted to match this achievement. Whereas 23 percent of industry in Tianjin was privately owned in 1955, by mid-January 1956 all industrial production had been "socialized." In 1955, just over half of all commerce and trade in Tianjin was in private hands. By the end of January, there was none. Guangzhou's silk industry celebrated its socialization with a performance of dancing lions on January 8.[96]

The same day that Beijing celebrated its transition to socialism with a massive rally, business and government leaders in Shanghai met and decided to complete the process in just five days. Altogether a total of 130,274 enterprises with more than 650,000 employees were "socialized" in six days, and on Friday, January 20, Shanghai officially "entered socialist society."[97] Shanghai celebrated the "transformation" with parades of gongs and drums, and banners announced the establishment of joint enterprises. Delegations of businessmen arrived at the headquarters of the GLU to "report the good news" (*baoxi*) and were received by vice chairman and former silk weaver Zhang Qi. Business leaders and union officials organized an event that evening to "celebrate the whole city's joint state-private merger" and the following day held a mass meeting in People's Square to "celebrate the victorious socialist transformation."[98] By the end of January, private industry and commerce in most Chinese cities was entirely socialized, but what that would entail for former capitalists and their employees remained to be seen.

In January and February of 1956, state agents and leaders of the Shanghai Silk Industry Association organized a Joint Operations Work Committee, with Zhu Zuxian of the CSC as chair and Song Baolin and

96. "Tientsin Achieves Task in Socialist Transformation," NCNA, 18 Jan. 1956, trans. in SCMP 1226, 9 Feb. 1956: 20; *People's Daily*, 8 Jan. 1956.

97. SMA C1-1-170.

98. SMA C1-1-166, C1-1-170.

four other association leaders as vice chairmen.[99] Few substantive changes were immediately apparent, however, either within individual silk factories or in the relationship between factories and the state company. Silk factories continued to collect thread from the CSC and deliver cloth at contracted prices. Loans still had to be repaid, and workers saw few immediate improvements in their working conditions or benefits. To justify the obvious lack of transformation the authorities put forward the slogan "joint operations first, transformation after" (*xian he hou gai*). This meant that the government would first approve factories' applications for joint state-private status and later carry out the practical work of appraising assets, reorganizing production, and making arrangements for personnel.[100]

Many workers employed in capitalist factories were impatient to receive the much-touted benefits of socialization, mainly improved working conditions and benefits. China's Communist leaders, however, expected increased productivity, improved management systems, and effective economic planning. In the weeks following the "socialist high tide," propaganda organs exhorted workers to unite with capitalists more than ever to improve production and presented several silk factories as models of labor-capital cooperation.[101] As with Liberation in 1949 and the Five Antis Campaign in 1952, the "socialist transformation" raised workers' expectations to great heights, only to result in frustration and disappointment. Although some workers enjoyed impressive improvements in working conditions and benefits, many others found that socialization meant stronger efforts to intensify labor and increase production.

Party and union leaders acted quickly to rein in workers' expectations and set them on the "correct" path to socialism. Union cadres were ordered to educate workers in the correct attitude of "masters of the factories" and to overcome the "blindly optimistic" attitude that "everything will be grand" (*wanshi daji*).[102] In February, union officials

99. SMA C48–2–1153; *Shanghai sichou zhi*, 222–23.
100. SMA C1–1–170; Frazier, *Chinese Industrial Workplace*, 133–35.
101. SMA S38–4–19.
102. SMA C1–1–170.

complained that "some employees still do not understand the socialist system and socialist management principles." But many silk workers had genuine practical concerns. One union report stated that "older workers feared they would not be able to keep up, while younger workers feared that discipline would become stricter" and that they would not have the same freedoms they had enjoyed under capitalist management. Party and union leaders promoted "correct" views by quoting statements like "the capitalists have handed over their enterprises, shouldn't the working class possess even more of the spirit of greatness?" According to a report from March, however, these efforts were less than successful, and workers' high expectations and anxieties about the future persisted.[103]

In a speech in June 1956, Vice Premier Chen Yun[104] called for patience and caution, stating, "The approval at one stroke of the switchover to joint state-private ownership and cooperatives does not mean the completion of the transformation; it is only the beginning. There are still many problems we have to solve one by one in this transformation."[105] An article in the journal *Commercial Work* stated: "All that is required at present is to change the signboard of private enterprises into the signboard of joint public-private operation and for specialized companies to take over and lead them."[106] One concern was that overly ambitious attempts to transform the economy would prove disastrous. Even the superficial "transformation" achieved in January disrupted supply and production relationships and credit and sales arrangements. In some cases, management systems were discarded overnight, and the

103. SMA C1-1-166. On the problem of reduced budgets, wages, and welfare benefits for workers employed in joint state-private enterprises, see Frazier, *Chinese Industrial Workplace*, 141–43.

104. Originally a print worker in Shanghai, Chen Yun joined the CCP in 1924. In the 1950s, he was one of the main architects of China's socialist economy. He served as vice premier and vice chairman of the party, and as a member of the Politburo, until he was removed from his positions during the Cultural Revolution. Klein, *Biographic Dictionary*, 149–53.

105. Chen Yun, "On the Socialist Transformation of Private Industry and Commerce," NCNA, 18 Jun. 1956, trans. in *Current Background* 393, 28 Jun. 1956, 14.

106. "The Upsurge of Socialist Transformation," 16.

transition wreaked havoc on enterprise accounts.[107] In Shanghai's silk weaving industry, such problems were generally avoided because little changed but the enterprise name and the top administrator. In many factories, however, even these changes did not materialize, as it was impossible for state companies to appoint new managers for every enterprise, and most owners continued to manage production as best they could.

Some things changed immediately, however, as Shanghai's leaders launched a campaign to increase production in newly socialized factories even before the sound of gongs and drums had faded. As one GLU report put it, "The purpose of the socialist transformation of capitalist industry and commerce and the alteration of the relations of production of the capitalist system of ownership is the further liberation of productive forces."[108] In the first month following the "socialist high tide," there were attempts to reorganize and intensify silk weaving, as the Second United Factory increased the number of spindles operated by each spooling worker in the prep department from 370 to 1,000 and implemented a three-shift system to utilize existing equipment more intensely.[109] Silk weaving factories in Shanghai's Jiangning District launched a "campaign to increase production and practice economy" to reduce the rate of defective cloth and conserve raw materials. By the end of the month, thirty-two Shanghai silk factories had exceeded December quality standards by 4.7 percent, but other statistics show that the overall rate of defective cloth remained at 12.85 percent by the end of January and was as high as 20 or 30 percent for many varieties of cloth.[110] As in the past, production competitions were mainly sloganeering and had little real impact.

Union reports stated that, even after all these years, workers' understanding of the "purpose, significance, and methods of socialist competitions" remained deficient. Echoing statements from the Korean War, party leaders criticized the competitions in early 1956 for over-

107. "Decisions on Socialist Transformation of Private Industry, Commerce, and Handicrafts," NCNA, 10 Feb. 1956, trans. in SCMP 1232, 21 Feb. 1956: 16.

108. SMA C1–1–170.

109. SMA S38–4–19.

110. SMA C1–1–166, S38–4–19, S39–4–83.

emphasizing output at the expense of quality, promoting competition rather than cooperation among workers (which led to resentment toward advanced producers), and relying too heavily on intensification of labor rather than improved techniques. Union leaders also claimed that the "old system of management" hindered production competitions, but they nonetheless urged factory-level cadres and workers to cooperate with management staff to improve production and foster the "unified strength of labor and technique."[111]

Despite party leaders' exhortations to factories to rely on "raising consciousness" or "improving technique" as the means of developing production, intensifying labor by increasing production norms remained one of the most effective ways of increasing productivity. In the months following socialization, state administrators and union cadres in Shanghai's silk weaving industry launched an effort to increase the number of looms each weaver operated from one or two to as many as six at one time. This coincided with the political struggle against "rightist conservatism" in agricultural collectivization and the economic "small leap" of 1956.[112] In a June 1956 experiment, the Meiya Silk Weaving Factory doubled the number of looms worked by seven weavers producing *jiuxian* satin. Productivity and quality remained the same, and production costs were reduced overall. Other factories, however, found that productivity per shift declined. The Jiuchang Silk Factory experienced an overall drop in production of 5 percent, and output of synthetic soft satin fell by more than 20 percent. The Futian Factory adopted the method of three weavers operating five looms to produce complex georgette velvets, such that only thirteen weavers were needed to operate twenty looms. Although quality improved, overall productivity declined.[113]

Silk weavers faced potentially conflicting incentives in this campaign. Although wages increased, incomes did not double for weavers operating two looms at once, and many weavers had to handle three or more looms. Almost from the beginning, there was resistance, and mentions of "poor discipline" appear frequently in reports. In other

111. SMA C1-1-166, C1-1-170, C1-2-1890.
112. *Shanghai sichou zhi*, 236.
113. SMA S38-4-19.

cases, however, weavers did not resist the reforms outright, but sought to manipulate them to their advantage, much like machine workers "making out" in Michael Burawoy's studies of US factory workers in the 1970s.[114] For example, some silk weavers, anticipating the shift to a double-loom system, increased the speed of their looms to set a higher average for the three months preceding the changeover, which resulted in a higher basic wage under the new system. This also meant that weavers operating only one loom sometimes earned higher wages than those operating two looms. Many weavers complained that they had to work harder for little or no benefit. Most weavers at the Meiwen Factory, particularly older workers, preferred to operate just one loom even when offered higher wages to operate more than one loom.

By November the production situation in Shanghai silk weaving factories had deteriorated, and most were unable to achieve output quotas or quality standards. Although the Futian Factory had changed from a two-shift to a three-shift system, and the factory's total work hours had increased by 20 percent, output only increased 6 percent. At the Yuesheng Factory, production did not increase at all and in some instances even declined.[115] Because of these problems, exacerbated by complications in adjusting wages due to the influx of new weavers from other factories, plans to expand the double-loom system were shelved, only to be revived during the production drives of the Great Leap Forward.

Even after the "socialist transformation" of the silk weaving industry, norms and standards continued to vary widely, and there was little progress toward standardization and rationalization of management systems. The means of rewarding advanced producers and workers who made technical improvements also varied widely. The Yongda Factory offered only material rewards, while the Yuesheng Factory offered only "honors" (*rongyu*) such as red flags and public commendation. Most factory administrators found these methods too troublesome, however, and simply ordered workers to "guarantee" the achievement of production quotas and quality standards.[116] As a result, many silk workers

114. Burawoy, *Politics of Production*, chapter 4.
115. SMA S38-4-19.
116. SMA S38-4-19, S38-4-78, C1-2-1890.

resisted state administration and "socialist competitions" as a means of increasing work norms without meaningful incentives. Other recurring problems included "formalism," or simply going through the motions in carrying out competitions, poor understanding of goals and methods among workers and administrators, difficulties in calculating wages and bonuses, and lack of concern for workers' health. In some cases, factory administrators did not even inform the employees that they were participating in a competition.[117]

Presaging developments during the Great Leap Forward, overtime work and constant meetings during the "small leap" of 1956 led to fatigue and health problems among workers, as well as high rates of absenteeism, declining product quality, and injuries. Overtime pay also increased production costs, although some factory administrators attempted to get around this by mobilizing workers for "voluntary" labor as during the Korean War. Union leaders, however, considered such policies "dangerous," as they could undermine workers' enthusiasm for socialism and their faith in the Communist Party. Given the choice between alienating workers and failing to achieve state-mandated production targets, however, state administrators sought to please their superiors by achieving the targets, and they tried to get workers to cooperate by any means necessary.[118]

Workers in private firms had been led to expect more than production campaigns from the "socialist transformation." Most viewed socialization as desirable not because it would enable them to improve production, but because they anticipated bringing working conditions and wage standards up to the level of state-run enterprises. Years of propaganda preceding the "socialist high tide" had created these expectations, but the realities of life in state-run factories often fell short of this ideal. Many workers hoped that socialization would include participatory systems of management that would give meaning to the old saw that workers were "masters of the factory." Although the party had earlier called upon workers to "supervise" capitalist management, it was not considered necessary for them to supervise the representatives of the workers' state. On the contrary, employees in joint state-private

117. SMA C1–2–1855.
118. SMA C1–2–1890.

enterprises were now expected to assist state administrators in every way.[119] Workers' management of newly socialized enterprises took the form of Production Management Committees (*Shengchan guanli weiyuanhui*), the main purpose of which was to organize production competitions and to bring managers and workers together to discuss and resolve key problems in production. The PMCs thus played a supportive role rather than supervising the factory administration, and the scope of their authority was much more limited than that of the LCCCs described in chapter 4.[120]

Most Shanghai silk factories established PMCs between July and September 1956, but these bodies often did not include any worker representatives. A December 1956 report by the Shanghai GLU revealed that most PMCs did not play a significant role in factory administration. Many factories did not even confirm the members of the committee or schedule regular meetings. According to a union report on the Meiwen Silk Factory, the state administrators had little understanding of "democratic management" and considered the PMC merely a forum for "state-private consultation." Meiwen's PMC included only one worker representative until CSC criticism compelled the committee to add three more representatives. Out of a total of nineteen committee members, only four were production workers. Eight were former factory owners and seven were party, state, or union cadres. None of the committee members were elected as called for in the relevant regulations.[121]

Compared with earlier experiments with "democratic management" in Shanghai's silk industry, Meiwen's PMC did little to enhance worker participation in management or to protect workers' interests. Of the four hand-picked worker "representatives," two did not attend a single meeting. Because of the high proportion of former capitalists on the committee, meetings tended to be dominated by their concerns, and by points of conflict between the state and private sides. The PMC at the Jiafeng Silk Weaving Factory had the opposite problem. Only four members of the committee were "private-side" personnel, and

119. *People's Daily*, 9 Sep. 1954.
120. SMA C1-2-1890.
121. SMA C1-2-1976.

promoted workers were appointed to all major managerial positions. The former capitalists found this unacceptable, but the state representative, preferring to "rely on the working class," ignored their protests and recommendations. State and party cadres attributed friction between capitalists and their former employees to workers persisting in the "old attitude of struggle." For example, when a "private-side" manager at the Qianlihe Silk Factory raised the issue of shortfalls in quality and productivity in a meeting, one worker simply said, "We don't know what defective cloth is," and then left before the meeting had concluded. Relations between former capitalists and production workers remained contentious at several other silk weaving factories in the fall of 1956.[122]

One of the most significant changes in the Shanghai silk weaving industry following socialization was the industry's reorganization through a series of factory mergers. It began in September 1956 and took almost a year to complete. The Silk Industry Association had drafted comprehensive plans for factory mergers in consultation with owners in 1955,[123] but these were never implemented. The process ultimately failed to address many anticipated difficulties such as conflicts among owners and workers from different factories, employment arrangements for "private-side personnel," and concerns about taking on other factories' debt.[124] The consolidation of Shanghai's silk industry involved 328 factories, of which 251 were silk weaving factories. Smaller factories were gradually merged with thirty "core" factories, becoming "satellites."[125] Most of these mergers were carried out with little or no preparation, however, and in some cases factory owners were informed of plans just one day in advance. This left no opportunity for negotiations or arrangements for personnel and equipment, and the lack of planning and consideration annoyed both owners and workers.[126]

Factory mergers could potentially benefit workers, and some factories established cafeterias, dormitories, clinics, and cultural centers

122. SMA S38–4–19.

123. SMA A66–1–18–1, A66–1–18–15, B123–2–1195.

124. SMA S39–4–110. See also *Shanghai sichou zhi*, 222. The gazetteer's claim that factory mergers had been "accelerating" since 1950 is questionable considering that there were only three factory mergers between 1950 and 1956.

125. SMA S38–4–71; *Shanghai sichou zhi*, 222–23, 226–27.

126. SMA S38–4–71.

in the process of combining operations. However, in the 1950s only a minority of Shanghai's silk weavers received such benefits. Furthermore, combining several factories' equipment resulted in crowded and unsafe workspaces. Weavers in one factory commented, "Now we work in a snail's shell."[127] Merging factories also created conflicts among workers concerning wages, work assignments, and living arrangements. Incoming workers were treated as "outsiders" or temporary workers. Workers in larger, more successful factories feared that those from smaller factories would not be able to achieve the same production norms or would consume more of the factory's resources. Workers in smaller factories feared that their skills would not be up to par in the larger factories, or resented the implication that "their" factory was inferior. Wage disparities were a major source of conflict. In one case, workers from a small factory earned thirty-five to forty-five yuan per month, while workers in the core factory earned fifty-five to ninety yuan per month. Differences in factories' equipment, management systems, procedures, and cultures also bred conflicts and disrupted production. Because of these conflicts and disruptions, rates of defective cloth generally increased following mergers, reaching as high as 97 percent in one factory.[128]

Over the next decade, socialization and mergers did benefit most employees in the silk weaving industry as work hours and wages became more standardized, more employees gained access to cafeterias, medical clinics, nurseries, and educational opportunities, and most workers received labor insurance.[129] In the winter of 1956, however, the problems described above caused considerable friction among workers and between workers and administrators. The party urged union cadres to combat workers' "factionalism" and lack of collective spirit with propaganda and political education, but it often proved difficult to convince silk workers to sacrifice their "individual short-term interests" or to tolerate perceived injustices while also being asked to work harder.[130]

127. SMA C1-1-166.
128. SMA C1-1-166; S38-4-71.
129. *Shanghai sichou zhi*, 236–53.
130. SMA C1-1-166.

Shanghai's former capitalists also voiced criticisms of the process of socialization and mergers in 1956. Many complained of material hardship including hunger and illness. As capitalists (even dispossessed ones), these men and women were not permitted to join union organizations or receive labor insurance or rice subsidies. Despite promises to the contrary, the lack of employment arrangements for "private-side personnel" and their families was a common problem. One man wrote to the Silk Industry Association that he could not support his wife and seven children on only 102 yuan per month. Although he had requested a job for his wife, this did not materialize, and he was told that he was "not the only one in this situation." He retorted, "Do we have to starve to death before we are considered to be in economic difficulties?"[131]

According to the guidelines for mergers, all "private-side" personnel were supposed to receive appropriate work assignments. But when factories merged, many were without work for months. At the same time, some positions remained unfilled, and some "core" factories reported a shortage of managerial personnel because the "satellite" factories were reluctant to give up their few staff members.[132] Ultimately, employment arrangements were made for 566 former owners and private-side personnel in Shanghai's silk weaving industry. Eleven became managers, engineers, or other staff at the new state-run Shanghai Silk Industry Company.[133] Another 134 became factory directors, vice-directors, department heads, or assistant department heads. The majority were assigned to "ordinary management work," transforming former factory owners into shop-floor supervisors. Some production workers also received promotions to supervisory positions, but in 1957 only about

131. SMA S39-4-77.

132. SMA S38-4-19.

133. The Shanghai Silk Industry Company was created on September 25, 1956, under the East China Textiles Industry Management Bureau. In January 1957, the company was brought under the control of the Ministry of the Textiles Industry's Wool, Hemp, and Silk Textiles Management Bureau. Then, on April 24, the company again came under the Shanghai Textiles Industry Bureau, and on May 7 became the Shanghai Municipal Silk Industry Company. *Shanghai sichou zhi*, 225–26.

10 percent of supervisors in Shanghai silk factories were promoted workers.[134]

One of the most prominent problems following socialization, widely discussed in the press along with models for emulation, was friction between the state and private-side representatives in the new joint enterprises.[135] In July 1956, the Silk Weaving Industry Association reported that state-private relations in Shanghai's silk industry, although still far from ideal, were relatively peaceful and cooperative compared with the city's other industries. The report stated that the most effective state administrators were those who "respected the private-side personnel and were good at utilizing them, encouraging them, praising their accomplishments, and giving them their due." In contrast, cadres in factories with "abnormal" state-private relations did not do enough to support the "private-side" personnel, such that the latter "do not dare to wield their administrative authority and cannot give play to their initiative."[136]

In general, relations between former capitalists and state-appointed administrators exhibited mistrust, resentment, and even hostility. Serious conflicts appeared in several core silk weaving factories, including Dacheng and Huaqiang. Personality conflicts accounted for much of the friction. Former capitalists and party cadres were usually proud men with strong opinions, more used to giving orders than taking them, and resistant to any form of "democracy" that infringed their authority. The wider political climate, especially the attacks on "conservatism" among party cadres in 1956, also made party cadres reluctant to associate too closely with former capitalists for fear of being corrupted by "bourgeois influence."

One of the most common complaints by "private-side" personnel was that, contrary to official policy, they were not involved in or even informed of managerial decisions; as a result, they felt that their skills and knowledge were going to waste. Many were also highly critical of the state representatives. For example, the former owners of the Dayaxiang Factory lobbied the state company to replace the man sent to run

134. *Shanghai sichou zhi*, 222–23; SMA S38–4–17, C16–2–192.
135. NCNA, 12 Jul. 1956.
136. SMA S38–4–19, S38–4–77.

(what used to be) their factory. At a symposium in September 1956, several former capitalists complained that some of the state-side personnel were incompetent or that their skills simply did not match the factories' needs. They expressed hope that the state company would help each factory to resolve its personnel problems without appointing "illiterate cadres," which would only cause more problems.[137]

In some cases, state and private-side personnel adapted and worked out a *modus vivendi*. A January 1957 report by the Silk Industry Association, perhaps overly optimistic, claimed that silk factories were "considered a model among textiles industries in Shanghai," and that state representatives frequently consulted with private-side personnel and showed concern for their economic difficulties. Nonetheless, even as late as March 1957 some "private-side personnel" remained "unwilling to accept the leadership of the state representative," while some cadres' work style was still considered too "raw and hard" (*shengying*).[138] Although the situation may have improved somewhat, one of the main complaints voiced by Chinese capitalists during the "blooming and contending" in the spring of 1957 was that they were not permitted to utilize their skills or play an active role in managing joint state-private industry.[139]

Overall, the agglomeration of Shanghai's scattered silk weaving workshops into larger enterprises coincided with improvements in production, and in comparison with what followed, 1957 was a peak year for silk production. In that year, China's silk industry produced a total of 144.54 million meters of silk cloth, of which 47.21 million meters was produced in Shanghai. Jiangsu and Zhejiang Provinces produced 14.71 and 31.81 million meters respectively.[140] In 1957, China produced a total of 9,913 tons of all varieties of silk thread, including mulberry and tussah. Shanghai filatures produced a total of 857 tons, while Jiangsu and Zhejiang Provinces produced 1,948 and 2,523 tons

137. SMA S38-4-77, S38-4-19.

138. SMA S38-4-77.

139. MacFarquhar, ed., *Hundred Flowers*, 207–8.

140. *Zhongguo sichou tongji*, 76–79. According to the *Jiangsusheng cansang sichou zhi*, 304, in 1957, Jiangsu Province produced a total of 19.99 million meters of silk cloth, overtaking the previous record for annual output. The average rate of defective cloth dropped to just 9 percent.

respectively.[141] Of the total for Jiangsu Province, 1,472 tons was produced in Wuxi.[142]

Even as production improved, the silk industry's problems in raw materials supplies and finances continued or worsened despite the establishment of joint state-private operations, and the complaints recorded in Silk Industry Association symposia in the fall of 1956 express similar concerns about state contracting as had documents from 1951. China continued to export the highest-quality filature silk and sent the lower-grade silk to weaving factories. The CSC supplied the Meiya Number Nine Factory with silk labeled as Shanghai product, but which turned out to be a mixture of Sichuan silk of inferior quality and "grade A" filature silk containing bits of cocoon husk. Because of poor-quality thread, prep workers who could normally operate 120 spindles at a time could only work forty. After socialization, silk weaving factories also had difficulty obtaining parts or repairs in a timely fashion and were sometimes forced to cannibalize existing machinery or to try to make the needed parts themselves.[143]

The inefficiencies created by replacing direct purchasing relationships with bureaucratic allocation, especially for supplies of raw materials, caused financial losses for many joint state-private silk factories, which were forced to borrow funds to pay wages just as they had done under private management. Shanghai silk factories continued to suffer losses due to shortcomings in the state pricing system. One of the main reasons for this was the irrational distribution of profits between industry and commerce. In 1956, the state retail price for satin quilt covers was 19.35 yuan and the wholesale price was 15.75 yuan. But the state purchasing price was only 9.06 yuan. With raw materials costing 6.55 yuan per quilt cover, the factory earned only 2.51 yuan to meet its other expenses, including workers' wages. The Dacheng Silk Weaving Factory lost 2.31 yuan for each quilt cover produced, while the wholesaler

141. *Zhongguo sichou tongji*, 42–45. According to Shanghai Statistics Bureau, *Xin Shanghai gongye tongji ziliao*, 37, in 1957, Shanghai produced 1,039 tons of filature silk and 47.22 million meters of silk cloth.

142. The peak year for Wuxi silk production in the 1950s was 1956, when the city's filatures produced 1,591 tons. Qian, *Wuxishi sichou gongye*, 84.

143. SMA S38–4–19.

made a profit of 6.50 yuan. Former factory owners, now employees of joint state-private enterprises, suggested that purchasing prices be increased to guarantee an average profit of 10 percent.[144]

In the spring of 1957, when the CCP announced a period of "blooming and contending" (*daming dafang*), also known as the Hundred Flowers Campaign, workers and former capitalists voiced criticisms and publicized many shortcomings of the developing socialist system.[145] In February 1957, Chairman Mao spoke to an enlarged session of the Supreme State Conference and described the continuing "contradictions" in China's socialist society. In his now famous speech, titled "On the Correct Handling of Contradictions among the People," Mao called for "mass supervision" of the party by the people, including non-party intellectuals and members of the Democratic Parties.[146] Mao stated that following agricultural collectivization and the socialization of private industry and commerce, "antagonistic" contradictions in Chinese society were reduced to a minimum. The remaining contradictions were primarily "non-antagonistic" contradictions or "contradictions among the people," which could be worked out through dialogue, criticism, and self-criticism rather than violent class struggle.

The combination of "class struggle" with "supervision of the party by the masses" sounded terrible to party leaders, who resisted Mao's campaign as best they could. Although Mao's opponents in the party leadership—mainly Liu Shaoqi and Deng Xiaoping—prevented the text of his speech from being published without revision and delayed its release until June, word of its content circulated among party cadres and intellectuals in the spring of 1957. Taking policy debates straight to the people and inviting "rectification" of the party by non-party intellectuals put the CCP leadership in a very difficult position. They could not openly oppose Chairman Mao's policy of "letting a hundred flowers bloom, a hundred schools of thought contend." Nonetheless,

144. SMA S38-4-19.

145. For a summary of the Hundred Flowers Campaign, see Meisner, *Mao's China and After*, 170–74.

146. For the text of Mao's speech of February 27, 1957, see MacFarquhar, *Secret Speeches of Chairman Mao*, 131–89.

the movement gained ground slowly because party leaders dragged their feet and because earlier "rectification" campaigns had taught China's intellectuals to be cautious.

Despite their initial reluctance, by the spring of 1957 more and more writers, academics, scientists, workers, and former capitalists were criticizing the party's policies and accomplishments.[147] Members of the "national bourgeoisie" mainly complained about their meager compensation and poor living standards, as well as their treatment at the hands of state administrators and the press. Many "private-side" personnel protested the "suppression of democracy" because when they raised suggestions or criticisms in the context of the joint state-private enterprise, party cadres condemned them for being "anti-leadership."[148] When the cadres in question were themselves incompetent, the situation could be especially frustrating.

At a "blooming and contending" symposium on May 28, 1957, some of Shanghai's silk capitalists suggested that it might be possible to recall the state representatives from the joint state-private factories and to leave factory management to the workers and redeemed capitalists. Other criticisms focused on the inefficiencies of economic planning, the irrational price system, and the unequal treatment of different social classes under the law.[149] At a similar symposium in Wuxi, former filature owner Gu Tinghuai suggested that the "state side should learn business operations from the private side, and the private side should learn politics from the state side. The state side should not lead business operations."[150] This amounted to a call for the removal of state representatives from positions of responsibility in the factories and the restoration of management by professionals, i.e., former capitalists.

The Hundred Flowers Campaign elicited a wave of labor unrest more widespread and intense than any since 1949, including strikes,

147. For excerpts from public criticisms of the party's policies and complaints by students, farmers, workers, and businesspeople, see MacFarquhar, *Hundred Flowers*, and Doolin, *Politics of Student Opposition*.

148. MacFarquhar, *Hundred Flowers*, 203–8.

149. SMA S38-4-77.

150. WMA D5-5-101.

protests, and even physical attacks on party and union cadres.[151] Workers questioned the party's claims concerning the "socialist transformation" because to them, little seemed to have changed. Workers' demands included restoring the legal right to strike and reviving the defunct Labor Bureaus as a means of mediating conflict between labor and management.[152] One union document urged cadres to explain to workers that because administrative control over the means of production had been "grasped by the representatives of the workers state," capitalist enterprises had progressed from "the situation of the workers supervising production to the state, led by the working class, directly managing production."[153] As far as workers were concerned, however, state management was no better at addressing their needs than private management and was even less responsive than the former capitalists.

Yangzi Delta silk workers do not seem to have engaged in strikes or protests on a large scale in the spring of 1957, but this is difficult to assess given the disappearance of relevant sources from Chinese archives. The phenomenon of workers striking against the Communist Party was, after all, extremely embarrassing for the "vanguard party of the proletariat," and there are few traces of documentation remaining of these events.[154] It is possible that silk workers did not engage in strikes to the same extent as other newly socialized Shanghai workers because many problems were resolved by the spring of 1957. But even if silk workers did not strike extensively, they complained vocally, and some of their complaints are recorded in archival documents.

151. Perry, "Shanghai's Strike Wave of 1957." See also Gipouloux, *"Cent Fleurs" à l'usine*; Frazier, *Chinese Industrial Workplace*, 197–99; Sheehan, *Chinese Workers*, 47–70.

152. Howe, *Wage Patterns and Policy*, 94–95.

153. SMA C1-1-171.

154. As of the 2010s, archival documents relating to the "strike wave" of 1957 are difficult to obtain, and the sources cited in Perry's article on the topic are no longer available to researchers. One of the few documents in the Shanghai Municipal Archives that even hints that such strikes took place concerns workers requesting back pay and travel expenses. According to the document, issued by the State Council on September 23, 1957, the government was unwilling to pay most workers back wages and travel expenses incurred during strikes in the spring of 1957. SMA B45-2-333.

One of the main sources of discontent was the (still) irrational wage system, despite the attempt at a nationwide wage reform in 1956. Inspired by Soviet reforms, the CCP sought to address problems like disparities between state and joint state-private enterprises, the provision of non-wage goods in lieu of wages, and the lack of clear standards and incentives for improvement. The wage reform both standardized wages and increased disparities among occupations and grades, especially for managers and technicians, to encourage skill acquisition and improvements in production. Driven by mass campaigns, the reform effort resulted in a 20 percent increase in overall wages and pitted party and union cadres against management staff who resisted increasing wages.[155] Other unintended effects included shortages of goods and price inflation, increased rural-urban migration, and a proliferation of night clubs and restaurants in cities like Shanghai as urban demand increased. By late 1957, however, wage increases were prohibited, and enterprise discipline intensified as statements supporting wage reform in 1956 suddenly came under attack as "rightist deviations."[156]

In Shanghai's silk weaving industry, factory mergers in the year following the socialist transformation highlighted ongoing disparities in pay scales, bonuses, and benefits.[157] In the spring of 1957, silk workers were more likely to bring these issues up with factory management than they were to walk out on strike.[158] One incident that reveals some silk workers' willingness to engage in strikes, however, is a "disturbance" by the basin workers (*pengong*) at Wuxi's Yongtai Filature in May 1957, at the height of "blooming and contending." On May 14, twenty-one basin workers, led by a young woman named Zhao Huiying, went on strike for half a day, just when the factory was busiest organizing the reeling

155. On the 1956 wage reform in the Wuxi silk industry, see Qian, *Wuxishi sichou gongye*, 229–30. Despite leaders' intentions, this wage reform resulted in an average increase of 89.62 percent for 12,726 silk workers, most of whom worked in newly formed joint state-private enterprises.

156. Howe, *Wage Patterns and Policy*, 89–95.

157. A document by the Labor and Wage Department of the Shanghai Silk Industry Company dated January 1958 indicates that even then, there remained considerable variation in wage systems in Shanghai's joint state-private silk industry, including day rates, hourly rates, and piece rates. B133-2-255.

158. SMA S38-4-77.

of spring cocoons. The basin workers demanded that the wage department promote them to positions as silk reelers. Through "persuasion and education," as well as promises to address their grievances, management convinced the basin workers to return to work by the end of the day.

The basin workers had raised the same demands the previous year and had been told that the problem would be resolved after "further research." When the basin workers again requested promotions, they were again told that it required "further research," which inspired them to strike. Because of this incident, factory leadership criticized cadres in the wage department for their "bureaucratism." According to the leading cadres at Yongtai, what the head of the wage department should have done was "correctly educate the workers as to how to handle the relationship between the individual and the collective to raise the workers' consciousness."

At the same time, Yongtai's leaders also criticized the striking workers for their "serious individualism" and "lack of socialist consciousness," as well as for not considering things from the viewpoint of the enterprise. In other words, although their demands were reasonable, they were not behaving according to the collectivist and patriotic ethos the Communist Party promoted for workers. While the half-day strike drew upon filature workers' traditions of spontaneous action going back to the 1920s or earlier, it was considered an "erroneous" act, inappropriate in the new context of factory management by the "workers state." Party leaders criticized the basin workers for engaging in "big democracy" (*daminzhu*) to cause trouble, with adverse effects on production. In a bizarre application of class categories, the factory's leaders characterized the workers' action as a manifestation of "petit bourgeois thinking."[159] It is ironic that just eight years after "Liberation," the party considered workers who went on strike to demand fair treatment and a living wage "bourgeois."

The "blooming and contending" lasted only a few months before the flood of criticism became intolerable and the CCP leadership reversed course. In June 1957, Vice Premier Deng Xiaoping launched an Anti-Rightist Campaign (*Fanyou yundong*) to suppress dissent and restore unity and party hegemony. As national figures like Zhang Naiqi

159. Yongtai Manuscript, 67.

and Li Kangnian came under attack,[160] the party mobilized former capitalists in the Yangzi Delta silk industry to criticize and repudiate opinions that were now considered "rightist." Unsurprisingly, there was much confusion, but they did their best to comply and produced some impressive rhetorical acrobatics in the process.[161]

The party also launched an ideological education campaign among factory workers and took steps to reform the unions, implementing a system of workers representative congresses to redress some grievances.[162] Because the unions led these bodies, however, most workers viewed them with disdain, and in practice they were little more than window dressing for the exclusive authority of state managers. Many of the demands workers voiced during the period of "blooming and contending" represented official policy in 1956, but by the autumn of 1957 these same demands were condemned as "rightist errors."[163] In the Anti-Rightist Campaign, entire social groups, especially former capitalists and their families, were subjected to continuous "education meetings" and were required to write self-criticisms and guarantees of their future political behavior, activities that continued into the spring of 1958 and merged with the disastrous experiment known as the Great Leap Forward.[164]

The Great Leap Forward and After

By the end of the First Five-Year Plan in 1957, workers employed in state-run industry enjoyed more benefits than in the past, but they were also subject to intense pressure to increase productivity. By the end of

160. MacFarquhar, *Hundred Flowers*, 197–99, 203–4.

161. For detailed accounts taken from archival documents see Cliver, "Surviving Socialism."

162. MacFarquhar, *Hundred Flowers*, 242–47; Sheehan, *Chinese Workers*, 72–75.

163. Howe, *Wage Patterns and Policy*, 95n3, gives two examples of statements that had been official policy in 1956 but were condemned in late 1957: "The enthusiasm of the workers for production depends on cash stimulation" and "some people think that engineers should be paid more than workers" (*Laodongbao*, 20 Jul. 1957, and *Zhongguo qingnian*, 1 Oct. 1958).

164. WMA D5-2-248, D5-2-250.

the Second Five-Year Plan, known as the Great Leap Forward (1958–61), many silk workers had become "second-class" workers employed as part-time, seasonal, or rural-contract workers. The collapse of sericulture resulting from the "Leap" created yet another crisis in China's Yangzi Delta silk industry that resulted in widespread layoffs and dramatic changes in the gendered division of labor.

By 1957, the CCP had achieved organizational and political dominance over China's economy, society, and government. Factories, farms, and commercial and handicrafts enterprises were brought under state administration. Labor unions and factory administrations toed the party line, knowing that any deviation would be criticized and punished. Whether sincere or coerced, support for the party and its policies was universal and opposition nearly impossible. Firmly in control after nearly a decade in power, Mao Zedong and the CCP attempted to mobilize the Chinese people to address the new problems created by agricultural collectivization and the socialization of private industry.

The process of formulating the Second Five-Year Plan was complex and entailed considerable debate within the party leadership during the two years preceding its launch.[165] At that time, China's economic planning system remained incomplete, and the resulting plans included contradictory goals such as increasing agricultural production without investing in agriculture and maintaining very high levels of investment in industry and construction. Mao threw his prodigious weight behind the plan in 1958, and is closely identified with its policies, especially agricultural collectivization and the "People's Communes" (*renmin gongshe*). Communalization of the rural economy, combined with the state's enhanced capacity to extract resources from agriculture, resulted in hardship and famine for millions of rural Chinese.[166] At the same time, China's political leaders continued to pour investment into construction and heavy industry, which

165. For records of these discussions at the Eighth National Congress of the CCP in 1956, see *Eighth National Congress*.

166. On the "Leap" famine, see Yang Jisheng, *Tombstone*, and Thaxton, *Catastrophe*.

resulted in financial collapse and unemployment for millions of industrial workers.[167]

Despite its initiatives to develop sericulture and silk production, the Great Leap Forward was a catastrophe for the silk industry. The stated goal was to "catch up with Japan and overtake France" in quality standards and productivity in three years.[168] In December 1958, the Ministry of Agriculture set a goal of "doubling or tripling" cocoon production in 1959; this was typical of the exaggerated "satellite" production goals of the "Leap" mentality. The silk industry recorded some impressive achievements in 1958. By carefully selecting the best cocoons, workers at Wuxi's Yongtai and Number Two filatures produced 5A and 6A grade thread, overtaking Japanese quality standards in April 1958. One silk reeler at the Number Three Filature produced thread without a single break, setting a new world record for continuously unbroken thread. By the end of November, three Wuxi filatures had produced thread of grade 8A, achieving the peak of world silk production.[169] As in the production campaigns of the Korean War, however, these achievements were not sustained.

The production of higher grades of silk was accomplished only through tremendous effort as well as political pressure to overcome the objections of silk reelers and technical staff. When the party committee at the Yongtai Filature first proposed the target of producing 5A grade silk in March 1958, many technicians said it could not be done while running the machines at high speeds and using poor-quality cocoons. Some silk reelers asked, "To expect a horse to excel without eating grass, how is this possible?" (*You yao maer hao, you yao maer bu chi cao, zenme neng zuodao ne?*). Several initial attempts to achieve 5A quality standards convinced the filature's technicians that the goal was impossible under the circumstances.

The party committee would not accept failure, however, and organized a meeting of leading cadres, technical staff, and production workers to criticize the technicians' "conservative" way of thinking. It took

167. Hollister, "Capital Formation in Communist China," 39–55.

168. SMA B48-2-94.

169. *Jiangsusheng cansang sichou zhi*, 253; Qian, *Wuxishi sichou gongye*, 23, 46, 341–43.

twenty-one attempts of carefully selecting the best cocoons and constantly modifying equipment to produce a small amount of 5A grade silk. At the national silk conference in Shanghai, however, Yongtai's party cadres claimed that this great victory was the result of "relying on the workers" and Communist Party leadership to overcome the technicians' "negative superstition" and conservatism. Over the following months, the factory's leaders raised the goals to 6A and 7A grade silk, standards that were achieved at high costs. If these results can be believed (and in the politicized climate of the "Leap," statistical reporting was subordinated to cadres' need to demonstrate enthusiasm and success), in November 1958, following similar accomplishments at the Wuxi Number One Filature, Yongtai's workers produced 8A grade silk for the first time. By the end of December, Yongtai had produced a total of twenty-five *liang* of 7A grade silk and seven *liang* of 8A grade silk. The filature also achieved its production goals for the year seventy days early.[170]

Unrealistic output targets and the domination of factory management by political cadres adversely affected quality and resulted in tremendous waste of labor, materials, and finances. Factory employees not only worked longer hours, but also had to contribute "voluntary" labor after hours, as if the country were at war. In their off hours, silk workers excavated air-raid shelters, produced bricks, and smelted steel in "backyard furnaces." Filatures ran machines at excessive speeds and did not maintain their equipment properly. By 1959 as many as 40 percent of the machines in some filatures had broken down.[171]

After two years, filature workers' enthusiasm was wearing thin, but the Wuxi Textiles Bureau only offered the slogan, "One year's bitter war to get through five passes, struggle hard to triple output." Calculating the time and effort they were putting into the production drive, some workers at the Yongtai Filature demanded overtime pay and pointed out, "In the past, working twelve hours was exploitation. Now what do we call working twelve hours?" However, political pressure (and the promise of advancement as a party activist) inclined other Yongtai

170. A *liang* is about fifty grams. Qian, *Wuxishi sichou gongye*, 342–43; Yongtai Manuscript, 82–86.

171. *Jiangsusheng cansang sichou zhi*, 304–5; Qian, *Wuxishi sichou gongye*, 38–40; Interview with Qian Binhua, 12 Feb. 2004.

workers to refuse overtime pay and to "volunteer" two hours a day to produce ever-higher grades of silk. The filature's party committee enthusiastically accepted workers' voluntary labor but ignored their demands for overtime pay.[172] In the climate of idealism and opposing "conservatism," workers could do little to resist constantly escalating production targets. The production drive resulted not only in a more intensive and politicized factory regime, but also in illness, injury, and even loss of life. In one example, a kerosene storage tank at Wuxi's Number Three Filature exploded on April 25, 1958, killing a woman worker named Fang Yuezhen.[173]

Similar trends appeared in Shanghai's silk weaving industry, with a few activists leading the way in intensifying work and the majority having no option but to comply. The attempt in 1956–57 to increase the number of looms each weaver operated foundered and the effort was shelved until March 1958, when the Shanghai Silk Industry Company ordered factories to increase the number of shifts and the number of looms (or spindles) for which each worker was responsible.[174] The state company guaranteed that weavers would not lose wages because of these changes, but increased wages were not commensurate with the additional effort required. The unit rate for workers on piece-rate wages was increased 15–20 percent, but workers had to achieve daily output standards as much as 50 percent higher than before, and most weavers were not paid overtime. Most of the labor models honored in Shanghai's silk weaving industry in 1959 and 1960 were recognized for their willingness to take the lead in operating up to three looms simultaneously, demonstrating their determination to "catch up with Japan and overtake France" in production of silk cloth.[175]

This goal proved elusive, however, as the "Leap" became a disaster. By 1959, the work of raising silkworms was collectivized under agricultural communes. Sericulture was particularly unsuited to collectivization, however, as raising silkworms and high-quality cocoons required painstaking effort. If sericulturalists could not earn a reasonable return,

172. Yongtai Manuscript, 93–94.
173. Qian, *Wuxishi sichou gongye*, 343.
174. SMA B134–6–102.
175. SMA B134–6–102, C1–2–2974, C1–2–2888, C1–2–2889, C1–2–2892.

they had little incentive to attend carefully to their silkworms.[176] As the situation in the countryside devolved into one of the worst famines in human history, sericulturalists stopped raising silkworms and converted mulberry fields to grain and vegetables. In 1960, total cocoon purchases in Jiangsu Province reached 191,400 tons, but by 1962 supplies had dwindled to just 92,700 tons, a decline of 52 percent in two years. By 1963, mulberry acreage had contracted by fifty thousand *mu* as compared with 1957, and production of fresh cocoons did not even reach five thousand tons.[177]

Shanghai's rural hinterland achieved only 35.9 percent of the production plan for cocoons for 1961. In desperation, the Shanghai Municipal People's Committee pleaded for all responsible parties in the region to address the problem. Although there is no mention of declining agricultural production or starvation, the document states that sericulture must "recover" to support Shanghai's silk industry, and that the difficulty lay in the distribution of income. For example, in a commune in Jinshan County, sericulturalists earned just two yuan per day, less than those raising cotton or vegetables, despite the intense day-and-night labor of raising silkworms. A report by the Shanghai Silk Industry Company stated that more than half of mulberry acreage had been converted to growing other crops and that agricultural communes were selling mulberry leaves and twigs to pharmaceuticals companies because they could earn twelve yuan (New Renminbi) per *dan* of mulberry, more than they could earn from raising silkworms.[178] As in the "Leap" economy as a whole, state-mandated prices did not support the stated goals of the production drive, and political exhortation proved inferior to economic incentives.

The collapse of sericulture naturally had a deleterious effect on silk production and exports. By the end of 1958, filatures were already cutting back work hours and shifts, and some filatures closed for lack of supplies.[179] From 1959 to 1963, Wuxi filatures could only operate for half the year. Total production of filature silk in 1961 in Wuxi was only

176. Geddes, *Peasant Life in Communist China*, 41–44.
177. *Jiangsusheng cansang sichou zhi*, 258; Qian, *Wuxishi sichou gongye*, 30–31.
178. SMA A72-2-343.
179. *Zhejiangsheng sichou zhi*, 30.

Table 7.2
Silk production statistics, 1949–1966

	Silk Cloth (million meters)				Silk Thread (tons)				
Year	**China**	Shanghai	Zhejiang	Jiangsu	**China**	Shanghai	Zhejiang	Jiangsu	Wuxi
1949	**50.00**	nd	nd	nd	**1,738**	nd	nd	nd	173
1950	**52.00**	nd	nd	nd	**3,382**	nd	nd	nd	783
1951	**63.00**	nd	nd	nd	**4,741**	nd	nd	nd	1,131
1952	**64.76**	17.91	14.03	10.53	**5,587**	528	1,758	1,528	1,232
1953	**74.00**	nd	nd	nd	**6,640**	nd	nd	nd	1,353
1954	**78.00**	nd	nd	nd	**6,716**	nd	nd	nd	1,452
1955	**94.00**	nd	nd	nd	**7,741**	nd	nd	nd	1,451
1956	**119.00**	nd	nd	nd	**9,386**	nd	nd	nd	1,591
1957	**144.54**	47.21	31.81	14.71	**9,913**	857	1,948	2,523	1,472
1958	**203.28**	61.52	52.19	33.25	**11,298**	1,014	3,573	1,962	1,437
1959	**277.83**	68.21	69.21	60.14	**10,219**	866	2,760	1,537	977
1960	**283.25**	71.17	64.72	67.92	**8,349**	807	2,258	1,086	682
1961	**252.60**	65.24	77.96	58.46	**5,249**	585	1,634	759	394
1962	**225.00**	55.51	59.62	50.32	**4,667**	501	1,273	562	329
1963	**245.84**	54.79	65.46	52.80	**4,685**	493	1,480	518	280
1964	**276.64**	58.77	67.63	57.27	**7,050**	784	1,713	829	527
1965	**341.85**	70.26	81.53	65.95	**9,149**	936	2,292	1,056	664
1966	**379.16**	79.28	81.90	66.89	**11,824**	905	3,341	1,334	801

SOURCE: *China Silk Statistics*, 42–45, 76–79; *Wuxishi sichou gongye zhi*, 84.

27.3 percent of the peak figure for 1956 (see table 7.2). In 1962, reduced supplies prompted a new round of mergers and consolidation. The thirteen filatures remaining after socialization in 1955 were consolidated into just five. The number of silk reeling machines was reduced from 3,122 in 1957 to just 1,690 in 1962. By 1964 the number of reeling machines in operation in Wuxi filatures had fallen to 1,558, just 47 percent of the 1956 number.[180]

One result of the crisis in sericulture was mass layoffs of filature workers, who faced unemployment and the prospect of being "sent down" to survive in rural villages. From 1961 to 1963, a total of 5,602 Wuxi filature workers were laid off. Of these, 2,600 were sent to rural villages where conditions were abysmal.[181] The total number of Wuxi filature employees dropped by more than half, from 15,534 in 1957 to 7,212 in 1963. Production of silk thread fell from 1,472 tons in 1957 to just 280 tons in 1963. In that year, provincial and municipal party committees decided to make silk reeling a seasonal industry, displacing the burden of risk onto filature workers just as silk capitalists had done in the 1930s. When the filatures were not in operation, employees received 40 percent of their regular wages.[182]

Chinese silk production recovered slowly from the "Leap." In 1964, Jiangsu Province began compensating sericulturalists for one hundred *jin* of fresh cocoons with one hundred *jin* of fertilizer, three hundred *jin* of grain, three cloth coupons, and four *jin* of kerosene. By this method, the province collected 135,400 tons of cocoons. By 1966, the cocoon harvest had increased to 246,600 tons, but mulberry acreage did not recover as quickly, and from 1966 to 1976, Jiangsu cocoon production was sufficient to meet just two-thirds of filature capacity. Sericulture's slow recovery, combined with the construction of new filatures

180. *Jiangsusheng cansang sichou zhi*, 304; Qian, *Wuxishi sichou gongye*, 40, 343.

181. Audrey Donnithorne reports that between 1959 and 1963, the urban population declined from 130 million to 110 million through the loss of "sent-down" workers. Rural migrants hired during the expansion of industry in 1958 were the first to go. "Sent-down" workers were given severance pay, travel allowances, and "farewell meetings" in their honor. Despite these measures, the policy was widely unpopular and, as rural famine worsened, proved difficult to enforce. Donnithorne, *China's Economic System*, 185–86.

182. Qian, *Wuxishi sichou gongye*, 30–31, 230, 344.

in northern Jiangsu, meant that Wuxi's output of filature silk never again reached the level of 1956.[183]

Silk weaving factories fared better than filatures during the "Leap" because they could utilize synthetic fibers, which China began to produce in 1957. But even as sericulture began to revive in the mid-1960s, the deterioration of Sino-Soviet relations necessitated finding new export markets in the capitalist world. The Cultural Revolution of 1966–76 interrupted silk production with its frequent political campaigns, during which silk suffered the stigma of being a luxurious "bourgeois" cloth.[184] The recovery of silk weaving in the 1960s and 1970s was slow and fitful, but by 1978 China had become the world's leading producer of silk, a position held by Japan since the First World War. By the 1990s, Chinese silk dominated world markets once again, and the boom in silk exports fueled a revival of household handicraft weaving, which produced almost half of China's silk cloth in the mid-nineties.[185]

Employment expanded apace with the restoration of production, but the composition of the workforce changed dramatically. It is unclear how many of the workers laid off during the "Leap" crisis returned to their jobs in the 1960s. Many of them surely did, but with the implementation of the *hukou* household registration system, many "sent-down" workers could only return to their jobs as temporary workers employed through contracts between urban factories and village cadres.[186] In the silk weaving industry, young women gradually replaced veteran male weavers, such that by the end of the 1960s, cloth factories predominantly employed women. By the 1980s, industrial silk weaving was again coded as "women's work," and the only jobs in silk factories that employed men were managerial or technical positions, or as

183. *Jiangsusheng cansang sichou zhi*, 254, 258; Qian, *Wuxishi sichou gongye*, 31.

184. On the Cultural Revolution in a Hangzhou silk factory, see Rofel, *Other Modernities*, 153–77.

185. Glasse, *Textiles and Clothing in China*; Grove, "Rural Manufacture in China's Cotton Industry," 450–58.

186. Donnithorne, *China's Economic System*, 186–87; *Zhongguo fangzhi*, no. 1, 10 Jan. 1965.

machinists and drivers.[187] The economic reforms of the 1990s led to the migration of silk weaving factories away from cities like Shanghai to smaller towns where costs were lower and cheap rural labor was available. The Meiya Number Four Silk Weaving Factory, with its storied history, was the last silk factory to leave Shanghai, moving to the Songjiang suburb in 2005.

Conclusion

Both the Chinese Communists and their critics present the process of the "transition to socialism" as if it played out according to a well-planned strategy to squeeze China's capitalists through control of finances, raw materials, and markets, leaving them no choice but to join the emerging socialist economy. This is a reasonable interpretation on the face of it, but it fails to explain the diversity of experiences and outcomes, the accelerated pace of reform, or the fact that many capitalists were more enthusiastic about joint state-private operations than were government officials. Even factory owners who were consistently hostile to the Communists were willing to go along with socialization because they recognized the advantages of obtaining a good position in the emerging socialist economy rather than clinging to rapidly vanishing markets and enterprise autonomy. In fact, after their experiences in the 1940s and 50s, many Chinese capitalists had grown to mistrust markets and prefer planning and state leadership, as long as it was rational and effective. Furthermore, the difficulties of managing class-conscious workers in the socialist economy were far more apparent to China's capitalists than to the PRC's Communist leaders.

The results of the "socialist transformation" were, more or less, what Mao Zedong and the central party leadership desired, but the pace of change caught them by surprise. This was in part because of the unanticipated enthusiasm for joint state-private mergers among private businesspeople as early as 1954. The fact that the process took as long as it did can be attributed to uncertainty about exactly what

187. Rofel, *Other Modernities*, 53–55, 119–23; F. Xu, *Women Migrant Workers*.

socialization would mean, as well as the limited capacity of local and provincial governments to administer China's thousands of industrial and commercial enterprises.

Unfortunately for those who had been led to expect great things, the "socialist transformation" frequently entailed no immediate or meaningful transformation at all, leading to widespread dissatisfaction and protests among workers and former capitalists in newly socialized enterprises. When the state took over management of formerly private factories, some aspects of factory work changed while others remained the same. In many cases, earlier brutal management practices (including bodily searches or beatings) continued under state management. Problems with supplies, credit, and labor relations also persisted beyond 1956. Despite years of revolution and transformation, by the end of the decade workers continued to work for wages and managers continued to manage them. The party-state attempted to address the problems created in the aftermath of the "socialist high tide," but remedies such as wage reform, mergers and agglomerations, workers representative congresses, and institutions for state management were generally ineffective and were just getting started when the Great Leap Forward derailed these plans, producing more chaos, disaster, and hardship.

In other respects, "socialist transformation" brought radical change to factory life. Although mass mobilization for production campaigns was not widespread in the early 1950s, by the end of the decade this had become a ubiquitous aspect of factory work. Similarly, by the end of the decade labor unions were staffed by loyal Communists and were more oriented toward production and labor discipline than representing the needs and interests of their worker-constituents. The failure of the workers representative congresses is indicative of the low regard in which most workers held the vacillating and powerless unions, and few workers considered these organizations to be "theirs" by the end of the decade.

During the 1950s, the kinds of collective action and political agitation that both silk weavers and filature workers had engaged in before were now prohibited. Opportunities to serve as a political activist or union cadre provided new means by which individual workers could advance themselves. For the most capable and experienced, working hard and becoming a labor model could bring real benefits in the form of income and opportunities. Similarly, demonstrating one's "political consciousness" and becoming an activist or party member was another avenue for advancement. Even if those promoted from the working class in the 1950s represented only a small minority of all industrial managers and technicians, this too presented a means of advancement for working-class people who took advantage of the political changes and the increased access to educational opportunities that the CCP provided.[188]

China's revolutionary transformation created new opportunities for those who were willing and able to toe the party line, demonstrate their activism and enthusiasm, and commit to doing whatever the party-state or factory management demanded of them. The vagaries of Chinese Communist politics provided some opportunities for workers to protest and voice their interests, especially during the "Blooming and Contending" of 1957 and the Cultural Revolution toward the end of the Maoist era.[189] But these were sporadic, exhibited little working-class solidarity, and were generally unsuccessful at achieving lasting change.

For many Chinese workers, the Communist-led revolution and "socialist transformation" brought impressive benefits, such as improved working conditions, health and injury insurance, and education and housing. But these came at the cost of almost complete dependency on one's place of employment—contributing to what Andrew Walder has called China's "Communist Neo-Traditionalism."[190] Permanent employment in socialist enterprises (which excluded a great many workers) bound factory employees into an almost "feudal" relationship with union and party cadres that involved patronage relationships and political support. Under the socialist *danwei* system, workers were rewarded for loyalty and activism and punished for independence and opposition. This system brought fully employed workers unprecedented

188. A report by the Shanghai GLU Women Workers Department stated that because of their activism in the Three Antis and Five Antis Campaigns, more than 1,200 women workers in the textiles industries were promoted to positions as management staff, department heads, and factory directors. SMA C1-2-854.

189. Perry and Li, *Proletarian Power*.

190. Walder, *Communist Neo-Traditionalism*.

job security, and the growth of China's industrial economy (in fits and starts) improved living conditions for Chinese industrial workers in the 1960s and 1970s. Even these benefits came under threat in the 1980s and 1990s, however, as the CCP began the process of restoring and developing China's capitalist economy, once again transforming labor relations, the organization of factory production, and state-society relations in pursuit of national wealth and power.

CONCLUSION

The Chinese Revolution in the Yangzi Delta Silk Factories

The process was complex and convoluted, and the results were surprising, but by the end of the 1950s the Yangzi Delta silk industry was decidedly "red." Communist Party cadres dominated all important positions in government, labor unions, factory administrations, and agriculture and commerce. By the end of the 1950s, having achieved ideological hegemony and organizational dominance, the CCP unfortunately proceeded to run the economy into the ground during the "Great Leap Forward," with disastrous consequences for the Chinese people. Although the death toll and economic losses were huge, the Chinese economy nonetheless recovered quickly, and by the 1970s was on its way to becoming the global powerhouse it is today. Indeed, China's current economic successes would not have been possible without the hard work and sacrifices of the generation that built a New China in the 1950s. Without the manufacturing, educational, infrastructure, and other foundational developments of this earlier era, China would likely still lag behind the more advanced capitalist countries.[1]

Like many aspects of Maoist China, both the short-lived era of New Democracy and the more radical policies implemented from the late 1950s on were experimental. The experiments of the early 1950s were more open to negotiation and provided greater opportunity for pursuit of collective interests, as long as these did not conflict with the

1. Richard Kraus, *Cultural Revolution*, 82–83.

overarching goals of the party-state. The ideological conformity and organizational hegemony that the party had achieved by the end of the decade, however, eliminated these possibilities, instead offering "politics in command," with welfare benefits and job security for some (mainly urban workers) and deprivation and exploitation for many (especially agricultural workers).

Conceptions of class and gender also changed during the 1950s, trending toward the party's vision of self-sacrificing proletarians and equality between men and women. As was the case with economic institutions and political organizations, however, class and gender were not constructed solely by the party leadership nor accepted unquestioningly by the populace. On the contrary, these were sites of intense conflict and contestation, as well as resistance; some elements in Chinese society strenuously opposed new, liberated conceptions of women's social and economic roles, and others sought to define working-class interests beyond economic development and service to the revolutionary state.

Most industrial workers in China enjoyed new benefits under socialism, especially compared with what they could access in the decades preceding the revolution. Throughout the 1960s and 1970s, however, China's socialist proletariat remained divided, with those employed in state-run factories receiving benefits and privileges that were denied to employees in the cooperative sector and to temporary or contracted workers in state enterprises. Later events, such as the Cultural Revolution and the reforms of the 1980s, produced new crises and provided new opportunities for China's workers to contest the terms of their employment and their place in socialist industry.[2] However, the restricted political discourse and the dependency created through the work unit (*danwei*) system of employment and benefits limited what was possible for workers to achieve through activism even under the chaotic conditions of the Cultural Revolution. Although the CCP did not create these divisions among the working class *ex nihilo*, workers remained divided and in conflict with their employers throughout the twentieth century.

2. On conflicts among Shanghai workers during the Cultural Revolution, see Perry and Li, *Proletarian Power*, and Walder, *Chang Ch'un Ch'iao*.

In the early 1950s, during the period of New Democracy, there were significant differences among Chinese workers that derived from the historical development of China's economy and society and conditioned the subsequent evolution of Chinese socialism. In the context of the Yangzi Delta silk industry, the most important distinction was between Shanghai silk weavers and filature workers in Wuxi and other smaller Jiangnan cities. Because of these historical differences, filature workers faced intense resistance from their male supervisors, who successfully opposed many of the Communists' policies in industry in the first years of the revolution.

Shanghai silk weavers had already established relatively strong and independent unions before 1949. The leaders of the Shanghai Silk Workers Union were experienced, competent, and had risen to positions of leadership in the course of the earlier labor movement. The union leadership also included many members of the Communist Party, who had an advantage in dealing with the party hierarchy following the seizure of power. Their location in the great industrial metropolis of Shanghai was also advantageous, as the political leaders in Shanghai were among the best the CCP had to offer, and unions could utilize the city's superior material resources in their efforts to improve workers' lives. Because of their loyalty and reliability, Shanghai silk workers were granted considerable autonomy to pursue their interests within the overall framework of party policy. As a result, in terms of pursuing democratic management, equal wages for men and women, and better working conditions and welfare, Shanghai's unionized silk weavers were among the most active and successful of China's industrial workers in the early 1950s.

By contrast, the Wuxi filature workers' union was newly established in 1949. The industry-level union organization was a product of the city's General Labor Union and was controlled by the GLU, while the factory-level unions were usually controlled by capitalist employers or their agents. Combined with filatures' financial difficulties and the relative neglect of Wuxi filature workers by the revolutionary ruling party, the lack of independent or genuinely representative union organizations inhibited the reform or democratization of management systems. This, in turn, delayed improvements in welfare, working conditions, and safety in Wuxi's silk reeling industry for more than two years following the Communist seizure of power. Furthermore, during the period of New Democracy in the early 1950s, union officials' emphasis on developing production and the policy of "benefiting both labor and capital" negated filature workers' traditional tactics of spontaneous action and informal networks of association. As a result, these women workers had few effective and legitimate means of expressing their needs or pursuing their interests under CCP rule.

Gender was another contested category, both as a locus of revolutionary struggle and as an important aspect of life at work and at home.[3] Although gender was not the only factor conditioning the experiences of different groups of workers, it is clearly a key part of any explanation of the significant differences in labor relations and working conditions in the two branches of the Yangzi Delta silk industry. The leadership of the Shanghai Silk Workers Union was largely male, but this did not prevent the union from advancing women's interests in Shanghai's silk industry, even in the face of opposition to gender equality on the part of male silk weavers. Given the social and cultural prejudices against women, especially young, working-class women, it was much easier for experienced, literate, male silk weavers to negotiate and cooperate with male factory owners in the context of a strong union enjoying the support of political leaders and relatively robust organs for democratic management.

In contrast, in the Wuxi filatures, gender conflict exacerbated class conflict and made the struggle for liberation that much more intense and difficult. Years of abuse, manipulation, and exploitation left a legacy of suspicion and animosity that prevented the implementation of democratic management and other reforms. Management in Wuxi filatures, especially the notoriously brutal shop-floor supervisors, had little respect for the young women who operated the silk reeling machines. Given the degree to which their authority was based on coercion, manipulation, and patriarchal privilege, these supervisors had much to lose from "liberation" and "democratization," and they strenuously resisted efforts at reform. For their part, many women workers

3. For an excellent article that analyzes rural production competitions through a gendered lens, see Eyferth, "Women's Work and the Politics of Homespun," 365–91.

in the filatures mistrusted both private and state managers, and were not confident in the newly established union organizations' ability to represent or support their interests. These circumstances, combined with existing factors such as worker hierarchies, manipulation by supervisors, low rates of literacy, lack of experience in union affairs or Communist Party politics, and separation from the sources of political power, undermined filature workers' ability to protect or advance their collective interests during the 1950s. No matter how much the party leadership in Beijing might have talked about liberating China's women workers, without effective organizations, there were few ways for the party to reach them.

Even if the filature workers' unions had not been co-opted by capitalist management in the early 1950s, the focus of union work was not necessarily the advancement of women workers' interests, and union reports on "woman work" (*funü gongzuo*) from 1952 and 1953 reveal serious ongoing shortcomings. Despite directives from the national leadership, many union organizations neglected to establish women worker departments, and those that existed usually did not enjoy the support of the industry and branch union committees. As late as 1953, union officials continued to criticize "woman work" for being unplanned, failing to grasp "core tasks," and paying insufficient attention to women's most pressing concerns.[4] A 1953 report stated that the Wuxi unions had managed to resolve several issues of importance to women workers, including providing childcare, improving the health of infants and expectant mothers, and reducing the workload of pregnant workers, all of which served to "push forward women workers' enthusiasm for production." However, the report also mentioned many persistent problems, for example poor working conditions and a lack of basic safety for women and children employed in industry. Despite the party's constant promotion of health education and access to labor insurance, by 1953 miscarriages were still very common, educational efforts were not sustained, and women workers continued to suffer from preventable diseases. Even when union documents paid attention to the needs of women workers, they emphasized production more than anything; efforts at liberating women workers or improving their welfare

4. SMA C1-2-854.

had to serve the goal of economic development. Recommendations for improving "woman work" in the unions overwhelmingly focused on increasing production, improving political education, and "following the leadership of the Communist Party."[5]

As the years progressed, the party's leadership became more prominent in all aspects of China's economy and society, even if it did not become more effective. Because the capabilities and reach of the revolutionary state expanded during the early 1950s, the timing of reforms was sometimes just as important to their outcomes as were factors like factory regime or workforce characteristics. The establishment of institutions for "democratic management" in the Shanghai silk weaving industry immediately followed the bombing of Shanghai's main power plant on February 6, 1950. The ensuing crisis encouraged the recognition of common interests among silk weavers and factory owners, which facilitated labor-capital cooperation in a manner that did not disadvantage workers. Furthermore, in 1950 the Communist Party had not yet initiated the "patriotic production campaigns" that developed during the Korean War. Even when these campaigns came to Shanghai's silk weaving industry, they were not very widespread, and their impact was limited. Working mainly in small, scattered, privately owned workshops with no significant CCP presence, most silk weavers remained beyond direct Communist influence for years following the seizure of power. Thus, both silk weavers and their union leaders retained a relatively high degree of autonomy and achieved many of their own goals in the early 1950s.

In contrast, the Democratic Reform Campaign in Jiangnan filatures in the autumn of 1951 was initiated and directed by Communist labor officials at a time when the party was extending its influence through state contracting and political campaigns. Differences in the timing of "democratic reform" in these two contexts strongly affected the capacity of each group of workers to pursue their goals. Furthermore, the party's "patriotic campaigns" conducted during the winter of 1950–51 immediately and directly influenced Wuxi filature workers. Because of the filatures' large size, concentration, close ties to the state, and the favorable attitude of management toward the campaigns, efforts

5. WMA D2-1-10.

to mobilize workers produced more immediate and tangible results despite the filatures' lack of democracy and obvious absence of "liberation" in a brutal factory regime. The fact that the production campaigns were less apparent in Shanghai silk weaving factories is another sign that silk weavers were more in control of their own destinies than were filature workers.

Similarly, in contrast with the Labor-Capital Consultative Conference (LCCC) in the Shanghai silk industry, the Democratic Reform Campaign in the Wuxi filatures in the autumn of 1951 was very much a top-down affair. Municipal labor officials organized and orchestrated the movement in Wuxi as part of a national campaign to eliminate the party's "enemies" in industry and purge disloyal elements from the unions. In this context, Democratic Reform served to increase the party's control over the unions and its ability to implement production campaigns more than to empower women workers to participate in management or to define and pursue their own interests independently.

It is important to take seriously the Communists' stated goals of liberating Chinese workers, and especially women, from past oppression. In the end, it was not a lack of commitment but diverse circumstances and conflicting imperatives that produced divergent outcomes. Beginning in 1952, the Communist Party and the Wuxi General Labor Union adopted some important measures to improve working conditions and protect the livelihoods of women workers in the Wuxi filatures. The improvements achieved in restoring production and employment, providing a living wage, and eliminating some of the worst abuses of management were not inconsequential. The party was far more successful, however, in developing silk production and extending its control over previously independent filature workers and their employers than it was at achieving a meaningful form of "liberation" for these women workers.

Despite the diversity of workers' experiences and opportunities in the early 1950s, the years 1952 through 1956 saw a convergence toward Communist Party hegemony and top-down political mobilization in both silk weaving factories and filatures. The years of the Korean War witnessed the gradual extension of a mobilizational factory regime, including "patriotic agreements," production competitions, and the identification and reward of model workers, that was very different from either capitalist production or the forms of "democratic management" established under New Democracy. National economic planning and political mobilization, the extension of the party's presence into virtually all private factories, and the nationalization of private industry and commerce by 1956 eliminated the last vestiges of both capitalist production and autonomous proletarian politics in the Yangzi Delta silk industry. Whether they themselves believed it or not, China's industrial workers found it necessary to conform to the party's vision of class and gender—self-sacrificing proletarians and gender equality that entailed the identification of many aspects of "feminine" identity with "bourgeois" deviation and decadence. Former members of the "National Bourgeoisie," although they lost the material basis for this class identity through the "socialist transformation," were never allowed to stop being capitalists and were forced to retain their "bourgeois" label throughout the Maoist period.[6]

Party domination of all aspects of politics, society, and the economy produced disaster by the end of the 1950s. Political loyalty in pursuit of unrealistic goals replaced technical expertise and cost accounting. In this context, the pursuit of working-class interests was branded as "petit bourgeois individualism," and any criticism or dissent was ruthlessly crushed. During the "Great Leap Forward," the party whipped the populace into a frenzy of wasted effort, millions died, and the Yangzi Delta silk industry, so recently recovered from war and economic crisis, again descended into a crisis from which it took years to recover.

6. Richard Kraus puts it this way: "That the most vital functions of class designations had been assumed by other measures [such as political labels and the wage-grade scale introduced in 1956] made these designations, and the class concept upon which they were based, a weak but not quite empty shell. As a ranking of one-time relationships to the means of production, the class designations retained considerable historical interest. Socialist transformation had borne in its wake new and more meaningful bases for reckoning inequality, but these were not to collide with the now frozen class designations until Mao endeavored to reformulate the concept of class for a society without large-scale private property." Richard Kraus, *Class Conflict in Chinese Socialism*, 58–61.

Because of the diversity of conditions and the many unintended consequences of China's revolutionary transformations, the socialist system that took shape by the 1960s was not solely the product of Communist Party ideology and policies. It bore the imprint of struggles, conflicts, and compromises within the developing system of the early 1950s. For example, Wuxi filature workers found themselves left out of Liberation because of their male supervisors' successful resistance to change in the early years of the revolution; these women workers never enjoyed the same opportunities as silk weavers in Shanghai. Elizabeth Perry, commenting on the ways in which the goals and interests of labor aristocrats, like the Shanghai silk weavers, influenced the development of China's socialist system, writes:

> The exclusivity and paternalism of the socialist enterprise were reminiscent of the artisan guild. One needed the introduction of friends or relatives to join these selective organizations, which offered lifetime benefits to their privileged members. Like its guild forerunner, the socialist factory also stipulated certain behavioral norms for its membership. But whereas the traditional guild had relied on the authority of its patron deity to enforce these values, the new state enterprise claimed legitimacy from the Communist Party.[7]

The origins of "Communist neo-traditionalism"[8] in China can thus be traced to these long-standing traditions, including patriarchal authority in the workplace and the exclusive organizations of privileged male artisans who comprised the most active working-class members of the Communist Party. Such influences were not simply atavistic holdovers from "traditional" Chinese society, however. As Mark Frazier has shown, many characteristics of factory management and labor relations in China's socialist workplaces, for example the direct provision of basic goods to factory workers, derive from more proximate causes and are recent "traditions" that emerged from the years of war and

7. Perry, "Labor Divided," 163.
8. Walder, *Communist Neo-Traditionalism*.

economic crisis in the decades preceding the 1949 revolution.[9] In short, the influences shaping the development of Chinese socialism in its seminal decade were much deeper, more complex, and far-reaching than merely the plans and visions of Communist Party leaders. China was never a "blank slate," and the developments and changes of the preceding decades inevitably conditioned and constrained the possibilities open to China's Communist revolutionaries in the second half of the twentieth century.

When China abandoned the principles of state-socialist labor relations in the last decades of the twentieth century, moving even farther away from the "traditions" that shaped the socialist system, the diversity within China's working class again produced varying responses and actions among different groups of workers. Faced with unemployment and poverty, workers in the old socialist enterprises (many of whom are men) resorted to strikes and protests, but also to petitions and appeals to a socialist moral economy, including conceptions of working-class interests and labor relations instilled in Chinese workers from the 1950s.[10] As in the early years of the revolution, the traditions of this group of workers influenced their actions in response to new crises.

On the other hand, the fastest growing group of industrial workers at century's end—those employed in private enterprises in the "Sun Belt" of the south and east (many of whom are young women)—faced different challenges. Confronted with an alliance between investment-hungry local governments and exploitative employers struggling to maintain their margins in an increasingly competitive global economy, these workers had to struggle to win the employment conditions and benefits supposedly guaranteed them under the law. The tactics they adopted—spontaneous action, walkouts, informal networks, and demands that during the Maoist period were criticized as "economistic," "petit bourgeois," and incompatible with the goal of socialist industrialization—recall those of the pre-1949 labor movement among the less privileged workers of the Yangzi Delta silk reeling industry. At

9. Frazier, *Chinese Industrial Workplace*, 244–46.
10. Hurst and O'Brien, "China's Contentious Pensioners," 345–60.

the same time, the legal basis for these workers' actions has improved immensely; and in recent years, more and more workers have turned to the legal system to protect and advance their interests. One of the most important changes in the context of capitalist restoration and foreign investment is that, when compared with the 1950s, the Communist Party's continuing calls for workers to sacrifice for the good of the nation and the revolution and to accept the leadership of a party that seems more bourgeois than proletarian in its makeup sound weak and hypocritical, and have little legitimacy among these very materialistic and independently class-conscious workers.[11]

Chinese workers today are more active in pursuing their collective interests than they were sixty years ago, but they are also poorly organized and subject to the repressive power of the party-state and the exploitation of China's new capitalists (often one and the same). One can only speculate where China's labor movement will progress from here. Perhaps the recovery of past tactics and methods of action and organization, combined with new technologies, will benefit China's workers today as they negotiate the transition to capitalism just as their predecessors negotiated the transition to socialism. Whatever new developments appear in the People's Republic of China, workers' actions are sure to include a wide range of tactics and strategies as these men and women adapt to changes in the economy, politics, and society, resist efforts to impose hegemony, and struggle to protect their interests in China's rapidly changing social, political, and economic landscape. Whether employed in state industries or in China's "Sun Belt," from Haier to Honda, Wahaha to Walmart, Chinese workers will continue to organize, speak out, and struggle for the right to define and advance their own interests.

11. Ching Kwan Lee, *Against the Law*; Chan, *China's Workers under Assault*; Leslie Chang, *Factory Girls*; Hurst, *Chinese Worker after Socialism*; Philion, *Workers' Democracy*; and Pun, *Made in China*.

Glossary

This glossary provides Chinese characters and English translations for important Chinese names, words, and phrases used in the text. This does not include factory names (which are far too numerous) or the names of authors, publications, and newspapers cited in the footnotes.

aiguo gongyue 爱国公约 patriotic agreements/compacts
Anhui 安徽 Anhui Province
Bagong ribao 罢工日报 *Strike Daily*
baoben zigei 保本自给 break even / self-sufficiency
baoxi 报喜 report the good news
Beijing 北京 Beijing Municipality
Bo Yibo 薄一波
bu da, bu chengren 不打不成人 If you don't beat them, they won't grow up
buke 补课 remedial study
Cai Chang 蔡畅
Cai Shengbai 蔡声白
caidianzhi 採点制 point picking system
Caizheng jingji jieguan weiyuanhui maoyi chu 财政经济接管委员会贸易处 Trade Department of the Finance and Economics Reconversion Commission
Cansi chanxiao xiedao weiyuanhui 蚕丝产销协导委员会 Silk Production and Marketing Assistance and Leadership Commission
Cansi gailiang hui 蚕丝改良会 Silk Reform Association
Chang Kia-Ngau 张嘉璈
Chen Ciyu 陈慈玉
Chen Jiyuan 陈纪元
Chen Lifu 陈立夫
Chen Yi 陈毅
Chen Yun 陈云
chetou 车头 female supervisors in silk filatures
Chiang Kai-shek 蒋介石
chongchang 充场 factory storming
Chongqing 重庆 Chongqing Municipality
chuliju 处理局 disposition bureaus
chumeitou 触霉头 encounter misfortune / bring bad luck
Cunjian yisi daisao ji fudao minying sichang fuye 存茧易丝代缫及辅导民营丝厂复业 exchanging stores of cocoons for silk reeled on contract,

and leading private filatures to restore production
Daishan 岱山 Daishan Islands
Dali 大利 Dali Silk Filature
daming dafang 大鸣大放 blooming and contending
daminzhu 大民主 big democracy
dan 担 a Chinese unit of weight equal to 50 kg
danwei 单位 work unit
Deng Xiaoping 邓小平
dengjing dengwei 等经等纬 waiting for warp and weft
dingxi 定息 fixed dividends
Dongxi 东溪 Dongxi, Jiangsu
dou 斗 a Chinese unit of volume equal to 10.35 L
fabi yuan 法币元 Nationalist currency
fanyou yundong 反右运动 Anti-Rightist Campaign
fangliao dingzhi banfa 方料定织办法 loom leasing system
feichu fengjian guanli zhidu 废除封建管理制度 abolishing the feudal management system
funü gongzuo 妇女工作 woman work (in union organizations)
Fuyihui 福益会 Workers' Welfare Society
gaizao 改造 transformation
ganbu 干部 cadre
Gelaohui 哥老会 Brotherhood Society
gexing 个性 personal character
gongchang de zhurenweng 工厂的主人翁 masters of the factory
gongshen dahui 公审大会 public trial meetings
gongsi heying qiye 公司合营企业 joint state-private enterprises
gongtou 工头 labor-gang boss
guanche 管车 male supervisors in silk filatures
Guangdong 广东 Guangdong Province
Guangzhou 广州 Guangzhou Municipality
gudao 孤岛 lonely island (wartime Shanghai)
Guojia jieshou weiyuanhui 国家接收委员会 National Reconversion Commission
Guomindang 国民党 Nationalist Party
Guomindang dui hanjian kuanda, Gongchandang dui tewu kuanda 国民党对汉奸宽大，共产党对特务宽大 The GMD was lenient with traitors, the CCP is lenient with enemy agents
Guomindang fandongpai 国民党反动派 Nationalist Party reactionary clique
guxiangduan 古香缎 *guxiang* satin
hang 行 brokerage
Hangzhou 杭州 Hangzhou, Zhejiang
Hankou 汉口 Hankou Hubei
helihua jianyi 合理化建议 rationalization suggestions
Hongkou 虹口 Hongkou District, Shanghai
Huachang sichang 华昌丝厂 Huachang Filature
Huazhong cansi gongsi 华中蚕丝公司 Central China Sericulture Company
huchangdui 护厂队 factory protection team
hukou 户口 household registration (system)
huochezhan 火车站 railway station

Huzhou 湖州 Huzhou, Zhejiang
jiagong daisao 加工代缫 processing and contract reeling
jiagong dinghuo 加工订货 contract processing and production (for the state company)
Jiang Weicheng 江蔚成
Jiangnan 江南 Lower Yangzi Valley
Jiangning 江宁 Jiangning District, Jiangsu
Jiangsu 江苏 Jiangsu Province
Jiangxi 江西 Jiangxi Province
jiaoqing lishi 交清历史 clarify (one's) history
jiating xiao sichang 家庭小丝厂 household microfilatures
Jiaxing 嘉兴 Jiaxing, Zhejiang
Jiefang 解放 Liberation
jieguan 接管 take over/reconvert
Jieguan weiyuanhui 接管委员会 Reconversion Commission
jieshou 接收 receive
jin 斤 a Chinese unit of mass equal to 500 g
jingbuqi kaoyan 经不起考验 cannot pass the test
Jinling 金陵 Jingling District, Nanjing, Jiangsu
Jinshanxian 金山县 Jinshan County, Shanghai
jiu zhidu 旧制度 old system
jiuxiaduan 九霞缎 nine clouds satin
juanfangchang 绢纺厂 silk spinning factory
Kang Mei yuan Chao yundong 抗美援朝运动 Campaign to Resist America and Aid Korea
kangRi houyuantuan 抗日后援团 anti-Japanese rear assistance groups
kongsu dahui 控诉大会 accusation meeting
laoban xianzai yao fa juanxian cai 老板现在要发捐献财 now the boss is getting rich on 'donations'
laodong jiufen 劳动纠纷 labor dispute
laodong mofan 劳动模范 labor model
laozi gongcun 劳资共存 mutual survival of labor and capital
laozi liangli 劳资两利 benefit both labor and capital
laozi xieshang huiyi 劳资协商会议 labor-capital consultative conference (LCCC)
laozi xietiao cujin hui 劳资协调促进会 conference for the promotion of labor-capital compromise
Leizu 嫘祖
Li Kangnian 李康年
Li Lisan 李立三
Li Weihan 李维汉
liang 两 a Chinese unit of mass equal to 50 g
lisaoche 立缫车 "standing" reeling machine
Liu Shaoqi 刘少奇
liuxiang 留香 charmeuse
Lu Jingshi 陆京士
Mao Sen 毛森
Mao Zedong 毛泽东
Meiya 美亚 Meiya/Mayar Silk Company
Ming 明 Ming dynasty
minzhu gaige 民主改革 democratic reform
minzhu guanli 民主管理 democratic management
minzhu pingyi weiyuanhui (minping) 民主评议委员会（民评）democratic appraisal committee
minzu zibenjia 民族资本家 national capitalists

minzu zichanjieji 民族资产阶级 national bourgeoisie
mofangong 模范工 model workers
moyanggong 磨洋工 loafing and dawdling
mu 亩 a Chinese unit of land area equal to two-thirds of a square kilometer
Nanhai 南海 Nanhai District, Foshan, Guangdong
Nanjing 南京 Nanjing, Jiangsu
nügongbu 女工部 women workers' departments (of unions)
peijian tingche 配茧停车 distribute cocoons and shut down machines
pengong 盆工 basin workers
poxie 破鞋 broken shoes
Qin 秦 Qin dynasty
Qing 清 Qing dynasty
Qingdao 青岛 Qingdao, Shandong
qingxi 清洗 purge
quan diqu zhi gongchao 全地区之工潮 regional labor tide
Renmin baoandui 人民保安队 People's Peace Preservation Corps
renmin dazhong 人民大众 popular masses
renmin gongshe 人民公社 people's communes
Renminbi 人民币 People's Money (RMB)
rongyu 荣誉 honors
Sanfan yundong 三反运动 Three Antis Campaign
Sansheng shoujian daikuan lianhe guanli chu 三省收茧贷款联合管理处 Three Province Cocoon-Purchasing Loans Unified Management Office
Shanghai 上海 Shanghai Municipality
Shanghai gongren fuli weiyuanhui 上海工人福利委员会 Shanghai Workers Welfare Committee
Shaoxing 绍兴 Shaoxing, Zhejiang
Shen Gendi 申跟第
shenyi weiyuanhui 审议委员会 deliberation committees
Shenzhen 深圳 Shenzhen, Guangdong
sheng 升 a Chinese unit of volume equal to one liter
Sheng Peisheng 盛佩绑
shengchan guanli weiyuanhui 生产管理委员会 production management committees (PMCs)
shengli 胜利 victory
shengying 生硬 raw and hard
shiyanchang 试验厂 experimental factory
shumai 赎买 buying out
Shunzhi 顺治 Shunzhi Emperor (r. 1644–61)
shuoli douzheng dahui 说理斗争大会 mass struggle meeting
shusan 疏散 disperse
Sichuan 四川 Sichuan Province
Song 宋 Song dynasty
Song Baolin 宋保林
Song Ziwen 宋子文
Songjiang 松江 Songjiang District, Shanghai
Subei 苏北 Northern Jiangsu Province
Sun Chuanfang 孙传芳
suoshou suojiao 缩手缩脚 become overly cautious
Suzhou 苏州 Suzhou, Jiangsu
Taiping 太平 Taiping Rebellion (1850–64)
Taiwan 台湾 Taiwan Island
tewu 特务 enemy agent

Tianjin 天津 Tianjin Municipality
Tong Xinbai 童莘佰
tongyangxi 童养媳 child daughters-in-law
tongye gonghui 同业公会 industry associations
touji 投机 speculation
tu 土 rustic/native
tugai 土改 land reform
Wahaha 娃哈哈 Wahaha Corp.
wanshi daji 万事大吉 everything will be grand
Wang Hao 王浩
Wang Jingwei 汪精卫
Wu Kaixian 吴开先
Wufan yundong 五反运动 Five Antis Campaign
Wuhan 武汉 Wuhan, Hubei
Wujiang 吴江 Wujiang District, Suzhou
Wujin 武进 Wujin District, Changzhou
Wuxi 无锡 Wuxi, Jiangsu
xian he hou gai 先合后改 joint operations first, transformation after
Xin minzhuzhuyi 新民主主义 New Democracy
xingzheng gongshu 行政公署 administrative office
Xinhua 新华 New China News Agency
Xinzha 新闸 Xinzha District, Shanghai
xuanchuan jiaoyu 宣传教育 propaganda and education
Xue Shouxuan 薛壽萱
Xue Zukang 薛祖康
Yan'an 延安 Yan'an, Shaanxi
Yancheng 盐城 Yancheng, Jiangsu
Ye Jianying 叶剑英
yichou yisi 以绸易丝 exchange silk cloth for thread
Yiguandao 一贯道 a religious movement in twentieth-century China
yisi yijian 以丝易茧 exchange silk for cocoons
Yongtai 永泰 Yongtai Silk Filature, Wuxi
You yao maer hao, you yao maer bu chi cao, zenme neng zuodao ne? 又要马儿好，又要马儿不吃草，怎么能做到呢？ To expect a horse to excel without eating grass, how is this possible?
yuan 元 Chinese currency
Yuan 元 Yuan dynasty
yuqing jiaxin 舆情加薪 plead for higher wages
Yunlin 云林 Yunlin Silk Factory, Shanghai
zagong 杂工 general laborer
zengjia shengchan, laoban facai 增加生产，老板发财 we increase production and the boss gets rich
Zhabei 闸北 Zhabei District, Shanghai
zhangfang 账房 accounting house/broker
Zhang Naiqi 章乃器
Zhang Qi 张祺
Zhejiang 浙江 Zhejiang Province
Zhenya fan geming yundong 镇压反革命运动 Campaign to Suppress Counter-Revolutionaries
zheshi danwei 折实单位 parity units
zhijin 织锦 brocade silk
Zhongguo cansi gongsi 中国蚕丝公司 China Sericulture Company (CSC)
Zhongguo renmin kang Mei yuan Chao weiyuanhui 中国人民抗美援朝委员会 Chinese People's

Committee to Resist America and Aid Korea
Zhongguo sichou gongsi 中国丝绸公司 China Silk Company (CSC)
Zhongguo zhongyang xintuoju 中国中央信托局 Central Trust of China
Zhonghua cansi gongsi 中华蚕丝公司 Central China Sericulture Company (CCSC)
Zhou 周 Zhou dynasty
Zhou Enlai 周恩来
Zhoushan 舟山 Zhoushan Islands
Zhu Xuefan 朱学范
Zhu Zuxian 朱祖贤
zuo sixiang zhunbei 做思想准备 make thought preparation/prepare oneself mentally
zuoqing maoxianzhuyi 左倾冒险主义 leftist adventurism
zuosaoche 坐缫车 "sitting" reeling machine

Bibliography

Archives

Meiya Factory Archives.

Meiya Manuscript. "Shanghai Meiya zhichouchang gongren yundong shi (taolungao)" (A history of the workers' movement at Shanghai's Meiya Silk Weaving Factory [review draft]). Edited by Shanghai disi dijiu zhichou chang gongren yundong lishi bianji weiyuanhui. Shanghai: Meiya Company Offices, 1993. Meiya Factory Archives.

Shanghai Municipal Archives (SMA)

Wuxi Municipal Archives (WMA)

Yongtai Manuscript. "Yongtai sichang fazhan shi, 1896–1958 (chugao)" (A history of the development of the Yongtai filature, 1896–1958 [preliminary draft]), 1959. Edited by the Yongtai Filature Factory History Editorial Group. Wuxi Municipal Archives.

Zhejiang Provincial Archives (ZPA)

Newspapers and Magazines Cited or Referenced in Text

China Monthly Review

Current Background

Dagongbao

Dalu

Dazhong

Dongnan ribao

Heping

Jiefang ribao

Jinrong

Laodongbao (translated as *Labor Daily* in text)

New York Times

North China Daily News (NCDN)

People's China

Renmin ribao (translated as *People's Daily* in text)
Shangbao
Shenbao
Shishi
Sunan ribao
Tianjin minguo
Wenhuibao
Xinhua (translated as New China News Agency [NCNA] in text)
Xinwenbao
Zhengyan
Zhongguo fangzhi
Zhongguo qingnian
Zhongyang

Other Sources

Andors, Phyllis. *The Unfinished Liberation of Chinese Women, 1949–1980.* Bloomington: Indiana University Press, 1983.

Andreev-Khomiakov, Gennady. *Bitter Waters: Life and Work in Stalin's Russia.* Translated by Ann E. Healy. Boulder, CO: Westview Press, 1997.

Arthur, W. Brian. "Competing Technologies, Increasing Returns and Lock-in by Historical Events." *Economic Journal* 99 (1989): 106–31.

Avrich, Paul. "The Bolshevik Revolution and Workers' Control in Russian Industry." *Slavic Review* 22, no. 1 (1963): 47–63.

Ba Tu. *Guomindang jieshou Riwei caichan* (The Nationalist takeover of Japanese and puppet properties). Beijing: Qunzhong chubanshe, 2001.

Ba kang Mei yuan Chao yundong tuijin dao xin de jieduan (Take the Campaign to Resist America and Aid Korea to a new stage). Edited by Zhongguo renmin baowei shijie heping fandui Meiguo qinlue weiyuanhui. Beijing: Renmin chubanshe, 1951.

Barber, Noël. *The Fall of Shanghai.* First American ed. New York: Coward, McCann & Geoghegan, 1979.

Barnett, A. Doak. *China on the Eve of the Communist Takeover.* New York: Praeger, 1963.

———. *Communist China: The Early Years, 1949–1955.* New York: Praeger, 1964.

Barnett, Robert W. *Economic Shanghai: Hostage to Politics, 1937–1941.* New York: International Secretariat, Institute of Pacific Relations, 1941.

Bell, Lynda S. *One Industry, Two Chinas: Silk Filatures and Peasant-Family Production in Wuxi County, 1865–1937*. Stanford, CA: Stanford University Press, 1999.

Bennett, Gordon A. *Yundong: Mass Campaigns in Chinese Communist Leadership*. Berkeley: University of California Press, 1976.

Bergère, Marie-Claire. *Shanghai: China's Gateway to Modernity*. Translated by Janet Lloyd. Stanford, CA: Stanford University Press, 2009.

Bian, Morris L. *The Making of the State Enterprise System in Modern China: The Dynamics of Institutional Change*. Cambridge, MA: Harvard University Press, 2005.

———. "The Sino-Japanese War and the Formation of the State Enterprise System in China: A Case Study of the Dadukou Iron and Steel Works, 1938–1945." *Enterprise and Society*, no. 3 (Mar. 2002): 80–123.

Bloodworth, Dennis. *The Messiah and the Mandarins: Mao Tsetung and the Ironies of Power*. New York: Atheneum, 1982.

Bo Yibo. "Wei shenrude pubiande kaizhan sanfan yundong er douzheng." *Shanghai Xinwen Ribao*, 11 Jan. 1952.

Bray, Francesca. *Technology and Gender: Fabrics of Power in Late Imperial China*. Berkeley: University of California Press, 1997.

Breth, R. M. *Mao's China: A Study of Socialist Economic Development*. Melbourne: Longman Cheshire, 1977.

Brook, Timothy. *Collaboration: Japanese Agents and Local Elites in Wartime China*. Cambridge, MA: Harvard University Press, 2005.

Brown, Jeremy, and Paul G. Pickowicz, eds. *Dilemmas of Victory: The Early Years of the People's Republic of China*. Cambridge, MA: Harvard University Press, 2007.

Brugger, William. *Democracy and Organisation in the Chinese Industrial Enterprise (1948–1953)*. Cambridge: Cambridge University Press, 1976.

Burawoy, Michael. *The Politics of Production: Factory Regimes under Capitalism and Socialism*. London: Verso, 1985.

Burawoy, Michael, and Janos Lukács. *The Radiant Past: Ideology and Reality in Hungary's Road to Capitalism*. Chicago: University of Chicago Press, 1992.

Burdekin, Richard, and Fang Wang. "A Novel End to the Big Inflation in China in 1950." *Economics of Planning* 32 (1999): 211–29.

Cain, Frank. "The US-Led Trade Embargo on China: The Origins of CHINCOM, 1947–1952." *Journal of Strategic Studies* 18, no. 4 (1995): 33–54.

Cell, Charles P. *Revolution at Work: Mobilization Campaigns in China*. New York: Academic Press, 1977.

Chan, Anita. *China's Workers under Assault: The Exploitation of Labor in a Globalizing Economy*. New York: M. E. Sharpe, 2001.

Chan, Anita, Richard Madsen, and Jonathan Unger. *Chen Village under Mao and Deng: Expanded and Updated Edition*. Berkeley: University of California Press, 1992.

Chang, John K. *Industrial Development in Pre-Communist China: A Quantitative Analysis*. Chicago: Aldine Publishing Company, 1969.

Chang Kai et al., eds. *Zhongguo gongyun shi cidian* (Historical dictionary of China's labor movement). Beijing: Laodong renshi chubanshe, 1990.

Chang Kia-Ngau. *The Inflationary Spiral: The Experience in China, 1939–1950*. Cambridge, MA: Technology Press of MIT, 1958.

Chang, Leslie T. *Factory Girls: From Village to City in a Changing China*. New York: Spiegel & Grau, 2008.

Chao Kuo-chun. *Economic Planning and Organization in Mainland China: A Documentary Study (1949–1957)*. 2 vols. Cambridge, MA: Harvard University Press, 1963.

Chen Boda. *Mao Tse-tung on the Chinese Revolution: Written in Commemoration of the 30th Anniversary of the Communist Party of China*. Peking: Foreign Languages Press, 1953.

Chen Ciyu. *Jindai Zhongguo de jixie saosi gongye, 1860–1945* (Modern China's machine filature industry, 1860–1945). Taibei: Zhongyang yanjiu yuan, 1989.

Chen, Feng. "Against the State: Labor Protests in China in the 1950s." *Modern China* 40, no. 5 (Sept. 2014): 488–518.

Chen Jian. *China's Road to the Korean War: The Making of the Sino-American Confrontation*. New York: Columbia University Press, 1994.

———. *The Sino-Soviet Alliance and China's Entry into the Korean War*. Washington, DC: Cold War International History Project, Woodrow Wilson International Center for Scholars, 1992.

Chen, Theodore Hsi-En. "The Liquidation of Private Business in Communist China." *Far Eastern Survey* 24, no. 6 (June 1955): 81–89.

Chen, Tina Mai. "Female Icons, Feminist Iconography? Socialist Rhetoric and Women's Agency in 1950s China." *Gender & History* 15, no. 2 (2003): 268–95.

Chen, Wen-hui Chong. *Wartime "Mass" Campaigns in Communist China: Official Country-Wide "Mass Movements" in Professed Support of the Korean War*. Lackland Air Force Base, TX: USAF, 1955.

Cheng Chu-yüan. *Communist China's Economy, 1949–1962: Structural Changes and Crisis*. South Orange, NJ: Seton Hall University Press, 1963.

Chesneaux, Jean. *The Chinese Labor Movement, 1919–1927*. Stanford, CA: Stanford University Press, 1968.

Chi, Ch'ao-ting. *Wartime Economic Development of China*. New York: Garland Publishing, Inc., 1980.

China Number Two Historical Archives. "Kangzhan shengli hou diwei chanye chuli gaikuang" (A survey of the expropriation of Japanese and puppet government property after victory in the War of Resistance against Japan). *Minguo dang'an* (Republican archives), no. 3 (1993).

Chinese Workers' Movement Institute, ed. *Li Lisan yu Lai Ruoyu lun gonghui* (Li Lisan and Lai Ruoyu on the trade unions). Beijing: Dang'an chubanshe, 1987.

Clayton, David. "Free Trade, Protection and the British Empire in the 1950s: Some Evidence from a Hong Kong Case Study." Discussion Papers in Economics, No. 99/10, University of York, 1999.

Cliver, Robert. "China." In *The Ashgate Companion to the History of Textile Workers, 1650–2000*, edited by Lex Heerma van Voss, Els Hiemstra-Kuperus, and Elise van Nederveen Meerkerk. Surrey, UK: Ashgate, 2010.

———. "*Minzhu guanli*: The 'Democratization' of Factory Management in the Chinese Revolution." *Labor History* 50, no. 4 (Nov. 2009): 409–35.

———. "Surviving Socialism: Private Industry and the Transition to Socialism in China, 1945–1958." *Cross-Currents: East Asian History and Culture Review*, no. 16 (Sept. 2015): 139–64.

Coble, Parks M. *Chinese Capitalists in Japan's New Order: The Occupied Lower Yangzi, 1937–1945*. Berkeley: University of California Press, 2003.

———. *The Shanghai Capitalists and the Nationalist Government, 1927–1937*. 2nd ed. Cambridge, MA: Harvard University Press, 1986.

Cochran, Sherman. "Capitalists Choosing Communist China: The Liu Family of Shanghai, 1948–56." In Brown and Pickowicz, *Dilemmas of Victory*.

Cohen, Jerome Alan. "Reflections on the Criminal Process in China." *Journal of Criminal Law and Criminology* 68, no. 3 (Sept. 1977): 323–55.

Croll, Elisabeth. *Feminism and Socialism in China*. New York: Shocken Books, 1978.

Dangdai Zhongguo gongren jieji gonghui yundong (Contemporary China's working class union movement). Vol. 1. Beijing: Dangdai Zhongguo chubanshe, 1997.

Davin, Delia. *Woman Work: Women and the Party in Revolutionary China*. Oxford: Clarendon Press, 1976.

Diamant, Neil J. *Revolutionizing the Family: Politics, Love, and Divorce in Urban and Rural China, 1949–1968*. Berkeley: University of California Press, 2000.

Diamant, Neil, and Feng Xiaocai. "The PRC's First National Critique: The 1954 Campaign to 'Discuss the Draft Constitution,'" *China Journal*, no. 73 (Jan. 2015): 1–37.

Ding Kangshi. "Woguo cansi chanxiao gaikuang" (The situation regarding China's silk production and sales). *Jinrong* (Finance), 18 July 1947.

Dirlik, Arif. "Beyond Chesneaux: Workers, Class, and the Socialist Revolution in Modern China." *International Review of Social History* 48, no. 1 (Apr. 2003): 79–99.

Donnithorne, Audrey. *China's Economic System*. New York: Praeger, 1967.

Doolin, Dennis, ed. *Communist China: The Politics of Student Opposition*. Hoover Institution Studies. Stanford, CA: Hoover Institution on War, Revolution and Peace, Stanford University, 1964.

DuBois, Thomas David. *The Sacred Village: Social Change and Religious Life in Rural North China*. Honolulu: University of Hawai'i Press, 2005.

Dutton, Michael Robert. *Policing Chinese Politics: A History*. Durham, NC: Duke University Press, 2005.

Eastman, Lloyd E. *Seeds of Destruction: Nationalist China in War and Revolution, 1937–1949*. Stanford, CA: Stanford University Press, 1984.

Ecklund, George N. "Protracted Expropriation of Private Business in China." *Pacific Affairs* 36, no. 3 (Autumn 1963): 238–49.

Eckstein, Alexander. *China's Economic Revolution*. New York: Cambridge University Press, 1977.

Eighth National Congress of the Communist Party of China. 3 vols. Beijing: Foreign Languages Press, 1956.

Eng, Robert. *Economic Imperialism in China: Silk Production and Exports, 1861–1932*. Berkeley: Institute of East Asian Studies, University of California Press, 1986.

Engel, Jeffrey A. "Of Fat and Thin Communists: Diplomacy and Philosophy in Western Economic Warfare Strategies toward China (and Tyrants, Broadly)." *Diplomatic History* 29, no. 3 (June 2005): 445–74.

Esherick, Joseph W. "War and Revolution: Chinese Society during the 1940s." *Twentieth Century China* 27, no. 1 (Nov. 2001): 1–37.

———. "The Ye Family in New China." In Brown and Pickowicz, *Dilemmas of Victory*.

Eyferth, Jacob. *Eating Rice from Bamboo Roots: The Social History of a Community of Handicraft Papermakers in Rural Sichuan, 1920–2000*. Cambridge, MA: Harvard University Asia Center, 2009.

———. "Women's Work and the Politics of Homespun in Socialist China, 1949–1980." *International Review of Social History* 57, no. 3 (2012): 365–91.
Ezpeleta, Mariano. *Red Shadows over Shanghai*. Quezon City, Philippines: Zita Publishing, 1972.

Fantanwu, fanlangfei, fanguanliaozhuyi (Oppose corruption, waste, and bureaucratism). Beijing: Renmin chubanshe, 1952.
Feng Xiaocai. *Cai Shengbai xiansheng zhuanlüe* (Tsai Hsiung: A biography). Hong Kong: Yang Yuanlong Education Foundation, 2007.
———. "Rushing toward Socialism: The Transformation and Death of Private Business Enterprises in Shanghai, 1949–1956." In *The People's Republic of China at 60: An International Assessment*, edited by William C. Kirby. Cambridge, MA: Harvard University Asia Center, 2011.
———. "Shenfen, yishi yu zhengzhi: 1956 nian hou zhonggong dui zibenjia de sixiang gaizao" (Identity, ideology, and politics: CCP thought reform of capitalists after 1956). *Journal of East China Normal University, Philosophy and Social Science*, no. 1 (2012): 32–38.
Feuerwerker, Albert. *Economic Trends in the Republic of China, 1912–1949*. Ann Arbor: University of Michigan Center for Chinese Studies, 1977.
Fletcher, Merton Don. *Workers and Commissars: Trade Union Policy in the People's Republic of China*. Bellingham: Western Washington State College, 1974.
Food and Agriculture Organization of the United Nations (http://www.fao.org/home/en/). *Silk Reeling and Testing Manual*, Chapter 11: "Raw Silk Testing." http://www.fao.org/3/x2099e/x2099e12.htm. Accessed 29 October 2019.
Forman, Harrison. *Blunder in Asia*. New York: Didier, 1950.
Frazier, Mark. *The Making of the Chinese Industrial Workplace: State, Revolution, and Labor Management*. New York: Cambridge University Press, 2002.
Friedman, Edward, Paul G. Pickowicz, and Mark Selden, with Kay Ann Johnson. *Chinese Village, Socialist State*. New Haven, CT: Yale University Press, 1991.

Gao Huamin. *Gongheguo nianlun 1955* (Yearbook of the People's Republic, 1955). Shijiazhuang: Hebei renmin chubanshe, 2001.
Gao, James. *The Communist Takeover of Hangzhou: The Transformation of City and Cadre, 1949–1954*. Honolulu: University of Hawai'i Press, 2004.
Gao Jingyue and Yan Xuexi, eds. *Jindai Wuxi cansiye ziliao xuanji* (Selected materials on the modern Wuxi silk industry). Nanjing: Jiangsu renmin chubanshe, 1987.

Gao Jun et al., eds. *Zhongguo gongren yundong shi jiaocai jianbian (1919–1949)* (Teaching materials for the short course on the history of the Chinese workers movement, 1919–1949). Shanghai: Huadong shifan daxue chubanshe, 1988.

Gardner, John. "The Wu-fan Campaign in Shanghai: A Study in the Consolidation of Urban Control." In *Chinese Communist Politics in Action*, edited by A. Doak Barnett. Seattle: University of Washington Press, 1969.

Gaulton, Richard. "Political Mobilization in Shanghai, 1949–1951." In *Shanghai: Revolution and Development in an Asian Metropolis*, edited by Christopher Howe. New York: Cambridge University Press, 1981.

Geddes, W. R. *Peasant Life in Communist China*. New York: Society for Applied Anthropology, Columbia University, 1963.

Gipouloux, Francois. *Les "Cent Fleurs" à l'usine: Agitation ouvrière et crise du modèle Soviétique en Chine, 1956–1957* (The "Hundred Flowers" in the factory: Workers agitation and the crisis of the Soviet model in China, 1956–1957). Paris: Éditions de l'École des hautes études en sciences sociales, 1986.

Glasse, James. *Textiles and Clothing in China: Competitive Threat or Investment Opportunity?* London: Economist Intelligence Unit, 1995.

Goodman, Bryna. *Native Place, City, and Nation: Regional Networks and Identities in Shanghai, 1853–1937.* Berkeley: University of California Press, 1995.

Grasso, June, Jay Corrin, and Michael Kort. *Modernization and Revolution in China: From the Opium Wars to the Olympics*. 4th ed. Armonk, NY: M. E. Sharpe, 2009.

Grove, Linda. "Rural Manufacture in China's Cotton Industry, 1890–1900." In *The Fibre That Changed the World: The Cotton Industry in International Perspective, 1600–1990s*, edited by Douglas A. Farnie and David J. Jeremy. Oxford: Oxford University Press, 2004.

Gu Guoda and Wang Zhaorong. *Riben qinhua shiqi dui zhongguo cansiye de tongzhi yu ziyuan lueduo* (The control and pillaging of China's silk industry during the Japanese occupation). Hangzhou: Zhejiang daxue chubanshe, 2010.

Guanche zhixing san da aiguo haozhao (Carry out and implement the Three Great Patriotic Slogans). Edited by Zhongguo renmin baowei shijie heping fandui Meiguo qinlue weiyuanhui. Beijing: Renmin chubanshe, 1951.

Hangzhou Silk Company, ed. *Hangzhou sichou zhi* (Hangzhou Silk gazetteer). Hangzhou: Zhejiang kexue jishu chubanshe, 1999.

Harper, Paul F. "The Party and the Unions in Communist China." *China Quarterly*, no. 37 (1969): 84–119.

———. "Trade Union Cultivation of Workers for Leadership." In *The City in Communist China*, edited by J. W. Lewis. Stanford, CA: Stanford University Press, 1971.

He Li. "Getting through Difficulties Is Glorious: The Difficulties and Future of Shanghai Industry and Commerce." In *Siying gongshangye de xinsheng* (A new life for private industry and commerce), edited by Xinhua. Hankou: Xinhua shudian, 1950.

Henriot, Christian. "A Neighborhood under Storm: Zhabei and Shanghai Wars." *European Journal of East Asian Studies* 9, no. 2 (2010): 291–319.

———. "Shanghai Industries under Japanese Occupation: Bombs, Boom, and Bust (1937–1945)." In Yeh and Henriot, *In the Shadow of the Rising Sun*.

Hershatter, Gail. *The Gender of Memory: Rural Women and China's Collective Past*. Berkeley: University of California Press, 2011.

———. *The Workers of Tianjin, 1900–1949*. Stanford, CA: Stanford University Press, 1993.

Hinder, Eleanor M. *Life and Labour in Shanghai: A Decade of Labour and Social Administration in the International Settlement*. New York: International Secretariat, Institute of Pacific Relations, 1944.

Hinton, William. *Fanshen: A Documentary of Revolution in a Chinese Village*. New York: Vintage Books, 1966.

Hoffmann, Charles. *The Chinese Worker*. Albany: State University of New York Press, 1974.

Hollister, William W. "Capital Formation in Communist China." In *Industrial Development in Communist China*, edited by Choh-Ming Li. New York: Frederick A. Praeger, 1964.

Honig, Emily. "Burning Incense, Pledging Sisterhood: Communities of Women Workers in the Shanghai Cotton Mills, 1919–1949." *Signs: Journal of Women in Culture and Society* 10, no. 4 (1985): 700–714.

———. *Sisters and Strangers: Women in the Shanghai Cotton Mills, 1919–1949*. Stanford, CA: Stanford University Press, 1986.

Hooton, E. R. *The Greatest Tumult: The Chinese Civil War 1936–49*. McLean, VA: Brassey's, 1991.

Howard, Joshua. *Workers at War: Labor in China's Arsenals, 1937–1953*. Stanford, CA: Stanford University Press, 2004.

Howe, Christopher. *Employment and Economic Growth in Urban China, 1949–1957*. Cambridge: Cambridge University Press, 1971.

———. *Wage Patterns and Wage Policy in Modern China, 1919–1972*. Cambridge: Cambridge University Press, 1973.

Hsia, Ronald. *Economic Planning in Communist China*. New York: Institute of Pacific Relations, 1955.

Hsu, Yung Ying, trans. *Chinese Views of Wartime Economic Difficulties.* New York: Institute of Pacific Relations, 1942.

Hu, Aiqun. *China's Social Insurance in the Twentieth Century: A Global Historical Perspective.* Leiden: Brill, 2016.

Hu Minjian. "Waishang yanghang kongzhi de huasi chukou" (The export of Chinese silk controlled by foreign merchants). In *Ershi shiji Shanghai wenshi ziliao wenku* (A collection of essays on the history of Shanghai in the twentieth century), edited by Lu Jianxin and Wanyan Zhaoyuan. Vol. 4. Shanghai: Shanghai Bookstore Publishing House, 1999.

Hu, Teh-wei. "Hyperinflation and the Dynamics of the Demand for Money in China, 1945–1949." *Journal of Political Economy* 79, no. 1 (Jan.–Feb. 1971): 186–95.

Hunter, Edward. *Brain-washing in Red China: The Calculated Destruction of Men's Minds.* Tokyo: Charles E. Tuttle, 1952.

Hurst, William. "Chinese Labor Divided." *Dissent* 62, no. 2 (Spring 2015): 127–36.

———. *The Chinese Worker after Socialism.* Cambridge: Cambridge University Press, 2009.

Hurst, William, and Kevin J. O'Brien. "China's Contentious Pensioners." *China Quarterly* 170 (June 2002): 345–60.

Huzhou sichou zhi (Huzhou silk gazetteer). Edited by Huzhou sichou zhi bianzuan weiyuanhui. Haikou: Hainan chubanshe, 1998.

Important Labour Laws and Regulations of the People's Republic of China. Enl. ed. Beijing: Foreign Languages Press, 1961.

Jiangsusheng zhi: Cansang sichou zhi (Jiangsu provincial gazetteer: Sericulture and silk gazetteer). Edited by Jiangsusheng difangzhi bianzuan weiyuanhui. Nanjing: Jiangsu guji chubanshe, 2000.

Jiefanghou de Shanghai laozi guanxi (Shanghai's labor relations after liberation). Shanghai: Shidai shuju, 1949.

Jiefanghou Shanghai gongyun ziliao (Materials on Shanghai's postliberation labor movement). Edited by Shanghai zonggonghui mishuchu. Shanghai: Laodong chubanshe, 1950.

Johnson, Kay Ann. *Women, the Family, and Peasant Revolution in China.* Chicago: University of Chicago Press, 1983.

Jordan, David K., and Daniel L. Overmyer. *The Flying Phoenix: Aspects of Chinese Sectarianism in Taiwan.* Princeton, NJ: Princeton University Press, 1986.

Ju Zhifen. "Labor Conscription in North China: 1941–1945." In *China at War: Regions of China, 1937–1945*, edited by Stephen R. MacKinnon et al. Stanford, CA: Stanford University Press, 2007.

Kaple, Deborah A. *Dream of a Red Factory: The Legacy of High Stalinism in China*. Oxford: Oxford University Press, 1994.

Kirby, William C. "The Chinese War Economy." In *China's Bitter Victory: The War with Japan, 1937–1945*, edited by James C. Hsiung and Steven I. Levine. New York: M. E. Sharpe, 1992.

———, ed. *Realms of Freedom in Modern China*. Stanford, CA: Stanford University Press, 2004.

Kirchheimer, Otto. "Confining Conditions and Revolutionary Breakthroughs." *American Political Science Review* 59 (1965): 964–74.

Klein, Donald W., and Anne B. Clark. *Biographic Dictionary of Chinese Communism*. Cambridge, MA: Harvard University Press, 1971.

Koo, Shou-eng. *Tariff and the Development of the Cotton Industry in China, 1842–1937*. New York: Garland Publishing, 1961.

Kratoska, Paul H., ed. *Asian Labor in the Wartime Japanese Empire: Unknown Histories*. Armonk, NY: M. E. Sharpe, 2005.

Kraus, Richard Curt. *Class Conflict in Chinese Socialism*. New York: Columbia University Press, 1981.

———. *The Cultural Revolution: A Very Short Introduction*. New York: Oxford University Press, 2012.

Kraus, Willy. *Economic Development and Social Change in the People's Republic of China*. Translated by E. M. Holtz. New York: Springer-Verlag, 1982.

Laodong chubanshe, ed. *Qiye guanli minzhuhua* (The democratization of enterprise management). Shanghai: Laodong chubanshe, 1951.

Lee, Ching Kwan. *Against the Law: Labor Protests in China's Rustbelt and Sunbelt*. Berkeley: University of California Press, 2007.

———. *Gender and the South China Miracle: Two Worlds of Factory Women*. Berkeley: University of California Press, 1998.

———. "What Was Socialism to Chinese Workers? Collective Memories and Labor Politics in an Age of Reform." In Lee and Yang, *Re-envisioning the Chinese Revolution*.

Lee, Ching Kwan, and Guobin Yang, eds. *Re-envisioning the Chinese Revolution: The Politics and Poetics of Collective Memories in Reform China*. Washington, DC: Woodrow Wilson Center Press, 2007.

Lee Lai To. *Trade Unions in China, 1949 to the Present*. Singapore: Singapore University Press, 1986.

Lenin, V. I. *Collected Works*. Moscow: Progressive Publishers, 1965.

Lewis, Joan Johnson. "Chinese Empress Discovers Silk Making." ThoughtCo., www.thoughtco.com/chinese-empress-discovers-silk-making-3529402. Accessed 1 July 2019.

Lewis, John W. *Leadership in Communist China*. Ithaca, NY: Cornell University Press, 1963.

Li, Choh-ming. *Economic Development of Communist China: An Appraisal of the First Five Years of Industrialization*. Berkeley: University of California Press, 1959.

Li, Hua-yu. *Mao and the Economic Stalinization of China, 1948–1953*. Lanham, MD: Rowman & Littlefield, 2006.

Li Jiaqi et al., eds. *Shanghai gongyun zhi* (Shanghai workers' movement gazetteer). Shanghai: Shanghai Academy of Social Sciences Publishing House, 1997.

Li, Lillian. *China's Silk Trade: Traditional Industry in the Modern World, 1842–1937*. Cambridge, MA: Harvard University Press, 1981.

Li Lisan. "Directive on Establishing LCCCs in Private Enterprises." In *Gongren ribao*, ed. *Laozi xieshang huiyi* (Labor-capital consultative conferences). Beijing: Gongren chubanshe, 1950.

———. "Xuehui guanli qiye" (Learn how to manage enterprises). In *Qiye guanli minzhuhua* (The democratization of enterprise management), edited by Laodong chubanshe. Shanghai: Laodong chubanshe, 1951.

Li Weihan. *Tongyi zhanxian wenti yu minzu wenti* (United Front issues and the nationalities question). Beijing: Renmin chubanshe, 1981.

Liao Gailong (Liao Kai-lung). *Aiguo yundong lunji* (A collection of essays on the Patriotic Campaign). Beijing: Haiyan shudian, 1951.

Liao Kai-lung (Liao Gailong). *From Yenan to Peking: The Chinese People's War of Liberation from Reconstruction to First Five-Year Plan*. Beijing: Foreign Languages Press, 1954.

Lieberstein, Samuel. "Technology, Work, and Sociology in the USSR: The NOT Movement." *Technology and Culture* (January 1975): 48–66.

Lieberthal, Kenneth G. *Revolution and Tradition in Tientsin, 1949–1952*. Stanford, CA: Stanford University Press, 1980.

Lieu, D. K. *China's Economic Stabilization and Reconstruction*. New Brunswick, NJ: Rutgers University Press, 1948.

———. *The Silk Industry of China*. Shanghai: Kelly and Walsh, 1941.

Lin Wei. "Shanghai Industry and Commerce Is Improving Gradually." In *Siying gongshangye de xinsheng* (A new life for private industry and commerce), edited by Xinhua. Hankou: Xinhua shudian, 1950.

Lin Yilan et al. *Soushan dahu chue wujin* (Search the mountains and beat the tigers, eliminate the evil and complete the mission). Guangzhou: Huanan renmin chubanshe, 1952.

Lincoln, Toby. *Urbanizing China in War and Peace: The Case of Wuxi County*. Honolulu: University of Hawai'i Press, 2015.

Liu, Alan P. L. *Communications and National Integration in Communist China*. New enl. ed. Berkeley: University of California Press, 1971.
Liu Dajun et al., eds. *Zhongguo gongye diaocha baogao* (Report on an investigation of China's industry). Vol. 2. Nanjing: Jingji tongji yanjiusuo, 1937.
Liu, Ta-chung, and Kung-chia Yeh. *The Economy of the Chinese Mainland: National Income and Economic Development, 1933–1959*. Princeton, NJ: Princeton University Press, 1965.
Lü, Xiaobo, and Elizabeth J. Perry, eds. *Danwei: The Changing Chinese Workplace in Historical and Comparative Perspective*. Armonk, NY: M. E. Sharpe, 1997.

Ma Junya. "Kangzhan shiqi Jiangnan nongcun jingji de shuaibian" (The decline of Jiangnan's rural economy during the Anti-Japanese War). *Kangrizhanzheng yanjiu* (Anti-Japanese War research), no. 4 (2003): 44–85.
MacFarquhar, Roderick, ed. *The Hundred Flowers*. London: Stevens and Sons, 1960.
———. *Origins of the Cultural Revolution*. 3 vols. New York: Columbia University Press, 1983.
MacFarquhar, Roderick, Timothy Cheek, and Eugene Wu, eds. *The Secret Speeches of Chairman Mao: From the Hundred Flowers to the Great Leap Forward*. Cambridge, MA: Council on East Asian Studies, Harvard University, 1989.
Malik, Rashid. *Chinese Entrepreneurs in the Economic Development of China*. Westport, CT: Praeger, 1997.
Mao Dun. *The Shop of the Lin Family and Spring Silkworms*. Translated by Sidney Shapiro. Beijing: Foreign Languages Press, 2001.
Mao Zedong. *Mao Zedong wenji, diliujuan (Oct. 1949–Dec. 1955)* (Selected works of Mao Zedong. Vol. 6 [Oct. 1949–Dec. 1955]). Beijing: Renmin chubanshe, 1999.
———. "On the People's Democratic Dictatorship." Marxists Internet Archive, https://www.marxists.org/reference/archive/mao/selected-works/date-index.htm. Accessed 1 November, 2019.
———. "Report to the Second National Congress of Workers' and Peasants' Representatives," 23 January 1934. Marxists Internet Archive, https://www.marxists.org/reference/archive/mao/selected-works/volume-6/mswv6_18.htm. Accessed 31 October, 2019.
———. *Selected Readings from the Works of Mao Tsetung*. Beijing: Foreign Languages Press, 1971.
———. *Selected Works of Mao Tse-Tung*. Vols. 2–4. Beijing: Foreign Languages Press, 1961.

Mao Zedong et al. *Xin minzhuzhuyi jingji de gongye fazhan fengzhen* (Guiding policy for the development of industry in the new democratic economy). Shenyang: Jilin chubanshe, 1949.

Mao Zedong, Deng Xiaoping, Jiang Zemin lun gongren jieji he gonghui gongzuo (Mao Zedong, Deng Xiaoping, and Jiang Zemin on the working class and union work). Edited by Zhonghua quanguo zonggonghui and Zhonggong Zhongyang wenxuan yanjiushi. Beijing: Zhongyang wenxuan chubanshe, 2002.

The Marriage Law of the People's Republic of China. Beijing: Foreign Languages Press, 1973.

Meisner, Maurice. *Mao's China and After: A History of the People's Republic*. 3rd ed. New York: Free Press, 1999.

Melby, John F. *The Mandate of Heaven: Record of a Civil War, China 1945–49*. New York: Doubleday & Co., 1971.

Meliksetov, Arlen, and Alexander Pantsov. "The Stalinization of the People's Republic of China." In Kirby, *Realms of Freedom in Modern China*.

Meng Xianzhang, ed. *Zhong-Su maoyi shiliao* (Historical materials on Sino-Soviet trade). Beijing: Chinese Foreign Economics and Trade Publishing House, 1991.

Montgomery, David. *Workers' Control in America: Studies in the History of Work, Technology, and Labor Struggles* Cambridge: Cambridge University Press, 1979.

Moore, W. J. *Shanghai Century*. Devon, UK: Arthur H. Stockwell, 1966.

Mustanduno, Michael. *Economic Containment: COCOM and the Politics of East-West Trade*. Ithaca, NY: Cornell University Press, 1992.

Myrdal, Jan. *Report from a Chinese Village*. New York: Pantheon Books, 1965.

Ong, Shao-er. *Labor Problems in Communist China (to February 1953)*. Lackland Air Force Base, TX: Air Force Personnel and Training Research Center, 1955.

Ono, Kazuko. *Chinese Women in a Century of Revolution, 1850–1950*. Edited and Translated by Joshua A. Fogel. Stanford, CA: Stanford University Press, 1978.

Pepper, Suzanne. *Civil War in China: The Political Struggle, 1945–1949*. 2nd ed. Lanham, MD: Rowman & Littlefield, 1999.

Perkins, Dwight. *Market Control and Planning in Communist China*. Cambridge, MA: Harvard University Press, 1966.

Perry, Elizabeth J. "Labor Divided: Sources of State Formation in Modern China." In *State Power and Social Forces: Domination and Transformation*

in the Third World, edited by Joel S. Migdal, Atul Kohli, and Vivienne Shue. Cambridge: Cambridge University Press, 1994.
———. *Patrolling the Revolution: Worker Militias, Citizenship, and the Modern Chinese State*. Lanham, MD: Rowman & Littlefield, 2006.
———. *Shanghai on Strike: The Politics of Chinese Labor.* Stanford, CA: Stanford University Press, 1993.
———. "Shanghai's Strike Wave of 1957." *China Quarterly* 137 (1994): 1–27.
———. "Workers' Patrols in the Chinese Revolution: A Case of Institutional Inversion." In Kirby, *Realms of Freedom in Modern China*.
Perry, Elizabeth, and Li Xun. *Proletarian Power: Shanghai in the Cultural Revolution*. Boulder, CO: Westview Press, 1997.
Philion, Stephen E. *Workers' Democracy in China's Transition from State Socialism*. New York: Routledge, 2009.
Pirani, Simon. *The Russian Revolution in Retreat, 1920–24: Soviet Workers and the New Communist Elite*. New York: Routledge, 2008.
Pun, Ngai. *Made in China: Women Factory Workers in a Global Workplace*. Durham, NC: Duke University Press, 2005.

Qian Yaoxing et al., eds. *Wuxishi sichou gongye zhi* (Wuxi silk industry gazetteer). Shanghai: Shanghai renmin chubanshe, 1990.
Qin Xiaoyi, ed. *Zhonghua Minguo jingji fazhan shi* (A history of the economic development of the Republic of China). Taibei: Jindai Zhongguo chubanshe, 1983.

Raeburn, John R., and Ko Fuh-Ting. "Prices Paid and Received by Farmers in Wuchin, Kiangsu." *Economic Facts*, no. 6 (July 1937): 251–61.
Rawski, Thomas G. *Economic Growth in Prewar China*. Berkeley: University of California Press, 1989.
Richman, Barry M. *Industrial Society in Communist China*. New York: Random House, 1969.
Riskin, Carl. *China's Political Economy: The Quest for Development since 1949*. Oxford: Oxford University Press, 1987.
Rofel, Lisa. *Other Modernities: Gendered Yearnings in China after Socialism*. Berkeley: University of California Press, 1999.
Rossi, Paolo Alberto. *The Communist Conquest of Shanghai: A Warning to the West*. Denver, CO: Twin Circle Publishing, 1970.
Roux, Alain. "From Revenge to Treason: Political Ambivalence among Wang Jingwei's Labor Union Supporters." In Yeh and Henriot, *In the Shadow of the Rising Sun*.
Rowan, Roy. *Chasing the Dragon: A Veteran Journalist's Firsthand Account of the 1949 Chinese Revolution*. Guilford, CT: Lyons Press, 2004.

Schoppa, R. Keith. "Patterns and Dynamics of Elite Collaboration in Occupied Shaoxing County." In *Chinese Collaboration: The Limits of Accommodation with Japan, 1932–1945*, edited by David Barrett and Larry Shyu. Stanford, CA: Stanford University Press, 2000.

Schram, Stuart, and Marianne Bastid, eds. *Authority, Participation and Cultural Change in China: Essays by a European Study Group*. Cambridge: Cambridge University Press, 1973.

Schurmann, Franz. *Ideology and Organization in Communist China*. 2nd ed. Berkeley: University of California Press, 1968.

Sears, Kathrin. "Shanghai's Textile Capitalists and the State: The Nationalization Process in China." PhD diss., University of Michigan, 1985.

Selden, Mark. *The Yenan Way in Revolutionary China*. Cambridge, MA: Harvard University Press, 1971.

Shanghai fangzhi gongren yundong shi (A history of the textiles workers movement). Edited by Shanghai fangzhi gongren yundong shi bianzuan weiyuanhui. Shanghai: Zhongguo gongchandang lishi chubanshe, 1991.

Shanghai fangzhi gongye zhi (Shanghai textiles industry gazetteer). Edited by Shanghai fangzhi gongye zhi bianzuan weiyuanhui. Shanghai: Shanghai shehui kexue yuan chubanshe, 1998.

Shanghai gongren kang Mei yuan Chao xingdong gangling (Shanghai workers resist America aid Korea action program). Shanghai: Laodong chubanshe, 1951.

Shanghai jiefang (Shanghai liberation). Edited by Shanghaishi dang'anguan. Beijing: Dang'anguan chubanshe, 1989.

Shanghai Labor Bureau, ed. *Laozi xieshang huiyi xuanji* (Selections on Labor-Capital Consultative Conferences). Shanghai: East China People's Press, 1951.

Shanghai Municipal Archives, ed. *Riben zai Huazhong jingji lueduo shiliao* (Historical materials on Japan's economic pillaging of central China). Shanghai: Shanghai Shiji chuban jituan, 2005.

Shanghai sichou zhi (Shanghai silk gazetteer). Edited by Shanghai sichou zhi bianzuan weiyuanhui. Shanghai: Shanghai shehui kexue yuan chubanshe, 1998.

Shanghai Statistics Bureau, ed. *Xin Shanghai gongye tongji ziliao (1949–1990)* (New Shanghai industrial statistics [1949–1990]). Shanghai: China Statistics Publishing House, 1992.

Shanghai tong (Shanghai expert). http://www.shtong.gov.cn. Accessed 21 Sept. 2015.

"Shanghaishi sizhi gongye wei wancheng fan hongzha renwu dingli laozi jiti xieyi" (Shanghai's silk weaving industry establishes collective agreement to complete the anti-bombing tasks). In Shanghai Labor Bureau, ed., *Laozi xieshang huiyi xuanji* (Selections on Labor-Capital Consultative Conferences).

Sheehan, Jackie. *Chinese Workers: A New History.* New York: Routledge, 1998.

Sheng, Michael. "Mao Zedong and the Three-Anti Campaign (November 1951 to April 1952): A Revisionist Interpretation." *Twentieth-Century China* 32, no. 1 (2006): 56–80.

Sheridan, Mary. "The Emulation of Heroes." *China Quarterly* 33 (Mar. 1968): 47–72.

Shih Ping. *Life of Workers under Chinese Communist Persecution.* Taibei: World Anti-Communist League, China Chapter, 1973.

Shue, Vivienne. *Peasant China in Transition: The Dynamics of Development toward Socialism, 1949–1956.* Berkeley: University of California Press, 1980.

Sichuan shinian wenxue yishu xuanji bianji weiyuanhui, ed. *Sichuan gongchang shi zuopinxuan* (A selection of works on the history of Sichuan factories). Chengdu: Sichuan renmin chubanshe, 1960.

Simkin, C. G. F. "Hyperinflation and Nationalist China." In *Stability and Inflation: A Volume of Essays to Honour the Memory of A. W. H. Phillips*, edited by A. R. Bergsttrom et al. New York: Wiley, 1978.

"Sizhiye laozi xieshang huiyi qingkuang" (The situation of the silk weaving industry Labor-Capital Consultative Conference). In Shanghai Labor Bureau, ed., *Laozi xieshang huiyi xuanji* (Selections on Labor-Capital Consultative Conferences).

Skocpol, Theda. *States and Social Revolutions: A Comparative Analysis of France, Russia, and China.* New York, NY: Cambridge University Press, 1979.

Smith, Aminda M. *Thought Reform and China's Dangerous Classes: Reeducation, Resistance, and the People.* Lanham, MD: Rowman & Littlefield, 2013.

Smith, S. A. *Like Cattle and Horses: Nationalism and Labor in Shanghai, 1895–1927.* Durham, NC: Duke University Press, 2002.

———. *Revolution and the People in Russia and China: A Comparative History.* New York, NY: Cambridge University Press, 2008.

———. "Talking Toads and Chinless Ghosts: The Politics of 'Superstitious' Rumors in the People's Republic of China, 1961–1965." *American Historical Review* 111, no. 2 (Apr. 2006): 405–27.

———. "Taylorism Rules OK? Bolshevism, Taylorism and the Technical Intelligentsia in the Soviet Union, 1917–1941." *Radical Science Journal* 13 (1983): 3–27.

So, Alvin Y. *The South China Silk District: Local Historical Transformation and World-System Theory.* Albany: State University of New York Press, 1986.

So, Bennis Wai-yip. "The Policy-Making and Political Economy of the Abolition of Private Ownership in the Early 1950s: Findings from New Material." *China Quarterly* 171 (2002): 682–703.

Sochor, Zenovia A. "Soviet Taylorism Revisited." *Soviet Studies* 33, no. 2 (1981): 246–64.

Spurr, Russell. *Enter the Dragon: China's Undeclared War against the U.S. in Korea, 1950–51.* New York, NY: Newmarket Press, 1988.

Stacey, Judith. *Patriarchy and Socialist Revolution in China.* Berkeley: University of California Press, 1983.

Stalin, Joseph. *Problems of Leninism.* Moscow: Foreign Languages Publishing House, 1954.

Strauss, Julia. "Paternalist Terror: The Campaign to Suppress Counter-revolutionaries and Regime Consolidation in the People's Republic of China, 1950–1953." *Comparative Studies in Society and History* 44, no. 1 (Jan. 2002): 80–105.

———. *Strong Institutions in Weak Polities: State Building in Republican China, 1927–1940.* Oxford: Clarendon Press, 1998.

Taire, Lucian. *Shanghai Episode: The End of Western Commerce in Shanghai.* Hong Kong: Rainbow Press, 1957.

Tang Jianxun. *Xin minzhu zhuyi wenda sanbai tiao* (Three hundred questions and answers on New Democracy). Hong Kong: Minhua chubanshe, 1949.

Tang Kentang. "Dali sichang jianshi" (A brief history of the Dali filature). *Shanghai wenshi ziliao xuanji*, no. 53 (1986): 233–36.

Tao Jie, Zheng Bijun, and Shirley L. Mow, eds. *Holding Up Half the Sky: Chinese Women Past, Present, and Future.* Translated by Amy Russell. New York: Feminist Press at the City University of New York, 2004.

Thaxton, Ralph A., Jr. *Catastrophe and Contention in Rural China: Mao's Great Leap Forward Famine and the Origins of Righteous Resistance in Da Fo Village* Cambridge: Cambridge University Press, 2008.

Thompson, E. P. *The Making of the English Working Class.* New York: Vintage, 1966.

Topley, Marjorie. "Marriage Resistance in Rural Kwantung." In *Women in Chinese Society*, edited by Margery Wolfe and Roxanne Witke. Stanford, CA: Stanford University Press, 1975.

The Trade Union Law of the People's Republic of China together with Other Relevant Documents. Beijing: Foreign Languages Press, 1951.

Tsukiyama, Gail. *Women of the Silk.* New York: St. Martin's Press, 1991.

Unger, Jonathan, and Anita Chan. "Memories and the Moral Economy of a State-Owned Enterprise." In Lee and Yang, *Re-envisioning the Chinese Revolution.*

United States Department of State. *The China White Paper, August 1949.* Stanford, CA: Stanford University Press, 1967.

"The Upsurge of Socialist Transformation of Private Commerce in Cities." *Commercial Work*, 19 Jan. 1956. Trans. in SCMP 1226, 9 Feb. 1956: 16–17.

Vogel, Ezra. *Canton under Communism: Programs and Politics in a Provincial Capital, 1949–1968*, with a new preface by the author. Cambridge, MA: Harvard University Press, 1980.

Wakeman, Frederic, Jr. "'Cleanup': The New Order in Shanghai." In Brown and Pickowicz, *Dilemmas of Victory.*

Walder, Andrew G. *Chang Ch'un Ch'iao and Shanghai's January Revolution.* Ann Arbor: Center for Chinese Studies, University of Michigan, 1978.

———. *China under Mao: A Revolution Derailed.* Cambridge, MA: Harvard University Press, 2015.

———. *Communist Neo-Traditionalism: Work and Authority in Chinese Industry.* Berkeley: University of California Press, 1986.

———. "The Remaking of the Chinese Working Class, 1949–1981." *Modern China* 10, no. 1 (1984): 3–48.

Wang Chaobin. *Sanfan shilu* (A veritable record of the Three Antis). Beijing: Jingguan jiaoyu chubanshe, 1992.

Wang, Fei-Ling. *Institutions and Institutional Change in China: Premodernity and Modernization.* Basingstoke, UK: Macmillan, 1998.

Wang He. "Wei fazhan Zhongguo siye er xiangji fendou" (The development of the Chinese silk industry and its struggles). *Jiangsu wenshi ziliao*, no. 34 (1989).

Wang Xiang. "Cong Yunjin gongsuo dao tieji gonghui: Jindai Suzhou sizhiye tongye zuzhi de shanbian" (From Yunjin Guild to Iron Loom Association: The evolution of the organization of modern Suzhou's silk weaving industry association). *Jindaishi yanjiu* (Modern Chinese history studies), no. 3 (2001): 109–36.

Wang Zheng. *Finding Women in the State: A Socialist Feminist Revolution in the People's Republic of China, 1949–1964.* Oakland: University of California Press, 2017.

Wei Leshan. *Xin minzhu zhuyi jiben renshi* (Basic understanding of New Democracy). Hong Kong: Qiushi chubanshe, 1951.

Weidner, Terry M. "Local Political Work under the Nationalists: The 1930's Silk Reform Campaign." *Illinois Papers in Asian Studies*, no. 2 (1983): 67–86.

Westad, Odd Arne. *Decisive Encounters: The Chinese Civil War, 1946–1950*. Stanford, CA: Stanford University Press, 2003.

Whiting, Alan. *China Crosses the Yalu: The Decision to Enter the Korean War*. New York: Macmillan, 1960.

Whyte, Martin K. *Small Groups and Political Rituals in China*. Berkeley: University of California Press, 1974.

Winn, Peter. *Weavers of Revolution: The Yarur Workers and Chile's Road to Socialism*. Oxford: Oxford University Press, 1989.

Wright, Tim. "Coping with the World Depression: The Nationalist Government's Relations with Chinese Industry and Commerce, 1932–1936." *Modern Asian Studies* 25, no. 4 (Oct. 1991): 649–74.

Wuxi ji geming lieshi yingminglu (List of heroic names of revolutionary martyrs of Wuxi). http://wap.wuxi.gov.cn/wap/mlxc/wxrw/wxls/6903831.shtml. Accessed 21 Sept. 2015.

Xin gongshang zhengce ji qi zhishi (The New Industrial and Commercial Policy and its directives). Shanghai: Xinhua shudian, 1949.

Xinhua. "Party History Researcher Warns against 'Historical Nihilism.'" Chinadaily.com.cn. http://www.chinadaily.com.cn/china/2017-07/03/content_29975661.htm. Accessed 2 July 2019.

Xu Dixin and Wu Chengming, eds. *Zhongguo zibenzhuyi fazhan shi* (A history of the development of Chinese capitalism). Beijing: Renmin chubanshe, 2003.

Xu, Feng. *Women Migrant Workers in China's Economic Reform*. New York: St. Martin's Press, 2000.

Xu Xinwu, ed. *Jindai Jiangnan sizhi gongye shi* (A history of the modern Jiangnan silk weaving industry). Shanghai: Renmin chubanshe, 1991.

———. *Zhongguo jindai saosi gongye shi* (A history of China's modern silk reeling industry). Shanghai: Shanghai renmin chubanshe, 1990.

Yan Zhongping et al., eds. *Zhongguo jindai jingji shi tongji ziliao xuanji* (A selection of statistical materials for the history of China's modern economy). Beijing: Kexue chubanshe, 1955.

Yang Jisheng. *Tombstone: The Great Chinese Famine, 1958–1962*. Translated and edited by Stacey Mosher, Guo Jian, and Edward Friedman. New York: Farrar, Straus, and Giroux, 2008.

Yang Kuisong. "Reconsidering the Campaign to Suppress Counterrevolutionaries." *China Quarterly* 195 (Mar. 2008): 102–21.

Yeh, Wen-hsin, ed. *Wartime Shanghai*. New York: Routledge, 1998.

Yeh, Wen-hsin, and Christian Henriot, eds. *In the Shadow of the Rising Sun: Shanghai under Japanese Occupation*. New York: Cambridge University Press, 2004.

Young, Arthur N. *China's Wartime Finance and Inflation, 1937–1945*. Cambridge, MA: Harvard University Press, 1965.

Yu, Frederick T. C. "Campaigns, Communications, and Development in Communist China." In *Communication and Change in the Developing Countries*, edited by Daniel Lerner and Wilbur Schramm. Honolulu: East-West Center Press, 1967.

Yu Jin. *Shanghai: 1949 da bengkui* (Shanghai: The great collapse of 1949). Vol. 2. Beijing: PLA Press, 1993.

Yu, Miin-ling. "Labor Is Glorious: Model Laborers in the PRC." In *China Learns from the Soviet Union, 1949–Present*, edited by Thomas P. Bernstein and Hua-yu Li. Lanham, MD: Lexington Books, 2010.

"Zenyang gaohao laozi xieshang huiyi: Lushi laozi xieshang huiyi gaikuang he zuoyong" (How to handle well the Labor-Capital Consultative Conference: The general situation and role of LCCCs in Shanghai). In Shanghai Labor Bureau, ed., *Laozi xieshang huiyi xuanji* (Selections on Labor-Capital Consultative Conferences).

Zhang Jiangming. *Xin minzhu zhuyi jianghua* (Talks on New Democracy). Guangzhou: Minjian shuwu, 1950.

Zhang Jinping. "Baiwan zhigong touru baowei dashanghai de zhandou" (A million workers join the battle to defend greater Shanghai). *Jingbei da Shanghai* (Greater Shanghai garrison). Shanghai, 1994.

Zhang Qi. *Shanghai gongyun jishi* (A record of the Shanghai workers movement). Shanghai: Zhongguo da baike quanshu chubanshe, 1991.

Zhang, Xiaoming. *Red Wings over the Yalu: China, the Soviet Union, and the Air War in Korea*. College Station: Texas A&M University Press, 2002.

Zhang Yan. *Qingdai jingji jianshi* (A brief history of the economy of the Qing dynasty). Beijing: Zhongguo guji chubanshe, 1998.

Zhao Ma. "Female Workers, Political Mobilization, and the Meaning of Revolutionary Citizenship in Beijing, 1948–1950." *Frontiers of History in China* 9, no. 4 (2014): 558–83.

Zhejiang gongren yundong shi (A history of the Zhejiang labor movement). Edited by Zhejiangsheng zonggonghui. Hangzhou: Zhejiang renmin chubanshe, 1988.

Zhejiangsheng sichou zhi (Zhejiang Province silk gazetteer). Edited by Zhejiangsheng sichou zhi bianzuan weiyuanhui. Beijing: Fangzhi chubanshe, 1999.

Zhongguo sichou gongye tongji ziliao huibian: 1949–1990 (A compendium of statistics on China's silk industry: 1949–1990). Edited by Zhongguo sichou gongye zonggongsi. Beijing: Zhongguo sichou gongye zonggongsi, 1993.

Zhongguo zhigong yundong wenxuan (Selected works on China's labor movement). Edited by Zhonghua quanguo zonggonghui. Beijing: Workers Press, 1949.

Zhongguo zibenzhuyi gongshangye de shehuizhuyi gaizao, Shanghai. Vol. 1. Beijing: Chinese Communist Party Press, 1993.

Zhou Dehua. "Lunxian shiqi de Wujiang sichouye" (Wujiang's silk industry during the occupation). *Jiangsu lishi dang'an* (Jiangsu historical archives), no. 2 (1995): 44–46.

Zhou Enlai. *Selected Works of Zhou Enlai*. 2 vols. Beijing: Foreign Languages Press, 1989.

Zhu Bangxing et al. *Shanghai chanye yu Shanghai zhigong* (Shanghai industry and Shanghai employment). Shanghai: Shanghai renmin chubanshe, 1984. Originally published in 1939.

Zhu Xinyu, ed., *Zhongguo sichou shi (tonglun)* (A history of Chinese silk). Beijing: Fangzhi gongye chubanshe, 1991.

Zhu Xinyu et al. eds. *Zhejiang sichou shi* (A history of Zhejiang silk). Hangzhou: Zhejiang renmin chubanshe, 1985.

Zhuang Jianping. "Japan's Exploitative Labor System in Qingdao: 1933–1945." In *China at War: Regions of China, 1937–1945*, edited by Stephen R. MacKinnon et al. Stanford, CA: Stanford University Press, 2007.

Index

Note: Page numbers in bold indicate a table; page numbers in italics indicate an illustration on the corresponding page.

Harvard East Asian Monographs
(most recent titles)

406. Michal Daliot-Bul and Nissim Otmazgin, *The Anime Boom in the United States: Lessons for Global Creative Industries*
407. Nathan Hopson, *Ennobling the Savage Northeast: Tōhoku as Japanese Postwar Thought, 1945–2011*
408. Michael Fuller, *An Introduction to Chinese Poetry: From the Canon of Poetry to the Lyrics of the Song Dynasty*
409. Tie Xiao, *Revolutionary Waves: The Crowd in Modern China*
410. Anne Reinhardt, *Navigating Semi-Colonialism: Shipping, Sovereignty, and Nation- Building in China, 1860–1937*
411. Jennifer E. Altehenger, *Legal Lessons: Popularizing Laws in the People's Republic of China, 1949–1989*
412. Halle O'Neal, *Word Embodied: The Jeweled Pagoda Mandalas in Japanese Buddhist Art*
413. Maren A. Ehlers, *Give and Take: Poverty and the Status Order in Early Modern Japan*
414. Chieko Nakajima, *Body, Society, and Nation: The Creation of Public Health and Urban Culture in Shanghai*
415. Pu Wang, *The Translatability of Revolution: Guo Moruo and Twentieth-Century Chinese Culture*
416. Hwansoo Ilmee Kim, *The Korean Buddhist Empire: A Transnational History, 1910–1945*
417. Joshua Hill, *Voting as a Rite: A History of Elections in Modern China*
418. Kirsten L. Ziomek, *Lost Histories: Recovering the Lives of Japan's Colonial Peoples*
419. Claudine Ang, *Poetic Transformations: Eighteenth-Century Cultural Projects on the Mekong Plains*
420. Evan N. Dawley, *Becoming Taiwanese: Ethnogenesis in a Colonial City, 1880s–1950s*
421. James McMullen, *The Worship of Confucius in Japan*
422. Nobuko Toyosawa, *Imaginative Mapping: Landscape and Japanese Identity in the Tokugawa and Meiji Eras*
423. Pierre Fuller, *Famine Relief in Warlord China*

424. Diane Wei Lewis, *Powers of the Real: Cinema, Gender, and Emotion in Interwar Japan*
425. Maram Epstein, *Orthodox Passions: Narrating Filial Love during the High Qing*
426. Margaret Wan, *Regional Literature and the Transmission of Culture: Chinese Drum Ballads, 1800-1937*
427. Takeshi Watanabe, *Flowering Tales: Women Exorcising History in Heian Japan*
428. Jürgen P. Melzer, *Wings for the Rising Sun: A Transnational History of Japanese Aviation*
429. Edith Sarra, *Unreal Houses: Character, Gender, and Genealogy in the* Tale of Genji
430. Yi Gu, *Chinese Ways of Seeing and Open-Air Painting*
431. Robert Cliver, *Red Silk: Class, Gender, and Revolution in China's Yangzi Delta Silk Industry*
432. Kenneth J. Ruoff, *Japan's Imperial House in the Postwar Era, 1945–2019*